STUDY GUIDE

ABNORMAL PSYCHOLOGY

STUDY GUIDE

Arthur G. Olguin
Santa Barbara City College

ABNORMAL PSYCHOLOGY
UNDERSTANDING HUMAN PROBLEMS

Second Edition

Philip C. Kendall
Temple University

Constance Hammen
University of California, Los Angeles

HOUGHTON MIFFLIN COMPANY   BOSTON   NEW YORK

Sponsoring Editor: David C. Lee
Senior Associate Editor: Jane Knetzger
Senior Manufacturing Coordinator: Marie Barnes
Marketing Manager: Pamela J. Laskey

Printed in the U.S.A.

ISBN: 0-395-87693-1

123456789-VG-01 00 99 98 97

Contents

Contents

To the Student

Human behavior and all its complexity are fascinating to observe. We notice tremendous variability in human behavior and how people adapt to complex situations in unique and creative ways. Human behavior is also very difficult to fully understand. We struggle to understand ourselves, our family members, friends, co-workers, and even strangers. Sometimes we think we understand others. At other times, the reasons for their actions are less clear. Not only is this the case when we look outwardly but also when we turn inwardly and reflect on our own thoughts, feelings, and actions.

As humans, we are sometimes troubled by mild challenges or serious difficulties in life. Although humans are adaptable and insightful problem solvers, these difficulties sometimes may result in profound suffering. The core of abnormal psychology involves how to describe, understand, and ameliorate human suffering. This textbook and *Study Guide* serve as tools to help you understand human suffering, from its genesis to its resolution. You are fortunate to have one of the best abnormal psychology textbooks currently on the market. Professors Kendall and Hammen accomplished the difficult task of writing about the wide range of abnormal behaviors in an engaging writing style. Their text is targeted toward an intelligent audience, and their treatment of abnormal behavior is current, accurate, and thorough.

How to Get the Most Out of this *Study Guide*

This *Study Guide* serves as a resource to help you master the concepts in Kendall and Hammen's textbook and to help you consolidate your learning. Each *Study Guide* chapter contains several sections:

1. *Learning Objectives*—These objectives identify issues/concepts that students should be able to address. After reading a section of the text, go to the Learning Objectives and answer the relevant questions. These objectives provide an opportunity for you to reflect on your learning. You also may use these questions to prepare for essays or to give you term paper ideas. Page numbers are given that reference the section where the material is discussed in the textbook.

2. *Chapter Outline*—A detailed outline is provided that highlights major points of the chapter. Review the outline *after* you have read the text. Don't be tempted to use the chapter outline as a substitute for reading the textbook—You will shortchange not only yourself but also the potential clients with whom you may work in the future. The chapter outlines also will serve as a good review prior to an examination. By studying the outlines, you will see how one point relates to others in the chapter.

3. *Key Terms Review*—These help you to check your understanding of important terminology or concepts.

4. *Multiple-Choice Questions*—Three sets of multiple-choice questions are provided. First, *Factual Multiple-Choice Questions* quiz your basic recall of key points in the chapter. *Conceptual Multiple-Choice Questions* add a degree of challenge by assessing your understanding of abnormal psychology concepts. These questions typically involve comparisons and contrasts and the use of cognitive skills at a level somewhat higher than simple factual recall. Last, *Application Multiple-Choice Questions* present situations in which you will assess, diagnose, or treat the problem at hand. These application questions pose situations faced by practitioners or researchers and challenge you to reason like a psychologist.

In order to improve your understanding of the material, answers to the questions are provided with corresponding textbook page numbers referenced. In addition, a justification is provided for the incorrect answers. Don't be a passive learner. Study the reasons why you made an incorrect response. The feedback will help you sharpen your analytical skills in this class and also in other classes where similar assessment methods are used.

Students sometimes feel overwhelmed with the sheer number of mental disorders that are covered in an abnormal psychology text. One framework that may be helpful in organizing the material is to consider each mental disorder in terms of its (1) phenomenology (i.e., a description of the disorder), (2) etiology (or the presumed causes of the disorder), and (3) treatment methods.

Although the textbook and *Study Guide* are the primary references for this course, students also may find work in small groups helpful in learning this material. In addition, there are numerous examples in films, books, and television to which you may apply your knowledge of abnormal behavior. Last, don't forget to use the excellent resources built into the textbook—the glossary at the end of the book, summary tables and charts, etc.

Study Skills

Although each student may have his or her preferred way to study a subject, research shows that many students use ineffective learning methods. Educational psychologists have studied various techniques that result in improved academic performance. If you would like to enhance your academic performance, perhaps a study skills course would be useful. Check with your professor to see whether or not your college has a learning assistance center. Typically, these centers have services to help students improve their academic success. In addition to workshops that may be offered by your college learning assistance center, an excellent printed resource is Pauk and Fiore's (1989) *Succeed in College!* Although targeted toward psychology courses, this book is recommended for all college students in any discipline and has excellent material on time management, note taking, learning from textbooks, and test-taking strategies, as well as a section on psychology and careers. One method discussed in the book is *SQ3R*, a method designed to help students read and study textbooks effectively.

The SQ3R method was developed by Francis P. Robinson, a psychologist at Ohio State University. Professor Robinson's research demonstrated that students' understanding and performance in academic courses increased by using the SQ3R method. SQ3R stands for *Survey, Question, Read, Recite, Review*, and the method is outlined below.

• *Survey*. Page through the chapter, looking at the main headings and the organization of the chapter. Read the final summary of the chapter. Try to get a *gestalt* of the chapter—an overall picture of how the chapter is organized and what's to come. Why is this important? Scanning a chapter helps you develop a cognitive schema of the chapter. When you begin to read the chapter, you will have a better idea of how ideas are linked to one another, and you will organize the information you encounter more efficiently.

- *Question.* Based on your survey of the chapter, formulate some questions about the material. One way to develop questions is to turn the chapter headings into questions. Another strategy is to read the Chapter Objectives in the *Study Guide* prior to reading the text material. Why is this important? When we have a question in mind, we seek to resolve the question. Presumably, this strategy makes us more active readers.

- *Read.* Actively read the chapter. Have your *Study Guide* nearby so that you can look periodically at the Chapter Outline. Break your reading into smaller segments. Don't read the entire chapter in one sitting, since there is too much material to absorb. While reading, take small breaks in between major sections of the chapter. During your break (e.g., while jogging), actively reflect on what you've read. See if you can answer the question(s) you formulated. After you have read several sections, and certainly before you quit your studying, review the Chapter Outline.

- *Recite.* Looking away from the book, briefly recite out loud the main points of the section you've read. Try to create an original example that would illustrate the concept under discussion. If a research study is discussed, summarize the main points of the research study. Another recitation strategy is to use the Key Terms Review in the *Study Guide.*

- *Review.* The Chapter Outlines in the *Study Guide* serve as a useful tool for review prior to an examination. Again, be active in your review. Look at the major headings, but try to actively recite the subpoints under the heading.

You are about to embark on a fascinating journey into the world of abnormal behavior. I hope you find this *Study Guide* a helpful resource as you commence your study.

Art Olguin, Ph.D.
Santa Barbara, California

References

Pauk, W., & Fiore, J. P. (1989). *Succeed in college!* Boston: Houghton Mifflin (ISBN 0-395-51408-8).

Robinson, F. P. (1970). *Effective study* (4th ed.). New York: Harper & Row.

CHAPTER 1
Abnormal Behavior in Context

LEARNING OBJECTIVES

1. Discuss the difficulty of defining abnormal behavior. (p. 4)

2. Define abnormality using a variety of definitional standards. (pp. 4–5)

3. Describe the difficulty of distinguishing between normal and abnormal behavior. (pp. 6–8)

4. Describe abnormal behavior in the context of epidemiological, functional, statistical, and behavioral criteria. (pp. 6–8)

5. Describe mental disorders from a historical perspective and the evolution of our beliefs. (pp. 10–16)

6. Explain the multicultural dimension of abnormal behavior, including the differences in symptoms and biases. (pp. 10–15)

7. Describe the early treatment of the mentally disturbed. (pp. 13–15)

8. Discuss the scientific basis for psychological abnormality and the development of modern treatment. (pp. 15–16)

9. Describe the effect of cultural and social factors on the emergence, severity, and prevalence of mental disorders. (pp. 17–22)

10. Discuss the effect of cultural differences on the shaping of symptoms in children. (pp. 20–21)

11. Describe the effects of gender on psychological disorders. (pp. 23–24)

12. Describe the effects of age on the symptoms and expression of mental disorders for the elderly. (pp. 24–26)

13. Discuss the changing nature of the family and its effect on modern psychopathology. (pp. 26–27)

14. Discuss the effect of age in the development and expression of mental disorders. (pp. 25–26)

15. Discuss the possibility of biases in the diagnostic system based on cultural factors (pp. 21–22), gender (pp. 23–24), and age (pp. 27–28).

1

CHAPTER OUTLINE

I. Myths and Definitions of Psychological Abnormality

    A. Myths and Misunderstandings

- No single definition of psychological abnormality.

- Many myths are associated with mental illness.

        1. Does infrequency define abnormality?

            a. Statistical infrequency is a poor criterion.

            b. Infrequent behavior may be desirable, and frequent behavior may be undesirable (e.g., alcohol consumption).

        2. Does suffering define abnormality?

            a. Distress alone does not define abnormality.

            b. Many mentally disordered persons do not appear to suffer at all.

        3. Does strangeness define abnormality?

            a. Many people report odd or unusual experiences.

            b. Much psychological abnormality is common rather than bizarre (e.g., fears).

        4. Does the behavior itself define the abnormality?

            a. The meaning of a behavior depends on its context.

        5. Is normality a guideline?

            a. Efforts to define normality have not generated wide acceptance.

    B. What's Normal? Is Abnormality Normal?

        1. Aim is to distinguish clinically significant dysfunction from common human experience.

        2. Epidemiological surveys consider responses from large numbers of people using standard, consistent methods.

        3. Surveys found that about 30 percent of adults reported experiencing a diagnosable disorder currently or within the last 6 months, and 48 percent of the population reported a disorder at some time during their life.

        4. Research with children indicates that over 20 percent of children reported a diagnosable mental disorder within the past year.

        5. Psychological difficulties are extremely common.

    C. Behavior in Context: A Practical Approach to Abnormality

        1. Impaired functioning

            a. Difficulty in performing appropriate and expected roles.

            b. A criterion for psychological abnormality.

c.   Judgment about impairment must be made in the context of the person's background.

2.   *The Diagnostic and Statistical Manual* (DSM-IV)

a.   A widely accepted system in the United States and around the world for classifying psychological problems and disorders

b.   DSM establishes diagnostic criteria for behaviors that fit a pattern, cause dysfunction or subjective distress, are present for a specified duration, and are not otherwise explainable.

3.   A definition of psychological abnormality

a.   Impaired functioning with respect to expected performance suitable for the person in a relevant context.

b.   *Psychological disorder* is used interchangeably with *psychological abnormality.*

c.   *Mental illness* is another term, but it is not preferred because few DSM disorders are truly medical problems.

d.   *Psychopathology* is the scientific study of psychological disorders.

II.   Changing Historical Views of Psychological Abnormality

•   Major psychological disorders occur in all cultures during all time periods.

•   Disorders had differing interpretations.

A.   Greek and Roman Contributions to Understanding Mental Illness

1.   Greeks held a pluralistic view regarding the cause of mental disorders:

a.   Recognition of psychological factors apart from bodily functioning.

b.   Considered mental disorder a physical illness with biological causes.

2.   Emphasized an individual's life experiences.

3.   Hippocrates developed humoral theory: a disease caused by an excess or imbalance of blood, phlegm, yellow bile, and black bile.

B.   Asian and African Views of Psychological Disorder

1.   Chinese views of mental health

a.   Mental disorders were viewed as an imbalance between the forces of yin and yang, the two forces in the universe: good and bad, male and female, dark and light, positive and negative.

b.   Remedies for restoring balance included herbs, acupuncture, and folk remedies.

c.   No stigma attached to mental disorders.

d.   Other explanations involved possession by spirits or retribution for sinful deeds.

       e.   Modern practice is an eclectic combination of traditional remedies and modern treatments.

    2. Middle Eastern cultures and mental illness

       a.   Mental disorders seen as impulsive, uncontrolled, and unreasonable conditions inflicted by supernatural powers.

       b.   Folk medicine and healing practices developed and handed down by the common people were advocated.

    3. African views of mental disorder

       a.   Diversity of beliefs of causes of illness means a variety of remedies.

       b.   Little stigma attached to mental disorder, and community support provided.

       c.   Folk healers serve an important function, treating both psychological and physical disorders.

C. European Traditions of Understanding Mental Illness

   • Demonology: The study of the influence of demons

    1. Witchcraft and demonology: Mentally ill often were persecuted and killed in medieval Europe.

    2. Growth of scientific concepts of mental disorder

       a.   Medical and scientific knowledge about mental illness replaced demonology, magic, and folk treatment.

       b.   Psychoanalysis, a talking-based treatment using principles from Freud's theories, developed.

       c.   Despite advances in knowledge, mentally ill were warehoused in large hospitals in frightful conditions.

    3. Public treatment of the mentally ill

       a.   Insane asylums, the first mental hospitals, were built in Europe in the Middle Ages.

       b.   Patients chained, provided little humane treatment.

       c.   Hospitalized patients put on display; people bought tickets to go see the mentally ill.

       d.   Moral treatment, including treating patient kindly and respectfully, ushered in an era of enlightened and humane treatment in the nineteenth century.

D. Mental Illness in the Late Twentieth Century

    1. Strong emphasis on the biological basis of psychological disorders; also on how social behaviors are acquired through learning.

    2. Maladaptive ways of thinking and behaving also explored.

    3. Psychotropic medications, used to control symptoms of mental disorder, were developed in the 1950s.

4. Mental health care professionals emerged.

5. Ongoing debate over causes: biological or psychogenic (originating from psychological factors)

III. Cultural Factors in Psychological Abnormality

A. Cultural Issues in the Experience and Meaning of Psychological Disorders

1. Different cultures view emotions and emotional experiences very differently.

2. Sense of individual self in Western thought is different from family or community emphasis in other cultures.

3. Cultural meanings shape what is viewed as normal or abnormal.

4. Increasing Western affluence has generated new internal private disorders.

B. Cultural Issues in the Expression of Psychological Disorders: Different cultures are associated with different frequencies of specific disorders, e.g., suicide, alcoholism, and eating disorders.

C. Focus on Research: Does culture influence children's disorders?

1. Weisz proposed that mental disorders are influenced by different cultural expectations. Adult distress threshold model: Discouraged behaviors in children will be viewed as more problematic and will be treated in clinics most often because parents are less tolerant of them.

2. Theorized problems of overcontrolled behavior (inhibition, anxiety, fearfulness) in countries like Thailand and problems of undercontrolled behavior (aggression, impulsiveness, distractibility) in countries like the United States.

3. Study concluded that individuals will perceive behaviors as problems according to cultural patterns.

D. Consequences of Cultural Differences in the Expression of Symptoms

1. Help seeking (entering treatment for a disorder) varies considerably among cultural groups.

2. Effectiveness of services varies.

3. The course of a disorder also may be affected by cultural differences.

E. Biases Due to Cultural Factors in Psychological Disorder

1. Culturally sensitive factors should be considered to avoid diagnostic bias.

2. Bias may occur in tests and assessment procedures.

IV. Gender and Psychological Abnormality

• People expect boys and girls, men and women to behave differently in the same situation.

A. Sex Differences in the Experience and Expression of Psychological Disorder

1. Men and women experience and express psychological disorders in different ways.

a. Women more likely to have "emotional" disorders such as depression.

        b.   Men more likely to have "behavioral" disorders such as antisocial conduct.

     2.   Difference in expectation gives women greater freedom to express emotions.

  B.   Biases Due to Gender Differences

     1.   Different disorder rates in men and women due to

        a.   Biology.

        b.   Gender socialization: The process of learning expected feminine and masculine behaviors and attitudes.

        c.   Experiences.

     2.   Four potential sources of bias:

        a.   Diagnostic system.

        b.   Judgments by clinicians.

        c.   Measurement methods.

        d.   Sampling: The process of selecting populations for study.

           1.   Studies may be biased if based only on people seeking treatment.

           2.   Women more willing than men to seek treatment.

V.   Age and Psychological Abnormality

  A.   Age Differences in the Experience and Expression of Disorders

     1.   Children and adults differ in how they express and cope with distress.

        a.   Children's disorders such as depression are now being studied in greater depth.

        b.   Additional research is needed with older adults.

  B.   Age Trends and Sources of Bias in Psychological Disorders

     1.   Age of onset reflects at what point in life certain disorders are most likely to appear.

     2.   Several types of mental disorders are likely to develop between late adolescence and early adulthood (e.g., depression, bipolar, obsessive-compulsive disorder, substance-use disorders, and schizophrenia).

  C.   Family Matters: The Importance of Family in Mental Health

     1.   Family experiences important in overall mental health functioning and adjustment.

     2.   Dramatic changes in family life in the United States threatens optimal mental health functioning.

        a.   Increasing number of children being raised in single-parent families, caused by divorces and births to unmarried women.

        b.   High teenage birth rate.

c. Stressors associated with being single, including poverty, increase children's risk of maladjustment and mental disorders.

D. Age-Related Biases

1. Issue of possible age-related bias must be addressed.

2. Until recently most psychological research neglected the elderly.

VI. What Lies Ahead?

A. Changing social norms will continue to influence the definition of psychological conditions.

B. Greater understanding is needed about the effects of age, culture, and gender on psychological disorders.

KEY TERMS REVIEW

1. Mental hospitals were once called _____.

2. Conditions originating from psychological factors are said to be _____.

3. The process of learning expected feminine and masculine behaviors and attitudes is called _____.

4. Surveys in which researchers, using standard, consistent methods of interviewing, interview large numbers of randomly selected people who represent all segments of the population—different sexes, ages, races, and socioeconomic status—are called a(n) _____.

5. In Chinese belief, the two forces within the universe—good and bad, male and female, dark and light, positive and negative—that must be maintained in balance are called _____.

6. A term used interchangeably with *psychological abnormality* is _____.

7. Psychological abnormalities such as inhibition, anxiety, and fearfulness are examples of _____.

8. Epidemiological surveys indicate that about _____ percent of adults are affected with mental disorders at some time during their life.

9. A method of treating the hospitalized mentally ill that emerged in the early nineteenth century and included treating patients kindly and respectfully, offering guidance and support, and encouraging fresh air and activity is called _____.

10. Difficulty in performing appropriate and expected roles is called _____.

11. _____ is a personality disorder characterized by a history of callousness, disregard for social conventions and others' rights and feelings, and illegal conduct.

12. The process used by ancient societies of surgically cutting a hole in the skull to permit the release of demons is known as _____.

13. A person who exhibits no symptoms of distress but who is judged by a clinician as being mentally unhealthy is said to have _____.

14. Entering treatment for a disorder is called _____.

15. The study of the influence of demons is called _____.

16. Healing practices developed and handed down by the common people are called _____.

17. The process of selecting groups of people from populations for study is called _____.

18. A term sometimes used interchangeably with *psychological abnormality* is _____.

19. Psychological abnormalities such as aggression, impulsivity, and distractibility are called _____.

20. Though not a part of modern mental health systems, they were observers of psychological disorders in traditional societies who used healing rituals and exorcism as well as herbal medicines to try to alleviate distress and are called _____.

21. A view of health originated by Hippocrates in which the body is seen as being composed of four fluids produced by various organs—blood, phlegm, yellow bile, and black bile—and disease or disorder is seen as developing as a result of excesses or imbalance of these substances from internal or external causes and is called the _____.

22. The most widely accepted system in the United States and around the world for classifying psychological problems and disorders is the _____.

23. Medicines used to control symptoms of mental disorder and to reduce distress associated with psychological problems are called _____.

24. A personality disorder characterized by traits such as excessive emotionality, flamboyance, and attention seeking is called _____.

25. Impaired functioning with respect to expected performance suitable for the person in a relevant context, which includes consideration of the situation in which the behaviors occur as well as gender, age, cultural values, and historical perspective, is called _____.

26. The scientific study of psychological disorders is called _____.

FACTUAL MULTIPLE-CHOICE QUESTIONS

1. Psychological abnormality
   a. is a matter of widely accepted truths.
   b. is related to definitions developed in the last twenty-five years.
   c. is not subject to confusion.
   d. is associated with myths and misconceptions.

2. Which criterion for defining abnormality is best illustrated by the renowned qualities possessed by Mother Teresa and Albert Einstein?
   a. infrequency
   b. strangeness
   c. suffering
   d. behavior

3. Epidemiological surveys
   a. focus on a small group of people.
   b. focus on one segment of the population.
   c. survey people who represent all segments of the population.
   d. use individualized methods of gathering the data.

4. The most widely accepted system in the world for classifying psychological problems is
   a. the *International Classification of Diseases.*
   b. *The Diagnostic and Statistical Manual.*
   c. *The Physician's Desk Reference.*
   d. *The Mental Measurements Yearbook.*

5. Psychopathology is
   a. the scientific study of psychological disorders.
   b. the study of psychopaths.
   c. the study of psychological diagnosis.
   d. the scientific study of illness based primarily on autopsy results.

6. The Greek physician who believed that psychological problems were due to an imbalance of bodily humors of fluids was
   a. Pinel.
   b. Homer.
   c. Hippocrates.
   d. Kraeplin.

7. The London hospital of St. Mary at Bethlehem was popularly known as
   a. the Asylum.
   b. Pandemonium.
   c. Bedlam.
   d. the Sanitorium.

8. The founder of moral treatment was
   a. Charcot.
   b. Breuer.
   c. James.
   d. Pinel.

9. Which group is more likely to make use of psychological services?
   a. Hispanics
   b. European Americans
   c. Asian Americans
   d. African Americans

10. Which of the following is more characteristic of the gender?
    a. women=depression, men=alcoholism
    b. women=drug abuse, men=manic-depression
    c. women=antisocial personality disorder, men=depression
    d. women=alcoholism, men=depression

CONCEPTUAL MULTIPLE-CHOICE QUESTIONS

1. Which of the following was *not* used by the Chinese to restore the balance between yin and yang?
   a. herbal medicines
   b. acupuncture
   c. folk remedies
   d. bloodletting

2. Cross-cultural research on children's mental health indicates that
   a. there are few differences in the type of mental disorders seen in children from various cultures.
   b. cultures emphasizing obedience tend to produce children with aggressive and undercontrolled symptoms.
   c. cultures emphasizing aggressiveness and self-expression tend to produce children with internalized and overcontrolled symptoms.
   d. what is considered a psychological disorder is influenced by the values and expectations of one's culture.

3. In late medieval Europe and in the American colonies, witches were burned, hanged, and drowned in an effort to
   a. exorcise the demon.
   b. save their souls.
   c. punish them for their sins.
   d. cure their mental illness.

4. The reason certain disorders are more prevalent in some countries than in others is primarily because of
   a. different cultural values.
   b. genetics.
   c. intelligence.
   d. physical condition.

5. In the United States, parents are tolerant of aggressiveness. This might encourage behaviors characterized by
   a. overcontrol.
   b. undercontrol.
   c. depression.
   d. school phobia.

6. Research on children's psychological disorders has shown that
   a. they are virtually identical to adult disorders.
   b. children cope with distress in the same way as adults.
   c. understanding childhood disorders is quite advanced.
   d. children and adults differ in how they cope with distress.

7. Dr. Miller works with a late adolescent population. Lately she has noticed that the problems in this age group
   a. have diminished.
   b. are of a less serious nature than other age groups.
   c. are unrelated to gender.
   d. seem to be more serious because of more severe stress.

8. Kenny is interested in learning how to help people solve their personal problems. He was surprised to learn
   a. that there are so few training progams available.
   b. that there are many training programs available.
   c. that little training is needed to become a mental health professional.
   d. that the training is of short duration.

9. Dr. Henri's client, Stella, demonstrated callous disregard for the rights of others and criminal activity. The doctor said his diagnosis would not be antisocial personality disorder (APD) because
   a. the diagnostic system is imperfect anyway.
   b. men and women are different and the diagnosis doesn't matter that much.
   c. APD is not typically a female disorder.
   d. everyone knows that women are emotional and men are aggressive.

10. Mark is entering graduate school in psychology and has discovered that issues of potential bias
    a. have virtually disappeared.
    b. don't apply to children or the elderly.
    c. have been under intense scientific scrutiny for some time.
    d. still exist with regard to gender, culture, and age.

APPLICATION MULTIPLE-CHOICE QUESTIONS

1. Marianne reports regular communication with the saints and Jesus. In all other aspects of her life she seems normal. She would be diagnosed as
   a. schizophrenic.
   b. abnormal.
   c. normal.
   d. insane.

2. A psychiatric group met to evaluate Mr. Smith. His behaviors were certainly unusual and disturbing to his family. He was having real difficulty performing basic tasks, and his internist had declared him physically sound. The diagnosis was
   a. eccentric but not abnormal.
   b. normal.
   c. psychological disorder.
   d. a medical problem.

3. Mr. Kwan, a citizen in ancient China suffering from a mental illness, was likely to be
   a. persecuted.
   b. cared for by his family.
   c. not tolerated by the community.
   d. jailed.

4. Willy Boy, a Native American from the Southwest, wants to find a therapist to help him with depression. He wants to find a Native American therapist because
   a. of cultural considerations.
   b. of the differences in training.
   c. of the extensive research on the importance of cultural sensitivity in therapy.
   d. of the overly broad view taken on agreed-on physical reality by most Western culture-tradition therapists.

5. Dr. Kim was especially concerned about Mr. Lee's excessive use of alcohol because
   a. it was unusual for a Korean male to drink so much.
   b. in Korea the use of alcohol is strictly forbidden by religious law.
   c. studies have shown that Korean men have very high rates of alcohol disorders.
   d. cultural influences rarely shape the use of alcohol.

6. Julie's parents tolerated her aggressive and sometimes intrusive behavior. Julie probably lives in
   a. the United States.
   b. Thailand.
   c. Jamaica.
   d. Great Britain.

7. Kwasi was diagnosed with schizophrenia. His family decided to keep him at home in their small village in Ghana. The course of his illness is likely to be good because
   a. of the tolerant/supportive environment of the village.
   b. of advances in the treatment of the illness.
   c. of psychotherapy, which will delve into his childhood experiences.
   d. his disorder is not biologically based.

8. Darryl, an African American, was picked up by the police near an affluent neighborhood acting in a strange, although nonviolent manner. He is likely to
   a. be released after a few questions.
   b. receive a psychological evaluation and treatment.
   c. be charged with a crime.
   d. be given a test that will fairly evaluate his psychological condition.

9. Jane and Jeremy were going through a difficult divorce. Jane told her friends that she was depressed and was crying several times a day. Jeremy is more likely to express his distress by
   a. weeping.
   b. going to good friends and telling them of his sadness.
   c. asking his friends for help because the situation was out of his control.
   d. using alcohol and other drugs to ease his pain.

10. Marie is nine years old and told her doctor that she always got a stomachache when Mommy and Daddy had fights. Her doctor should consider treating Marie for
    a. depression.
    b. schizophrenia.
    c. autism.
    d. conduct disorder.

ANSWER KEY: KEY TERMS REVIEW

1. insane asylums (13)
2. psychogenic (16)
3. gender socialization (23)
4. epidemiological surveys (6)
5. yin and yang (11)
6. psychological disorder (9)
7. overcontrolled behavior (20)
8. forty-eight (6–7)
9. moral treatment (14)
10. impaired functioning (8)
11. antisocial personality disorder (APD) (24)
12. trephining (10)

13. illusory mental health (7)
14. help seeking (21)
15. demonology (13)
16. folk medicine (11)
17. sampling (24)
18. psychological disorder or mental illness (9)
19. undercontrolled behavior (20)
20. folk healers (11)
21. humoral theory (11)
22. *Diagnostic and Statistical Manual,* 4th edition (DSM-IV) (8)
23. psychotropic medications (16)

24. histrionic personality disorder (HPD)   25. psychological abnormality (9)
    (24)   26. psychopathology (9)

ANSWER KEY: FACTUAL MULTIPLE-CHOICE QUESTIONS

1. *d. is associated with myths and misconceptions (p. 4)
   a. There is no single, final, widely accepted truth about what constitutes psychological abnormality.
   b. The definitions in use today have evolved over centuries.
   c. Most people are confused about what psychological abnormality is.

2. *a. Infrequency (p. 5)
   b. Strangeness is departure from normal sensory experience. Mother Teresa and Einstein are not known for such experiences.
   c. Neither Mother Teresa nor Einstein were (are) noted for their suffering.
   d. Their behaviors and accomplishments are unusual, but not shocking or disgusting.

3. *c. survey people who represent all segments of the population (p. 6)
   a. Epidemiological surveys consider large numbers of people.
   b. The researchers sample many segments of the population.
   d. Standardized methods are used to gather the data.

4. *b. *The Diagnostic and Statistical Manual* (p. 8)
   a. The World Health Organization publishes the ICD, which is similar to the DSM, but is not the most widely accepted system.
   c. The PDR is a general reference work for physicians and not a diagnostic manual.
   d. The MMY is a compendium of information on psychological tests and not a diagnostic manual.

5. *a. the scientific study of psychological disorders (p. 9)
   b. Psychopathy is just one category of mental disorder.
   c. Psychopathology is the study of all aspects of disorders.
   d. Psychopathology is based upon information derived from many sources.

6. *c. Hippocrates (p. 11)
   a. Pinel ushered in the era of moral treatment in France during the eighteenth century.
   b. Homer was not a physician but is credited with writing the *Odyssey*.
   c. Kraeplin developed a diagnostic classification system during the late 1800s.

7. *c. Bedlam (p. 14)
   a. St. Mary's was an asylum, but was known popularly as Bedlam.
   b. Pandemonium is the name of the capital of hell in Milton's *Paradise Lost*.
   d. Sanitorium is a term associated with health resorts, some of which dealt with mental disorders.

8. *d. Pinel (p. 14)
   a. Charcot was one of the early experimenters with hypnotism.
   b. Breuer influenced Freud in the development of the cathartic method, later psychoanalysis.
   c. William James was a psychologist-philosopher and influential in the early days of psychology.

9. *d.   African Americans (p. 21)
   a.   Hispanics underutilize services.
   b.   European Americans underutilize services.
   c.   Asian Americans underutilize services.

10. *a.   women=depression, men=alcoholism (p. 23)
    b.   Women are more associated with emotional disorders.
    c.   Men are associated with behavioral disorders.
    d.   There are proportionally far fewer female than male alcoholics.

ANSWER KEY: CONCEPTUAL MULTIPLE-CHOICE QUESTIONS

1. *d.   bloodletting (p. 11)
   a.   Herbal medicines were used to restore the balance of the two forces.
   b.   Acupuncture is another technique used when the humors were thought to be out of balance.
   c.   Folk remedies of many types were used for physical and mental problems.

2. *d.   what is considered a psychological disorder is influenced by the values and expectations of one's culture. (pp. 20–21)
   a.   Weisz's research shows differences in symptomatology between children from the U.S. and Thailand.
   b.   Such cultures exhibit higher levels of internalized or overcontrolled symptoms.
   c.   Such cultures exhibit higher levels of externalized or undercontrolled symptoms.

3. *b.   save their souls (p. 13)
   a.   These people were thought of as agents of the devil, not possessed.
   c.   These policies were designed to rid the populace of heretics and the devil, not to punish sinners.
   d.   It was not until social conditions changed that some of those accused of witchcraft were recognized as mentally ill.

4. *a.   different cultural values (p. 19)
   b.   Genetics only pass the biological material from one generation to the next.
   c.   Intelligence is a factor that is highly variable and may be symptomatic of mental retardation if it is found to be low.
   d.   Physical condition may contribute to certain disorders, but it is not associated with different frequencies of disorders.

5. *b.   undercontrol (pp. 20–21)
   a.   Overcontrol behaviors are associated with cultures that value quiet, controlled behavior.
   c.   Depression would more likely be associated with problems of overcontrol.
   d.   School phobia would be associated with overcontrol.

6. *d.   children and adults differ in how they cope with distress (p. 25)
   a.   Children may "act out" to release tension, while an adult might turn to drugs.
   b.   Children cope with distress in very different ways than adults.
   c.   Researchers have only recently begun to study children's disorders.

7. *d. seem to be more serious because of more severe stress (pp. 25–26)
   a. Recent research shows increasing stress on young adults.
   b. Some of the most serious disorders have age of onset between thirteen and twenty-five.
   c. There are gender-related differences, such as age of onset for depression.

8. *b. that there are many training programs available (p. 16)
   a. The twentieth century has seen the emergence of many mental health care professional training programs.
   c. Most programs require a minimum of a bachelor's degree and many require more advanced degrees and training.
   d. The training may last from six years to twelve years for an M.D. or Ph.D.

9. *c. APD is not typically a female disorder. (p. 24)
   a. The diagnostic system is functional, but bias distorts some evaluations.
   b. Diagnostic criteria were not designed to be differentially applied according to stereotypical attitudes about gender.
   d. Application of diagnostic labels may be biased by clinicians with this attitude.

10. *d. still exist with regard to gender, culture, and age (p. 27)
    a. The potential for bias in such areas as alcoholism, homosexuality, and antisocial conduct is very real.
    b. Potential for bias applies specifically to children and the elderly.
    c. Scientific study of these issues has not answered all the questions regarding the effects of culture, age, and gender bias on psychological disorders.

ANSWER KEY: APPLICATION MULTIPLE-CHOICE QUESTIONS

1. *c. normal (p. 5)
   a. Such experiences as hearing voices in and of themselves do not necessarily signal psychological abnormality.
   b. Unusual behaviors and experiences are often greatly valued.
   d. Insanity is a legal term often used in defense of persons who have committed crimes.

2. *c. psychological disorder (p. 8)
   a. Mr. Smith's impaired functioning would go beyond mere eccentricity.
   b. Both aspects of Mr. Smith's behavior argue for a diagnosis of a mental disorder.
   d. There is no evidence that his behavior is prompted by a medical problem.

3. *b. cared for by his family (p. 11)
   a. There was no stigma attached to mental disorders in ancient China, because such disorders were thought to be related to physical imbalances.
   c. Communities were quite tolerant if they felt the victims had been singled out for no apparent reason.
   d. Families and communities were fairly tolerant of persons with mental disorders.

4. *a. of cultural considerations (p. 17)
   b. The ethnicity of the therapist will not determine the level of formal training.
   c. The recognition of the importance of culture has only recently gained a research following.
   d. Western culture-tradition therapy is not tolerant of departures from agreed-on physical reality.

5. *c. studies have shown that Korean men have very high rates of alcohol disorders (p. 19)
    a. Under certain circumstances, Korean men are known to consume large quantities of alcohol.
    b. Religious law does not forbid the use of alcohol in Korea.
    d. Some cultures stress the use of large quantities of alcohol under certain conditions.

6. *a. the United States (p. 20)
    b. Thai children are taught to be polite, modest, and deferential toward others.
    c. Jamaican children are expected to be polite, obedient, and unaggressive.
    d. The British emphasize respect for authority.

7. *a. of the tolerant/supportive environment of the village (p. 21)
    b. Any advances in the treatment of the illness would not reach his village.
    c. That approach to therapy would likely be of little interest to someone living in a poor village.
    d. Schizophrenia is at least partially biologically based, but the tolerant environment of the village will provide important support for Kwasi.

8. *c. be charged with a crime (p. 22)
    a. African American men who exhibit aberrant behavior are likely to be treated as criminals.
    b. African American men are often sent to prison rather than diagnosed as mentally ill and needing psychiatric care.
    d. Bias may occur in the test and assessment procedures.

9. *d. Men are particularly prone to "behavioral" disorders. (p. 23)
    a. Men are less apt to weep; they are expected to be strong and not display emotion.
    b. Men are expected to be dominant and in control of situations and are less apt to share needy situations.
    c. Men are expected to be independent and are less apt to seek help.

10. *a. depression (p. 25)
    b. Schizophrenia is usually later onset than age nine and with more bizarre symptoms.
    c. Marie does not demonstrate any of the symptoms of autism.
    d. Conduct disorder would have symptoms of aggression and hostility.

CHAPTER 2
Models of Psychopathology

LEARNING OBJECTIVES

1. Explain the importance of using paradigms and theories to understand abnormal behavior. (p. 32)

2. Describe the biomedical model of psychopathology. (pp. 32–33)

3. Describe the anatomy of the brain. (pp. 33–34)

4. Describe the action of neurotransmitters in the brain. (pp. 34–35)

5. Describe the physical reactions to situations controlled by the autonomic nervous system. (pp. 35–37)

6. Discuss the effect of genetic transmission and inherited biological predispositions. (pp. 37–39)

7. Describe the diathesis-stress model of interaction between biological predispositions and environmental influences. (p. 38)

8. Discuss the pros and cons of using a biomedical model to explain the causes of mental disorders. (p. 40)

9. Describe behaviorism and the learning models, including classical conditioning, operant conditioning, and modeling. (pp. 40–45)

10. Discuss the pros and cons of using the behaviorist model to explain the causes of mental disorders. (p. 45)

11. Describe the cognitive models, including Ellis's irrational beliefs and Beck's cognitive theory of depression. (pp. 45–48)

12. Describe the cognitive-behavioral model. (pp. 48–49)

13. Discuss the pros and cons of using the cognitive model to explain the causes of mental disorders. (pp. 48–49)

14. Describe the psychodynamic model of human behavior, including the mental structures, levels of consciousness, defense mechanisms, and psychosexual stages of development. (pp. 49–52)

15. Discuss the neo-Freudians and their contributions to basic psychodynamic theory. (pp. 53–54)

16. Describe the pros and cons of using the psychodynamic model to explain the causes of mental disorders. (pp. 54–55)

17. Describe the humanistic model, including the theories of Rogers and Maslow. (pp. 55–56)

18. Discuss the pros and cons of using the humanistic model to explain the causes of mental disorders. (pp. 56–57)

19. Discuss how each of the theories would describe normal functioning. (pp. 57–59)

CHAPTER OUTLINE

- Model (paradigm): A guiding framework that helps conceptualize and organize available information.

- In addition to a model, a methodology is also needed to empirically test assumptions and hypotheses.

I. Biomedical Models: Psychological Disorders and Biological Conditions

- The biomedical model assumes symptoms of psychological disorder are caused by biological factors.

- *General paresis* was one of the earliest recognitions of a mental illness caused by an underlying physical cause, syphilis bacteria.

A. The Role of the Brain in Psychological Abnormality

1. Anatomy of the brain

a. *Neurons* (nerve cells) and *glial* (support) cells make up the brain.

b. *Cerebral cortex:* outer area of the brain, responsible for many functions. Has four regions:

(1) Frontal lobes contain motor cortex and are involved with higher-order mental processes such as thinking and planning.

(2) Temporal lobes involved in processing language, in memory, and in perception.

(3) Parietal lobes contain the somatosensory cortex and receive information about pain, pressures, and body temperature.

(4) Occipital lobes contain the visual cortex.

c. Three sections of brain: *forebrain, midbrain,* and *hindbrain.*

(1) Thalamus processes and relays information to areas in the cerebral cortex.

(2) Hypothalamus regulates hunger, thirst, sex drive, and temperature.

(3) Limbic system provides *homeostasis,* or constancy of internal environment. Regulates endocrine glands and autonomic nervous system.

2. Communication in the brain: neurotransmitters

    a. Neurotransmitter substances are chemicals used to transmit electrical impulses from neuron to neuron.

    b. More than 50 types of neurotransmitters in brain.

    c. Neurotransmission problems have many physiological as well as environmental causes.

B. Arousal and Overarousal

1. Autonomic nervous system regulates motivational and emotional states of the body and monitors its basic physiology.

    a. Sympathetic system mediates body's response to stress (fight-or-flight response).

    b. Parasympathetic system conserves body's resources and restores homeostasis.

C. Genes and Their Expression

1. Genetic transmission determines the inherited *biological predisposition* of a person toward psychopathology.

2. Genes: codes for the potential expression of characteristics, found in chromosomes.

3. Genes carry predisposition for certain psychological disorders.

    a. Monozygotic twins (identical)—have 100 percent genetic similarity.

    b. Dizygotic twins (fraternal)—have 50 percent genetic similarity.

D. Biological Predispositions and Interactions with the Environment

1. Sociocultural influences

    a. Biological predisposition is influenced by interactions with the environment and sociocultural influences.

    b. Culture has a strong influence.

    c. *Cultural relativity* is an extreme perspective that emphasizes importance of culture.

2. The diathesis-stress model

    a. Assumes the existence of a biological predisposition in conjunction with environmental factors.

    b. *Diathesis* refers to biological predispositions.

    c. *Stress* refers to current environmental factors that could contribute to abnormal behavior.

E. Focus on Research: Can the Role of the Environment in Development Be Experimentally Shown?

1. Research supports the importance of environment on individual differentiation.

2. Genes set certain limitations on characteristics that are influenced by the environment.

F. Pros and Cons of a Biomedical Model

1. Biological forces are not the sole cause of mental disorders.

2. Biomedical model more relevant to some problems than to others.

3. Gender differences not accounted for biomedically.

4. Biological differences do not indicate *causes* (could be results) of disorders.

II. Behaviorism: The Learning Models

• Behaviorists emphasize observable behavior and environmental factors.

• Focus on how behavior is acquired (learned) and maintained over time.

A. Classical conditioning

1. A form of learning in which once neutral stimuli, often repeated pairings over time, came to invoke involuntary responses.

2. *Unconditioned stimulus:* Dangerous location.

3. *Unconditioned response:* Fear response (unlearned).

4. *Conditioned stimulus:* A neutral stimulus (e.g., music) repeatedly paired with unconditioned stimulus (dangerous situation).

5. *Conditioned response:* The learned response that results from the conditioned stimulus.

B. Operant conditioning

1. Operant learning indicates that a response will be increased when it is followed by reinforcement and decreased when the response is followed by punishment.

a. Thorndike: learning produced by consequences (*law of effect*).

b. Skinner: operant conditioning includes *punishment* as a disincentive and *positive reinforcement* as reward to encourage certain behaviors.

c. Shaping is a gradual process, with reinforcement at interim steps.

d. Partial reinforcement: occasional reinforcement is more effective in maintaining a behavior.

e. Negative reinforcement: likelihood of a behavior increases by the removal of an unpleasant situation.

f. Avoidance learning is another strategy to avoid discomfort (but is used often when response is not necessary).

C. Modeling

1. Observational learning or modeling is the process of learning behaviors by observing others performing those behaviors.

2. Social learning theory: Behavior is the product of external stimulus events and internal cognitive processes.

    D. Pros and cons of the behavioral model

        1. Pro: sensitive to cultural and social factors.

        2. Con: oversimplified and unrealistic.

III. The Cognitive Model: Disordered Thought Processing

    • *Cognition:* How humans perceive, recognize, attend, reason, and judge

    • Cognitive model emphasizes that cognitive functioning contributes to any emotional or behavioral distress.

    • Cognition can be best understood in terms of cognitive structure, cognitive content, cognitive processes, and cognitive products.

    • Cognitive deficiencies (absence of thinking) and cognitive distortions (dysfunctional thought processes) are additional factors.

    A. Cognitive Distortions and the Emotional Disorders

        1. Irrational beliefs

            a. Misguided and inaccurate assumptions (Ellis's rational-emotive view).

            b. Events themselves don't cause distress, but the person's interpretation of them.

            c. Inaccurate silent assumptions result in psychological maladjustment.

        2. Cognition and depression

            a. Cognitive model of depression sees causes in individual distortion of experience.

            b. Negative distortions: Fatalistic view of reality

    B. Pros and Cons of the Cognitive Model

        1. Model is clinically useful.

        2. Biological and interpersonal factors are not considered.

        3. Overemphasizes the present.

        4. Many life circumstances not irrational, simply horrible.

        5. Verification difficult.

    C. Cognitive-Behavioral Model

        1. Emphasizes the learning process and the influences of the environment.

        2. Proposes treatments aimed at modifying client's perceptions while employing behavioral procedures.

        3. An integrated model

IV. Psychodynamics: An Intrapsychic Model

- Emphasizes internal mental processes and the role of early childhood experiences.

A. Elements of Freud's Theory

   1. Mental structures in conflict

     a. Called *psychodynamic* because he believed disorders result from mental conflict—intrapsychic conflict

     b. Based on his view of id (unorganized unconscious reservoir of forbidden wishes), superego (storehouse of moral and ethical standards, conscience), and ego (mediator of id and superego which satisfies id impulses in realistic ways).

   2. Levels of consciousness

     a. Conflicts occur at different levels: *preconscious, conscious,* and *unconscious* (mental activity outside a person's normal awareness).

     b. Freud believed the unconscious exercised profound effect on conscious thinking, emotions, and behavior, producing anxiety and guilt.

   3. Defense mechanisms

     a. These are unconscious processes used by the ego and aimed at reducing anxiety caused by uncomfortable or unacceptable id impulses.

     b. Example is repression, the unconscious but purposeful exclusion of painful thoughts from consciousness. If these defenses fail, the person develops a neurosis.

   4. Stages of psychosexual development

     a. Oral, anal, phallic, latency, and genital stages must supposedly be passed successfully or the adult may become fixated and then regress under stress.

     b. Fixation: Excessive attachment to someone or something appropriate to earlier stage.

     c. Regression: Reversion to an earlier form of behavior.

     d. Unsuccessful resolution of stages affect personality development and influence psychological disorders.

B. Neo-Freudian Reconsiderations

   1. Neo-Freudian views also based on intrapsychic conflict.

   2. Neo-Freudians placed less emphasis on sexuality and more on social interaction.

     a. Jung: collective unconscious.

     b. Adler: basic inferiority and compensation.

     c. Sullivan: security.

     d. Horney: childhood relationships important for secure psychological adjustment.

3. Object relations theory focuses on early interpersonal relationships, especially mother-child relationship.

C. Pros and Cons of the Psychodynamic Model

    1. Enduring contributions

        a. First to recognize the importance of child's early experiences.

        b. Internal conflict important source of psychological difficulty.

        c. Identified the unconscious as an influential motivator of human behavior.

    2. Unsupported ideas

        a. Sexual instincts as basis for all human behavior is a limiting concept; learned motives also influence behavior.

        b. No evidence of psychosexual stages.

        c. No evidence for id, ego, and superego.

    3. Underrepresentativeness of sample.

        a. Theories based on small limited sample of 20- to 45-year-old upper-middle-class Viennese women.

        b. Not based on empirical research.

    4. Sexism of Freud's views

        a. Depicts women as inferior.

        b. Did not study children.

V. Humanism: Self-Focused Views

- Humanistic view emphasizes each individual's values, free choices, and personal goals, values, and sense of purpose.

- Abnormality results from lack of self-acceptance, inauthentic living, and refusal to accept personal responsibility for one's actions.

A. Rogers's View of the Self

    1. Rogers valued personal authenticity, living in a way that reflects awareness and care of one's self and others.

    2. Noted for *client-centered* therapy.

B. Maslow's Self-Actualization

    1. Hierarchy of human needs with self-actualization (ongoing fulfillment of personal potential) at its pinnacle and physiological needs at the base.

    2. Postulated that basic needs must be met before more advanced needs.

    3. When needs are not met, conflict emerges, resulting in stress and psychological and physical disorders.

C. Pros and Cons of the Humanistic Model

1. Emphasizes individual's strengths, values, and personal goals; sensitive to individual differences, including cultural diversity.

2. Has lost much of its influence except in the area of group psychotherapy.

3. Humanistic disapproval of the scientific approach has weakened its influence.

VI. Family Matters: Models of Family Functioning and Psychopathology

1. Most models of psychological functioning locate psychopathology within the individual rather than within larger systems in which the individual operates (e.g., family).

2. Behaviorists emphasize importance of parents: Modeling, selectively rewarding, creating climate of acceptance or rejection.

3. Enmeshment: Family situation in which no member can have a separate identity.

4. Enmeshment, rigidity, and overprotection seen in families with an anorectic child.

5. Family systems assume that the individual does not have a disorder; rather, the family is viewed as dysfunctional.

VII. What's Normal? What the Models Have to Say About Healthy Functioning

1. Each model has different assumptions for what constitutes normal mentally healthy functioning.

2. Jahoda's notion of mental health stresses effective interpersonal problem-solving skills.

VIII. What Lies Ahead?

A. Modern approaches to models of psychopathology do not expect universal applicability.

B. Move toward micromodels to explain individual disorders.

C. Trend toward integration of models.

D. Trend toward greater attention to gender, and ethnic and cultural influences.

KEY TERMS REVIEW

1. According to Freudian theory, unconscious processes that try to protect the ego from anxiety, provoked by unwanted or unacceptable impulses, are called _____.

2. The operations or manners of operation by which the individual system inputs, stores, transforms, and governs the output of information are called _____.

3. Identical twins who share 100 percent of genetic makeup are also called _____.

4. The hypothesized mental structure that is said to be an unorganized reservoir of forbidden wishes and passions of our basic sexual and aggressive drives, which strives for immediate gratification that bypasses the demands of reality, order, and logic, is called the _____.

5. The absence of thinking, as when an individual's responses and emotional states do not benefit from careful thinking or planning, is called _____.

6. Mental activity outside a person's normal awareness is the _____.

7. A reversion to an earlier, and therefore more immature, form of behavior, said to be the result of some external stress or in response to internal conflict, is called _____.

8. A model that explains psychological abnormalities in terms of an active interaction between genetic and other biological dispositions and stressful environmental influences is called the _____.

9. Misguided and inaccurate assumptions, which influence one's perceptions and can lead to maladaptive behavior, are called _____.

10. Freud's second psychosexual phase, during which the focus of sexual attention is the anal area and the child derives pleasure from the retention and expulsion of feces, is called _____.

11. The unconscious but purposeful exclusion of painful thoughts or unacceptable desires or impulses from consciousness is called _____.

12. A form of learning in which once neutral stimuli, after repeated pairings over time, come to evoke involuntary responses is called _____.

13. The fifth—and last—of Freud's psychosexual stages, which begins with puberty and is characterized by a reawakening and maturation of the sexual drives, is the _____.

14. Thought processes that are dysfunctional, such as active misperceptions and misconstruals of the environment, are called _____.

15. Psychologists who emphasize observable behavior and the environmental forces that maintain the action are called _____.

16. Living in a way that reflects awareness and care of oneself and others, which includes being spontaneous, open to new experiences, self-directed, and accepting of personal responsibility, is _____.

17. The hypothesized mental structure that is the storehouse of the moral and ethical standards taught by parents and culture (what we generally think of as "conscience") is the _____.

18. The actual information that is stored in memory is called the _____.

19. Conflict among the ego, id, and superego, which, according to psychodynamic theory, contributes to thoughts, attitudes, and behaviors is called _____.

20. The type of response an organism makes to a conditioned stimulus as a result of learning is called the _____.

21. An explanation of psychopathology that emphasizes that an individual's cognitive functioning contributes to emotional or behavioral distress is called the _____.

22. The fourth psychosexual phase, during which sexual drives seem to be inactive, is the _____.

23. Chemicals used to transmit electrical impulses from neuron to neuron are called _____.

24. A part of the nervous system that regulates the motivational and emotional states of the body and monitors its basic physiology is called the _____.

25. The third psychosexual phase, during which a boy develops sexual attachment to his mother and views his father as a rival and a girl shifts away from her mother and toward her father, is called the _____.

26. A psychological model that emphasizes each individual's values, free choices, and personal sense of purpose, with central roles given to the notion of the self and the nature of human needs and personal growth experiences, is called the _____.

27. Defense mechanisms are unconsciously used by the ego to lessen _____.

28. Following initial escape responses (to stop a negative condition) as a strategy to alleviate discomfort, the individual gradually uses avoidance responses (to prevent a negative condition) even when the response is not necessary is called _____.

29. A description of depressive disorder, in which individuals distort experience through characteristic errors in perceiving and thinking about event outcomes, personal attributes, and interpersonal relations, is called the _____.

30. A region of the forebrain that regulates hunger, thirst, sex drive, and body temperature is called the _____.

31. A psychological view that emphasizes the learning process and the influences of the environment while underscoring the importance of cognitive-mediating and information-processing factors in the development and treatment of psychological disorders is called the _____.

32. Another word for *model* is _____.

33. If one's behavior has the effect of stopping a negative condition, then the behavior is called an _____.

34. According to Jung's theory, a collection of primitive ideas and images that are inherited and shared across the human race is called the _____.

35. A psychological model that explains behavior as the product of both external stimulus events and internal cognitive processes is called _____.

36. A view of human motivation as multileveled, ranging from basic human needs for food, drink, and sex at the bottom to the need for self-actualization at the top, is called the _____.

37. The internal organization of information that influences how new experiences are perceived and understood is called _____.

38. Predisposing factors, which include biological determinants and characteristic manners of responding that interact with stress to contribute to psychological disorders, are called _____.

39. The results of an individual's manipulation of the information within the cognitive system are called _____.

40. Freud's concept, indicating a stoppage or arrest at some point in the person's psychosexual development, is called _____.

41. A guiding framework (paradigm) that helps conceptualize and organize available information is called a(n) _____.

42. An area of the forebrain that is important in the processing and relaying of information between other regions of the central nervous system and the cerebral cortex is the _____.

43. Perceptions that distort reality in unnecessarily fatalistic ways are called _____.

44. A family situation in which no member can have a separate identity is called _____.

45. The part of the autonomic nervous system that mediates the body's response to stress, speeding up the heart rate, increasing blood pressure, and generally preparing for action, is the _____.

46. The process of learning behavior as a result of observing others is called _____.

47. Fraternal twins are also called _____.

48. The process of rewarding successive approximations of desired behavior, which does not require the learner to produce an entire new response pattern to receive the reinforcement, is called _____.

49. The part of the autonomic nervous system that works to conserve the body's resources and restore homeostasis by slowing the heart rate, reducing blood pressure, and preparing the body for rest is the _____.

50. The hypothesized mental structure that mediates the wishes of the id, the demands of reality, and the strictures of the superego is called the _____.

51. Reinforcements that occur only with some instances, rather than all occurrences, of desired behavior, which lead to behaviors that are more persistent than continually reinforced behavior, is called _____.

52. A psychodynamic theory of psychotherapy that deemphasizes *im*personal forces and counterforces and focuses on the influences of *inter*personal relationships stemming from early mother-child relationships is called _____.

53. A type of reinforcement in which the likelihood of a behavior increases by the removal of an unpleasant stimulus or situation is called _____.

54. Ongoing fulfillment of personal potentials and missions, a fuller acceptance of one's intrinsic nature, and a willingness to be oneself yet share fully with others is called _____.

55. The first psychosexual stage, during which the major source of pleasure is the mouth, is the _____.

56. Views of abnormal psychology that suggest that the symptoms of psychological disorders are caused by biological factors are called _____.

57. Codes for the potential expression of characteristics; found in chromosomes, they are called _____.

58. A theory that seeks to alter problem behaviors by applying positive and negative reinforcements and shaping by successive approximations is called _____.

59. A measure of the conductance of the skin, which is influenced by sweat, to determine a subject's emotional reactions is called a _____.

60. The area of the brain that includes parts of the cortex, the thalamus, and the hypothalamus; it provides *homeostasis*, or constancy of the internal environment, by regulating the activity of endocrine glands and the autonomic nervous system is the _____.

FACTUAL MULTIPLE-CHOICE QUESTIONS

1. The biomedical model suggests that the cause of psychological disorders is
   a. organic.
   b. intrapsychic.
   c. environmental.
   d. contagious.

2. Strong support for the biomedical model came with the discovery that syphilitic infection caused
   a. hysteria.
   b. neurosis.
   c. general paresis.
   d. dementia praecox.

3. Neurons transmit electrical impulses to other neurons by means of
   a. synapses.
   b. dendrites.
   c. synaptic gaps.
   d. neurotransmitters.

4. Physiological responses to the environment are controlled by the
   a. hypothalamus.
   b. central nervous system.
   c. autonomic nervous system.
   d. hormones.

5. The interaction of predisposing factors and environmental factors is called the
   a. biological-territorial model.
   b. genetic-cultural model.
   c. monozygotic-dizygotic model.
   d. diathesis-stress model.

6. The part of the mental structure that Freud thought contained forbidden wishes and passions is the
   a. superego.
   b. libido.
   c. ego.
   d. id.

7. The level of consciousness that controls a major portion of mental activity is the
   a. preconscious.
   b. unconscious.
   c. conscious.
   d. self-conscious.

8. The oral and anal stages are two of the five phases of
   a. psychodynamics.
   b. defense mechanisms.
   c. toilet training.
   d. psychosexual development.

9. Pavlov discovered
   a. positive reinforcement.
   b. operant conditioning.
   c. classical conditioning.
   d. negative reinforcement.

10. Thought processes that are dysfunctional may be called
   a. cognitive deficiencies.
   b. rational-emotive.
   c. unconscious.
   d. cognitive distortions.

CONCEPTUAL MULTIPLE-CHOICE QUESTIONS

1. Genetic material may create greater likelihood of mental disorders because of
   a. birth order.
   b. biological predisposition.
   c. id impulses.
   d. the unconscious.

2. The approach to understanding abnormal behavior emphasizing the role of internal mental processes is
   a. self-actualization.
   b. psychoanalysis.
   c. psychodynamic.
   d. neurosis.

3. Humanists oppose the medical model in their deemphasis of
   a. the client/therapist relationship.
   b. psychotherapy.
   c. diagnosis.
   d. individual responsibility.

4. Delivery of a reinforcer or punisher will determine the frequency of a behavior according to
   a. classical conditioning.
   b. operant conditioning.
   c. psychodynamic theory.
   d. humanistic theory.

5. James has been receiving psychotropic medication for over a year. The success of this treatment is not evidence of
   a. causal relationship.
   b. medical breakthrough.
   c. complete cure.
   d. biological causation.

6. Myrna and Jennifer are monozygotic twins. Myrna developed schizophrenia, inherited from her mother. Jennifer did not. This is an indication that
   a. biological predispositions are powerful predictors.
   b. genetic transmission must have been incomplete.
   c. other factors influence the development of disorders.
   d. dizygotic twins are equally at risk.

7. Dr. Young considered herself a neo-Freudian because she had rejected the master's belief in the primacy of sexuality as the determiner of human behavior in favor of
   a. religious experiences.
   b. learning theory.
   c. environmental and personal relations.
   d. the biomedical model.

8. Freud's system was completely deterministic in that all human action could be explained by a theory. Dr. Rogers refuses to accept the Freudian view and insists that we have
   a. to overcome our sexual natures.
   b. choice and self-determination.
   c. repressed our sexual needs.
   d. to recognize the importance of instinct.

9. Dr. Johnson's patient is terrified of fluffy animals. Dr. Johnson subscribes to Pavlov's explanation about the source of such fear, which is that
   a. neutral stimuli can elicit responses.
   b. neutral stimuli always remain neutral.
   c. stimulus-response is completely predictable.
   d. fear is the most easily learned response.

10. When Jane scolds her son Jimmy for reaching for the electrical outlet, she is applying the principles of
    a. Pavlov.
    b. Rogers.
    c. Skinner.
    d. Ellis.

APPLICATION MULTIPLE-CHOICE QUESTIONS

1. Dr. Schreber assigns the diagnosis *schizophrenia* and prescribes a powerful anti-psychotic drug. Her paradigmatic orientation is probably
   a. humanistic.
   b. behaviorist.
   c. cognitive.
   d. biomedical.

2. Driving on the freeway, Bernadette is cut off by a large truck. Her blood pressure goes up, pupils dilate, she begins to tremble and sweat. This response is caused by
   a. intrapsychic conflict.
   b. the autonomic nervous system.
   c. the central nervous system.
   d. the parasympathetic system.

3. Dr. Forbin was excited about the latest discoveries in treating schizophrenia. He was preparing a paper suggesting that soon all mental illnesses will be eradicated. His attitude toward the medicalization of treating mental illness may mean
   a. greater emphasis on non-biological factors.
   b. less concentration on developing more effective drugs.
   c. psychological problems will be treated as diseases with less emphasis on personal and interpersonal factors.
   d. fewer experiments will be done to search for defective genes and neuroregulatory disorders.

4. Dr. Fleiss, a psychoanalyst, interprets the dreams of her patients. This is an attempt to understand the patient's
   a. preconscious.
   b. id impulses.
   c. unconscious.
   d. ego.

5. Bill is unable to remember a large part of his painful childhood, even under intense therapy. This reaction is called
   a. amnesia.
   b. regression.
   c. repression.
   d. fugue.

6. Jane is under a great deal of stress at work. At home she often cries and refuses to talk to anyone, preferring to lie curled in her bed. This reaction might be called
   a. the oral stage.
   b. repression.
   c. regression.
   d. the Electra dilemma.

7. According to Thorndike's law of effect, Johnny learned to avoid the radiator that burned his hand and ran to his mother's outstretched arms because
   a. learning is concerned with all manner of stimuli.
   b. he is concerned with consequences of behavior.
   c. most responses are satisfying.
   d. most responses are unsatisfying.

8. Mike was laid off and feels that he is incompetent and will never be able to find another job. He is a victim of
   a. id impulses.
   b. cognitive deficiency.
   c. classical conditioning.
   d. negative distortion.

9. Joanna is able to solve problems in a logical and solution-oriented way, but she is exhausted by the process. Your diagnosis of her condition would be
   a. depression.
   b. normal.
   c. neurosis.
   d. obsessive/compulsive disorder.

10. Patricia feels depressed because her long-time boyfriend unexpectedly ended their relationship and married another woman. Patricia says that she will never trust any man again in the future because all men are dishonest. She says that she is going into therapy because there must be something personally wrong with her because her former boyfriend did not want to marry her. Which therapeutic perspective might best explain the causes of Patricia's depression?
    a. Biomedical model
    b. Behavioral model
    c. Psychodynamic model
    d. Cognitive model

ANSWER KEY: KEY TERMS REVIEW

1. defense mechanisms (50–51)
2. cognitive processes (45)
3. monozygotic twins (37)
4. id (49)
5. cognitive deficiencies (46)
6. unconscious (50)
7. regression (52)
8. diathesis-stress model (38)
9. irrational beliefs (46)
10. anal stage (52)
11. repression (51)
12. classical conditioning (40–41)
13. genital stage (52)
14. cognitive distortions (46)
15. behaviorists (40)
16. personal authenticity (56)
17. superego (49)
18. cognitive content (45)
19. intrapsychic conflict (49)
20. conditioned response (40–41)
21. cognitive model (45)
22. latency stage (52)
23. neurotransmitter substances (34)
24. autonomic nervous system (33)
25. phallic stage (52)
26. humanistic view (55)
27. anxiety or guilt (50)
28. avoidance learning (43–44)
29. cognitive model of depression (46–47)
30. hypothalamus (33)
31. cognitive-behavioral model (48–49)
32. paradigm (32)
33. escape response (43)
34. collective unconscious (53)
35. social learning theory (44)
36. hierarchy of human needs (56)
37. cognitive structures (45)
38. diatheses (38)
39. cognitive products (45)
40. fixation (52)
41. model (32)
42. thalamus (33)
43. negative distortions (46)
44. enmeshment (57)
45. sympathetic nervous system (36)
46. modeling (44)
47. dizygotic twins (37)
48. shaping (42)
49. parasympathetic nervous system (36)
50. ego (49)
51. partial reinforcement (43)
52. object relations (54)
53. negative reinforcement (43)
54. self-actualization (56)
55. oral stage (52)
56. biomedical models (32)
57. genes (37)
58. operant conditioning (42–44)
59. galvanic skin response (GSR) (54)
60. limbic system (33)

ANSWER KEY: FACTUAL MULTIPLE-CHOICE QUESTIONS

1. *a. organic (p. 32)
    b. The intrapsychic model deals with psychodynamics.
    c. Environmental factors may interact with biological predispositions.
    d. Psychological disorders are not contagious.

2. *c. general paresis (p. 33)
   a. Hysteria is caused by anxiety.
   b. Neurosis is also caused by anxiety.
   d. Dementia praecox is an early term for schizophrenia and is unrelated to syphilis.

3. *d. neurotransmitters (p. 34)
   a. Synapse is the point of contact between one cell and another.
   b. Dendrites are the short fibers of the nerve cell.
   c. Synaptic gaps are the spaces between nerve cells.

4. *c. autonomic nervous system (p. 36)
   a. The hypothalamus regulates hunger, thirst, sex, and body temperature.
   b. The central nervous system contains all the structures of the brain and spinal chord.
   d. Hormones are involved in controlling some bodily responses.

5. *d. diathesis-stress model (p. 39)
   a. Biological and territorial elements interact in the animal, not the human world.
   b. Cultural factors may protect the individual from the development of psychopathology.
   c. Monozygotic and dizygotic relate to the development of identical or fraternal twins and are not related to the environment.

6. *d. id (p. 49)
   a. The superego is also thought of as the conscience.
   b. The libido is the sexual energy that powers the psychical system.
   c. The ego is the structure that satisfies the impulses of the id in realistic ways.

7. *b. unconscious (p. 50)
   a. Preconscious thoughts are easily made conscious.
   c. Conscious material is what is in immediate awareness.
   d. Self-consciousness is in the conscious realm.

8. *d. psychosexual development (p. 52)
   a. Psychodynamics is the name for the entire system.
   b. Defense mechanisms protect the ego.
   c. Toilet training is important during the anal period.

9. *c. classical conditioning (pp. 40–42)
   a. Positive reinforcement is part of operant conditioning.
   b. Operant conditioning was discovered by Thorndike.
   d. Negative reinforcement is also part of operant conditioning.

10. *d. cognitive distortions (p. 46)
    a. Cognitive deficiencies show a lack of thought, not thought distortion.
    b. Rational-emotive is the name of a type of therapy developed by Albert Ellis to deal with cognitive distortions.
    c. Dysfunctional thought processes will be in the awareness of the individual.

ANSWER KEY: CONCEPTUAL MULTIPLE-CHOICE QUESTIONS

1. *b. biological predisposition (p. 37)
   a. Birth order does not change the genetic material we inherit.
   c. The id is the primitive part of Freud's psychical apparatus and its existence is not verifiable.
   d. The unconscious is part of the psychodynamic theory and its existence is not verifiable.

2. *c. psychodynamic (p. 49)
   a. Self-actualization is the highest goal in Maslow's hierarchy of human needs.
   b. Psychoanalysis is the method of therapy Freud developed.
   d. Neurosis is what develops from unresolved conflicts.

3. *c. diagnosis (p. 56)
   a. Humanists see the client/therapist relationship as central to the progress of therapy.
   b. Psychotherapy is what humanistically oriented therapists do.
   d. Individual responsibility is part of the philosophical underpinnings of the humanist orientation.

4. *b. operant conditioning (pp. 42–44)
   a. Classical conditioning deals with pairing unconditioned, conditioned, and neutral stimuli.
   c. Psychodynamic theory relates to instinctual forces, not learned responses to the environment.
   d. Humanistic theory emphasizes free will and responsibility, not reinforcement.

5. *a. causal relationship (p. 40)
   b. Medical breakthroughs are rare in psychopathology.
   c. Complete cures are rare and the fact that a drug treats a symptom does not mean it cures the illness.
   d. There may be biological causation, but efficacy of a particular drug is not evidence of this.

6. *c. other factors influence the development of disorders (p. 38)
   a. Biological predispositions are powerful, but not completely predictive.
   b. Genetic composition is identical in monozygotic twins.
   d. Dizygotic twins have about 5–15% chance of developing the same heritable disorder.

7. *c. environment and personal relations (pp. 53–54)
   a. Religious experiences were important to Jung, but not central to the departure from the psychoanalytic theory.
   b. Learning theory was used by the behaviorists in developing their theories.
   d. The biomedical model does not consider environmental and social factors.

8. *b. choice and self-determination (pp. 55–56)
   a. Our sexual natures are part of the self to be understood, not overcome.
   c. Repression is part of Freud's theory of defense mechanisms.
   d. Instinct is an important element in psychoanalytic theory.

9. *a. neutral stimuli can elicit responses (p. 40)
   b. Neutral stimuli can become conditioned.
   c. The response cycle may not be predictable if all the elements are not identifiable.
   d. Pleasure may be more easily learned than fear.

10. *c. Skinner (pp. 42–44)
    a. Pavlov's theory was classical conditioning, not operant conditioning.
    b. Rogers didn't care about stimulus-response.
    d. Ellis cared about thought content and distortions.

ANSWER KEY: APPLICATION MULTIPLE-CHOICE QUESTIONS

1. *d. biomedical (p. 32)
    a. Humanists don't like diagnoses.
    b. Behaviorists would use a learning/cognitive intervention.
    c. Cognitive therapy would also include psychotherapy.

2. *b. the autonomic nervous system (p. 35)
    a. Intrapsychic conflict alone would not cause this reaction.
    c. The autonomic nervous system is part of the peripheral nervous system.
    d. The parasympathetic system is part of the ANS, but works to conserve the body's resources.

3. *c. psychological problems will be treated as diseases with less emphasis on personal and interpersonal factors (p. 40)
    a. His attitude reflects greater emphasis on biological factors.
    b. It shows more concentration on drug development.
    d. There will be more research done to isolate defective genes and neurotransmitters with less research on sociocultural factors.

4. *c. unconscious (pp. 49–50)
    a. The preconscious is very close to awareness.
    b. Id impulses are unavailable to consciousness and have no easily discernible form.
    d. The ego is reflected in the behavior of the client.

5. *c. repression (p. 51)
    a. Amnesia is a more aggressive form of memory loss.
    b. Regression is returning to a more primitive level of functioning in the psychosexual stages of development.
    d. Fugue is the departure of a person under stress from home, accompanied by memory loss.

6. *c. regression (p. 52)
    a. The oral stage is the first of the psychosexual stages of development.
    b. Repression is another defense mechanism regarding memory.
    d. The Electra dilemma is the female equivalent of the Oedipus dilemma (complex), the desire to possess the opposite sex parent.

7. *b. is concerned with consequences of behavior (p. 52)
    a. Stimuli are just one part of the law of effect.
    c. Some responses are satisfying, others are not.
    d. Not all responses are unsatisfying.

8. *d. negative distortion (p. 48)
    a. Id impulses express themselves in times of stress and usually take the form of pleasure seeking.
    b. Cognitive deficiency is the absence of thinking.
    c. Mike's experience is a response in an operant mode, not a classical conditioning mode.

9. *b. normal (p. 58)
   a. She shows no symptoms of clinical depression.
   c. She is not overly anxious.
   d. Joanna demonstrates none of the symptoms of OCD.

10. *d. Cognitive model (pp. 45–48)
   a. The biomedical model stresses biochemical abnormalities, brain defects, or hormonal problems, none of which are indicated here.
   b. The behavioral model emphasizes classical conditioning, operant conditioning, and modeling.
   c. The psychodynamic model emphasizes unconscious conflicts and early childhood experiences, neither of which are indicated here.

CHAPTER 3

Approaches to Treatment

LEARNING OBJECTIVES

1. Describe the types of environments in which therapy is offered. (pp. 64–66)

2. Describe some of the common forms of therapy. (pp. 65–66)

3. Describe the techniques of traditional psychoanalysis, including free association, interpretation, analysis of dreams, resistance, and transference. (pp. 66–69)

4. Describe developments in contemporary psychodynamic therapy, including ego psychology, object relations, and interpersonal therapy. (pp. 68–69)

5. Discuss the humanistic approach to therapy, including person-centered therapy. (pp. 69–71)

6. Describe behavioral therapies, including systematic desensitization, operant procedures, and observational learning. (pp. 71–75)

7. Describe cognitive-behavioral therapies, including rational-emotive therapy. (pp. 75–79)

8. Discuss Beck's cognitive therapy for depression. (p. 78)

9. Describe the research on understanding the proper balance between positive and negative thinking. (pp. 79–80)

10. Discuss the problem-solving approaches to therapy. (pp. 80–81)

11. Discuss family and couples therapy and the various approaches to such treatment including insight-oriented and action-oriented models. (pp. 81–84)

12. Describe the different approaches taken to involve family members in therapy. (p. 84)

13. Describe the importance of such factors as ethnicity and gender in the outcome of therapy. (p. 86)

14. Discuss how the eclectic approach to therapy has become widely accepted among practitioners. (pp. 87–88)

15. Describe the biological and medical approaches, including chemical shock, psychosurgery, and electroshock. (pp. 88–91)

16. Describe the revolutionary development of psychotropic drugs, how they work, and what the unwanted side effects are. (pp. 91–92)

17. Discuss some of the perceptions and misconceptions about the use of psychotropic drugs. (pp. 92–94)

18. Discuss the need for caution in understanding the medical treatment of mental disorders. (p. 95)

CHAPTER OUTLINE

I. The Context of Therapy

    A. Until the 1950s, long hospitalizations (institutions used to be called *asylums*) were the norm for the treatment of mental disorders.

    B. Antipsychotic medications developed in the 1950s lessened the need for hospital care.

    C. Milieu therapy developed: a therapeutic approach that seeks to make the total hospital environment a therapeutic setting conducive to psychological improvement.

    D. Deinstitutionalization followed, partially replacing hospitals with community mental health centers.

        1. Many of the deinstitutionalized mentally ill became homeless.

        2. Those who do receive treatment are treated in a variety of ways (e.g., individual therapy, couples therapy, family therapy, group therapy), by psychologists, psychiatrists, social workers, and others.

II. Insight-Oriented Therapies

    • Insight: A person's ability to understand the basis of his or her thinking, behavior, emotions, and perceptions.

    • Psychodynamic therapy addresses the internal conflicts said to have been established in childhood and influential on adult adjustment.

    • Assumes that behavioral change follows from insights.

    A. Traditional Psychoanalysis

        • Psychoanalysis: A process through which the therapist's interpretation of the client's behavior allows unconscious feelings and thoughts to become conscious.

        1. Free association: Client expresses thoughts and feelings without fear of censure.

        2. Interpretations

            a. Therapist makes statements to identify elements of something the client has done or said about which the client is unaware.

            b. Goal: To increase the client's self-understanding.

        3. Analysis of dreams

            a. Manifest content: content of the dream as remembered by the client.

b. Latent content: contains repressed conflictual material in a disguised form.

4. Resistance

   a. Client's unwillingness to express true feelings, divulge actual thoughts, or accept therapist's interpretations or directives.

5. Transference: reliving relationships

   a. Client reexperiences the thoughts and feelings toward the therapist that were experienced in childhood when relating to an authority figure such as a parent.

   b. Replays client's unconscious internal conflicts.

   c. Countertransference refers to the therapist's unconscious feelings about the client.

   d. Working through refers to client's acceptance of formerly unconscious experiences and relating to therapist and thus to patient in a positive way.

6. Interpersonal therapy

   a. Therapist's essential task is to disrupt the client's vicious cycle of self-defeating interpersonal interactions.

   b. Therapists are more directive and active compared with psychoanalysis.

7. Evaluation

   a. Hypotheses have not been well examined and outcomes not adequately tested.

   b. Method more suitable for verbal and intelligent people with mild psychological problems.

B. A Humanistic Approach to Therapy

   • Humanistic therapy assumes an inherent human tendency toward growth and self-actualization.

   • Therapists' goal is to set the stage for clients to improve themselves.

   1. Person-centered therapy (Carl Rogers)

      a. Originally called *client-centered therapy*

      b. Nondirective, nonjudgmental

      c. Facilitative environment fostered by therapist includes

         (1) Therapist genuineness

         (2) Accurate empathy (understanding the world as the client sees it)

         (3) Unconditional positive regard (acceptance and valuing of the client)

   2. Evaluation

      a. Sometimes called simple-minded.

b.   Patients whose therapists showed high levels of genuineness, empathy, and unconditional positive regard showed significant improvement.

c.   Mixed findings; may be appropriate for certain client types and problems but not others.

III.   **Action-Oriented Therapies**

- Emphasize observable behavior rather than subconscious processes.

- Assumes that behavioral symptoms require change rather than intrapsychic insights.

A.   **Behavior Therapies**

- Assume that human action is acquired through learning.

- Applies learning theories to the treatment of mental disorders (classical conditioning, operant conditioning, observational learning).

1.   **Systematic desensitization**

a.   Therapy based on classical conditioning.

b.   Employs counterconditioning, in which the client is taught to replace an undesirable anxiety response with a relaxation response.

c.   Exposure: Patients directly confront once-feared objects or situations.

2.   **Operant procedures**

a.   Operant conditioning procedures seek to alter behavior by applying positive and negative reinforcements such as token economies, where tokens are earned for desired behavior and can be used like money.

b.   May be combined with other therapies.

3.   **Observational Learning**

a.   Modeling is learning that occurs by observing and imitating others.

b.   Mastery model demonstrates ideal behavior.

c.   Coping model demonstrates difficulties and then models strategies to overcome these difficulties.

d.   Self-efficacy: confidence in one's ability to cope with difficulties.

4.   **Evaluation**

a.   Behavioral approaches are conscientious in using scientific evaluation of their therapies.

b.   Criticized for being mechanical in application and limiting itself to changes in observable behavior.

c.   Recent models have incorporated cognition.

B.   **Cognitive-Behavioral Therapy**

- A combination of performance-based interventions and strategies that address the client's thinking.

- Uses collaborative empiricism: client participates, actively suggesting ideas, trying new behaviors, and reporting back.

1. Rational-Emotive therapy

   a. Seeks to teach clients to identify and change the irrational notions that underlie their distressing symptoms.

   b. Focuses on changing patterns of irrational thinking.

   c. Uses shame-attacking exercises to challenge need for conventionality.

   d. Problems with RET:

      (1) One set of irrational beliefs for all people.

      (2) Equating rationality and adaptiveness.

      (3) Pays little attention to diagnosis.

      (4) Does not address the application of RET to different forms of psychopathology.

2. Cognitive therapy for depression (Aaron Beck)

   a. Modifies the client's depressive emotional state by altering his or her cognitive and behavioral functioning.

   b. Active, structured, time-limited approach.

   c. Beck believes that maladaptive beliefs are tied to depressed states.

   d. Automatic negative thoughts: Self-critical negative statements clients make without testing accuracy.

   e. Prospective hypothesis-testing used: Clients are guided by therapists to formulate and test specific predictions related to dysfunctional beliefs.

3. Evaluation

   a. Research results have demonstrated the efficacy of Beck's approach in the treatment of depression.

   b. Cognitive therapy is comparable in effectiveness to treatment with medications and is more potent in preventing relapse.

   c. Cognitive therapy criticisms include that the procedure does not address comorbidity nor explain the origins of maladaptive cognitive functioning. Sometimes seen as a simple promotion of the power of positive talk.

C. What's Normal? The Power of Negative Thinking

- Some negative thinking is normal.

- The ideal ratio of positive to negative thinking, or healthy thinking, is approximately 2:1.

1. Problem-solving approaches to therapy

      a.   Problem-solving treatments help clients overcome thought *deficiencies*.

      b.   Target specific problems.

      c.   Steps include

          (1)   Identifying the problem.

          (2)   Generating alternative solutions.

          (3)   Anticipate consequences of alternative solutions.

          (4)   Making a decision.

          (5)   Implement and evaluate the plan.

      d.   Has been applied in preventive treatment.

   2.   Although can be applied to many disorders, questions about generalizability remain.

IV.   Family and Couples Therapy

   A.   Insight-Oriented Family and Couples Therapy: Focus on the disturbed relationships within the family and on the resolution of conflict.

   B.   Action-Oriented Family and Couples Therapy

      •   Emphasize active and direct involvement in interpersonal system to produce change.

      1.   Action-oriented family therapy

         a.   Conjoint family therapy requires participation of the entire family to work on disturbed patterns of communication.

         b.   Parents learn skills for managing their children and obtain coaching and feedback from therapist.

      2.   Action-oriented couples therapy

         a.   Couples therapy with an action orientation has been called behavioral marital therapy (BMT), which has an emphasis on skills training, homework, communications, problem-solving, and practice.

         b.   Validation, or acknowledgment that a person has been heard, altering attribution of negative states to a partner, and changing negative self-talk are important elements of BMT.

   C.   Evaluation

      1.   Action-oriented family therapy for child disorders has been evaluated favorably.

      2.   Less is known about BMT for diagnosed adult disorders.

   D.   Family matters: Encouraging Family Involvement in Individual Treatment. Using family members in therapy is often useful, and the types of involvement can vary from direct treatment to collaboration.

V. The Art and Science of Psychotherapy

- Many mental health professionals debate whether or not therapy is an art that cannot be subjected to scientifically controlled investigations.

A. Ethnic Status and Therapy

1. Asian Americans see therapy as stigmatizing.

2. Different ethnic values present potential barriers between client and mental health service.

3. Various ethnic minorities differ in their use of mental health services and in pattern of termination of use.

B. Gender and Therapy

1. Gender similarity is associated with positive client perception of therapist.

2. Effect on therapy outcome from gender matching is minimal.

C. Eclecticism

1. Eclecticism is the incorporation of elements from several treatment modalities to treat clients.

2. May include different types of psychotherapies and psychoactive medications.

VI. Biological and Medical Approaches

A. Nonpharmacologic Somatic Treatments

1. Insulin shock therapy: Effects were temporary.

2. Electroconvulsive therapy (ECT)

   a. Indiscriminate use resulted in memory impairment, physical damage, and occasional death.

   b. Currently limited use for severe, intractable depression.

3. Psychosurgery

   a. An operation on the brain to alter symptoms of a severe psychological disorder, called lobotomy.

   b. Risks include substantial damage to other mental capacities, occasionally death.

   c. Criticism grew with the indiscriminate use, uneven results; use of the procedure has virtually disappeared.

B. Psychotropic Medications

- Use of psychotropic drugs (or psychopharmacology) has revolutionized the treatment of mental disorders.

   a. Antipsychotics, such as chlorpromazine (Thorazine), reduce psychotic behavior such as hallucinations and delusions.

       b.   Antidepressants, such as imipramine (Tofranil), elevate mood and increase activity but are not a cure.

       c.   Antianxiety drugs have a calming effect but can cause drowsiness.

  1. How do the drugs work?

       a.   Researchers know more about what the drugs do than why they do it.

       b.   Affect neurotransmitters by blocking, increasing, or altering receptors or increasing the amount of a neurotransmitter.

       c.   More research needed.

  2. Side effects

       a.   Unwanted effects of medication include

           (1)   Dry mouth, blurred vision, lethargy.

           (2)   Tardive dyskinesia (TD): Irreversible side effect includes involuntary facial movements and motor activity.

           (3)   Taken with alcohol can be toxic.

           (4)   Some can cause tolerance (need for increased dosages) and *dependence*.

  3. Perceptions about medications

       a.   Clients often expect medication to cure.

       b.   Symptoms may be relieved, but unless they are the cause of the problems, difficulties remain.

       c.   Many prescriptions for psychotropic medications are written not by psychiatrists but by primary care physicians who are not trained in psychological disorders and their treatment.

       d.   Medications frequently prescribed improperly, expecially overprescription.

C. Related Considerations

  1. The Treatment-Etiology fallacy: Error of logic in which treatment mode is (incorrectly) assumed to imply the mechanism of the cause of the disorder.

  2. Can we afford our enthusiasm for medical breakthroughs?

       a.   We expect too much from the medical world.

       b.   Simple solutions do not solve complex problems.

D. Focus on Research: Can Science Test Psychotherapy?

  1. There is a need for greater empirical testing of treatments.

  2. *Consumer Reports* survey indicates that therapy is effective, but methodological problems with the study.

  3. Disagreement exists about whether to use only therapies that have been demonstrated empirically to be effective.

VII. What Lies Ahead?

    A. Psychological treatments will be focus of research.

    B. Movement toward development of treatments for specific disorders.

    C. Integrative treatments needed.

KEY TERMS REVIEW

1. A therapeutic approach in which a therapist (model) initially demonstrates difficulties similar to the observer's and then subsequently models strategies to overcome difficulties and eventually models the desirable behavior is called the _____.

2. An approach in which patients confront the once-feared objects or situations is called _____.

3. The need for increased dosages of psychotropic medications to experience the same effects is called _____.

4. A therapeutic approach that modifies depressive emotional states by altering the client's cognitive and behavioral functioning is called _____.

5. Unwanted effects that come with certain treatments are called _____.

6. A person's acknowledgment that he or she heard what another person just said is called _____.

7. Psychologists who are more concerned with the functions of the ego than with the superego or the id are called _____.

8. A therapeutic process within cognitive-behavioral theory by which the client participates actively in suggesting ideas, trying out new behaviors, and reporting back to the therapist is called _____.

9. The characteristic of therapists in person-centered therapy, in which therapists come to see and understand the world the way the client experiences it, is called _____.

10. The movement to replace the huge mental hospitals that often served an entire state with community outpatient and aftercare facilities for short-term care that enable patients to be more fully integrated into their own communities is called _____.

11. An error of logic in which the treatment mode is assumed to imply the mechanism of the original cause of a disorder is called _____.

12. A process, such as in systematic desensitization, in which the client is gradually taught to replace an undesirable response—the anxiety response—with a response that is incompatible with the undesirable response—the relaxation response—is called _____.

13. Psychotropic medications that elevate mood and increase activity are called _____.

14. The unwillingness of a client in therapy to express true feelings, divulge actual thoughts, or accept the therapist's interpretations is called _____.

15. Repressed conflictual material in a dream, interpreted by the therapist in relation to the client's personality, daily activities, and symbolic meaning of events and objects in the dream is called _____.

16. An action-oriented therapeutic approach used with couples is called _____.

17. A pattern of thinking that is associated with a 2:1 ratio of positive thinking to negative thinking is called _____.

18. Using different treatments for clients with different disorders or using a rational combination of various treatments for the same client; a dominant force in the provision of psychological treatments is called _____.

19. The process of learning behavior as a result of observing others is called _____.

20. Targeting and treating clients at risk for the later development of disorders is called _____.

21. The characteristic of therapists in person-centered therapy in which therapists actively accept the client as a valued person regardless of the client's own motivation and ability to improve is called _____.

22. A therapeutic approach in which it is assumed that human action is acquired through the learning process. Therapy emphasizes the acquisition and practice of appropriate behaviors in the relevant situation and is called _____.

23. A person's ability to understand the basis of his or her thinking, behavior, emotions, and perceptions is called _____.

24. A therapeutic approach that requires all family members to be seen together as a single group with the goal of changing their dysfunctional patterns of communication is called _____.

25. Psychotropic medications that reduce muscular tension and have a calming and soothing effect on the emotions but can cause drowsiness and lethargy are called _____.

26. A method of inducing convulsions by applying electricity to the brain with the aim of resolving depression is called _____.

27. Therapeutic approaches that combine behavioral performance-based interventions with strategies that address the client's thinking are called _____.

28. A therapeutic approach in which the therapist demonstrates successful adjustment and nondisturbed behavior is called the _____.

29. Statements made by a therapist, typically psychodynamic, that identify features of something the client has said or done, of which the client had not been fully aware, are called _____.

30. Self-critical, pessimistic, or exaggerated negative statements that clients make to themselves without testing their accuracy are called _____.

31. The acceptance by a client in therapy of formerly unconscious experiences and coming to relate to the therapist and, by extension, to the parent in a positive way is called _____.

32. A talking-based psychodynamic treatment based on principles from Freud's theories of personality is called _____.

33. A surgical procedure in which nerve fibers that connect to the frontal cortex are severed; used as treatment for extremely disturbed patients and rarely practiced today is called _____.

34. An old-fashioned term for mental hospitals is _____.

35. The craving for continued doses of a substance; continued use despite adverse consequences and the belief that the substance is needed for continued well-being is called _____.

36. A therapeutic approach that emphasizes that each person has an inherent tendency toward growth and self-actualization is called _____.

37. A process by which a client in therapy reexperiences the thoughts and feelings toward the therapist that were experienced in childhood when relating to an authority figure such as a parent is called _____.

38. An irreversible, undesirable neurological side effect of antipsychotic medications marked by involuntary movements and motor activity in the hands and feet is called _____.

39. A therapeutic approach in which the therapist's essential task is to disrupt the client's vicious cycle of self-defeating interpersonal interactions is called _____.

40. Public facilities in many communities that provide outpatient services and, sometimes, short-term inpatient care are called _____.

41. The characteristic of therapists in person-centered therapy, in which they allow their true inner feelings and thoughts to emerge honestly and openly, is called _____.

42. A technique of psychoanalysis in which a client expresses thoughts and feelings as they come to mind and without fear of censure, which helps reveal unconscious conflicts, is called _____.

43. The content of a dream as it is recalled by the dreamer is called the _____.

44. A therapeutic approach based on learning principles in which patients earn tokens as rewards for accomplishing specific desirable behaviors; the tokens may be exchanged for privileges and items of value to the patient; this is called a _____.

45. An operation on the brain intended to alter the symptoms of severe psychological disorder is called _____.

46. The therapist's unconscious feelings about the client are called _____.

47. A therapeutic approach that seeks to alter problem behaviors by applying positive and negative reinforcements and shaping by successive approximations is called _____.

48. A term for the use and study of *psychotropic medications* is _____.

49. A behavioral therapy based on classical conditioning in which fear responses are paired with relaxation is called _____.

50. Therapeutic approaches that aim to help clients overcome deficiencies in thinking by teaching the process (steps) useful in solving problems are called _____.

51. Expectations of success in a given situation and confidence in one's ability to cope with difficulties is called _____.

52. A therapeutic approach that seeks to teach clients to identify and change the irrational notions that underlie their distressing symptoms is called _____.

FACTUAL MULTIPLE-CHOICE QUESTIONS

1. A later enduring change in the treatment of the severely mentally disturbed was
   a. deinstitutionalization.
   b. asylum treatment.
   c. insulin shock therapy.
   d. electroconvulsive therapy.

2. Searching for the underlying causes of maladaptation is the goal of
   a. behavior modification.
   b. cognitive restructuring.
   c. systematic desensitization.
   d. psychodynamic therapy.

3. The mother-child relationship is particularly important for
   a. object relations therapy.
   b. person-centered psychotherapy.
   c. cognitive-behavior therapy.
   d. interpersonal therapy.

4. The goal of the humanist therapist is for the clients to
   a. follow their advice.
   b. uncover forgotten conflict.
   c. learn new coping skills.
   d. improve themselves.

5. Behavior therapists assume human action is acquired through
   a. unconscious conflict.
   b. the learning process.
   c. defense mechanisms.
   d. instinctual drives.

6. In his therapy, Albert Ellis assumes that psychological disturbances arise from
   a. defective parent-child relationships.
   b. cognitive distortions.
   c. cognitive deficiencies.
   d. lack of meaning in life.

7. Beck's therapy has been shown to be particularly effective with
   a. schizophrenia.
   b. obsessive-compulsive disorder.
   c. hysteria.
   d. depression.

8. Virginia Satir was a pioneer in
   a. cognitive therapy.
   b. family therapy.
   c. humanistic therapy.
   d. psychodynamic therapy.

9. Psychotherapy integration is another term for
   a. rational-emotive therapy.
   b. person-centered therapy.
   c. behaviorism.
   d. eclecticism.

10. Electroconvulsive therapy (ECT) use has declined dramatically, but is still used in some cases of
    a. mania.
    b. obsessive-compulsive disorder.
    c. schizophrenia.
    d. depression.

CONCEPTUAL MULTIPLE-CHOICE QUESTIONS

1. For the first half of this century, hospitalization for those with mental disorders was thought to be
   a. brutal.
   b. therapeutic.
   c. remedial.
   d. efficient.

2. The first major enduring change in the treatment of mental disorder in the twentieth century was the introduction of
   a. psychosurgery.
   b. chemical shock treatment.
   c. antipsychotic medications.
   d. deinstitutionalization.

3. Psychotherapists agree that therapy should be
   a. of short duration.
   b. based on the medical model.
   c. a corrective and helpful experience.
   d. conducted by people with doctorates.

4. The psychoanalytically-oriented therapist subjects all types of client behavior to
   a. free association.
   b. evaluation.
   c. interpretation.
   d. questioning.

5. The use of psychotropic medications was an important advance in treating mental disorders because
   a. scientists know exactly how they work.
   b. they always treat the underlying causes of the disorders.
   c. they often treat the symptoms of the disorders effectively.
   d. they are not dangerous to the client.

6. Mr. Smyth is tearfully recounting events from his childhood in therapy. The therapist's orientation is probably
   a. psychoanalytic.
   b. behaviorist.
   c. humanistic.
   d. rational-emotive.

7. Dr. Martin, a psychologist, reads the psychoanalytic literature, but treats many of her clients with cognitive-behavior therapy. Her approach to therapy might be called
   a. person-centered.
   b. biomedical.
   c. eclectic.
   d. humanistic.

8. Dr. Hillary is concerned about prescribing Thorazine to a newly admitted, actively hallucinating patient for fear it may
   a. cause legal problems.
   b. increase the hallucinations.
   c. not cure the problem.
   d. cause side effects.

9. A primary difference between insight-oriented and action-oriented psychotherapies is that
   a. insight-oriented therapies assume that self-awareness and understanding of one's problems are necessary conditions for achieving behavioral change.
   b. action-oriented therapy emphasizes understanding one's subconscious processes as a necessary precursor to action.
   c. action-oriented therapy has been found to be less effective than insight-oriented therapy.
   d. insight-oriented therapy views the client's problems as a result of faulty learning patterns.

10. Which of the following situations best illustrates the "treatment-etiology fallacy"?
    a. Maria stopped taking her antidepressant medication even though the drug seemed effective because she was afraid there might be undesirable side effects.
    b. The judge ordered Juan to receive therapy from a cognitive-behavioral therapist because he thought Juan's faulty thinking patterns were the primary cause of his antisocial conduct.
    c. Quyen states that behaviorally oriented therapies that target specific symptoms do not address the real underlying causes of a mental disorder.
    d. After taking the drug lithium carbonate and finding relief from extreme mood states, Janice says the cause of her bipolar disorder was a biochemical imbalance in the brain.

APPLICATION MULTIPLE-CHOICE QUESTIONS

1. Dr. Johnson works with two people to improve structure and communication patterns in their relationship. She is probably a
   a. clinical psychologist.
   b. couples therapist.
   c. family therapist.
   d. counseling psychologist.

2. Julie wants a therapist who will help her make decisions and understand her options in an ambivalent relationship. What would be the least appropriate type of therapist for her to consult?
   a. rational-emotive
   b. person-centered
   c. psychoanalytic
   d. cognitive-behavioral

3. Heidi has an inordinate fear of heights. She is desperate to find a therapist who will help her conquer her fear as soon as possible. What type of intervention would you recommend?
   a. psychoanalysis
   b. rational-emotive therapy
   c. person-centered therapy
   d. systematic desensitization

4. Scott is an inmate at the Juvenile Correction Center and he wants to hit someone he thinks gave him trouble. He doesn't do it because he is afraid he will lose his television privileges. This is an example of what type of intervention?
   a. counterconditioning
   b. cognitive-behavioral
   c. modeling
   d. token economy

5. Dr. Franken points out to Robert that his constant refrain of "I am no damn good because I lost my job" is an irrational response to the situation. Dr. Franken is probably using what technique?
   a. rational-emotive therapy
   b. operant conditioning
   c. shaping
   d. modeling

6. Mr. Roberts is working with Dr. Davis to understand why he always sees himself in such a negative light. The two are working toward finding ways to change his reactions to his problems. Dr. Davis probably subscribes to the tenets of
   a. Carl Rogers.
   b. B. F. Skinner.
   c. Sigmund Freud.
   d. Aaron Beck.

7. Dr. Rashid is working with the Simpson family and refuses to concentrate on Billy alone, who is in trouble at school. Rather, she considers the entire group to be in need of help and requires the whole family to be seen together. This is typical of
   a. psychoanalysis.
   b. preventive treatment.
   c. conjoint family therapy.
   d. validation.

8. Miriam, an African American, found therapy difficult. She terminated after only two sessions. One possible reason for her quick cessation of treatment might be
   a. lack of ethnic match.
   b. African Americans rarely seek treatment.
   c. underrepresented populations in general show negative responses to therapy.
   d. because there has been no cultural responsiveness in the system.

9. Mr. Miller spent many years in a mental hospital in the late 1950s. As a result of a procedure he underwent, he became docile and childlike. That procedure might have been
   a. ECT.
   b. lobotomy.
   c. insulin shock.
   d. milieu therapy.

10. Ms. Appleton has agreed to participate in an experiment in which a drug treatment is combined with a psychological approach. This style of treatment is called
   a. biomedical.
   b. conjoint.
   c. double-blind.
   d. integrated.

ANSWER KEY: KEY TERMS REVIEW

1. coping model (74)
2. exposure (72)
3. tolerance (90)
4. cognitive therapy for depression (78)
5. side effects (90)
6. validating (83)
7. ego psychologists (68)
8. collaborative empiricism (75)
9. accurate empathy (70)
10. deinstitutionalization (64)
11. treatment-etiology fallacy (92)
12. counterconditioning (71)
13. antidepressants (89)
14. resistance (67)
15. latent content (67)
16. behavioral marital therapy (BMT) (83)
17. healthy thinking (79–80)
18. eclecticism (86)
19. modeling (74)
20. preventive treatment (81)
21. unconditional positive regard (70)
22. behavioral therapy (71)
23. insight (66)
24. conjoint family therapy (81)
25. antianxiety drugs (89)
26. electroconvulsive therapy (87–88)
27. cognitive-behavioral therapies (75)
28. mastery model (74)
29. interpretations (67)
30. automatic negative thoughts (78)
31. working through (68)
32. psychoanalysis (66)
33. lobotomy (88–89)
34. asylums (64)
35. dependence (90)
36. humanistic therapy (69–70)
37. transference (68)
38. tardive dyskinesia (90)
39. interpersonal therapy (69)
40. community mental health center (64)
41. genuineness (70)
42. free association (66–67)
43. manifest dream (67)
44. token economy (73)
45. psychosurgery (88–89)
46. countertransference (68)
47. operant conditioning procedures (73)
48. psychopharmacology (89)
49. systematic desensitization (71)
50. problem-solving treatments (80)
51. self-efficacy (75)
52. rational-emotive therapy (RET) (76)

ANSWER KEY: FACTUAL MULTIPLE-CHOICE QUESTIONS

1. *a. deinstitutionalization (p. 66)
   b. Asylums were the old warehouse type of care.
   c. Insulin shock therapy was supplanted by autopsychotic medications.
   d. The use of electroconvulsive therapy has declined.

2. *d. psychodynamic therapy (p. 66)
   a. Behavior modification treats the symptoms.
   b. Cognitive restructuring treats the thought process.
   c. Systematic desensitization treats the fear.

3. *a. objects relation therapy (p. 68)
   b. Person-centered therapy is concerned with the present.
   c. Cognitive-behavior therapy is concerned with thought process and action rather than relationship.
   d. Interpersonal therapy centers around disrupting the patient's self-defeating interpersonal interactions and does not focus on childhood.

4. *d. improve themselves (p. 69)
   a. Humanistic therapists rarely give advice.
   b. Humanistic therapists are interested in the present.
   c. This is an outcome of the behaviorist approach.

5. *b. the learning process (p. 71)
   a. Learning-based therapies are not concerned with the unconscious.
   c. Defense mechanisms are part of the psychoanalytic theory.
   d. Instinct is part of the psychodynamic theory.

6. *b. cognitive distortions (p. 76)
   a. Parent-child conflict is a factor in object relations theory.
   c. Cognitive deficiencies, or the absence of thinking, are very different from Ellis's concern with irrational beliefs.
   d. Lack of meaning in life is not distorted thinking.

7. *d. depression (p. 78)
   a. Schizophrenia is a thought disturbance and responds less well to psychotherapy.
   b. OCD requires a different therapeutic approach, helping clients deal with their anxiety, which could be quite rational.
   c. Hysteria, rarely seen today, is related to anxiety.

8. *b. family therapy (p. 81)
   a. Ellis and Beck were pioneers in cognitive therapy.
   c. Rogers and Maslow were pioneers in humanistic therapy.
   d. Freud developed psychodynamic therapy.

9. *d. eclecticism (pp. 86–87)
   a. Rational-emotive therapy does not borrow from other approaches.
   b. Person-centered therapists tend for the most part to use their techniques exclusively.
   c. Behaviorists tend to stay focused on their paradigm in therapy.

10. *d. depression (pp. 87–88)
    a. Mania is not affected by ECT.
    b. OCD is not treated with shock techniques.
    c. Schizophrenia is usually treated with medication.

ANSWER KEY: CONCEPTUAL MULTIPLE-CHOICE QUESTIONS

1. *b. therapeutic (p. 64)
   a. The treatment was not effective, but it was not considered brutal.
   c. No actual treatments were offered, just custodial care.
   d. These hospitals were overcrowded, understaffed, and underfunded.

2. *c. antipsychotic medications (p. 64)
   a. Psychosurgery was an early change, but it lost favor when the results were less than earlier reported.
   b. Shock treatments also were found to be ineffective.
   d. Deinstitutionalization emerged as a trend in the 1960s.

3. *c. a corrective and helpful experience (p. 66)
   a. Some therapies take years.
   b. The medical model is one of many therapeutic approaches.
   d. Much effective therapy is done by people without doctorates.

4. *c. interpretation (p. 67)
   a. Free association is one of the techniques used in therapy.
   b. Therapist responses are nonjudgmental.
   d. The therapist may ask some questions, but interpretation is the key.

5. *c. they often treat the symptoms of the disorder effectively (pp. 89–91)
   a. No one knows exactly how these chemicals work.
   b. They usually only affect the symptoms.
   d. Many of these drugs have dangerous side effects.

6. *a. psychoanalytic (pp. 67–69)
   b. Behaviorists are concerned about the present.
   c. Humanists are also primarily concerned with the present.
   d. RET deals with irrational thoughts rather than memories of childhood.

7. *c. eclectic (p. 86)
   a. Her theoretical orientation is probably cognitive rather than person-centered.
   b. Medical approaches usually include the use of medications.
   d. Humanists would not use cognitive-behavior techniques.

8. *d. cause side effects (p. 90)
   a. Such a prescription is not illegal if there is a doctor to prescribe the drug.
   b. Thorazine controls positive symptoms such as hallucinations.
   c. The antipsychotics do not cure schizophrenia, they control the symptoms.

9. *a. insight-oriented therapies assume that self-awareness and understanding of one's problems are necessary conditions for achieving behavioral change.
   b. Action-oriented therapy does not emphasize subconscious processes.
   c. Both action- and insight-oriented therapies have shown some effectiveness, depending on client and type of problem.
   d. Action-oriented therapy, particularly behavioral therapy, assumes faulty learning patterns.

10. *d. After taking the drug lithium carbonate and finding relief from extreme mood states, Janice says the cause of her bipolar disorder was a biochemical imbalance in the brain.
    a. Drug therapy may result in side effects and should be reported to one's physician, but this does not exemplify the treatment-etiology fallacy.
    b. Faulty thinking patterns are the focus of cognitive therapy.
    c. This criticism of behavioral therapies is commonly made by insight-oriented therapists.

ANSWER KEY: APPLICATION MULTIPLE-CHOICE QUESTIONS

1.* b. couples therapist (p. 81)
   a. They work with many combinations of people.
   c. Family therapists work with the entire family, including children and others.
   d. Counseling psychologists often work in school settings.

2. *b. Person-centered (p. 72)
   a. Cognitive approaches are more directive.
   c. Psychoanalysts provide interpretations that might help her with her immediate problems.
   d. Cognitive-behaviorists would be more problem-oriented in their approach.

3. *d. systematic desensitization (pp. 71–72)
   a. Psychoanalysis may take years.
   b. Rational-emotive therapy does not deal specifically with fears.
   c. Person-centered therapy would also take too long and be too nondirective.

4. *d. Token economy (p. 73)
   a. Counterconditioning procedures are used to reduce anxiety.
   b. Cognitive-behavior therapy refers to modification of thought processes.
   c. Modeling is based on observational principles.

5. *a. Rational-emotive therapy (p. 76)
   b. Operant conditioning deals with behavior, not thought processes.
   c. Shaping is another of the operant techniques.
   d. Modeling is based on observational principles.

6. *d. Aaron Beck (p. 78)
   a. Rogers's therapy does not focus on negative issues.
   b. Skinner would have worked on behavior.
   c. Freud would have dealt with unconscious conflict and childhood trauma.

7. *c. conjoint family therapy (pp. 81–82)
   a. Psychoanalysis typically has a therapist with an individual client.
   b. This is too late for preventive treatment, because Billy is already in trouble.
   d. Validation refers to acknowledging what someone has just said.

8. *a. lack of ethnic match (pp. 85–86)
   b. African Americans seek help at higher rates than other groups.
   c. There is great variability in the rate different ethnic groups seek mental health services.
   d. There have been improvements in cultural responsiveness.

9. *b. lobotomy (pp. 88–89)
    a. ECT usually leaves patients with temporary memory loss, not with a change in personality.
    c. Insulin shock did not have any long-lasting effects.
    d. Milieu therapy refers to the environment of the patients.

10. *d. integrated (pp. 86, 93)
    a. Biomedical treatment usually does not include psychotherapy.
    b. Conjoint refers to seeing a family together in therapy.
    c. Double-blind is an experimental control technique to remove the placebo effect.

CHAPTER 4
Assessment and Diagnosis of Psychological Disorders

LEARNING OBJECTIVES

1. Discuss the issues associated with the measurement and assessment of human behavior and the importance of inference in making these decisions. (p. 98)

2. Describe the importance of reliability in evaluating assessment procedures. (pp. 98–99)

3. Describe the importance of validity in evaluating assessment procedures. (pp. 99–101)

4. Describe the importance of utility in evaluating assessment procedures. (p. 101)

5. Discuss how misclassification of mental disorders may occur, especially when low base rates are present. Differentiate between false positives and false negatives in the classification of mental disorders. (p. 101)

6. Discuss the advantages and disadvantages of interviewing, questionnaires, and personality inventories in psychological assessment. (pp. 102–107)

7. Discuss the advantages and disadvantages of intelligence tests, neuropsychological assessments, and projective tests. (pp. 107–110)

8. Discuss the advantages and disadvantages of observation techniques and self-monitoring. (pp. 110–114)

9. Describe the difficulties associated with gathering data on families. (pp. 112–114)

10. Describe neuroimaging assessment techniques such as CT scans, PET scans, and MRI. (p. 114)

11. Describe the functioning and use of psychophysiological methods such as the polygraph. (pp. 114–115)

12. Discuss the advantages of combining assessment procedures. (pp. 115–116)

13. Discuss ethical issues such as invasion of privacy, informed consent, consideration of client characteristics, and the possibility of error in making evaluations. (pp. 116–119)

14. Discuss the potential effect of human bias in assessment. (pp. 117–119)

15. Discuss the advantages and potential difficulties of diagnosing psychological disorders. (pp. 118–119)

16. Describe the diagnostic manuals such as the ICD and the DSM and how their classification systems work. (pp. 119–121)

17. Describe how the field trial technique was used to improve reliability in the DSM-IV. (pp. 122–124)

18. Describe the features of the DSM-IV. (pp. 119–124)

19. Discuss the controversies surrounding diagnosis, such as the potential dangers of labeling, reification, culture, and gender bias. (pp. 124–125)

CHAPTER OUTLINE

I. Criteria for Successful Assessment

- Assessment procedures help us to describe, classify, explain, predict, plan, and evaluate treatments for mental disorders.

- Establishing criteria for psychological disorders is difficult.

- Temporary conditions influenced by situations are *states;* enduring characteristics that show consistency across situations are *traits.*

   A. Reliability

   1. Reliability refers to the consistency or repeatability of results of a measurement.

   2. Types of reliability include

      a. Test-retest reliability: consistency of test results over time.

      b. Internal consistency: correspondence between test items designed to measure the same concept.

      c. Interrater reliability: consistency among separate scorers or observers rating the same behavior or characteristic.

   B. Validity

   1. Validity is the degree to which a measuring procedure measures what we say it measures.

   2. Types of validity:

      a. Content validity: The degree to which the items of an assessment device represent examples of what the test is targeting.

      b. Face validity: The degree to which items on a test appear on face value to measure what the test purports to measure.

      c. Criterion-related validity: The degree to which a measure agrees with an external standard.

         (1) Predictive validity: To what extent does an assessment measure or predict a future criterion?

(2) Concurrent validity: Agreement between a measure of a variable and some criterion that is obtained at the same time.

    d. Construct validity shows that the measure is related in consistent ways to other characteristics as specified by the theory.

3. Many factors can interfere with reliability and validity: sampling, questionnaire problems, scoring methods, and attitude of subjects toward the evaluation procedure, or response biases.

C. Utility

1. Utility: The degree to which an assessment procedure is useful and provides unique information not otherwise available or available only at greater cost.

2. Assessment procedures should be valid, reliable, economical, and give better information than not using the procedure at all.

3. Care must be exercised in making judgment errors due to false positives and false negatives, especially where low base rates are found.

II. Common Methods for Assessing Psychological Disturbance

A. Interview Procedures

1. Interviews are oral means of collecting information from someone.

2. Can be sensitive, flexible, and efficient.

3. Types of interviews include

    a. Unstructured: Open-ended and do not follow any particular format.

    b. Structured: Provide specific questions and an interview format.

    c. Semistructured: Interviewer may explore certain areas as needed.

4. The Diagnostic Interview Schedule (DIS; DISC for children) and Structured Clinical Interview for DSM-III-R (SCID) are widely used structured interview instruments.

B. Questionnaires

1. Questionnaire: A written set of questions to which the person provides written replies.

2. Advantages: provide much information, are economical, easily administered, and can be adapted to address specific issues.

3. Personality inventories are questionnaires with numerous items scored on multiple scales that, in a self-report, attempt to derive complex pictures of a person's overall personality.

    a. Personality inventories derived from three methods: the rational, empirical, and statistical.

    b. One of the most widely used is the MMPI-2.

4. Disadvantages: potential for invalid conclusions and interpretations.

C. Performance Tests

- Psychological measures that involve completion of tests believed to indicate cognitive abilities.

- May include manipulation of objects and mental tasks, or reveal personality characteristics by telling stories about or stating perceptions of ambiguous stimuli.

1. Tests of intelligence

    a. Intelligence tests are tests of intellectual functioning most widely used to place children in academic settings or to screen adults for occupational placement.

    b. Among the most widely used tests are the Wechsler for children and adults (WISC-III, the WAIS-R) and the Stanford-Binet.

    c. Performance of increasingly difficult tasks is compared to that of others in the same age category to derive an overall verbal and performance IQ.

    d. Controversies regarding these tests include innate capacity versus achievement, global or specific aspects of intelligence, fairness, and cultural bias.

2. Tests of cognitive impairment

    a. Neuropsychological assessment: An approach to cognitive assessment that tests numerous types of cognitive functioning to identify the nature and extent of possible brain impairment.

    b. Useful in diagnosis, planning, and evaluating.

    c. Can identify subtle neurological impairment.

    d. Examples: Luria-Nebraska test, Halstead-Reitan test.

3. Projective tests

    a. A performance test that seeks to reveal a person's underlying personality by measuring how he or she responds to an ambiguous task.

    b. The best known are the *Rorschach Ink Blot Test* and the *Thematic Apperception Test (TAT)*.

    c. Theory behind tests is that a person given an ambiguous task will project unconscious motives, feelings, and personality characteristics.

    d. May reveal information, but the interpretations are not empirically validated.

D. Observational Methods

1. Observational techniques are assessments achieved by actually watching and recording what a person does in a particular setting.

2. Most often used by clinicians with a behavioral or cognitive-behavioral orientation.

3. Can be structured, in a clinical setting, or naturalistic, in a setting such as school or hospital.

4. Reactivity and interrater reliability can be weakness in this technique.

E. Family Matters: Measuring Families

1. Most family research is limited by retrospective reports, which are limited by bias, memory, and accuracy.

2. Scales used with families include the Family Adaptability and Cohesion Evaluation Scales (FACES), the Family Environment Scale (FES), the Parental Bonding Instrument, and the Family Interaction Coding Scale.

3. Weaknesses include

   a. Possible contamination of ratings by person's current mood.

   b. Combining differing views of mother and father leads to inaccuracy.

   c. Unclear which dimensions of family functioning are most important to assess.

   d. There are few widely used research procedures to allow comparisons across deficient studies.

4. Self-monitoring

   a. A behavioral observation procedure in which the individual observes herself or himself in certain contexts.

   b. Limitation is that the procedure may cause reactivity.

F. Biological Assessment Techniques

   • Their use assumes that mental disorders have biological causes, but direct, clear-cut biological causal links are not established.

1. Neuroimaging techniques

   a. Methods of measuring the brain based on computerized synthesis of highly sensitive detection methods.

   b. Computerized axial tomography (CT) scans pass a radioactive ray through bone and brain tissue to show structures of the brain.

   c. Positron emission tomography (PET) scans show actual brain activity by measuring radiation in the brain from radioactive water injected into the blood stream.

   d. Nuclear magnetic resonance imaging (NMR or MRI) uses alterations in the electromagnetic field of the body created by a magnet.

   e. Functional MRI (fMRI) provides views of brief changes in brain activity without injection of radioactive material.

2. Psychophysiological techniques

   a. Psychophysiological techniques are assessment instruments based on the assumption that emotional states involve changes in the autonomic nervous system. Example: polygraph.

   b. Used primarily in research.

G. Selecting and Combining Procedures: Procedures usually combined because any one by itself is limited.

H. Using Psychological Assessment Appropriately

1. Crucial issues include *invasion of privacy* and *informed consent.*

2. Assessment procedures must be applied in appropriate situations where the procedure has been validated.

3. Important not to draw conclusions beyond information given.

4. Fundamental attribution error: The tendency of people, when explaining the behavior of others, to generally underestimate the influence of situations and overestimate the influence of personality traits.

I. What's Normal?: Human Error in Clinical Assessment

1. Human mind makes many errors resulting in inaccurate clinical judgment.

2. Mistakes include *confirmatory bias, first impressions, illusory correlation,* and *availability bias,* among others.

III. Diagnosis of Psychological Disorders

- Diagnosis: Determining the constellation of symptoms and how they fit the classification system for mental disorders

- Diagnosis helps understand the problem.

- Permits communication among professionals

- Assists in scientific study

- Complexity of psychological disorders makes classification difficult.

A. *The Diagnostic and Statistical Manual* (DSM)

- For thousands of years cultures have recognized differences between madness, melancholia, dementia, and criminality.

- DSM-IV is a uniform manual of diagnosis, a widely accepted system for classifying psychological problems and disorders.

1. Features of the DSM

a. DSM revisions are guided by research including literature reviews, reanalysis of existing data, and field trials designed to answer particular diagnostic questions.

b. The DSM is multiaxial, providing evaluations on five different scales, or axes, each representing different aspects of the person's adjustment and life: Axis I (diagnosed disorder), Axis II (chronic and stable patterns of impaired functioning, such as personality disorders and mental retardation), Axis III (physical conditions), Axis IV (psychosocial stressors), and Axis V (global assessment of functioning).

c. Disorders are defined in terms of observable features, not their causes.

d. Based on *prototypes* that represent the *essential features* of a disorder.

e.   Diagnoses and criteria are empirically validated.

2.   Major categories of the DSM: The DSM-IV provides clinical criteria and basic information on over two hundred mental disorders, which are broken down into fourteen major categories.

B.   Focus on Research: How Do Field Trials Shape Our Diagnostic System?

1.   DSM-IV field trials included thousands of psychiatrists; were used to establish reliability and validity of proposed diagnostic categories.

2.   Diagnosis and criteria are empirically validated.

C.   Diagnosis: Controversies and Unresolved Issues

1.   In search of the perfect system.

a.   Comorbidity, the presence of more than one condition, is a significant difficulty in assessment.

b.   Many disorders have indistinct, overlapping boundaries and may exist as dimensions of one rather than several disorders.

2.   It may be reliable, but is it valid? Clinicians disagree about diagnoses because criteria for validation not well established.

3.   Labeling and reification. Problems with diagnoses: Labeling and *reification* (treating a disorder as if it were an object).

4.   Cultural and gender bias

a.   Cultural variation addressed in DSM-IV.

b.   Gender bias continues to generate controversy.

IV.   What Lies Ahead?

A.   Future refinements of diagnostic tools (particularly biomedical instrumentation and medical testing).

B.   Further validation of diagnoses.

KEY TERMS REVIEW

1.   Research projects specifically aimed at testing particular diagnostic questions by examining relevant populations are called _____.

2.   Interviews that provide specific questions and an interview format are called _____.

3.   The tendency of the client to represent himself or herself in a particular but not accurate way, such as acknowledging only socially desirable responses, or saying "yes" to any symptoms, is called _____.

4.   The co-occurrence of different types of disorders in one person is called _____.

5.   Consistency among separate scorers or observers rating the same characteristic is called _____.

6. Tests of intellectual functioning, most widely used to place children in academic settings or to screen adults for occupational placement are called _____.

7. A behavioral observation procedure in which an individual records for herself or himself the frequency of behavior or thoughts in certain contexts is called _____.

8. Validity based on agreement between an assessment measure and a criterion (future indicator of a behavior) is called _____.

9. The degree to which a measuring procedure (assessment test) measures what we say it measures is called _____.

10. Oral means of collecting information from someone is called a(n) _____.

11. The tendency of people, when explaining the behavior of others, generally to underestimate the influence of situations and overestimate the influence of personality traits is called _____.

12. The degree to which the items of an assessment device represent examples of what the test is targeting is called _____.

13. Agreement between a measure of a variable and some criterion that is obtained at about the same time is called _____.

14. A performance test that seeks to reveal a person's underlying personality by measuring how he or she responds to an ambiguous task is called a _____.

15. A form of psychometric reliability; correspondence between test items intended to measure the same concept is called _____.

16. Self-report questionnaires with numerous items scored on multiple scales that attempt to derive complex pictures of a person's overall characteristics or traits are called _____.

17. Methods of measuring the brain based on computerized synthesis of highly sensitive detection methods are called _____.

18. Determining the constellation of symptoms and how they fit the classifications system for mental disorders is called _____.

19. The consistency of a test's results over time is called _____.

20. The degree to which an assessment procedure is useful and provides information not otherwise available or obtained more cheaply is called _____.

21. A neuroimaging technique that passes a radioactive ray through bone and brain tissue to show structures of the brain is called _____.

22. The degree to which items on a test appear to measure what the test purports to measure is called _____.

23. The best-known projective test, in which the subject is presented with a series of ten inkblots and asked to describe what he or she "sees"; intended to reveal the underlying personality and its dynamics, it is called the _____.

24. A widely accepted system in the United States and around the world for classifying psychological problems and disorders is the _____.

25. A feature of the DSM-IV designed to provide a comprehensive picture of the characteristics and functioning of the person by providing an evaluation on five different scales, or axes, each representing different aspects of the person's adjustment and life, is called _____.

26. Interviews that are open-ended and do not follow any particular format so that two interviewers might obtain very different information are called _____.

27. An advanced neuroimaging technique for evaluating brain structure that produces sharp images and does not require radioactive substances is called _____.

28. The degree to which test results and the theoretical construct (or concept) the test is attempting to measure are related is called _____.

29. An approach to cognitive assessment that tests numerous types of cognitive functioning to identify the nature and extent of possible brain impairment is called _____.

30. The consistency or repeatability of results of a measurement is called _____.

31. Psychological measures that involve the completion of tasks believed to indicate cognitive abilities and include manipulation of objects and mental tasks, or reveal personality characteristics by telling stories about or providing perceptions of ambiguous stimuli, are called _____.

32. Biological assessment that shows actual brain activity is called _____.

33. A written set of questions to which a person provides written replies is called a _____.

34. Assessment achieved by actually watching and recording (coding) what a person does in a particular setting is called _____.

35. Assessment instruments based on the assumption that emotional states involve changes in the autonomic nervous system are called _____.

36. The degree to which a measure agrees with an external standard or criterion is called _____.

FACTUAL MULTIPLE-CHOICE QUESTIONS

1. If a characteristic cannot be measured directly, assessment requires the use of
   a. laboratory.
   b. inference.
   c. observation.
   d. diagnosis.

2. Unchanging characteristics such as sociability and psychopathy are referred to as
   a. states.
   b. traits.
   c. anxiety.
   d. moods.

3. A test that produces consistent results after repeated administrations is said to have
   a. interrater reliability.
   b. internal consistency.
   c. test-retest reliability.
   d. criterion validity.

4. If a test has scientific evidence that it measures what it says it measures, this is called
    a. reliability.
    b. accuracy.
    c. utility.
    d. validity.

5. A test containing items that appear to measure what it purports to measure is said to have
    a. content validity.
    b. criterion-related validity.
    c. face validity.
    d. construct validity.

6. Interviews in which questions are asked in the same way, following the same order, are called
    a. personal.
    b. unstructured.
    c. educational.
    d. structured.

7. A questionnaire used to compile a picture of a person's traits, characteristics, and tendencies is a
    a. personality inventory.
    b. test of intelligence.
    c. performance test.
    d. projective test.

8. A widely used, recently revised personality inventory is the
    a. DACL.
    b. POMS.
    c. 16PF.
    d. MMPI.

9. The creator of one of the most widely used intelligence tests for adults and children is
    a. Thorndike.
    b. Beck.
    c. Wechsler.
    d. Terman.

10. Tests that measure responses to ambiguous stimuli are called
    a. inventories.
    b. intelligence tests.
    c. projective tests.
    d. test batteries.

11. When a person agrees to participate in a research project after understanding the procedure and being assured of confidentiality, he or she is said to have given
    a. permission.
    b. informed consent.
    c. authorization.
    d. subject approval.

12. The publisher of the DSM is the
    a. American Psychological Association.
    b. World Health Organization.
    c. American Medical Association.
    d. American Psychiatric Association.

13. The diagnostic system of the DSM incorporates several evaluations. This system is called
    a. multimodal.
    b. multidirectional.
    c. multiaxial.
    d. multivariate.

14. A person often has more than one disorder. This is called
    a. symptom overlap.
    b. mixed conditions.
    c. comorbidity.
    d. reification.

15. An assessment procedure that provides unique information that is not available through other means, or at a reasonable cost, is said to have
    a. reliability.
    b. utility.
    c. predictive validity.
    d. concurrent validity.

CONCEPTUAL MULTIPLE-CHOICE QUESTIONS

1. The schoolchildren whispered to each other about the person watching them and making notes. This could represent a problem in research called
    a. fundamental attribution error.
    b. placebo effect.
    c. reification.
    d. reactivity.

2. Dr. Mallory is perplexed by the confusing symptoms presented by her patient. She calls a colleague who treated the client before. They disagree on the DSM-IV diagnosis. This is an example of
    a. low reliability.
    b. low validity.
    c. professional bias.
    d. difficulty of diagnosis.

3. Beverly's psychiatrist determined that her symptoms reflected both depression and anxiety, a condition that is an example of
    a. comorbidity.
    b. prototypes.
    c. the multiaxial approach.
    d. essential features.

4. Dr. Adams saw that in addition to agoraphobia, her patient was suffering from asthma. She noted this condition on the evaluation, reflecting an example of the DSM's
   a. validity.
   b. multiaxial approach.
   c. prototype system.
   d. field-trial system.

5. Bill has been turned down numerous times in his job search because he was recently hospitalized for depression. This is an example of
   a. misdiagnosis.
   b. gender bias.
   c. labeling.
   d. cultural bias.

6. Nancy was told by a friend that she was neurotic, but on examining the DSM she found that the term did not exist. Why?
   a. Field trials.
   b. Neurosis has just been discovered.
   c. Neurosis is an outdated term.
   d. There was a political lobby to exclude the term.

7. Kevin was picked up by the police for exhibiting bizarre and disruptive behavior in public. He was taken to a local community mental health center. The staff interviewed Kevin, observed his behavior, administered some performance tasks, and after a few hours released Kevin from the center. What procedure has occurred?
   a. DSM diagnosis
   b. predictive validity
   c. psychological assessment
   d. retrospective report

8. Keith and Greg are colleagues. Greg commented that Keith's absence from departmental meetings reflected a strong hostility motive. Keith objected and said that the reason he was absent from the last meeting was that he was attending a conference. Greg's comment illustrates:
   a. the fundamental attribution error.
   b. an illusory correlation.
   c. low interrater reliability.
   d. the availability bias.

9. Which of the following factors, if present, would likely contribute to an inaccurate assessment and DSM diagnosis?
   a. a client exhibiting bizarre behavior that has a low base rate
   b. use of instruments that have high interrater reliability
   c. use of assessment procedures that have high predictive validity
   d. results from a standardized intelligence test

10. You overhear Dr. Jones talking about one of his patient's problems with alcohol. During the conversation, Dr. Jones frequently characterizes such patients as "alcoholics." Dr. Jones's characterization of individuals with alcohol problems as alcoholics reflects
    a. internal validity of the diagnosis.
    b. reification.
    c. comorbidity.
    d. the fundamental attribution error.

APPLICATION MULTIPLE-CHOICE QUESTIONS

1. Dr. Miller is interpreting Murray's responses to a personality inventory on the basis of ten clinical scales. The test she is interpreting is the
   a. Luria-Nebraska.
   b. MMPI-2.
   c. Halstead-Reitan.
   d. PET Scan.

2. As Dr. Johnson watched, Bill assembled the pieces of the puzzle to form an object. The test he was taking was probably measuring
   a. intelligence.
   b. personality.
   c. psychopathology.
   d. memory.

3. Jane looked at the photograph for several minutes before she described what she saw. The test was the
   a. Rorschach.
   b. TAT.
   c. Draw-A-Person.
   d. Bender-Gestalt.

4. Dr. Ferguson wanted to determine if Hillary's condition might be related to impaired brain functioning. He asked her to perform certain tasks and took a measure utilizing a
   a. CT scan.
   b. MRI.
   c. PET scan.
   d. EEG.

5. A school district administrator is planning a large-scale intelligence evaluation on a limited budget. She would probably not use the WISC-III because
   a. it has low reliability.
   b. it is individually administered and would therefore be expensive.
   c. it is culturally biased.
   d. it has low validity.

6. Laura's performance on the intelligence test was not good. Her therapist concluded that she was not a good candidate for therapy requiring high verbal skills. Which of the following is *not* a reason to reach such a conclusion?
   a. Intelligence tests are unreliable.
   b. Anxiety.
   c. Fatigue.
   d. Familiarity with the examiner.

7. Dr. Forsyth is not able to make a final diagnosis in Mrs. Choi's case because there are family factors that he feels the client has not expressed. His reluctance might reflect his fear of
   a. legal implications.
   b. cultural bias.
   c. labeling.
   d. reification.

ANSWER KEY: KEY TERMS REVIEW

1. field trials (123)
2. structured interviews (102)
3. response bias (101)
4. comorbidity (124)
5. interrater reliability (99)
6. intelligence (IQ) tests (107–108)
7. self-monitoring (114)
8. predictive validity (100)
9. validity (99)
10. interview (102)
11. fundamental attribution error (117)
12. content validity (100)
13. concurrent validity (100)
14. projective test (109–110)
15. internal consistency (99)
16. personality inventories (103)
17. neuroimaging techniques (114)
18. diagnosis (118)
19. test-retest reliability (98)
20. utility (101)
21. computerized axial tomography (CT) (114)
22. face validity (100)
23. Rorschach inkblot test (109–110)
24. *Diagnostic and Statistical Manual* (119)
25. multiaxial (119)
26. unstructured interviews (102)
27. nuclear magnetic resonance imaging (NMR or NMI) (114)
28. construct validity (100)
29. neuropsychological assessment (109)
30. reliability (98)
31. performance tests (107)
32. positron emission tomography (PET) (114)
33. questionnaire (103)
34. observation techniques (110)
35. psychophysiological techniques (114–115)
36. criterion-related validity (100)

ANSWER KEY: FACTUAL MULTIPLE-CHOICE QUESTIONS

1. *b. inference (p. 98)
   a. A laboratory would not provide more information on a characteristic that cannot be measured.
   c. Observation is a direct measure that can be quantified.
   d. Diagnosis follows assessment.

2. *b. traits (p. 98)
   a. States are temporary conditions.
   c. Anxiety is sometimes temporary and does not include sociability.
   d. Mood is a temporary condition subject to change.

3. *c. test-retest reliability (p. 98)
   a. Interrater reliability refers to consistency among scorers or observers, not repeated measures of the same test.
   b. Internal consistency is correspondence between test items, not between test administrations.
   d. Criterion validity involves validity by determining current or future agreement with the criterion.

4. *d. validity (p. 99)
   a. Reliability refers to consistency of results.
   b. Accuracy can be measured, but determining validity is a process, usually based on research.
   c. Utility means the instrument serves its purpose.

5. *c. face validity (p. 100)
   a. Content validity means the items of an assessment represent true examples of what the test is designed to measure.
   b. Criterion-related validity says the test predicts what will happen in a particular behavior (the criterion).
   d. Construct validity means that test results and the theoretical construct the test is measuring are related.

6. *d. structured (p. 102)
   a. A personal interview could be structured or unstructured.
   b. Unstructured interviews are not precise as to the presentation of questions.
   c. This type of interview is used extensively for diagnostic evaluations and could be structured or unstructured.

7. *a. personality inventory (p. 103)
   b. Personality inventories do not attempt to test intelligence.
   c. A performance test would measure cognitive abilities, not traits and characteristics.
   d. Projective tests use ambiguous cues, not questionnaires.

8. *d. MMPI (pp. 104–106)
   a. DACL is the Depression Adjective Check List.
   b. POMS is the Profile of Mood States.
   c. 16PF is the 16 Personality Factors.

9. *c. Wechsler (p. 107)
   a. Thorndike was a behaviorist, not a pioneer in intelligence testing.
   b. Beck works with depression.
   d. Terman was an early theorist in intelligence.

10. *c. projective tests (p. 109)
    a. Inventories ask specific questions to measure identifiable qualities.
    b. Intelligence tests seek specific responses.
    d. Test batteries are a group of tests designed to measure certain characteristics.

11. *b. informed consent (p. 116)
    a. Permission does not imply complete understanding of the procedure.
    c. Authorization does not imply complete knowledge.
    d. Informed consent requires much more than approval.

12. *d. American Psychiatric Association (p. 119)
    a. The American Psychological Association is made up of psychologists but did not publish the DSM.
    b. The World Health Organization publishes the ICD.
    c. The AMA includes psychiatrists, but did not publish the DSM.

13. *c. multiaxial (p. 119)
    a. Multimodal refers to approaches in therapy, not diagnosis.
    b. The diagnostic system is more than directional.
    d. Multivariate refers to a statistical technique.

14. *c.   comorbidity (p. 124)
    a.   Symptoms may indeed overlap, making an accurate diagnosis difficult, but this is not a term to describe the person with several disorders.
    b.   Clients often have mixed conditions, which are less serious than disorders.
    d.   Reification is treating a disorder as an "it," an object.

15. *b.   utility (p. 101)
    a.   Reliability deals with consistency of measures.
    c.   Predictive validity is the degree of agreement between an assessment measure and some future indicator of a behavior.
    d.   Concurrent validity is the degree of agreement between an assessment measure and a criterion obtained at about the same time.

ANSWER KEY: CONCEPTUAL MULTIPLE-CHOICE QUESTIONS

1. *d.   reactivity (p. 112)
    a.   Fundamental attribution error refers to underestimating the influence of situations and overestimating the influence of personality traits.
    b.   Placebos elicit effects because of the belief in the efficacy of a procedure, and do not reflect a self-conscious reaction to a researcher.
    c.   Reification is treating the diagnosis as something that truly exists, rather than as a convenient construct used by researchers and theorists.

2. *d.   difficulty of diagnosis (pp. 118–119)
    a.   The DSM may be highly reliable, but is still subject to professional interpretation.
    b.   The DSM may be valid while still allowing room for disagreement.
    c.   Differing diagnoses may not be bias, but an honest disagreement.

3. *a.   comorbidity (p. 124)
    b.   Prototypes are the typical characteristics that define the disorder.
    c.   Multiaxial is a feature of the DSM, referring to evaluations made on five scales, and is a measurement tool, not a set of disorders.
    d.   Essential features are defined in DSM-IV, but would not reflect an overlap of symptoms.

4. *b.   multiaxial approach (p. 119)
    a.   Validity is whether a test measures what it says it measures, and is not related to Dr. Adams's careful notations.
    c.   Prototype refers to the essential features of a diagnosis on Axes I and II and not to physical symptoms (reported on Axis III).
    d.   Field trials are used to determine the accuracy of diagnostic categories and the need for any changes.

5. *c.   labeling (pp. 124–125)
    a.   The diagnosis may be correct, but the reaction is of a discriminatory nature.
    b.   Gender does not seem to be a factor here.
    d.   The label of mental illness may overshadow other types of bias, such as cultured bias, which does not seem to be the issue here.

6. *c. neurosis is an outdated term (p. 120)
    a. Field trials do not define terms, but test the reliability of a diagnosis or of certain diagnostic categories.
    b. Neurosis was a term coined by Freud that has since been eliminated from the DSM.
    d. No political lobby excluded the term.

7. *c. assessment (p. 98)
    a. A DSM diagnosis may or may not be given following a psychological assessment.
    b. Predictive validity is the degree of agreement between an assessment measure and some future indicator of a behavior.
    d. A retrospective report is when the person discusses an event which has occurred in the past.

8. *a. the fundamental attribution error (p. 117)
    b. The illusory correlation is a predisposition to make associations between stimuli that are not actually related.
    c. Interrater reliability is the consistency among separate scorers or observers rating some characteristic.
    d. Greg ignores the circumstances of the situation and attributes personal characteristics to Keith.

9. *a. a client exhibiting bizarre behavior that has a low base rate. (p. 101)
    b. Instruments with a high interrater reliability are generally desirable, especially if the instruments are valid.
    c. Assessment procedures that have high predictive validity are generally valuable.
    d. Results from a standardized intelligence test would be helpful, depending on the type of behavior being considered.

10. *b. reification.
    a. Internal validity relates to experimental procedures.
    c. Comorbidity is the co-occurrence of different types of disorders in one person.
    d. The fundamental attribution error is the tendency for people to overemphasize personality traits and underemphasize situational influences when explaining the causes for others' behavior.

ANSWER KEY: APPLICATION MULTIPLE-CHOICE QUESTIONS

1. *b. MMPI-2 (pp. 104–106)
    a. Luria-Nebraska is a neurophysiological test, not a personality inventory.
    c. Halstead-Reitan is a test to measure possible brain injury.
    d. PET scan is a neuroimaging technique.

2. *a. intelligence (p. 107)
    b. Object assembly is not used with personality tests.
    c. Object assembly is not used in tests to determine psychopathology.
    d. Memory is not primarily tested by object assembly.

3. *b. TAT (pp. 109–110)
    a. The Rorschach uses inkblots, not photographs.
    c. Draw-A-Person is often used with children.
    d. The Bender-Gestalt is a measure of sensorimotor construction skills.

4. *c. PET scan (p. 116)
   a. CT scans provide only structural pictures of the brain.
   b. MRI gives a sharper image without radioactive substances but does not show actual brain activity.
   d. EEG is tracings of electrical activity in the brain.

5. *b. it individually administered and would therefore be expensive (p. 107)
   a. The WISC-III has high reliability.
   c. The WISC-III is one of the least biased intelligence tests.
   d. The validity of the WISC-III is high.

6. *a. Intelligence tests are unreliable results (p. 108)
   b. Anxiety can negatively affect test results.
   c. Fatigue is another factor that can negatively affect test results.
   d. Familiarity with the examiner will improve test results.

7. *b. cultural bias (p. 125)
   a. Legal implications are not a factor in this case.
   c. This is not a matter of labeling, but getting at the truth of her difficulty.
   d. The therapist has not made a diagnosis, hence reification would not be a factor.

CHAPTER 5
Research Methods

LEARNING OBJECTIVES

1. Discuss the strategies of science and how the scientific method applies to abnormal psychology. (pp. 130–131)

2. Explain the importance of validity in determining the strength of conclusions reached in scientific investigations. (p. 131)

3. Distinguish the factors that may affect internal and external validity. (p. 131)

4. Describe the methods used to differentiate between normal and abnormal behavior, such as the continuity and discontinuity theories. (pp. 131–132)

5. Describe data-gathering techniques and research methods. (pp. 132–134)

6. Describe the descriptive methods of research, including case studies and surveys. (pp. 134–136

7. Describe the research that is being conducted to determine the changing nature of the American family. (pp. 136–138)

8. Describe the correlational method, and discuss the reasons why correlational methods cannot be used to establish cause-effect relations. (pp. 138–141)

9. Articulate how the experimental method is used in making cause-effect claims. (pp. 141–145)

10. Describe the process of isolating the effects of the independent variable through control groups, randomization, matching, counterbalancing, and placebo control groups. (pp. 142–144)

11. Discuss the meaning of statistical significance. (pp. 143–144)

12. Describe how a study meets acceptable standards of internal and external validity. (pp. 144–145)

13. Describe the single-subject designs that compare baseline data with the same behavior under other conditions. (pp. 145–146)

14. Discuss some of the cautions to be used in single-subject-design research. (pp. 145–146)

15. Discuss some of the recurring themes associated with research in abnormal psychology, such as the distribution of disorders and the effectiveness of treatment. (p. 149)

16. Describe longitudinal designs, such as the Robins and Price (1991) study of antisocial behavior. (pp. 146–149)

17. Describe the research methods used to determine the possibility of genetic transmission of psychological disorders through family studies, twin/adoption studies, and the high-risk method. (pp. 150–152)

18. Describe methods used to determine the effectiveness of treatment, such as normative comparisons. (pp. 152–153)

19. Discuss meta-analysis as a tool for integrating a large body of research literature. (pp. 153–154)

20. Discuss ethical considerations related to research, such as informed consent of subjects and confidentiality. (pp. 154–155)

21. Discuss emerging trends in psychological research. (p. 155)

CHAPTER OUTLINE

I. Science and Psychopathology

- *Science:* Knowledge gained by observing, experimenting, testing, and revising.

- *Empiricism:* Assumes that the world can be known through observation.

- *Hypotheses:* Opinions that are open to verification.

- *Theory:* Organized system of assumptions that purport to explain a physiological phenomenon.

- *Operational definitions:* Define a concept by the steps used in measuring it.

A. Internal and External Validity

1. Internal validity: The extent to which the methodology of a study allows for strong conclusions to be drawn by eliminating rival explanations.

   a. Threats to validity include simultaneously occurring outside events, maturation, the effects of testing, and statistical regression.

   b. Confounds are eliminated.

2. External validity: The degree to which research findings can be generalized to situations, persons, or locations beyond those employed in the study.

3. Representativeness: The degree to which important characteristics of the sample of persons studied match these characteristics in the population.

B. What's Normal? Researchers Struggle with the Question

1. Continuity theory states that psychological dysfunctions and normal behavior form one continuum, from normal behavior, to mild disturbance, to moderate disturbance, to severe disturbance.

2. Discontinuity theory states that mild and severe psychological dysfunctions are distinct from each another and from normality; that they stem from different causes and follow different courses.

3. Conformity and discontinuity theories may apply specifically to different disorders.

C. Designing Research

1. Data-gathering techniques

a. Gathering meaningful data crucial to quality science.

b. Approaches include interviews and questionnaires, testing, collection of psychophysiological measures.

c. Analogue: A scaled-down facsimile of reality that contains certain basic characteristics of the real thing in a simplified and controlled manner; the basis of some research designs.

d. Research of Seligman on *learned helplessness* with dogs was the analogue study that helped our understanding of depression.

2. Research methods

a. Researchers have different goals that require them to use different methods.

b. Methods include descriptive, correlational, and experimental.

II. Descriptive Methods

• Descriptive approaches are general procedures used to summarize and organize samples of data

A. Case Studies

1. Examine and describe in depth an individual's current feelings, thoughts, and behaviors.

2. Freud and Kraepelin were early users of the case study approach.

3. Used for new and rare disorders.

4. Case studies limited because they do not control variables.

5. Cases are not representative and thus limit external validity (generalizability).

6. Data may not be gathered systematically; thus biases are especially problematic.

B. Surveys

1. Provide information about the nature and scope of mental health problems across large populations or regions.

2. Important tool for epidemiology, the study of the incidence and prevalence of disorders in a specific population.

a. *Incidence:* The number of new cases of a disorder reported during a specified period of time.

        b.   Prevalence: The overall frequency of a disorder in a specified population.

      3.   Random sampling necessary to achieve external validity; means every member of the population has an equal chance of being selected.

  C. Focus on the Family: The Changing American Family

      1.   The American family is changing.

      2.   Research is needed to determine the effects of the changes on mental health adjustment.

III. Correlational Methods

  • Correlation studies: Approaches to research questions that focus on the relationship (covariation) among variables.

  • When two variables are highly related, knowledge about one variable helps to make predictions about the other.

  A. Assessing Correlations

      1.   Scatter plots: Graphs used to display data from correlational studies, in which values of one variable are shown on horizontal axis and values of the other variable are shown on the vertical axis.

      2.   Correlation coefficient: The measure, at a range from +1.0 to –1.0, used to express the direction and magnitude of the relationship between variables.

          a.   *Positive correlation*

          b.   *Negative correlation*

      3.   Statistically significant correlation is one that would not occur as a result of chance alone.

  B. Using Correlational Methods

      1.   Problem of the third variable: An unknown variable that may be responsible for the changes in the other two variables.

      2.   Problem of directionality: The question of which of two correlated variables caused the other.

      3.   Classification variables: Variables used to identify two groups of subjects, permitting a nonexperimental (correlational) or quasi-experimental study.

IV. Experimental Methods

  • In an *experiment*, researcher directly manipulates the variable(s) of interest.

  • Independent variable: The variable manipulated to determine effects on dependent variables.

  • Dependent variable: The measure or effect attributable to the manipulated independent variable.

  A. Controlling Variables

- A control group is a group of subjects exposed to all features of the experiment with the exception of the independent variable.

- Experimental (treatment) group is exposed to independent variable

- Responses of two groups are then compared.

1. Random assignment

    a. Assignment of subjects to experimental and control groups by chance.

    b. Reduces any preexisting differences between the experimental and control groups at the beginning of the experiment that may influence the dependent variable.

2. Matching: Ensuring that subjects in all conditions are comparable on key variables that may be related to the dependent variable.

3. Counterbalancing: Presentation of research events to subjects in different orders.

4. Placebo control groups

    a. Placebo: An inert pill or treatment given in such a way that the person believes the medication (or therapy) is active.

    b. Placebo effect: Improved health as a result of being given something believed to be helpful.

    c. Placebo effect can interfere with results unless controlled.

5. Statistical significance: An index of the probability that the effects of an experiment are explained not by chance but by the variable being investigated.

B. Internal and External Validity in Experimental Studies

1. Paul's study compared systematic desensitization and insight-oriented psycho-therapy.

2. Internal validity was emphasized to increase confidence in the findings.

3. External validity was limited by the sample of college students.

V. Single-Subject Designs

- Baseline: Measure of the frequency of naturally occurring target behavior.

- Compared with the frequency of the same behavior under other conditions (i.e., intervention).

A. The A-B-A-B Design

1. Also called *reversal designs,* used to assess effects of intervention by demonstrating that problem behavior changes systematically with the provision and removal of treatment.

2. A = baseline, B = treatment

    a. Baseline and treatment conditions are alternated.

    b. Following a baseline measure (A), treatment is applied (B) and terminated (A), and measures are taken to see if improvement is the result of B.

B. The Multiple Baseline Design: Two or more baselines recorded simultaneously and intervention is applied to only one.

C. Cautions Regarding Single-Subject Designs

1. Generalizability is limited.

2. Changes may be transitory.

3. Effects of treatment may spill over to the other baselines.

VI. Focus on Research: What Can Be Learned from Different Approaches to Studying a Particular Behavior?

A. Childhood conduct disorder associated with numerous adult disorders, including antisocial personality and alcohol abuse.

B. Psychopaths were found to be poor at inhibiting their reward-seeking behavior.

VII. Perennial Themes: Some Key Questions for Research

• Research studies reflect the underlying question of the researcher. Some questions include: What is the nature of the disorder? How widespread is the disorder? What is the effect of treatment?

A. Identifying the Course of Disorder: Longitudinal Research

1. Longitudinal designs: Study changes over time by repeatedly measuring the same subjects at select intervals.

2. Cross-sectional studies: Examine the same characteristics in different individuals at different ages.

3. Follow-up studies identify patients at a certain point and study them again later on.

4. Follow-back studies identify adult patients and examine earlier records.

5. High-risk studies look at children exposed to conditions thought to contribute to disorder.

6. Longitudinal studies useful because they

a. Permit causal inferences.

b. Identify precipitating factors.

c. Assess diagnostic stability.

d. Describe course of disorder.

e. Identify predictors of outcome.

7. Drawbacks

a. Take a long time.

b. Expensive.

c. Subjects may drop out.

B. Studying Genetic Transmission of Psychological Disorders

    1. Family studies

        a. Address the question of whether the frequency of a particular disorder is higher among family members than in the general population.

        b. High-risk method: Children of a parent with an identified disorder are studied.

        c. Cannot separate the effects of genetics from those of environment.

    2. Twin and adoption studies

        a. Used to separate the influence of nature and nurture.

        b. Twin studies: Researchers determine extent to which the sibling of twins with a disorder have the disorder.

            (1) If both have the disorder, they are *concordant*.

            (2) Researchers compare concordant a rate of monozygotic and dizygotic twin.

            (3) Higher concordance rate of monozygotic versus dizygotic twins is assumed to be due to genetic inheritance.

        c. In an adoption study, adopted children with diagnosable biological parents are studied.

        d. Cross-fostering: Children of normal biological parents who have been adopted and raised either by normal or disordered parents.

C. Are the Effects of Treatment Meaningful?

    1. Clinical significance used in addition to statistical significance to evaluate efficacy of treatment method.

    2. Normative comparisons require clients after treatment to be clinically indistinguishable from a nondisturbed group.

D. Meta-Analysis: Integrating Research

    1. Meta-analysis is a technique for comparing effects found in different studies.

    2. Effect size measures difference in means of experimental and control group, divided by standard deviation of control group.

    3. Useful technique for combining and comparing studies.

VIII. Research Ethics

A. APA provides ethical principles for researchers.

    1. No real risk for participating in the study.

    2. Informed consent of participants.

    3. Debriefing after the study is complete.

    4. Freedom to terminate at any time.

5. Right to confidentiality.

B. Researchers ethically required to remove or correct unwanted consequences.

IX. What Lies Ahead?

A. Research expanding on causes of psychopathology: the role of the family, genetics, and cognition.

B. Interest increasing in evaluating the treatment of disorders

C. Will examine diversity (gender, age, race, and culture) and its role in the development, expression, and treatment of disorders

D. New research methods being developed

KEY TERMS REVIEW

1. The variable that a researcher influences or manipulates in an experiment to investigate its effect on other dependent variables is called a(n) _____.

2. General procedures used to summarize and organize samples of data; two forms, case studies and surveys, are called _____.

3. A preferred research method in which a researcher directly influences or manipulates one or more of the independent variables and assesses the effects on other dependent variables is called a(n) _____.

4. Any aspect of a person, group, or setting that is measured for the purpose of a study is called a(n) _____.

5. Research that identifies adult patients and examines their earlier records at schools or treatment agencies is called a(n) _____.

6. Research techniques that assess the effects of an intervention by demonstrating that the problem behavior changes systematically with the provision and removal of treatment are called _____.

7. A relationship showing the value of one variable increasing accompanied by increases in the value of the other variable is called _____.

8. An unknown variable that may be responsible for the changes in two other variables, even when those variables have high correlation, is called a(n) _____.

9. A measure of the difference between mean (average) scores of the various conditions under investigation is called the _____.

10. The measure, at a range from +1.0 to –1.0, used to express the direction and magnitude of the relationship between variables is called the _____.

11. The overall frequency of a disorder in the specified population is called the _____.

12. A scaled-down facsimile of reality that contains certain basic characteristics of the real thing in a simplified and controlled manner that is the basis of some research designs is called a(n) _____.

13. A technique for comparing the sizes of the effects found in different studies and for examining the relationship between certain variables and the outcomes of different studies is called _____.

14. A method of selecting participants in the sample by which, regardless of the size of the sample, every member of the population being studied has an equal chance of being included is called _____.

15. A method of research that provides information about the nature and scope of mental health problems across large populations or regions is called a(n) _____.

16. Research that considers children who are exposed to conditions that can contribute to a disorder are called _____.

17. Used in addition to statistical significance, to evaluate the efficacy of a treatment method, sometimes determined by using *normative comparisons*, this is called _____.

18. A detailed examination of an individual's current feelings, thoughts, and behaviors is called a(n) _____.

19. Research that identifies patients at a particular point, such as when they are first diagnosed, and studies them again at a later time is called a(n) _____.

20. Research that attempts to test genetic hypotheses by determining the extent to which the twin sibling of a twin with a disorder also experience a disorder is called _____.

21. The degree to which important characteristics of the sample of persons studied match these characteristics in the population is called _____.

22. Research that compares the rates of disorder among adopted children whose biological parents had a diagnosable disorder with the rates among adopted children whose biological parents did not have disorders is called a(n) _____.

23. Approaches to research questions that focus on the relationship (covariation) among variables are called _____.

24. The principle that subjects' responses to psychological tests or tasks are not open to the public is called _____.

25. The extent to which the methodology of a study allows for strong conclusions to be drawn is called _____.

26. Graphs used to display data from correlational studies, in which values of one variable are shown on the horizontal axis and values of the other variable are shown on the vertical axis, are called _____.

27. The naturally occurring frequency of a target behavior is called the _____.

28. The study of the incidence and prevalence of disorders in a specific population is called _____.

29. The methods for determining the probability that the effects of an experiment are explained not by chance but by the variable being investigated are called _____.

30. A correlation or covariation between variables that would not occur as a result of chance alone is called _____.

31. Variables used to identify two groups of subjects—those who are grouped a certain way and those who are not—are called _____.

32. The variable used to measure the effects, if any, of the manipulated independent variable in an experiment is called the _____.

33. Assigning subjects to a condition in an experiment purely by chance is called _____.

34. Presenting research events to subjects in different orders, done to control unwanted sequence effects, is called _____.

35. A group of subjects exposed to all features of an experiment with the exception of the independent variable is called the _____.

36. In an experimental setting, inert pills or treatments given in such a way that the person believes that the medications or therapies are active are called _____.

37. Research that studies changes and stability over time by repeatedly measuring the same subjects at select intervals is called a(n) _____.

38. The question of which of two correlated variables caused the other is called the _____.

39. Research that studies the children of parents with known psychological problems or no problems who have been adopted and raised by either normal or disordered parents is called _____.

40. Research that addresses the question of whether the frequency of a particular disorder is higher among family members than in the general population is called a(n) _____.

41. A relationship showing the value of one variable increasing while the value of the other variable decreasing is called a _____.

42. To provide participants in a study with a clear statement of the rationale and methods of the study when their participation is completed is called _____.

43. The number of new cases of a disorder reported during a specified period of time is called the _____.

44. The attempt to ensure that the subjects in all conditions in an experiment are comparable by first defining the important ways that subjects could differ from one another and then putting an equal number of subjects of each type in each group is called _____.

45. The principle that, for a treatment to be clinically significant, clients after treatment must be indistinguishable from a representative nondisturbed group is called a(n) _____.

46. A view stating that mild and severe psychological dysfunction are distinct from each other and from normality, that they stem from different causes and follow different courses, is called the _____.

47. A research method used with single (or few) cases in which two or more baselines are recorded simultaneously and the intervention applied for only one of the baselines is called a(n) _____.

48. The principle that subjects in a study must be told about the study and give their permission to be involved before they participate is called _____.

49. The degree to which research findings can be generalized to situations, persons, or locations beyond those employed in the study is called _____.

50. Research that examines the same characteristics in different individuals at one point in time is called _____.

51. A view stating that psychological dysfunctions and normal behavior form one continuum, from normal behavior to mild disturbance to moderate disturbance, to severe disturbance is the _____.

FACTUAL MULTIPLE-CHOICE QUESTIONS

1. The methods of science are based on
   a. tradition.
   b. empiricism.
   c. the medical model.
   d. popular opinion.

2. A researcher who believes that normality and abnormality differ only as a matter of degree would subscribe to the
   a. discontinuity theory.
   b. continuity theory.
   c. validity theory.
   d. reliability theory.

3. Epidemiological studies are concerned with
   a. independent and dependent variables.
   b. internal validity.
   c. incidence and prevalence.
   d. control groups and placebo groups.

4. Correlational research measures the relationship between
   a. cause and effect.
   b. variables.
   c. unknown variables.
   d. experiments.

5. A member of a control group is not exposed to the
   a. experimental group.
   b. dependent variable.
   c. independent variable.
   d. placebo.

6. Saigh's study of posttraumatic stress disorder made use of
   a. baseline design.
   b. multiple baseline design.
   c. control groups.
   d. field studies.

7. Grove's study of schizophrenia was an example of a
   a. family study.
   b. case study.
   c. historical study.
   d. field study.

8. Freud built his theories and developed his therapy with the use of a relatively small number of clients. His research was based on
   a. case studies.
   b. field studies.
   c. longitudinal studies.
   d. historical studies.

9. Half the subjects in an experiment are given an inert substance, the other half are given an active drug. The active drug is called the
   a. placebo.
   b. dependent variable.
   c. independent variable.
   d. third variable.

CONCEPTUAL MULTIPLE-CHOICE QUESTIONS

1. If a study is not open to alternate explanations, it is said to be
   a. internally valid.
   b. statistically significant.
   c. clinically significant.
   d. externally valid.

2. When a study does not include important characteristics in the sample that match those characteristics in the population it is said to lack
   a. internal consistency.
   b. dependability.
   c. useability.
   d. representativeness.

3. Seligman's classic study of learned helplessness is an example of
   a. survey research.
   b. laboratory task research.
   c. EEG tracings.
   d. analogue research.

4. A researcher working on a new therapeutic intervention might test her theory by using the
   a. diagnostic approach.
   b. field study approach.
   c. double blind approach.
   d. case study approach.

5. The experimental approach to research has the advantage over other methods of permitting statements about
   a. cause and effect.
   b. reliability and validity.
   c. description.
   d. incidence and prevalence.

6. The effect caused by a placebo results from
   a. the medical model.
   b. the effect of the drug.
   c. the control group.
   d. expectation of relief.

7. A study of the effects of Alzheimer's disease would probably employ
   a. multiple baseline design.
   b. high-risk studies.
   c. longitudinal designs.
   d. single-subject experiments.

8. If a treatment allows the client to reach a level of functioning indistinguishable from a normal group, the treatment is said to have reached
   a. statistical significance.
   b. clinical significance.
   c. baseline.
   d. external validity.

9. Mary Ann first became homeless two years ago. Since then she has been in and out of institutions. She has been diagnosed as schizophrenic, paranoid type. Why can't we say there is a correlation between her homelessness and schizophrenia?
   a. independent variable
   b. randomization
   c. many schizophrenics are homeless
   d. directionality

10. Dr. Song wants to study the effects of substance abuse on homelessness. He has great difficulty identifying his groups because of the unpredictability of behavior on the part of his homeless subjects. He persists because using actual homeless persons will increase his study's
    a. external validity.
    b. internal validity.
    c. placebo control.
    d. randomization.

APPLICATION MULTIPLE-CHOICE QUESTIONS

1. Dr. Johnson prepared a study to determine if grade school achievement is related to income levels. He failed to administer an intelligence test as part of his design. This would threaten what aspect of his design?
   a. representativeness
   b. internal validity
   c. correlation
   d. clinical significance

2. Michelle reports to her therapist that the depression she has suffered has gotten worse with her return to college. She now feels that she cannot cope with the demands of college. Her experience would support which theory of abnormal behavior?
   a. discontinuity
   b. continuity
   c. baseline
   d. multiple baseline

3. Dr. Miller would like to study the effects of stress, but she is told by the Human Subjects Committee that administering electrical shocks to human beings is unacceptable. She still wants to measure the effects of electrical shock stress, so she will have to use
   a. case studies.
   b. longitudinal studies.
   c. epidemiological studies.
   d. analogue studies.

4. Jonathan received an invitation from Dr. Coolidge to participate in a paper and pencil psychology experiment. His name was chosen from a listing of all members of the freshman class. His selection is an example of what research technique?
   a. random sampling
   b. placebo control group
   c. epidemiological study
   d. family study

5. Keith was given medication to control his hyperactivity and then his behavior was monitored. The drug was removed for a period of time during which his behavior was monitored and then compared to the previous behavior sample. The drug was reapplied and behavior monitored again. This design is called
   a. multiple baseline.
   b. random sample.
   c. placebo control.
   d. A-B-A-B.

6. Inmates at the penitentiary who are identified as antisocial personality disordered are studied by reviewing their academic records and records of previous encounters with law enforcement. This type of study is called
   a. longitudinal.
   b. high-risk.
   c. follow-back.
   d. follow-up.

7. Susan's identical twin sister is institutionalized with schizophrenia. Susan has been participating in a study for the two years since her sister was hospitalized. This study is designed to learn about
   a. directionality.
   b. genetic transmission.
   c. external validity.
   d. epidemiology.

8. Diane's mother was diagnosed as manic-depressive soon after Diane was born. Diane has been the subject of a study since she was three. This is an example of a
   a. baseline design.
   b. adoption study.
   c. high-risk study.
   d. follow-back study.

9. Ryan's behavior in school improved noticeably after he began therapy yet he was still a problem for his classmates and teachers. The treatment may have been
   a. clinically significant.
   b. statistically significant.
   c. normative.
   d. unethical.

10. Juan was not told about the nature of the films he would see during the experiment. The graphic depiction of automobile accident injuries was upsetting since he was still recovering from a serious accident. This situation violated the ethical requirement of
    a. confidentiality.
    b. debriefing.
    c. placebo control group.
    d. informed consent.

ANSWER KEY: KEY TERMS REVIEW

1. independent variable (141)
2. descriptive approaches (134)
3. experiment (141)
4. variable (135)
5. follow-back studies (149)
6. A-B-A-B designs (145)
7. positive correlation (140)
8. third variable (140)
9. effect size (153)
10. correlation coefficient (139)
11. prevalence (135)
12. analogue (133)
13. meta-analysis (153)
14. random sampling (136)
15. survey (135)
16. high-risk studies (151)
17. clinical significance (153)
18. case study (134–135)
19. follow-up studies (149)
20. twin studies (151)
21. representativeness (131)
22. adoption study (152)
23. correlational studies (138–139)
24. confidentiality (155)
25. internal validity (131)
26. scatterplots (139)
27. baseline (145)
28. epidemiology (135)
29. inferential statistics (143–144)
30. statistically significant (140)
31. classification variables (141)
32. dependent variable (141)
33. randomization (142)
34. counterbalancing (142–143)
35. control group (142)
36. placebos (143)
37. longitudinal design (149)
38. directionality problem (140)
39. cross-fostering (152)
40. family study (150)
41. negative correlation (140)
42. debriefing (154)
43. incidence (135)
44. matching (142)
45. normative comparisons (153)
46. discontinuity theory (132)
47. multiple baseline design (145)
48. informed consent (154)
49. external validity (131)
50. cross-sectional studies (149)
51. continuity theory (132)

ANSWER KEY: FACTUAL MULTIPLE-CHOICE QUESTIONS

1. *b. empiricism (p. 130)
   a. Tradition has little to do with modern science.
   c. This is descriptive, not experimental.
   d. This has little to do with science.

2. *b. continuity theory (p. 132)
   a. The discontinuity theory states that disorders are distinct from one another.
   c. Validity is an assessment concept that does not consider issues of normalcy.
   d. Reliability is also a statistical term related to measurement and assessment.

3. *c. incidence and prevalence (p. 135)
   a. These studies are not concerned with treatment of a disorder.
   b. These studies are concerned more so with external validity and representativeness.
   d. Control groups and placebo groups apply to experimental research.

4. *b. variables (pp. 138–139)
   a. Correlations alone do not provide evidence for cause-effect conclusions.
   c. Unknown or third variables may be responsible for both other variables in a study, making causative arguments difficult.
   d. Correlations are measures of relationship within a study, not between studies or experiments.

5. *c. independent variable (pp. 141–142)
   a. They are members of different groups in the same experiment and would have no reason to be together.
   b. The dependent variable is not a matter of exposure, but an outcome measurement taken of both groups.
   d. Only those persons in a placebo control group would be exposed to the placebo.

6. *b. multiple baseline design (pp. 145–146)
   a. Saigh used multiple factors in the study.
   c. His study dealt with a single individual.
   d. Saigh's study was conducted with one person in a controlled setting.

7. *a. family study (p. 151)
   b. Grove used many subjects in his study.
   c. Grove was more concerned with current experience than history.
   d. This study focused on specific families, not a field approach.

8. *a. case studies (pp. 134–135)
   b. Freud did his work in his office and used his clinical experiences as his laboratory.
   c. Freud's case studies involved relatively short periods of time.
   d. Freud was concerned with insight, not history.

9. *c. independent variable (p. 141)
   a. Placebos are inert.
   b. The dependent variable is the outcome or effect of the drug.
   d. The third variable is an unknown variable that may be responsible for the other variables. Third variables are not factors in experimental designs.

ANSWER KEY: CONCEPTUAL MULTIPLE-CHOICE QUESTIONS

1. *a. internally valid (p. 131)
   b. The study may not reach statistical significance.
   c. The study may not have clinical applicability.
   d. External validity has to do with generalizability of findings, not security from alternate explanations.

2. *d. representativeness (p. 131)
   a. Internal consistency is a measure of the correspondence between test items, not a sampling factor.
   b. This is not a statistical or sampling term.
   c. A study may be usable although not representative.

3. *d. analogue research (p. 133)
   a. Questionnaires were not used by Seligman with his dogs.
   b. Laboratory tasks were not used because this was analogue research with animals.
   c. EEG tracings were not used, only observations of the dogs' reactions to the electric shocks.

4. *d. case study approach (pp. 134–135)
   a. Interventions are not diagnostic.
   b. Field studies would be applicable only if there were a large sample from which to draw.
   c. This would be used at a later stage in research.

5. *a. cause and effect (p. 142)
   b. Reliability and validity apply to many types of research, not specifically the experimental method.
   c. Descriptive studies are not experimental.
   d. Epidemiological studies deal with incidence and prevalence.

6. *d. expectation of relief (p. 143)
   a. The medical model is no more compelling than any theoretical model in determining the placebo effect.
   b. The placebo is an inert substance with no pharmacological effect.
   c. The effect is caused by the belief that the subjects are receiving the active drug.

7. *c. longitudinal designs (p. 151)
   a. Multiple baseline design would be unethical if it required removing treatment from an Alzheimer's sufferer.
   b. High-risk studies deal with children at risk.
   d. Experimental designs determine the effects of treatment, not the effects of the illness itself.

8. *b. clinical significance (p. 153)
   a. Statistical significance indicates that a relationship is not due to chance, but it may not imply clinical significance.
   c. A baseline is a beginning measure and doesn't speak to clinical significance.
   d. External validity has to do with generalizability, not clinical significance.

9. *d. directionality (p. 140)
    a. There is no independent variable in this case.
    b. There was no randomization in her case.
    c. There may be other unknown factors that are more important than schizophrenia in causing homelessness.

10. *a. external validity (p. 144)
    b. The internal validity will be weakened because of the difficulty in applying the independent variable to the subjects and obtaining the proper control groups.
    c. No placebos will be used in this type of study.
    d. Randomization is not possible because all members of the group are included.

ANSWER KEY: APPLICATION MULTIPLE-CHOICE QUESTIONS

1. *b. internal validity (p. 131)
    a. The study could still be representative, by including an accurate sample of the population.
    c. The correlations could still be high.
    d. This study is not dealing with a clinical intervention.

2. *b. continuity (p. 132)
    a. The discontinuity theory assumes that the mild form is different from the more serious form of the disorder.
    c. The baseline is a beginning measure of a factor.
    d. Multiple baselines are beginning measures of several factors.

3. *d. analogue studies (p. 133)
    a. Case studies would still involve the use of humans, who should not be shocked.
    b. Longitudinal studies are repeated measures over time.
    c. Epidemiological studies are concerned with incidence and prevalence.

4. *a. random sampling (p. 136)
    b. There will be no placebos used in an experiment of this type.
    c. This experiment involves measuring a response, not description of a population.
    d. This experiment is about Jonathan's responses and not about families'.

5. *d. A-B-A-B (p. 145)
    a. This is a single baseline design.
    b. This is a single subject design and not random.
    c. No placebos were administered in this design.

6. *c. follow-back (p. 149)
    a. There were no measures taken over time.
    b. This study was conducted with adults, not children.
    d. The information gathered is historical.

7. *b. genetic transmission (pp. 151–152)
    a. This study will not provide information on directionality.
    c. External validity deals with the generalizability of a study.
    d. This study is not concerned with prevalence or incidence.

8. *c. high-risk study (pp. 151)
   a. There are no baseline measures or applications of treatment in this study.
   b. Diane is with her biological mother.
   d. This is more similar to a follow-up study.

9. *b. statistically significant (p. 154)
   a. He is still not functioning normally, so clinically significant improvement is not shown.
   c. He doesn't meet the norm of his class behavior.
   d. The treatment and method were appropriate.

10. *d. informed consent (p. 154)
    a. There was no breach of confidentiality.
    b. Debriefing has to do with post-experiment explanation of the procedures and outcome.
    c. Juan was not part of a control group in this experiment.

CHAPTER 6
Anxiety Disorders

LEARNING OBJECTIVES

1. Describe the experience of anxiety. (p. 160)

2. Distinguish between anxiety and fear. (p. 161)

3. Describe what is a normal level of anxiety. (p. 161)

4. Describe the interaction of biological predisposition (trait) and environmental effects (state) in the stimulation of fear and anxiety. (pp. 161–162)

5. Describe the connection between anxiety and the body's physical systems of arousal. (pp. 163–164)

6. Discuss the genetic and constitutional factors that influence certain anxiety disorders. (pp. 163–165)

7. Explain the biological reactivity theory of anxiety. (p. 164)

8. Discuss the effect of neurotransmitter functioning on anxiety and how neurotransmitter systems are treated to alleviate anxiety disorders. (pp. 164–165)

9. Describe the psychodynamic theory of anxiety arousal, including objective, moral, and neurotic anxiety. (pp. 164–165)

10. Discuss the cognitive-behavioral explanation of anxiety, emphasizing the processes involved in the acquisition of anxiety responses and the dysfunctional efforts to organize the world as a cause of anxiety. (pp. 166–168)

11. Explain how the anxiety response is acquired by witnessing fear, as demonstrated by analogue experiments done with monkeys. (pp. 169–170)

12. Discuss the classification of anxiety disorders. (pp. 169–170)

13. Describe generalized anxiety disorder. (pp. 170–172)

14. Describe the features of phobias and their symptoms, specific phobia, social phobia, and agoraphobia. (pp. 172–176, Table 6.4)

15. Explain the various etiological explanations for phobias: psychodynamic, biomedical, learning, cognitive, and family systems views. (pp. 175–176)

16. Discuss various treatments for phobic disorders. (pp. 176–178)

17. Describe the elements of panic disorder and panic attacks. (pp. 178–179; Table 6.5; Figure 6.5)

18. Describe the research being conducted on panic attacks by using "challenges" such as hyperventilation. (pp. 179–181)

19. Discuss the defining features of and treatment approaches for obsessive-compulsive disorder. (p. 182)

20. Describe the elements that define posttraumatic stress disorder and related treatment approaches. (pp. 186–190)

21. Discuss the new approaches to studying and treating anxiety disorders. (pp. 195–196)

CHAPTER OUTLINE

I. What's Normal? Just How Mellow Should We Be?

- Anxiety disorders: Psychological disorders associated with pervasive and persistent symptoms of anxiety and avoidance behavior that cause clinically significant distress or impairment of functioning in social and work situations.

A. Fear is a reasonable and rational reaction to a genuinely alarming situation.

B. Anxiety is a feeling of apprehension over an anticipated situation or object that typically would not produce discomfort in rational individuals. When anxiety is prolonged, intense, distressing, unwanted, and interferes with life, it becomes a disorder.

II. People and Places: The Interaction of Person and Situation in Anxiety

A. Anxiety disorders include biological vulnerabilities interacting with personal, psychological, and environmental characteristics

1. This approach is called the *diathesis-stress model.*

2. Interactional perspective: Individual dispositions and situational influences interact in a causal way in the development and maintenance of psychological disorders.

3. Traits: Characteristic attitudes, beliefs, behaviors, reactions, and ways of thinking about oneself and the world that are enduring and unchanging

4. States: Characteristics of emotion/behavior/cognition that are temporary conditions affected by the situation.

5. Traits and states interact in the development of anxiety disorders and also in one's resilience to anxiety.

III. Theories about Anxiety Disorders

A. Biological Theories

- Cause of anxiety linked to the body's physical systems of arousal.

- Autonomic nervous system activates the body.

1. Genetic and constitutional factors

   a. Selective association, the tendency to learn fears as a result of natural selection.

   b. Studies show a significant, though modest, inheritance for some anxiety disorders.

   c. Evidence suggests a moderate degree of family transmission of anxiety disorders (could be influenced by learning).

2. Biological reactivity: Highly reactive autonomic nervous system does not fully explain the incidence of panic attacks.

3. Endocrinological and neurotransmitter factors

   a. Little clear evidence of a biological marker of anxiety disorders.

   b. Benzodiazepine and GABA have been linked to anxiety disorders.

   c. Obsessive-compulsive disorder is related to serotonin.

4. Brain anatomy and functioning: Neuroimaging techniques have been used to trace brain functioning in anxiety disorders.

B. Medical Therapies

- Barbiturates, sedatives, and benzodiazepines taken, but have unwanted side effects.

1. Benzodiazepines

   a. Inhibit the central nervous system.

   b. Called *anxiolytics* because they reduce anxiety.

   c. Most commonly used for specific anxiety-producing situations, insomnia, generalized anxiety disorder, and panic disorder.

   d. The drug binds to a neuroreceptor site and increases the activity of the neurotransmitter GABA, which has an inhibitory effect in the brain.

   e. Side effects include slowing of physical movement, drowsiness, toxicity, tolerance (dosages need to be increased to experience the same effects), and dependence (physical withdrawal symptoms and prolonged use to avoid such symptoms).

   f. Rebound effect: Anxiety symptoms appear worse when medication is stopped.

2. Other medications for anxiety disorders: Some antidepressants also reduce anxiety, obsessive-compulsive disorder, and panic attack.

C. Cognitive and Behavioral Theories

1. Cognitive causes

a. Assume that anxiety results from dysfunctional efforts to make sense of the world.

b. Strong relationship between irrational beliefs and anxiety.

c. Expectation of future negative events (anxious schema).

2. Behavioral causes: People learn to behave in an anxious manner through: classical conditioning, avoidance response, escape response, and modeling.

D. Family Matters: Witnessing Someone Else's Fear

1. Fear can be acquired through observational experiences.

2. Mineka's study suggests that anxiety is not caused simply by genetics.

E. Psychodynamic Theories of Anxiety

1. Freud's definitions:

a. Objective anxiety: The source of the unpleasant emotions is in the outside world (fear).

b. Moral anxiety: Superego is the source of individual's sense of threat of and worry about being punished for doing or thinking something that violates an accepted standard of behavior.

c. Neurotic anxiety: The threat that engenders the unpleasant emotional state is a sense of being overwhelmed by an uncontrollable urge to engage in some thought or behavior that might prove harmful or socially unacceptable.

2. Modern psychodynamic theory focuses on interpersonal influences, such as the mother-child relationship.

3. Psychodynamic treatment generally found to be effective.

F. Humanistic and Existential Theories and Therapies

1. Used with milder anxiety-related problems.

2. Existential approaches may include paradoxical intervention.

IV. Classifying and Treating Anxiety Disorders

• Anxiety disorders are among the most prevalent of all mental disorders.

1. Affect approximately 15 percent of the population.

2. Comorbidity is common.

A. Generalized Anxiety Disorder (GAD)

• Anxious apprehension: Chronic, persistent anxiety characteristic of GAD.

• Generalized anxiety disorder (GAD): An anxiety disorder marked by excessive anxiety and worry that do not appear to be linked to specific situations or external stressors.

• Sometimes called *free-floating anxiety.*

• Involves major emotional, physical, and cognitive symptoms.

- Diagnosis criteria include excessive, unrealistic anxiety for a minimum of six months; difficult to control; associated with restlessness, fatigue, difficulty concentrating, irritability, muscle tension, sleep disturbance.

1. Who is affected with GAD?

   a. Occurs twice as frequently among women as men.

   b. Higher frequency among black versus nonblack groups.

2. Causes of GAD

   a. Worry may be due to fears of social evaluation and loss of control.

   b. Relaxation-induced anxiety: Phenomenon among GAD patients in which the process of inducing relaxation paradoxically produces greater anxiety and tension.

3. Treating GAD

   a. Relaxation and cognitive-behavioral therapies superior to nondirective therapy.

   b. Cognitive-behavioral therapy superior to medication alone.

B. Phobias

- Phobias are intense, recurrent, and irrational fears that are disproportionate to the actual situation.

- Claustrophobia is the fear of closed places.

- Clients recognize their fear is excessive and actively avoid the fear-producing stimulus.

1. Who is affected with phobias?

   a. Most common of anxiety disorders; 14.2 percent lifetime prevalence.

   b. Women outnumber men 2 to 1; three times higher prevalence for African-Americans and Hispanics compared with whites.

   c. Typically begin in adolescence or early adulthood.

2. Specific (simple) phobia: A kind of phobia characterized by pathological (excessive and unrealistic) fears of specific animals, objects, or situations.

3. Social phobia

   a. Involves a persistent fear of being in a social situation in which one is exposed to scrutiny by others and doing something embarrassing.

   b. Shyness is much less acute than social phobia.

4. Agoraphobia

   a. Agoraphobia is a marked fear of being alone or in public places from which escape would be difficult.

   b. Ratio of female to male is 4 to 1.

    c.   Comorbidity is frequently observed.

  5.   Causes of phobias

      a.   Psychodynamic: phobia is a displacement of internal anxiety.

      b.   Some evidence of a family transmission pattern, but unclear whether this is genetic or learned.

      c.   More recent explanations relate to faulty learning and cognitive influences. Cognitive model: *anticipation of panic,* anxiety sensitivity (belief that anxiety experiences have negative implications), *uncontrollability.*

      d.   Family systems emphasize the symptom as a source of control in a dysfunctional marriage or family.

  6.   Treating phobias

      a.   Systematic desensitization has been found effective in treating phobic disorders. The procedure may include elements of exposure and flooding.

      b.   The mechanism underlying desensitization's effectiveness is unclear. Habituation, counterconditioning, and cognitive explanations (imaginal exposure, expectancy for positive gains, increase in self-efficacy) have been proposed.

      c.   Agoraphobia is also effectively treated with in vivo desensitization (exposure to the real environment).

C.   Panic Disorder

    •   An anxiety disorder characterized by a vulnerability to and the experience of frequent panic attacks.

    •   Panic attacks: Discrete periods of intense fear or discomfort, occurring unpredictably and without apparent provocation and not due to evaluation apprehension or scrutiny by others.

    •   Criteria for diagnosis of panic disorder include recurrent unexpected panic attacks followed by concern about the attacks.

    •   Panic attacks usually last a few minutes; often appear with agoraphobia.

  1.   Who is affected with panic disorder? Women to men, 2 to 1.

  2.   Focus on Research: Are Panic Attacks Biological?

      a.   Lactate infusion produces discomfort in control group and a panic attack in panic patients.

      b.   Biological model of panic disorder may be incorrect; cognitive interpretation seems to be the key.

      c.   Physiological symptoms precede fear.

      d.   Dysfunctional heart does not seem to be a precursor to panic attack.

  3.   Treating panic disorder: Relaxation, exposure, and modification of cognitive misinterpretations effective.

D. Obsessive-Compulsive Disorders (OCDs)

- True compulsions are not ends in themselves, but avoidance behaviors.

1. Features of OCD

    a. Obsessions: Persistent thoughts, ideas, or images unwanted and not created by the person.

    b. Compulsions: Ritualistic and repetitive behavior patterns, not ends in themselves, but undertaken to prevent or postpone other actions.

    c. Obsessives are described as worriers and doubters.

    d. Most common obsessional thoughts are about contamination.

    e. Most common compulsions are nonfunctional and ritualistic.

2. Who is affected with OCD?

    a. Lifetime prevalence 2 percent to 3 percent (4 million people)

    b. Often occurs with depression.

    c. Equal number of males and females.

3. Causes of OCD: OCD is not considered a genetic disorder. Learning and cognitive causes viewed as more plausible explanations.

4. Treating OCD

    a. Biological techniques include psychosurgery (cingulotomy) and medication (clomipramine, an antidepressant affecting serotonin).

    b. Behavioral explanations focus on learned avoidance and escape behaviors undertaken to reduce anxiety; therapy techniques include exposure and response prevention (blocking avoidant response). Behavioral therapies effective in reducing unwanted obsessions and compulsions and also effect changes in brain activity.

    c. Cognitive-behavioral techniques are aimed at helping clients to change dysfunctional beliefs and to reappraise situations more realistically.

    d. Psychodynamic perspective reflects helping the client to deal with unresolved unconscious conflicts.

E. Posttraumatic Stress Disorder (PTSD)

- A cluster of psychological symptoms that can follow a psychologically distressing event.

- Stressor outside the range of normal, common stressors.

- Typical symptoms follow intense fear and horror: reexperiencing, avoidance of reminders, and increased arousal. These persist for at least a month.

- Acute stress disorder: PTSD reactions that persist from two days to a month.

1. Who is affected with PTSD?

    a. Estimated lifetime prevalence 7.8 percent.

b. Military combat veterans, rape and battery victims, victims of natural and man-made disasters.

2. Understanding PTSD

a. Traumatic exposure, not pretrauma adjustment, is the primary factor contributing to the etiology of PTSD.

b. Loss in social support: Network of individuals with whom a subject has social or personal contact, especially the support related to emotional well-being.

c. Physiological response in PTSD resembles reaction to unavoidable shock.

d. Exaggerated neurotransmitter activity, conditioned reactions to trauma stimuli, perceptions of uncontrol and unpredictability, and inability to integrate the trauma characterize the onset of PTSD.

3. Treating PTSD: Cognitive-behavioral and exposure treatments seem to be helpful to PTSD sufferers, whether veterans or rape and battery victims.

V. What Lies Ahead?

A. Anxiety disorders are the largest domain in psychopathology.

B. Movement toward consolidation of biological, behavioral, and cognitive influences.

C. Treatments will become more sophisticated in addressing comorbid conditions.

KEY TERMS REVIEW

1. A marked fear of being alone or of being in public places where escape is difficult or help not readily available is called _____.

2. A method for treating anxiety disorders in which the client is exposed through images to the feared situation is called _____.

3. Distinguishing real from imagined events is called _____.

4. The craving for continued doses of a substance; tolerance and withdrawal symptoms is called _____.

5. A kind of phobia characterized by pathological fears of specific animals, objects, or situations is called _____.

6. A reasonable and rational reaction to a genuinely alarming situation is _____.

7. An anxiety disorder characterized by a vulnerability to and the experience of frequent panic attacks is _____.

8. The behaviors observed when anxiety symptoms appear to be worse after a medication is stopped is called the _____.

9. The intense and irrational fear of closed spaces is called _____.

10. Characteristics of emotion/behavior/cognition that are temporary conditions are _____.

11. A behavioral technique in which a client with OCD is placed in the real feared situation and the compulsive behavior is blocked is called _____.

12. Psychological disorders associated with pervasive and persistent anxiety that cause clinically significant distress are referred to as _____.

13. Persistent thoughts, ideas, or images that a person does not want, does not intentionally produce, and perceives as invading his or her thinking are called _____.

14. Surgical interruption of the cingulate bundles of the brain is called a(n) _____.

15. A kind of phobia characterized by a persistent fear of being in a social situation in which one is exposed to scrutiny by others and a related fear of acting in a way that will be humiliating or embarrassing is called _____.

16. The network of individuals with whom a subject has social or personal contact, especially the support related to emotional well-being, and which may be lost in PTSD, is called _____.

17. A diffuse and vague feeling of apprehension is _____.

18. PTSD-like reactions that persist for at least two days but less than four weeks are called _____.

19. GAD treatment in which the client practices coping while exposed to the real environment is called _____.

20. Intense, recurrent, and irrational fears that are disproportionate to the actual situation are called _____.

21. The need for increased dosages of psychotropic medications to experience the same effects is called _____.

22. Psychodynamic theory distinguishes three types of anxiety. They are _____, _____, _____.

23. A cluster of psychological symptoms that follow a psychologically distressing event is called _____.

24. Characteristic attitudes, beliefs, behaviors, reactions, and ways of thinking about oneself and the world that are enduring and unchanging are _____.

25. An anxiety disorder marked by unrealistic or excessive anxiety and worry that does not appear to be linked to specific situations or external stressors is called _____.

26. A behavioral therapy based on classical conditioning, in which fear responses are paired with relaxation, is called _____.

27. Chronic, persistent anxiety, characteristic of generalized anxiety disorder, is called _____.

28. Ritualistic and repetitive behavior patterns that are not ends in themselves but avoidance of other actions are called _____.

29. The belief that anxiety experiences have negative implications is called _____.

30. A view of anxiety, holding that individual dispositions and situational influences work together in a causal way in the development and maintenance of psychological disorders, is called _____.

31. That humans may be prepared to learn certain fears is referred to as _____.

32. An approach in treating phobias in which patients confront the once-feared objects or situations is called _____.

33. A treatment strategy in which the client with an anxiety disorder is instructed and encouraged to do or wish for exactly what is feared is called _____.

34. The phenomenon among patients with generalized anxiety disorder in which the process of inducing relaxation instead produces anxiety and tension is called _____.

35. A therapeutic philosophy, rather than a set of approaches, strategies, or techniques, for the treatment of psychological disorders is _____.

36. Discrete periods of intense fear, occurring unpredictably and without apparent provocation, are called _____.

37. Exposure to many cues or features of the fearful or phobic situation in which the client experiences maximum anxiety is called _____.

FACTUAL MULTIPLE-CHOICE QUESTIONS

1. The three types of anxiety Freud proposed are
   a. objective, subjective, moral.
   b. moral, spiritual, subjective.
   c. neurotic, objective, normal.
   d. objective, moral, neurotic.

2. According to Beck and Emery, the themes of danger or harm are reflected in
   a. anxious schema.
   b. panic disorder.
   c. phobia.
   d. panic attack.

3. *Free-floating anxiety* is another term for
   a. fear of flying.
   b. obsessive-compulsive disorder.
   c. generalized anxiety disorder.
   d. posttraumatic stress disorder.

4. Many sufferers of agoraphobia also suffer anxiety symptoms of
   a. repression.
   b. obsessive-compulsive disorder.
   c. panic attacks.
   d. generalized anxiety disorder.

5. Persistent thoughts, ideas, or images that the person does not want are typical of
   a. obsessions.
   b. compulsions.
   c. phobias.
   d. panic disorder.

6. A type of therapy that focuses on alleviating excessive anticipatory anxiety by encouraging the client to wish for what is feared is called
   a. paradoxical intervention.
   b. Gestalt therapy.
   c. psychoanalysis.
   d. cognitive-behavioral therapy.

7. An effect of the benzodiazepines that make their use problematic is
   a. arousal.
   b. hypertension.
   c. dependence.
   d. hyperventilation.

8. Cognitive-behavioral methods strive to correct faulty thinking and beliefs. This is particularly helpful in treating
   a. posttraumatic stress disorder.
   b. obsessive-compulsive disorder.
   c. generalized anxiety disorder.
   d. social phobia.

9. Theodore had to take a twelve-hour flight to Asia. He was terrified of the prospect, but had no choice. His psychiatrist is most likely to prescribe
   a. benzodiazepines.
   b. a placebo.
   c. barbiturates.
   d. neuroleptics.

10. When Allen stopped his medication for anxiety the symptoms returned with even greater intensity. This effect is called
    a. rebound.
    b. placebo.
    c. withdrawal.
    d. tolerance.

CONCEPTUAL MULTIPLE-CHOICE QUESTIONS

1. Fear is distinguishable from anxiety because fear relates to a
   a. vague feeling of apprehension.
   b. specific discernible object.
   c. different set of physical symptoms.
   d. genetic predisposition.

2. Marjorie raises her hand in class and responds to a question incorrectly and is embarrassed. Her reluctance to raise her hand again supports the theory called
   a. avoidance response.
   b. psychoanalytic.
   c. modeling.
   d. existential/humanistic.

3. Erin was fearful of small, furry animals. Her therapist decided to have her go to a petting zoo and sit down among a large number of rabbits. This approach to therapy is known as
   a. systematic desensitization.
   b. flooding.
   c. imaginal exposure.
   d. self-efficacy training.

4. Which of the following best illustrates the notion of "traits"?
   a. Carmen's mood changes from happy to sad whenever she sees her former boyfriend.
   b. Neil tells his sister that she has been suspicious of other people for most of her life.
   c. Patrick becomes extremely frightened when he goes on a fast amusement park ride.
   d. Eleanor feels her body change from relaxed to tense with anger because of the rude comment her sister made.

5. Jane says that anxiety disorders are the most widely prevalent mental disorder in the United States. She notes that research has found a moderate degree of family transmission of anxiety disorders, and this suggests that anxiety disorders are probably genetically caused. She argues that in order to treat the disorder, short-term anxiolytic drugs would be useful. What part of the statement would you disagree with?
   a. Anxiety disorders are not the most widespread mental disorder.
   b. Studies do show a family transmission for anxiety disorders, but this does not prove that the disorder is genetic.
   c. There is not a moderate degree of family transmission of anxiety disorders.
   d. Research has shown anxiolytic drugs to be ineffective unless they are taken long term.

6. What concept relates to both the psychodynamic and the behavioral explanations for the causes of obsessive-compulsive disorder (OCD)?
   a. avoidant behavior
   b. selective association
   c. free-floating anxiety
   d. anxious schema

7. Katherine is phobic about riding in elevators. Dr. Taylor told Katherine to intentionally increase her anxiety when she approaches an elevator. Dr. Taylor's recommendation is based on the principle of
   a. rebound effects.
   b. flooding.
   c. paradoxical intervention.
   d. counterconditioning.

8. A study by Power and associates compared the effectiveness of psychological and pharmacological treatments for general anxiety disorder. What conclusions can be drawn from their study?
   a. Cognitive-behavioral therapy was found to be ineffective at reducing anxiety symptoms.
   b. Medication treatment was found to be more effective than any of the psychological therapies.
   c. There were no decreases in anxiety symptoms when a placebo was administered.
   d. Clients reduced their anxiety substantially through cognitive-behavioral therapy or with a combination of cognitive-behavioral therapy and medication.

9. Dr. Kraemer's client, Jerry, is diagnosed with OCD. For the last three years, Jerry has continuously picked at a rather large scab on his forehead, preventing the scab from healing properly. The facial blemish has caused Jerry great anxiety and has interfered with his ability to maintain a job or be seen in public. What question should Dr. Kraemer consider as he begins treatment of Jerry?
   a. What is Jerry avoiding by engaging in scab picking?
   b. How many of Jerry's family members have also inherited OCD?
   c. Does Jerry's obsession result from a traumatic experience in the past?
   d. Would a medication that affects dopamine neurotransmitters be useful to treat this condition?

10. Dr. James works with war veterans diagnosed with PTSD. He believes that it is not a traumatic event that causes PTSD but rather the individual's overall poor coping skills before he or she joined the military. Dr. James argues that clients with PTSD are likely to have had poor psychological adjustment prior to the traumatic event. How would you respond to Dr. James's assertion?
   a. Agree with Dr. James because poor premilitary psychological adjustment is the single best explanation for the development of PTSD.
   b. Disagree with Dr. James because PTSD is generally caused by a biochemical imbalance in the brain.
   c. Disagree with Dr. James because the degree of combat exposure and adjustment to military life are stronger predictors of PTSD than is the veteran's premilitary adjustment.
   d. Agree with Dr. James because PTSD suggests that the person is psychologically weak, and cannot cope with normal stressors.

APPLICATION MULTIPLE-CHOICE QUESTIONS

1. Caroline was afraid of driving in crowded freeway conditions, but John was fearful of driving under any conditions. What would be your diagnosis of Caroline's condition?
   a. specific phobia
   b. generalized anxiety disorder
   c. normal
   d. agoraphobia

2. Bill spent hours rehearsing what he would do each day, and each night he reexamined the day's failures. His symptoms are characteristic of
   a. social phobia.
   b. obsessions.
   c. generalized anxiety disorder.
   d. specific phobia.

3. Claire refused to accept invitations to the beach because she was reluctant to be seen in a bathing suit. This fear became generalized to anything related to the beach and became so intense that an advertisement for a seaside hotel caused her to tremble and sweat. This condition is
   a. social phobia.
   b. agoraphobia.
   c. specific phobia.
   d. panic disorder.

4. As Mildred contemplated the trip to the doctor's office she imagined sitting in the car in traffic, the car stalling, and being unable to restart it. She began to feel nauseous and faint. Her condition could be described as
   a. agoraphobia.
   b. panic attack.
   c. GAD.
   d. specific phobia.

5. Howard was convinced that everything he touched was contaminated in some way. Because of this he refused to leave his room, prepared all his meals himself, and ate alone. His condition is an illustration of
   a. social phobia.
   b. specific phobia.
   c. agoraphobia.
   d. obsessive-compulsive disorder.

6. Frank found it necessary to clear his desk every day. If he discovered that the cleaning person had disturbed something he became very upset. He would often return to the office at night to be sure that everything was the way he had left it. Frank's behavior is
   a. obsessive.
   b. compulsive.
   c. GAD.
   d. specific phobia

7. Elena survived the airplane crash, but for months was plagued with terrifying nightmares of the incident. A diagnosis of her condition would be
   a. panic attack.
   b. panic disorder.
   c. posttraumatic stress disorder.
   d. generalized anxiety disorder.

8. Dr. Fischer was helping Jeremy recover from the psychological effects of his Vietnam combat experiences. He told Jeremy to
   a. forget about the war.
   b. increase his intake of Vitamin B.
   c. recall all the details of the trauma he could remember.
   d. spend more time alone.

9. As the test was distributed to the class, Marisela began to sweat. As she did she told herself not only to sweat, but to begin sweating buckets, to let her sweat fill the aisles, to sweat more than anyone had ever seen. This approach to controlling anxiety is called
   a. flooding.
   b. systematic desensitization.
   c. paradoxical intervention.
   d. Gestalt.

10. Dr. Michener used the cognitive-behavioral techniques of self-monitoring, discussion, and rehearsal of new thinking styles to treat what type disorder?
    a. generalized anxiety disorder
    b. panic attack
    c. posttraumatic stress disorder
    d. obsessive-compulsive disorder

ANSWER KEY: KEY TERMS REVIEW

1. agoraphobia (174)
2. imaginal exposure (177)
3. reality monitoring (186)
4. dependence (166)
5. specific phobia (173)
6. fear (161)
7. panic disorder (178)
8. rebound effects (166)
9. claustrophobia (172)
10. states (162)
11. response prevention (185)
12. anxiety disorders (160)
13. obsessions (180)
14. cingulotomy (185)
15. social phobia (174)
16. social support (188)
17. anxiety (161)
18. acute stress disorder (187)
19. in vivo exposure (178)
20. phobias (172)
21. tolerance (166)
22. objective, moral, and neurotic anxiety (168)
23. posttraumatic stress disorder (186)
24. traits (162)
25. generalized anxiety disorder (170)
26. systematic desensitization (176)
27. anxious apprehension (170)
28. compulsions (182)
29. anxiety sensitivity (176)
30. interactional perspective (162)
31. selective association (163)
32. exposure (177)
33. paradoxical intervention (169)
34. relaxation-induced anxiety (171)
35. existential therapy (169)
36. panic attacks (178)
37. flooding (177)

ANSWER KEY: FACTUAL MULTIPLE-CHOICE QUESTIONS

1. *d. objective, moral, neurotic (p. 168)
   a. Subjectivity is not associated with anxiety types.
   b. Spirituality does not relate to anxiety typing.
   c. Anxiety may be objective but it is not focused.

2. *a. anxious schema (p. 166)
   b. Panic disorder is a reaction to panic situations.
   c. Phobias are specific fear responses.
   d. Panic attack is a response to stressors, not a cognitive schema.

3. *c. generalized anxiety disorder (p. 170)
   a. Fear of flying is a specific phobic reaction.
   b. OCD is more specifically focused.
   d. Posttraumatic stress disorder is a reaction to an unusual stressor.

4. *c. panic attacks (p. 175)
   a. Repression is a psychodynamic defense mechanism not associated with agoraphobia.
   b. OCD is not usually comorbid with agoraphobia.
   d. GAD is less specific than agoraphobia.

5. *a. obsessions (p. 182)
   b. Compulsions are ritualistic acts, not thoughts.
   c. Phobias are reactions to specific objects or activities.
   d. Panic disorder is less related to cognitions.

6. *a. paradoxical intervention (p. 169)
   b. Gestalt therapy is advised for overly restrained clients.
   c. Psychoanalysis attempts to resolve hidden conflicts that cause anxiety.
   d. Cognitive-behavioral therapy addresses distorted thought processes.

7. *c. dependence (p. 165)
   a. The benzodiazepines reduce arousal.
   b. They do not affect hypertension.
   d. They reduce the likelihood of hyperventilation.

8. *b. obsessive-compulsive disorder (p. 186)
   a. Posttraumatic stress disorder is not related to faulty thinking, but to a genuinely terrifying experience.
   c. GAD is not associated with faulty thinking.
   d. Behavioral approaches seem to work best with social phobia.

9. *a. benzodiazepines (p. 165)
   b. He would need an active medication, not a placebo.
   c. Barbiturates are powerful, addictive drugs and unnecessary for a specific anxiety.
   d. Neuroleptics are used primarily for the positive symptoms of schizophrenia.

10. *a. rebound (p. 166)
    b. Rebound is a reaction to an active drug, not a placebo.
    c. Withdrawal has to do with the physiological response to the absence of the drug, not the return of psychological symptoms.
    d. Tolerance is the need for more of the drug to maintain the desired effect.

ANSWER KEY: CONCEPTUAL MULTIPLE-CHOICE QUESTIONS

1. *b. specific discernible object (p. 161)
   a. Anxiety is vaguely directed.
   c. The symptoms may be the same.
   d. There is no difference in genetic predisposition between the two.

2. *a. avoidance response (p. 167)
   b. Her behavior suggests a response learned in school, not an internal conflict from childhood.
   c. Marjorie was embarrassed by her own action, not by watching others be embarrassed.
   d. The humanist paradigm doesn't respond well to the example.

3. *b. flooding (p. 177)
   a. This approach does not follow Wolpe's systematic desensitization procedure.
   c. This technique is in vivo, the real world, and is not imaginary.
   d. The patient was exposed directly to the fear producing stimulus; no training was involved.

4. *b. Neil tells his sister that she has been suspicious of other people for most of her life. (p. 162)
   a. Carmen's mood is more affected by a situational influence on behavior.
   c. Fear of a fast amusement park ride might be expected from many people, and does not necessarily reflect their stable traits.
   d. There is no evidence that Eleanor's tension and anger is stable over different situations.

5. *b. Studies do show a family transmission for anxiety disorders, but this does not prove that the disorder is genetic. (p. 164)
   a. About 15 percent of the U.S. population is affected with anxiety disorders.
   c. A moderate degree of family transmission of anxiety disorders has been found, but this may be due to learning.
   d. Anxiolytic drugs are not generally recommended long term because of side effects, including dependence and rebound effects.

6. *a. avoidant behavior. (pp. 167, 169)
   b. Selective association refers to phobic disorders and suggests that humans may be prepared to learn certain fears rather than others.
   c. Free-floating anxiety is another term for generalized anxiety disorder.
   d. Cognitive psychologists suggest that people with anxiety disorders may develop anxious schemas.

7. *c. paradoxical intervention. (p. 177)
   a. Rebound is the tendency for anxiety symptoms to reappear and with greater intensity following discontinuation of an anxiolytic medication.
   b. Therapists may elicit flooding by exposing the client to many cues or features of the fearful situation.
   d. Counterconditioning is based on systematic desensitization procedures and is a different procedure than paradoxical intervention.

8. *d. Clients reduced their anxiety substantially through cognitive-behavioral therapy or with a combination of cognitive-behavioral therapy and medication. (p. 172)
   a. Cognitive-behavioral therapy did reduce anxiety symptoms.
   b. Medication alone was no more effective than a placebo.
   c. Subjects in the placebo control group also showed a decrease in anxiety symptoms, illustrating how important it is to include placebo conditions in an experiment.

9. *a. What is Jerry avoiding by engaging in scab picking? (p. 182)
   b. OCD is not currently considered a genetic disorder.
   c. PTSD may result from a traumatic experience in the past.
   d. Medications which have been found moderately effective in treating OCD, such as clomipramine, affect the neurotransmitter serotonin.

10. *c. Disagree with Dr. James because the degree of combat exposure and adjustment to military life are stronger predictors of PTSD than is the veteran's premilitary adjustment. (p. 188)
    a. Poor premilitary psychological adjustment is an inadequate explanation for the development of PTSD.
    b. PTSD is a reaction to an extremely stressful event, not a biochemical imbalance in the brain.
    d. The stressor is outside the range of normal, common stressors.

ANSWER KEY: APPLICATION MULTIPLE-CHOICE QUESTIONS

1. *c. normal (p. 161)
   a. Specific phobia might better describe John.
   b. The stressor is too specific for GAD.
   d. An agoraphobic would probably not drive under any conditions.

2. *c. generalized anxiety disorder (p. 170)
   a. The problem is unrelated to specific fears of social interaction.
   b. Bill's thoughts do not have the unwanted and intrusive character of obsessions.
   d. There is no specific focus to his anxiety.

3. *c. specific phobia (p. 173)
   a. In the example the fear is specific to the beach, not to the social interactions.
   b. The fear is not generalized to all public situations.
   d. Panic disorders usually have unknown causes or many causes, not just one.

4. *a. agoraphobia (p. 174)
   b. Panic attacks are unexpected.
   c. Generalized anxiety disorder does not take specific form.
   d. Specific phobias are not mingled with other fears. Marjorie is fearful of leaving her home as well as driving the car.

5. *d. obsessive-compulsive disorder (p. 183)
   a. Social phobia is fear of encounters with people or social situations, not contamination.
   b. Specific phobia refers to particular objects or situations.
   c. Agoraphobia is fear of being in public places or being alone.

6. *b. compulsive (p. 184)
   a. Obsessions are intrusive thoughts that the person does not want.
   c. Generalized anxiety disorder has no specific focus.
   d. This is not a fear of something, as a specific phobia would be, but a ritualistic behavior problem.

7. *c. posttraumatic stress disorder (p. 187)
   a. Panic attacks are usually not related to past events.
   b. Panic disorders are not necessarily related to a traumatic event.
   d. GAD is unfocused and vague with regard to the source of anxiety.

8. *c. recall all the details of the trauma he could remember (p. 189)
   a. Recalling, not forgetting, is part of the healing process for PTSD victims.
   b. Vitamin B consumption is unrelated to PTSD.
   d. Loss of social support is particularly painful to PTSD sufferers.

9. *c. paradoxical intervention (p. 169)
   a. Flooding is large-scale exposure to the fear-producing stimulus and is not the same technique as paradoxical intervention.
   b. Systematic desensitization pairs imaginal stressors to relaxation techniques.
   d. Gestalt works best with people who are moderately disturbed and tightly constrained.

10. *d. Obsessive-compulsive disorder (p. 186)
    a. GAD responds to a variety of therapeutic techniques.
    b. Panic attacks are not usually cognitive in nature.
    c. No extraordinary stressor was involved in this instance.

CHAPTER 7

Somatoform and Dissociative Disorders

LEARNING OBJECTIVES

1. Characterize somatoform disorders. (p. 194)

2. Describe the features of somatization disorder. (pp. 194–195)

3. Explain the difficulty involved in treating a client with somatization disorder. (pp. 196–197)

4. Describe the characteristics of hypochondriasis. (pp. 197–198)

5. Compare the subtle differences between somatization, hypochondriasis, factitious disorders, and malingering. (p. 198)

6. Explain the difficulties involved in treating these clients. (pp. 198–200)

7. Describe effective treatments for hypochondriasis. (pp. 199–200)

8. Define the characteristics of conversion disorder. (pp. 200–202)

9. Describe why conversion disorders are difficult to treat. (pp. 202–203)

10. List the qualities that typify a dissociative disorder. (p. 203)

11. Distinguish between forgetfulness and amnesia. (pp. 203–204)

12. Describe the different types of amnesia. (pp. 203–204)

13. Explain the theories of memory, forgetting, and repression and the controversy surrounding recovered memories. (pp. 204–206)

14. Describe the characteristics of dissociative (psychogenic) fugue and its treatment. (pp. 206–207)

15. Describe the characteristics of dissociative identity disorder (multiple personality disorder). (pp. 208–209)

16. Discuss the problems involved in determining whether or not there is a real increase in the number of DID cases, including the issue of false positives. (pp. 209–210)

17. Describe the research into the causes of DID. (pp. 211–212)

18. Describe the treatment of DID. (p. 212)

19. Discuss the new approaches being taken to understand these disorders with emphasis on new diagnostic and assessment techniques. (p. 210)

CHAPTER OUTLINE

I. Somatoform Disorders

   • Somatoform disorders involve physical symptoms that have no organic base.

   • Underlying emotional distress, psychological difficulties, and conflicts are thought to be tied to these disorders.

   A. Somatization Disorder

   • Is a disorder in which a person has a long-standing history of physical complaints that result in treatment for impaired social and occupational functioning.

   • Pattern of complaints include pain, gastrointestinal functions, sexual or reproductive issues, or the senses.

   • High comorbidity with anxiety, depression, and personality disorders.

   • Psychological conflict communicated in the form of somatic symptoms.

   1. Who is affected with somatization disorder?

      a. Most sufferers are female.

      b. Occurs across ethnic and social groups, but more prevalent in nonwhite, less educated, and poor.

   2. Course of somatoform disorder

      a. Long-standing history of complaints begins before age of thirty.

      b. Chronic condition does not dissipate over time.

   3. Cause of somatization disorder: Disorder runs in families, but unclear whether genetics or environment is involved.

   4. Treating somatization disorder

      a. Research is scant and optimal treatment not yet determined.

      b. Response prevention is one therapeutic technique in which the client is deflected from making the dysfunctional avoidance response.

   B. Hypochondriasis

   • Hypochondriasis is a preoccupation with, fear of, or belief that one has a serious medical condition.

      a. Clients continue to believe their self-diagnosis even in the face of medical diagnosis that shows no pathology.

   b.   May be disappointed when a physician finds nothing medically wrong.

   c.   Complaints are not purposely faked to gain exemption from responsibilities.

   d.   Undiagnosed physical illness is always a possibility.

   e.   Factitious disorders involve the feigning of symptoms in order to be considered sick. (Somatization disorder and hypochrondriasis are considered unintentional.)

   f.   Malingering is faking symptoms in order to avoid work or legal responsibility.

1.   Who is affected with hypochondriasis?

   a.   Hypochondriasis is one of the most common forms of somatoform disorder (3 to 13 percent).

   b.   Equally prevalent among men and women.

2.   Course of hypochrondriasis

   a.   Chronic condition.

   b.   Emerges between ages twenty and thirty.

3.   Cause of hypochondriasis

   a.   Learning theory: reinforcement for being ill, adopting the sick role, and parental modeling.

   b.   Psychodynamic: repressed conflicts.

   c.   Cognitive: misperception and misinterpretation of bodily functions.

   d.   *Somatosensory amplification* refers to fears and false beliefs about disease which may contribute to the disorder.

4.   Treating hypochondriasis: Exposure to the feared stimuli and response prevention have proven effective in reducing patients' reported distress.

5.   Comorbidity of hypochrondriasis: Common comorbidity with anxiety and depression

C.   Conversion Disorder

   •   Involves a loss or alteration of physical functioning that is an expression of a psychological problem.

   •   Symptoms not produced intentionally.

   •   Can simulate almost any physical disease.

   •   Glove anesthesia is a condition where the patient has no feeling in the hand.

   •   Aphonia is a conversion disorder in which the patient, though physically capable, is unable to speak above a whisper.

   •   *La belle indifference* refers to a nonchalant attitude toward one's physical symptoms.

1. Who is affected with conversion disorder? Diagnosed twice as often in women.

2. Course of conversion disorder

    a. First appears in adolescence or early adulthood.

    b. Seen in military medical wards.

3. Cause of conversion disorder: Psychodynamic, learning, family, and cognitive explanations are all suggested.

4. Treating conversion disorder: Studies of treatment are rare.

II. Dissociative Disorders

*   Dissociative disorders are severe disruptions or alterations in identity, memory, or consciousness.

*   Memory loss is not physically caused but psychologically caused.

A. Dissociative Amnesia and Fugue

1. Dissociative amnesia

    a. Not the same as forgetfulness.

    b. Selective, psychologically motivated forgetting.

    c. Selective dissociative amnesia: Forgetting some, but not all of what happened in a certain period of time.

    d. Generalized dissociative amnesia: Forgetting one's entire life history.

2. What's Normal?: Memory, forgetting, and repression

*   Four theories of memory loss

    a. Decay theory: Result of disuse and the passage of time.

    b. Interference theory: Memory has a limited capacity, and when its capacity is reached, it is susceptible to confusion and forgetting.

    c. Failure in retrieving information: The information is there, but a person cannot retrieve it.

    d. Motivated forgetting: Repression is the unconscious but purposeful exclusion of painful thoughts or unacceptable desires or impulses from consciousness.

    e. Unreliable formerly "repressed memories" of childhood physical and sexual abuse may be due to increased popularization of writings on the subject and to therapists' use of leading questions.

3. Dissociative fugue

    a. Sudden unexpected travel away from home or work with an inability to recall the past and confusion about personal identity.

    b. Psychological processes of dissociative amnesia and fugue are the same.

4. Who is affected with dissociative amnesia and fugue?

      a.   Both are rare.

      b.   Can appear any time, though less among the elderly.

5. Course of dissociative amnesia and fugue

      a.   Usually short-lived, lasting hours or days.

      b.   Recovery is rapid.

      c.   Recurrences are rare.

6. Cause of dissociative amnesia and fugue: Episodes often follow severe psychological stress for which there is no apparent solution.

7. Treating dissociative amnesia and fugue: Treatment usually begins after the episode and includes stress management techniques.

B. Dissociative Identity Disorder (formerly called *multiple personality disorder*)

1. Dissociative identity disorder (DID) is the alteration in one's sense of identity, memory, or consciousness.

      a.   DID is not related to personality disorders.

      b.   DID is not the same as schizophrenia.

      c.   The essential feature of the disorder is the presence of two or more distinct personalities or personality states within one individual.

      d.   Differences between personalities can be extreme: shy versus flamboyant, left-handed versus right-handed, heterosexual versus homosexual, etc.

2. Focus on Research: Has dissociative disorder really increased?

     •   There is controversy surrounding the prevalence of DID and whether some psychiatrists diagnose a disproportionately high number of DID cases.

     •   DID may occur more frequently than once believed, but reasons are unclear.

3. Who is affected with DID? Many times more often in women than in men; may reflect greater amount of exposure to sexual abuse, greater internalizing disorders among women, or greater help-seeking among women.

4. Course of DID

      a.   Difficult to separate from other diagnoses.

      b.   High rates of other psychiatric problems in such persons.

5. Family matters: DID and childhood physical and sexual abuse

     •   Dissociative disorders generally caused by traumatic experiences

     •   DID might be a defense against intensely painful and frightening experiences in childhood.

     •   Most common association is between DID and childhood physical and sexual abuse, but retrospective reports are limiting. Also, not all abused children develop DID.

6. Treating DID

    a. Psychotherapy aimed at unifying the personalities is one of the preferred courses of treatment for DID.

    b. Psychodynamic therapy has been applied.

    c. No systematic controlled studies of treatment outcomes available.

III. What Lies Ahead?

    A. Increased collaborative research and a more holistic approach to treatment.

KEY TERMS REVIEW

1. A dissociative disorder in which a person forgets some but not all of what happened in a certain period of time is called _____.

2. The phrase used to describe the tendency for hypochondriacal patients to report more fears and beliefs about disease and attend more to bodily sensations is _____.

3. A dissociative disorder in which a person suddenly and unexpectedly travels away from one's home or place of work and is unable to recall the past; often associated with the assumption of a new identity, this is called _____.

4. Physical symptoms that have no organic basis, and are associated with psychological conflicts and stress and are not produced voluntarily are called _____.

5. An explanation for memory loss suggesting that loss of memory results from disuse and the passage of time is called _____.

6. The unconscious but purposeful exclusion of painful thoughts or unacceptable desires or impulses from consciousness is called _____.

7. A nonchalant, matter-of-fact attitude of the patient reflecting a lack of concern about the patient's suffering or disability which used to be a requirement of conversion disorder is called _____.

8. A treatment for a disorder in which the client is deflected from making the dysfunctional avoidance response is called _____.

9. A dissociative disorder in which a person forgets his or her entire life history is called _____.

10. A long-standing history of physical complaints that results in treatment for impaired social and occupational functioning is called a(n) _____.

11. An explanation for memory loss suggesting that memory has a limited capacity and when its capacity is reached it is susceptible to confusion and forgetting is called _____.

12. Disorders, psychological in origin, that involve one or more symptoms or deficits affecting voluntary functioning that cannot be explained by a neurological or general medical condition are called _____.

13. Somatic disorders in which the patient intentionally produces physical or psychological signs or symptoms in order to assume the role of a sick person are called _____.

14. A somatic disorder in which the sufferer is preoccupied with fears about having disease is called _____.

15. A rare but famous disorder in which one person displays more than one identity, each of which acts and thinks in a different way, is called _____.

16. A severe disruption or alteration of a person's identity, memory, or consciousness is called _____.

17. When a patient reports not being able to feel anything with one hand in an area that resembles the shape of a glove this is called _____.

18. When symptoms are intentionally faked for an external incentive this is called _____.

19. A conversion disorder in which the patient, though physically capable, is unable to speak above a whisper is called _____.

20. Where forgetting is linked to a person's inability to retrieve stored information this is called _____.

FACTUAL MULTIPLE-CHOICE QUESTIONS

1. The root of the word *somatoform* refers to the
   a. mind.
   b. body.
   c. personality.
   d. illness.

2. A person who sees a series of medical doctors for a variety of physical complaints that have no organic base might be diagnosed with
   a. hysteria.
   b. conversion disorder.
   c. dissociative identity disorder.
   d. somatization disorder.

3. Somatization patients are often comorbid with
   a. phobia.
   b. schizophrenia.
   c. personality disorder.
   d. obsessive-compulsive disorder.

4. Hypochondriacal persons will ignore medical evidence to the contrary to insist on the correctness of their
   a. self-diagnosis.
   b. mental disorder.
   c. memory.
   d. identity.

5. A person who feigns an illness in order to avoid work is
   a. somatizing.
   b. malingering.
   c. hypochondriacal.
   d. phobic.

6. Hypochondriacs may have misperceptions of
   a. bodily sensations.
   b. the medical establishment.
   c. diagnostic criteria.
   d. their doctor's ability.

7. If a physical symptom appears at a time of great stress for an individual it may be
   a. phobia.
   b. generalized anxiety disorder.
   c. hallucination.
   d. conversion disorder.

8. In dissociative amnesia the memory loss is from
   a. physical causes.
   b. decay.
   c. aphonia.
   d. psychological causes.

9. Recovered memories may be caused by
   a. suggestion.
   b. truth drugs.
   c. family conflict.
   d. transference.

10. An important element in amnesia and fugue is
    a. recurrence of symptoms.
    b. avoidance of stress.
    c. physical symptoms.
    d. medical diagnosis.

11. Dissociative identity disorder is often confused with
    a. obsessive-compulsive disorder.
    b. fugue.
    c. generalized anxiety disorder.
    d. schizophrenia.

12. Dissociative states are possibly caused by
    a. early childhood physical or sexual abuse.
    b. hypnosis.
    c. overly protective parents.
    d. memory loss.

CONCEPTUAL MULTIPLE-CHOICE QUESTIONS

1. Somatization patients' symptoms are thought to be a way to communicate
   a. fear of medical doctors.
   b. psychological conflict.
   c. real fear of illness.
   d. imaginary fear of illness.

2. Marty developed blindness after he was exposed to toxic chemicals in a plant accident. He was unable to work and remained at home but showed little despondency over the situation. This clue to the possibility of a conversion disorder is called
   a. malingering.
   b. la belle indifference.
   c. somatizing.
   d. hypochondriasis.

3. Dr. James was convinced that Jake was faking dissociative identity disorder because one of the alternate personalities was female and gay. The diagnosis for Jake might be
   a. malingering.
   b. amnesia.
   c. somatization disorder.
   d. dissociative identity disorder.

4. Which of the following best illustrates the concept of dissociation?
   a. While traveling from home to work and thinking about an important meeting, Jonathan noticed that he traveled several miles without remembering anything about the drive.
   b. At a high school reunion, Kerry cannot remember the names of some of her former classmates.
   c. A nervous Marlene cannot remember her lines during the opening of a play.
   d. Even after two weeks in the hospital, Thomas remains unconscious following a motorcycle accident.

5. Which model is *least* likely to explain the causes of glove anesthesia?
   a. psychodynamic
   b. cognitive
   c. behavioral
   d. biomedical

6. Behavioral therapists frequently utilize response prevention strategies because they believe that
   a. a new conditioned stimulus-conditioned response link will be formed.
   b. by challenging a client's cognitive distortions, new schemas will be developed.
   c. shaping is an effective way to modify behavior.
   d. blocking avoidant and escape responses will prevent negative reinforcement.

7. Joshua is a rehabilitation counselor whose job is to help disabled people become reemployed in another appropriate occupation. Joshua is concerned that there has been an increase in the number of people claiming to be disabled by stress or feigning physical injuries in order to receive government disability payments. What concept best identifies Joshua's concern?
   a. factitious disorder
   b. malingering
   c. moral anxiety
   d. collaborative empiricism

8. Dr. Canfield has a new client, Tamara, who was treated by another therapist for depression. Tamara says that her former therapist helped her recover repressed memories of childhood sexual abuse by using hypnosis and age-regression techniques. Her parents, denying that any such abuse ever occurred, questioned the competence of the therapist and recommended that Tamara seek help for her depression from another therapist. Tamara feels confused because she does not have any clear memories of past abuse and depressed because her boyfriend has recently broken up with her. Dr. Canfield should
   a. accept that the childhood sexual abuse probably occurred and has made Tamara depressed and that Tamara's parents are in denial.
   b. inform Tamara that by using hypnosis, the former therapist used an inappropriate and unethical technique.
   c. avoid an uncritical acceptance of Tamara's depression being caused by childhood sexual abuse and consider that memories of childhood sexual abuse may have been created by the therapist's behavior.
   d. be suspicious of Tamara's lapse in memory and begin an aggressive recovered memory therapy regimen.

APPLICATION MULTIPLE-CHOICE QUESTIONS

1. Dr. Johnson reviewed Ellen's file and found that she had been hospitalized more than twelve times in the past seven years. But there was no record of any physiological causation. Ellen may be suffering from
   a. amnesia.
   b. conversion disorder.
   c. dissociative disorder.
   d. somatization disorder.

2. Mary refused to let her sister Catherine visit the doctor for the third time in the same week for a vague stomach complaint. She insisted that Catherine go to work. This approach was suggested by a psychiatrist Catherine's internist referred her to, although Catherine refused to see him. The psychiatrist referred to this treatment as
   a. existential therapy.
   b. response prevention.
   c. rational-emotive therapy.
   d. paradoxical intervention.

3. Jack Bernstein is 85 years old and a widower. He has chronic arthritis and sees his doctor about twice a month. His daughter complains about his hypochondriasis. His physician says he is
   a. neurotic.
   b. dissociating.
   c. normal.
   d. hypochondriacal.

4. Master Sergeant Grant accused Private Slocomb of malingering when Slocomb fainted during the morning run. After extensive tests that showed no physical abnormalities, Private Slocomb's doctor concluded he was
   a. amnesiac.
   b. malingering.
   c. hypochondriacal.
   d. suffering from fugue.

5. As Will approached the witness stand he stopped and clutched his throat. He had to leave the courtroom because he was unable to speak. His condition might be diagnosed as
   a. panic disorder.
   b. social phobia.
   c. agoraphobia.
   d. conversion disorder.

6. Michael awoke one morning after a particularly violent fight with his wife and could not remember his name or where he worked. He remembered the fight and going to bed but nothing else that had happened. His condition could be
   a. generalized dissociative amnesia.
   b. fugue.
   c. repression.
   d. selective dissociative amnesia.

7. Jody did not believe her therapist when she told her that she had called her last night in a suicidal rage. The therapist said that Jody called herself Irene and threatened to kill first Jody and then herself. Jody said her only memory of the night before was of a severe headache before she went to bed. Jody's condition could be
   a. amnesia.
   b. dissociative identity disorder.
   c. fugue.
   d. obsessive-compulsive disorder.

8. Dr. Newman used hypnosis to help Marianne return to her childhood and uncover a hidden trauma that might be causing her symptoms. Her therapeutic orientation is probably
   a. humanistic/existential.
   b. cognitive.
   c. psychodynamic.
   d. behaviorist.

9. Paula's relief for her partial paralysis after many therapy sessions supports the possibility that
   a. experiences must be relived to produce relief.
   b. psychotherapy works in all these somatoform cases.
   c. the skill of the therapist is the most important variable.
   d. Paula was malingering.

10. Dr. Baker shook her head at seeing Mrs. Jones on her client appointment list because she knew that this somatization patient would not
    a. go to the specialist she was going to recommend.
    b. follow her medical treatment recommendations.
    c. accept referral to a psychiatrist.
    d. offer her own diagnosis.

ANSWER KEY: KEY TERMS REVIEW

1. selective dissociative amnesia (203)
2. somatosensory amplification (199)
3. dissociative (psychogenic) fugue (206)
4. somatoform disorders (194)
5. decay theory (204–205)
6. repression (205)
7. la belle indifference (202)
8. response prevention (197)

ANSWER KEY: FACTUAL MULTIPLE-CHOICE QUESTIONS

1. *b. body (p. 194)
   a. The Greek word for mind is *psyche.*
   c. Some of these disorders have personality components.
   d. They all have to do with physical illness of a psychogenic nature.

2. *d. somatization disorder (p. 194)
   a. Hysteria is an outdated term related to conversion disorder.
   b. Conversion disorder implies physical symptoms related to some psychological causation.
   c. DID usually does not have a physical illness component.

3. *c. personality disorder (p. 194)
   a. They may have anxiety complaints that do not take phobic form.
   b. Schizophrenics often have somatic complaints, but somatization patients rarely suffer from schizophrenia.
   d. OCD sufferers may have physical problems such as hand-washing compulsion, but not medical problems.

4. *a. self-diagnosis (p. 197)
   b. They do not consider themselves to be mentally disturbed.
   c. They are concerned with their current "illness" and may have complete records and memory of all their treatments.
   d. Identity has to do with dissociative disorders and is not associated with hypochondriasis.

5. *b. malingering (p. 198)
   a. Somatization patients don't believe they are really ill.
   c. A person with hypochondriasis is more focused on a single disease and is not deliberately inventing symptoms.
   d. There is no evidence of an intense fear in the desire to avoid work.

6. *a. bodily sensations (p. 199)
   b. They believe they understand the medical establishment quite well.
   c. They are familiar with the symptoms of their supposed illness.
   d. They may question their doctor's ability, but want the confirmation of the medical profession.

7. *d. conversion disorder (p. 202)
   a. Phobias may appear at any time.
   b. GAD is not related to a particularly stressful time.
   c. Hallucinations are usually associated with schizophrenia.

8. *d. psychological causes (p. 203)
   a. In dissociative amnesia memory loss is unrelated to physical causes.
   b. Decay relates to disuse and passage of time, but current memory is lost with dissociative amnesia.
   c. Aphonia is the inability to speak above a whisper, though physically capable, and is unrelated to dissociative amnesia.

9. *a. suggestion (p. 206)
   b. The usual technique to help a client recover lost memory is hypnosis.
   c. Early childhood trauma is often seen as the source of recovered memories, not as the cause.
   d. Transference is the process of reexperiencing feelings toward the therapist that were experienced in childhood and is unrelated to recovering lost memory.

10. *b. avoidance of stress (p. 207)
    a. Symptoms rarely recur.
    c. Physical symptoms are not part of this condition.
    d. Dissociative disorders do not have a physiological component.

11. *d. schizophrenia (p. 208)
    a. OCD has to do with rituals and intrusive thoughts, not split minds.
    b. Fugue is fleeing home or work with memory loss and is different from DID.
    c. GAD has nothing to do with personality fragmentation.

12. *a. early childhood physical or sexual abuse (pp. 211–212)
    b. Hypnosis is often used to uncover repressed trauma, but is not a cause of dissociative states.
    c. Parental involvement is often associated with abuse, not excessive protection.
    d. Memory loss is symptomatic, not causative.

ANSWER KEY: CONCEPTUAL MULTIPLE-CHOICE QUESTIONS

1. *b. psychological conflict (p. 195)
   a. They seek out many medical doctors.
   c. The illnesses or complaints are metaphors for a deeper conflict.
   d. The concern for illness is a preoccupation, but the real unacknowledged complaint is psychological conflict.

2. *b. la belle indifference (p. 202)
   a. His symptoms were real.
   c. He did not have a history of many physical ailments.
   d. He was not focused on a particular disease.

3. *d. dissociative identity disorder (p. 208)
   a. There is no evidence that he was attempting to avoid work.
   b. Loss of memory was not mentioned.
   c. Jake did not have a series of physical complaints.

4. *a. While traveling from home to work and thinking about an important meeting, Jonathan noticed that he traveled several miles without remembering anything about the drive. (pp. 203–205)
   b. Kerry's failure in retrieval may be due to simple memory decay.
   c. There is no evidence of loss of consciousness, and nervousness may impede memory.
   d. Dissociation (due to psychogenic factors) and being unconscious (due to biogenic reasons) are not the same.

5. *d. biomedical. (p. 200)
   a. The psychodynamic model assumes the disorder is due to unconscious conflicts.
   b. A cognitive psychologist might emphasize information processing and cognitive distortions.
   c. Psychologists using a behavioral model might explain the problem as a function of reinforcement (secondary gain).

6. *d. blocking avoidant and escape responses will prevent negative reinforcement. (pp. 196–197)
   a. Response prevention is based on operant conditioning, not classical conditioning.
   b. The cognitive model stresses schemas and how information is cognitively processed.
   c. Therapists shape behavior by reinforcing successive approximations toward the target behavior.

7. *b. malingering. (p. 198)
   a. Factitious disorder implies that there is no economic gain.
   c. The Freudian concept of moral anxiety suggests that superego functions create anxiety when one's actions or thinking violates accepted standards of behavior.
   d. Collaborative empiricism is an approach in cognitive-behavioral therapy where the client actively suggests ideas, tries new behaviors, and reports back to the therapist.

8. *c. avoid an uncritical acceptance of Tamara's depression being caused by childhood sexual abuse and consider that memories of childhood sexual abuse may have been created by the therapist's behavior. (pp. 205–206)
   b. Hypnosis is not considered an unethical procedure, although states may regulate its practice by psychotherapists.
   d. Tamara's difficulty in remembering past instances of abuse may not be due to repression if those instances never occurred in fact.

ANSWER KEY: APPLICATION MULTIPLE-CHOICE QUESTIONS

1. *d. somatization disorder (p. 194)
   a. Her problem is associated with physical symptoms, not memory loss.
   b. Conversion disorder usually relates to a single symptom that is psychologically motivated.
   c. Dissociative disorders deal with problems of consciousness, identity, or memory.

2. *b. response prevention (p. 196)
   a. Existential therapy is more a philosophy than a specific approach, such as response prevention.
   c. RET attempts to teach clients to change irrational notions but does not involve direct intervention.
   d. Paradoxical intervention is a technique where clients purposely exaggerate their symptoms.

3. *c. normal (p. 197)
   a. Neurosis is an outdated term. There is no evidence of psychological abnormality here.
   b. There is no indication of loss of memory or identity confusion.
   d. His response to his condition is based on fact.

4. *b. malingering (p. 198)
   a. No loss of memory was mentioned.
   c. He was not focused on a particular illness.
   d. The private did not go on a long trip or suffer memory loss.

5. *d. conversion disorder (p. 200)
   a. There is no mention of the full spectrum of panic symptoms.
   b. He was prepared to testify before the symptom developed.
   c. He had no problem getting to the courtroom.

6. *d. selective dissociative amnesia (pp. 203–204)
   a. Generalized dissociative amnesia is forgetting one's entire life rather than one portion.
   b. Fugue is leaving home or work and forgetting who one is.
   c. There is no evidence of repressed memories returning.

7. *b. dissociative identity disorder (p. 208)
   a. DID sufferers often do not remember the appearance of alternate personalities.
   c. Jody did not travel far away.
   d. There is no evidence of OCD symptoms, such as persistent thoughts or ritualized behavior.

8. *c. psychodynamic (p. 212)
   a. This orientation is less concerned with childhood memories or traumas.
   b. There is no mention of cognitive concerns.
   d. Behaviorists would be interested in current activity, not childhood memory.

9. *a. experiences must be relived to produce relief (p. 202)
   b. Psychotherapy may work in some cases but not all.
   c. Therapist skill is a factor, but uncovering the trauma causing the symptoms appears to be most important.
   d. There is no evidence that she was trying to avoid work.

10. *c. accept referral to a psychiatrist (p. 196)
    a. Somatization clients will go to all manner of medical doctors for treatment of their symptoms.
    b. Mrs. Jones will follow the medical treatment regimen and ask for more.
    d. Most somatization patients will have their own diagnoses and explanations for their conditions.

CHAPTER 8
Mood Disorders and Suicide

LEARNING OBJECTIVES

1. Define the difference between normal human reactions and clinical mood states. (p. 216)

2. Explain the mood and cognitive symptoms associated with unipolar depression. (pp. 216–217)

3. Describe the physical symptoms and interpersonal difficulties of those suffering from unipolar depression. (pp. 217–218)

4. List the effects of depression on social, role, and physical functioning. (p. 218)

5. Distinguish the features of major depressive disorder, psychotic depression, melancholia, seasonal depression, and dysthymia. (pp. 219–220)

6. Describe the comorbidity of depression with other disorders. (p. 220)

7. Discuss the pervasiveness of unipolar depression by sex, ethnic group, and age. (pp. 221–224; Figure 8.5)

8. Describe the phenomenon of earlier onset of depression and its causes. (pp. 224–225)

9. Explain the course of unipolar depression and the likelihood of recurrence and chronicity. (pp. 225–226)

10. Discuss the roles of genetics, neurotransmitters, neuroendocrine functioning, biological rhythms, and hormones in causing depression. (pp. 226–228)

11. Discuss the roles of psychodynamic factors, cognitive vulnerability, stressful life events, and parent-child relations in causing depression. (pp. 228–232)

12. Describe the effect of depressed parents on children. (pp. 232–233)

13. Describe Suomi's experiments on the effects of loss on depression. (pp. 233–235)

14. Describe the treatments for unipolar depression, including the use and effectiveness of antidepressants, electroconvulsive therapy, light therapy, sleep deprivation, cognitive-behavioral therapy, and interpersonal therapy. (pp. 235–239)

15. Describe the clinical characteristics of bipolar disorder. (pp. 239–242)

16. Compare the prevalence of unipolar depression and bipolar disorder and which groups may be particularly affected by the disorders. (pp. 242–243)

17. Describe the outlook for eventual adjustment for sufferers of bipolar disorder. (p. 243)

18. Describe the biological causes of bipolar disorder, including genetic, neuroregulatory, and chronobiological. (pp. 244–245)

19. Discuss the psychological perspectives on bipolar disorder. (pp. 245–246)

20. Describe the use and effectiveness of treatments for bipolar disorder, including lithium carbonate, anticonvulsants, and psychotherapy. (pp. 246–247)

21. Discuss the reasons a person resorts to suicide. (p. 247)

22. Explain what the most common contexts of suicide are. (pp. 247–249)

23. List the psychological disorders that might impair a person's judgment and be associated with suicide. (p. 252)

24. Discuss the cultural and religious variations affecting suicide and the variations among gender, ethnic, and age groups in the United States who commit suicide. (pp. 249–252)

25. Explain the factors that contribute to suicide in children and youth. (p. 252)

26. Describe the biological and psychological factors associated with suicide. (pp. 252–253)

27. Describe efforts made to treat suicide attempters and suicide prevention efforts. (pp. 253–254)

CHAPTER OUTLINE

I. Features of Unipolar Depression

- Mood disorders: Conditions defined by intense emotional states as well as related behavioral, cognitive, and physical symptoms.

- Affective disorders: Another term for *mood disorders*.

- Syndrome: The entire set of defining symptoms of a condition.

A. Clinical Characteristics of Unipolar Depression

- Clinically significant depression persists for weeks or months.

- Unipolar depression: Depression without an extreme positive mood.

1. Mood symptoms: Being down, feeling everything is dull, gray, and flat, nothing is enjoyable, and irritability.

2. Cognitive symptoms: Depressive thinking

   a. Tendency to focus on negative thoughts.

   b. Perceive and interpret themselves as inadequate and world as rejecting.

   c. Impaired motivation.

   d. Hopelessness and perceived helplessness.

    e.   Negative memories and thinking make people feel worse.

    f.   Difficulties with concentration, memory, and decision making.

3.   Physical and behavioral symptoms

    a.   Difficulty in initiating activity.

    b.   Loss of energy and feelings of fatigue.

    c.   Persistent tiredness often accompanied by aches, pains, stomach problems, and other physical symptoms.

    d.   Overall slowing down of activity, including movement and speech.

    e.   Sleep disturbance and weight fluctuations.

    f.   Social withdrawal.

4.   Living with depression: Impaired functioning

    a.   Depression disrupts people's lives and makes their circumstances worse.

    b.   Interpersonal relations are impaired.

    c.   Depression leads to greater dysfunctionality than many chronic medical conditions.

B.   Diagnosing Unipolar Depression

- Clinically significant depression is so widespread that it has been called the "common cold" of psychiatric disorders.

- For diagnosis, a person cannot ever have had a manic episode.

1.   Major depressive disorder

    a.   A distinct period (episode) of at least two weeks of moderate to severe symptoms.

    b.   Psychotic depression may include severe symptoms as well as departures from reality including delusions and hallucinations.

    c.   Melancholia refers to a distinct quality of severe depressive experience; includes unresponsiveness and loss of pleasure in all activities.

    d.   Seasonal affective disorder refers to depression on a recurring basis in one season of the year (usually winter) when it gets dark early and light late.

2.   Dysthymic disorder: Mild, prolonged depression lasting at least two years (one year in children and adolescents).

3.   The heterogeneity of depression

    a.   Symptoms and patterns can vary enormously.

    b.   Some former distinctions included *endogenous, reactive, neurotic, psychotic,* but these divisions have less utility than subtype distinctions based on symptoms.

    c.   Depressive disorder not otherwise specified (NOS) is a collective term for a group of depressive conditions that are briefer and milder than the two main forms.

        (1)   Minor depression: Two weeks of depressive symptoms but less than five symptoms required for a major episode.

        (2)   Recurrent brief depression.

        (3)   Premenstrual dysphoric disorder.

  4.   Comorbidity: Quite high for both psychological and medical problems, particularly alcoholism, anxiety disorders, and personality disorders.

  5.   What's Normal? Mood "disorders" in the normal range

    a.   Depressed and elated moods are normal, but extreme moods approach disorder.

    b.   Even mild symptoms may lead to later depressive episode and cause significant impairment.

    c.   Chronic mild symptoms may suggest individual has a depressive personality.

C.   Who Is Affected with Unipolar Depression?

  •   Between 5 and 7 percent of population are depressed, and 2 to 4 percent are dysthymic.

  •   Lifetime prevalence is 17 percent for major depressive episode.

  1.   Depression as a disorder of women

    a.   Female to male ratio 2 to 1.

    b.   Women have more severe disorders and greater recurrence of episodes.

  2.   Cultural and ethnic differences in depression

    a.   Major depression occurs in all cultures.

    b.   Non-Western cultures may blend physical and emotional symptoms of depression.

  3.   Young people: The epidemic of depression

    a.   Rates of depression among young people and earlier onset of the disorder are increasing.

    b.   May be due to social and demographic changes.

D.   Course of Unipolar Disorders

  1.   Major depressive episodes usually improve whether treated or untreated within a few months.

  2.   Often recurrent or chronic.

II. Causes of Unipolar Depression

A. Biological Approaches to Depression

- Many depressive symptoms are physical, regulated by *limbic* system of the brain and its neural connections.

- Many medical illnesses and medications produce depression.

- Do biological factors cause depression or result from it?

1. Genetic studies

   a. Depression runs in families.

   b. Heritability plays a modest role, but unclear as to what is inherited.

   c. Environmental factors also important.

2. Neurotransmitter and neuroendocrine functioning

   a. Early theories suggested that depression resulted from too little and mania from too much of monoamine neurotransmitters, especially norepinephrine in the limbic system.

   b. A new model emerged that emphasizes dysregulation of neurotransmitter systems: A theory of biological cause for depression that claims that depression results from the instability, desynchronization, and abnormal reactivity of the monoamine neurotransmitter system.

   c. Neuroendocrine complexes may play an important role in controlling hormone secretions which contribute to depression.

   d. Neuroendocrine systems are complex interconnections between the brain, certain hormones, and various organs.

      (1) Hypothalamus-pituitary-adrenal (HPA) axis: A system highly important to body's mobilization in the face of stress and related to the production of cortisol, a hormone that prepares the body for stress.

      (2) Whether the proposed disregulation is genetically transmitted or due to sensitization and damage from earlier stress reactions is unclear.

3. Biological rhythm dysfunction

   a. Depressed people show disruptions in their circadian rhythms, or regular daily cycles of changes.

   b. They also show sleep abnormalities, particularly reduced REM latency, or shortened interval from beginning of sleep to onset of rapid eye movement (REM) stage.

4. The role of hormones

   a. Female prevalence of depression has been explained by a link between the disorder and female hormones.

   b. Postpartum depression, postpartum blues and premenstrual dysphoric disorder may reflect hormonal shifts.

5. Although there exist links between biology and depression, the research has not established clear causal connections.

B.   Psychological Perspectives on Depression

- Nearly all psychological models of depression take a diathesis-stress approach.

1.   Psychodynamic perspectives

   a.   Depression is like grief, and often follows the loss of an important relationship.

   b.   Low self-esteem results from a lost relationship from which the anger of the loss is turned inward.

   c.   Loss, interpretation of loss, self-worth, and family relationships are all important factors in instigating depression.

2.   Cognitive vulnerability

   a.   Beck proposed that depression is a disorder of thinking as well as of mood. Proposed a cognitive triad (a person's views of the self, the world, and the future) and the depressive schema (underlying negative beliefs that people use to distort information) to describe the depressive thought process.

   b.   Recently Beck described "domains of self-worth," sources of self-esteem such as jobs or close relationships.

   c.   Model suggests that negative thinking causes depressive reactions.

   d.   Seligman used the term *learned helplessness* to describe the erroneous expectation that one has no control over important outcomes and therefore takes no action even though action might be successful.

   e.   Hopelessness theory adds cognitive and environmental features to learned helplessness theory.

3.   Stressful life events

   a.   Trigger many unwanted reactions, both medical and psychological.

   b.   Contribute to relapse and recurrence of depression.

   c.   Cognitive appraisals (interpretation) of events are critical in determining the development of clinical depression.

      (1)   The person must interpret the event as a reflection of personal worthlessness to trigger depression.

      (2)   The ability to handle a negative situation distinguishes a nondepressive from depressive reaction.

   d.   Supportive relationships reduce the impact of negative events.

4.   Parent-child relations in childhood

   a.   Early childhood adversity has been linked to vulnerability to depression.

   b.   Early parent-child attachment bond is crucial to the formation of positive self-view.

   c.   What children learn to believe about themselves provides schemas that determine how they interpret themselves in their worlds.

Mood Disorders and Suicide 133

d. Depressed parents have difficult relations with their children and thus pass on their depression.

C. Family Matters: Children of Depressed Parents

1. Depression runs in families, and this may be due to psychological factors associated with the family environment.

2. Depression and stress go together.

3. Both undermine potential ability to function lovingly and responsively.

4. Depressed parents may feel overwhelmed and unable to deal with a difficult child.

5. Some children are resilient (showing no ill effects) in the face of these types of negative circumstances.

6. Diathesis-stress models

   a. A variety of factors are important in the causation of stress, and no one model accounts for all the patterns.

   b. Few of the diathesis-stress models clearly address the interrelationships between environmental and personal factors.

D. Focus on Research: What Can Monkeys Teach Us about Depression?

1. Suomi and colleagues used rhesus monkeys as human analogues to study reaction to separation.

2. They measured behavioral, emotional, and biological changes.

3. Monkeys reared by their biological mothers were better protected against stress than peer-reared monkeys.

4. High risk (highly reactive) monkeys were more successful with nurturant foster mothers but showed more severe reactions to separation than normals.

5. There appeared to be stable individual patterns of reactivity over life span suggesting a biological diathesis.

6. Antidepressant medication reversed many of the symptoms associated with separation.

III. Treatment of Unipolar Depression

• Many people seek help for depressive disorders from primary care physicians.

• Traditional psychotherapy not very successful.

A. Antidepressant Medications

• Tricyclic antidepressants work in complex ways to alter neurotransmitter systems.

• Serotonin reuptake blockers are antidepressants that block the reuptake (absorption) of serotonin so that more is available in the synaptic cleft.

• Monoamine oxidase inhibitors (MAOIs) block the effects of substances that break down the monoamine neurotransmitters, increasing their availability.

1. Use of antidepressants

    a. Recommended for moderate to severe levels of depression.

    b. Positive effects usually take two or three weeks.

    c. Continuation of treatment recommended for at least sixteen to twenty weeks and then the dosage is gradually reduced.

    d. Maintenance treatment recommended for patients with recurrent episodes.

    e. Side effects of the drug and type of depression affect choice of medication.

    f. Fluoxetine (Prozac) is one of the more controversial of the new generation of antidepressants.

2. Effectiveness of antidepressants

    a. Controlled blind trials, in which patients and doctors do not know whether the pills administered are active or placebo, have reported that antidepressants are effective in the reduction of acute depression.

    b. Some atypical and severe forms of depression do not respond well to antidepressants.

B. Other Biological Treatments for Depression

    1. Electroconvulsive therapy (ECT), inducing convulsions by applying electricity to the brain, is extremely effective for certain kinds of severe, otherwise-untreatable depressions.

    2. Light therapy, exposure to bright light (full-wavelength spectrum) for a prescribed time during the day, is a treatment for seasonal affective disorder.

    3. Sleep deprivation, an experimental treatment for depression in which patients are kept awake during part of the night, produces very temporary improvement.

C. Psychotherapies for Depression

    • Psychotherapies helpful in coping with difficult life circumstances.

    1. Characteristics of cognitive-behavioral therapy

        a. A treatment approach that focuses on reducing the depressive symptoms and resolving the contributory problems and personal vulnerabilities.

        b. Clients are taught specific techniques and given assignments to help them combat maladaptive assumptions or negative schemas (e.g., Three-column technique to "deautomatize" negative thinking).

    2. Characteristics of interpersonal therapy (IPT): Short-term therapy based on psychodynamic principles to explore relationship and other social problems.

    3. Effectiveness of psychotherapy for depression

        a. As successful as antidepressants.

        b. Reduces the likelihood of relapse.

        c. IPT effective in reducing acute symptoms.

    d.   Studies indicate that therapy in combination with medication may be more effective than either alone.

    e.   Contact with a supportive therapist rather than specific treatment technique is key to effectiveness.

    f.   Maintenance psychotherapy and medication may be needed to prevent relapse.

IV. Features of Bipolar Disorders

- Bipolar disorder, previously known as manic-depression, involves depression and mania.

- Mania is the opposite of depression, marked by grandiose or irritable mood, increased energy, activity, and distractibility.

- Hypomania is a mild version of mania.

A. Clinical Characteristics of Bipolar Disorder

    1. Mania, like depression, is defined by changes in cognitive functioning, physical state, and behaviors as well as by changes in mood.

        a.   Hypomania—sense of well-being, exhilaration, outgoing, confident, and enthusiastic or irritable.

        b.   Excessive emotional state may last for days or months.

        c.   Manic state more extreme: elated, expansive, or extremely irritable and angry.

        d.   Characterized by heightened self-esteem, grandiosity, overactivity, increased energy, and decreased need for sleep.

        e.   May become more productive, talkative, creative, center of attention.

        f.   Sometimes become dysfunctionally active, brawling, delusional, and incoherent.

B. Diagnosing Bipolar Disorders

- Overlap among symptoms of unipolar, bipolar, and schizophrenia has caused diagnostic problems.

    1. Diagnostic criteria for bipolar disorder

        a.   Therapist must examine entire history of client's episodes. A person is diagnosed as bipolar if there has ever been a manic or hypomanic episode.

        b.   Manic episodes with pronounced euphoria or irritability must last for at least one week with major impairment of functioning.

        c.   Additional symptoms include grandiosity, decreased need for sleep, increased talkativeness, racing thoughts, distractibility, increased activity, and excessive involvement in potentially harmful activities.

        d.   Three subcategories:

           (1)   Bipolar I: Bipolar disorder with manic episodes

(2) Bipolar II: with hypomanic episodes

(3) Cyclothymic disorder: with mild and frequent mood swings

2. Comorbidity: Substance abuse and personality disorders are common in patients with bipolar disorder.

C. Who Is Affected with Bipolar Disorder?

1. Relatively infrequent (about 1 percent)

2. Men and women diagnosed at about the same rate, with higher socioeconomic groups overrepresented.

3. Many writers, statesmen, and musicians are known to have experienced severe mood swings.

4. Younger people today may be at greater risk for developing the disorder.

D. Course of Bipolar Disorder

• Lifelong disorder often beginning in childhood or adolescence

1. The pattern of episodes

a. Great variability in number of episodes.

b. Best predictor of future episodes is number of previous episodes.

c. Each person has a different pattern of depression, normalcy, and mania.

2. Outlook for adjustment

a. Lithium helpful for some major mood symptoms, but relatively poor outcomes and recurrence for most patients.

b. Most have difficulties in social, marital, and work adjustment.

V. Causes of Bipolar Disorders

• At present, no theory clearly explains the disorder.

A. Biological Perspectives on Bipolar Disorder

1. Genetic studies

a. Evidence of heritability is strong for bipolar disorder, but what is inherited is unclear.

b. Failure to replicate genetic linkage studies suggests there may be multiple genetic pathways and more than one disorder.

2. Neuroregulatory processes

a. Catecholamine hypothesis is too simplistic an explanation for mood disorders.

b. Dopamine, a type of neurotransmitter, is hypothesized to play a role in the dysfunction of the behavioral facilitation system.

c. Behavioral sensitization is progressively more rapid and extreme behaviors in response to stimuli as a result of repeated administrations of the stimuli.

d. Kindling is repeated low-level electrical stimulation of the brain that eventually causes seizures to occur spontaneously.

e. Life event stress may cause the alteration of the brain which increases sensitivity to stress and eventually to spontaneous episodes of bipolar disorder.

f. Over time, episodes create episodes.

3. Chronobiological dysfunction

a. Disturbances of the circadian rhythm (naturally occurring biological and behavior rhythms of 24- or 25-hour cycles) systems may be the origin of mood disorders.

b. Links between circadian rhythm disturbances, light sensitivity, and neurotransmitter functioning can result in increased manias in summer and increased depressions in winter.

B. Psychological Perspectives on Bipolar Disorder

1. Psychological factors involve stress and coping.

2. High levels of stressors precede onset of manic or depressive episodes.

3. Stressful life events more common before the first episode of bipolar disorder, causing greater likelihood of later spontaneous mood swings.

4. Family problems may be both cause and result of bipolar disorder.

VI. Treatment of Bipolar Disorder

A. Characteristics and Effects of Lithium

1. Lithium carbonate: a naturally occurring salt that has antimanic properties

2. Revolutionized treatment of bipolar disorders

a. Reduces acute manic and depressive episodes.

b. Prevents (or lessens) manic and depressive episodes.

c. Indefinite maintenance suggested.

d. Effective in about 50 percent of users and less effective in patients with frequent episodes and comorbid substance use disorders.

3. Side effects of lithium

a. Major side effect is toxicity.

b. High lithium levels can damage kidneys and thyroid.

c. Thirst, fatigue, weight gain, diminished concentration and memory.

d. Kidney functioning must be monitored closely.

e. Noncompliance, a patient's tendency to refuse medication or fail to take it in prescribed amounts, is a major problem.

4. Anticonvulsant medications as mood stabilizers

   a. Two anticonvulsants, carbamazepine (Tegretol) and sodium valproate (Depakote), have successfully reduced acute manic symptoms.

   b. Decrease excitability of areas of brain involved in emotional regulation.

5. Psychotherapy for bipolar disorder

   a. Psychotherapy sometimes used to supplement medication.

   b. No systematic outcome studies yet available.

VII. Suicide

A. Meaning and Context of Suicide

   1. Suicides may be of five motivational types:

      a. Escape

      b. Revenge

      c. Altruism

      d. Risk-taking

      e. Mixed

   2. Contexts of suicides

      a. Most common form is individual.

      b. Occasionally occurs in couples (usually murder-suicide).

      c. Cluster suicides are imitations of a publicized suicide, particularly problematic with teens.

B. Who Commits Suicide?

   1. Cultural variations in suicide

      a. Suicide rates are highly influenced by culture.

      b. Religious prohibition against suicide lowers the suicide rate for Catholics and Muslims.

   2. Variations among U.S. ethnic groups

      a. Highest for Native American and white males.

      b. Trend of increasing suicide rate in African American males.

   3. Suicide and gender

      a. Men more likely to kill themselves than women in almost every country.

      b. Women more apt to communicate distress than to die.

    c.   Social isolation, role differences, alcoholism, and lethality of means all contribute to gender differences in suicide.

   4. Age patterns in suicide

    a.   Suicide more common in older adults than among younger persons.

      (1)   Social isolation a major cause.

      (2)   Sharp decrease in elderly suicides since 1933 with increasing economic security and health care.

    b.   Suicide in adolescents

      (1)   Rates have quadrupled since 1950.

      (2)   Associated with impulsiveness, access to guns, alcohol and substance abuse, and suggestibility.

      (3)   High rates of *suicide ideation* and nonlethal attempts.

    c.   Suicide in children

      (1)   Relatively rare but does exist.

      (2)   Young children may not understand consequences.

C. Causes of Suicide

   1. Suicide as an illness

    a.   Associated with mental disorders, especially depression and alcoholism.

    b.   Association does not mean that mental illness causes suicide (most people with mental disorders don't kill themselves).

   2. Risk factors for predicting suicide

    a.   Several psychological and demographic characteristics are associated with suicide, but they don't explain the causes of suicide.

    b.   Social isolation, hopelessness, and substance use with available lethal methods are associated with suicide.

D. Treatment of Suicidal Behavior

   1. Evaluation and intervention recommended.

   2. Psychiatric hospitalization may be recommended as safest way to contain and monitor the person.

   3. Crisis intervention: Brief therapies that attempt to identify and quickly resolve immediate crisis by drawing on person's own resources.

   4. Suicide prevention

    a.   Many people who attempt suicide never seek medical or psychological help.

    b.   Suicide prevention centers (organizations providing service to suicidal people) and telephone hot lines are supportive services. Effectiveness of such programs is difficult to determine.

c. Suicide prevention in teens

(1) School-based prevention programs: Education programs integrated into the curriculum that teach teens about the problems and myths of suicide.

(2) Effectiveness of these programs is hard to determine.

VIII. What Lies Ahead?

A. Increased prevalence of mood disorders, especially among elderly and youths, raises questions about the causes of these problems and what to do about these problems.

B. Should our society prevent suicide, and if so, how?

C. How will social changes including the increased availability of guns affect individuals, especially youths' perceptions and ability to cope with their lives?

KEY TERMS REVIEW

1. Regular daily cycles of changes in such functions as sleep-wake cycles, neuroendocrine activity, and body temperature are called _____.

2. A neurotransmitter substance that is thought to be related to certain psychological disorders such as depression is called _____.

3. An experimental treatment for depression in which patients are kept awake during part of the night is called _____.

4. Bipolar disorder with hypomanic episodes is called _____.

5. A person's views of the self, the world, and the future, which, according to Beck, make a person susceptible to depression if they are negative are called the _____.

6. _____ is a period of grandiose or irritable mood; increased energy, activity, and distractibility; and excessive engagement in pleasurable behaviors that might lead to painful consequences; phase of bipolar depression.

7. The entire set of defining symptoms of a condition is called a(n) _____.

8. A classification of unipolar depression characterized by a distinct period of at least two weeks of moderate-to-severe symptoms is called _____.

9. Programs integrated into the curriculum that teach teens about various problems and myths of suicide, the warning signs, and the resources for helping with problems are called _____.

10. _____ is an electrophysiological process in which repeated low-level electrical stimulation of the brain produces seizures, which eventually occur spontaneously when the stimulation has been sufficiently repeated.

11. Underlying negative beliefs that, according to Beck's theory of depression, people use to distort information so that they select interpretations that fit their beliefs while ignoring or reinterpreting information that does not fit those beliefs are called _____.

12. A disorder characterized by persisting disturbances of negative mood and cognition and altered energy, motivation, behavior, and bodily functioning affecting sleep and appetite and not accompanied by changes to an extreme positive mood, known as *mania*, is called _____.

13. Suicides committed in imitation of a publicized suicide are called _____.

14. Ways of thinking about or interpreting stressors, which may be linked to emotional disorders, are called _____.

15. Conditions defined by intense emotional states as well as related behavioral, cognitive, and physical symptoms are called _____.

16. _____ is a neurotransmitter that plays a critical role in regulating type and level of activity in the brain and is implicated in bipolar disorder.

17. Depressive episodes that occur after a woman gives birth and are more severe than postpartum blues are called _____.

18. The hormone produced in the adrenal glands that physiologically prepares the body for response to stress is _____.

19. Another name for *mood disorders* is _____.

20. A pattern of relatively brief spells of crying, sadness, anxiety, and upset experienced by the majority of women after they give birth is called _____.

21. A bipolar disorder characterized by mild and frequent mood swings is called a(n) _____.

22. _____ are complex interconnections between the brain, certain hormones, and various organs, one of which (HPA) may play a role in depression.

23. A distinct quality of severe depressive experience in which the person has lost pleasure in almost all activities or is unresponsive even when something good happens and suffers certain distinctive physical symptoms is called _____.

24. A neurotransmitter thought to be associated with various disorders, including impulsive aggressiveness, is called _____.

25. A depressive disorder in which a person becomes depressed on a recurring basis in one season of the year (usually winter) and improves in the following season is called _____.

26. Exposure to bright full-spectrum light for a prescribed period during the day; a treatment for seasonal affective disorder is called _____.

27. Bipolar disorder with manic episodes is called _____.

28. A type of major depressive disorder that may include severe symptoms plus departures from reality such as delusions or hallucinations that might have a depressive content is called _____.

29. The quality of the early parent-child relationship, said to be crucial to the formation of a positive view of the self, is called _____.

30. Mood disorders that include both depression and mania or hypomania are called _____.

31. Brief therapies, conducted either as inpatient or outpatient treatment, that attempt to identify and quickly resolve the immediate crisis by drawing on the person's own resources including friends and family support is called _____.

32. A mild version of mania is called _____.

33. A type of depressive disorder not otherwise specified marked by impaired functioning in women associated with mood and depressive syndrome changes limited to the late portion of the menstrual cycle is called _____.

34. _____ is a therapeutic approach in which the therapist's essential task is to disrupt the client's vicious cycle of self-defeating interpersonal interactions.

35. _____ is a shortened interval from the beginning of sleep to the onset of the rapid eye movement (REM) stage that appears to be relatively specific to depressed patients.

36. Organizations providing services to suicidal people, usually telephone help lines, are called _____.

37. A mild, prolonged depression; a category of unipolar depression is called _____ or _____.

38. A person characterized by showing no ill effects despite negative circumstances is said to be _____.

39. A type of depressive disorder not otherwise specified characterized by intense but brief periods of depression experienced at least monthly but not associated with the menstrual cycle is called _____.

40. A neuroendocrine system highly important to the body's mobilization in the face of stress and which may be involved in depression is called the _____.

41. A previously used term for *bipolar disorder* is _____.

42. Psychotropic medications that have been used to reduce acute manic symptoms are called _____.

43. _____ is a method of inducing convulsions by applying electricity to the brain, with the aim of resolving depression.

44. A class of drugs used to treat depression by blocking the effects of substances that break down the monoamine neurotransmitters are called _____.

45. The exhibition of progressively more rapid and extreme behaviors in response to stimuli as a result of repeated administrations of the stimuli is called _____.

46. A theory of a biological cause for depression that claims that depression results from the instability, desynchronization, and abnormal reactivity of the monoamine neurotransmitter system is called _____.

47. Studies in which patients and doctors do not know whether the pills administered are active or placebo are called _____.

48. _____ is a patient's tendency to refuse medication or fail to take it regularly in the prescribed amounts; a major problem for bipolar patients.

49. _____ is a theory of depression that extends learned helplessness theory by applying it to a subgroup of depressed persons whose thoughts are characterized by hopeless interpretations.

50. A type of depressive disorder not otherwise specified characterized by two weeks of depressive symptoms but less than the five required for a major depressive episode is called _____.

51. New antidepressants that are selective and block the reuptake of serotonin so that more is available in the synaptic cleft are called _____.

52. _____ is a cognitive model of depression that suggests that persons are susceptible to depression if they have an erroneous expectation that they cannot control important outcomes and that unchanging and pervasive negative qualities of the self are the causes of negative events.

53. A collective term for a group of depressive conditions that are briefer and milder than the two main forms; a type of unipolar depression is called _____.

54. Continuing use of psychotropic drugs at a level sufficient to prevent recurrence of episodes or symptoms is called _____.

55. A naturally occurring salt that has antimanic properties, used in preventing bipolar episodes, is _____.

56. Therapeutic approaches that combine behavioral performance-based interventions with strategies that address the client's thinking are called _____.

57. Continuing to administer antidepressant medication after the initial symptoms of depression have diminished for a period of at least sixteen to twenty weeks giving the initial dosage followed by a gradual reduction is called _____.

58. _____ are a class of medications used to treat depression.

59. Neurotransmitters (primarily norepinephrine, dopamine, and serotonin) known to be important in the limbic system of the brain and widely distributed into other areas that affect and integrate emotional, psychomotor, and biological functions are called _____.

FACTUAL MULTIPLE-CHOICE QUESTIONS

1. The primary mood symptom of unipolar depression is
   a. excitability.
   b. hypomania.
   c. workaholism.
   d. loss of pleasure.

2. A person suffering from severe depressive symptoms as well as delusions and hallucinations is most likely to be diagnosed with
   a. schizophrenia.
   b. brief reactive psychosis.
   c. hypomania.
   d. psychotic depression.

3. Mild, prolonged unipolar depression is known as
   a. cyclothymia.
   b. dysthymia.
   c. dysphoria.
   d. melancholia.

4. Two established trends in depression among the young are
   a. decreasing rates and later onset.
   b. increasing rates and earlier onset.
   c. decreasing rates and earlier onset
   d. increasing rates and later onset.

5. The subset of neurotransmitters that plays a central role in depression is called
   a. monoamines.
   b. hormones.
   c. tricyclics.
   d. neuroleptics.

6. The daily cycles of changes that ordinarily take place in the human body are called
   a. dysthymia.
   b. cyclothymia.
   c. biofeedback.
   d. circadian rhythms.

7. One of the most successful treatments for seasonal affective disorder is
   a. light therapy.
   b. cognitive-behavior therapy.
   c. interpersonal therapy.
   d. ECT.

8. If bipolar patients experience four or more episodes of depression or mania a year, they are called
   a. psychotic.
   b. bipolar II.
   c. comorbid.
   d. rapid cyclers.

9. The medication that revolutionized the treatment of bipolar disorder is
   a. dopamine.
   b. lithium carbonate.
   c. serotonin.
   d. norepinephrine.

10. Public attitudes that suicide is a "reasonable" response to unbearable problems might waver if it were known that most people who commit suicide
    a. have criminal records.
    b. are from lower socioeconomic groups.
    c. are primarily young women.
    d. have a diagnosable mental illness.

11. One of the factors that accounts for higher suicide rates for men than women is
    a. a higher rate of psychopathology for men.
    b. inaccuracies in reporting suicide statistics.
    c. men are more likely to plan a suicide than women.
    d. men use more lethal methods.

12. When there is major suicide risk the recommended intervention is
    a. treatment for depression.
    b. psychiatric hospitalization.
    c. psychoanalytic therapy.
    d. family therapy.

CONCEPTUAL MULTIPLE-CHOICE QUESTIONS

1. If major depressive episodes are left untreated, the patient will usually
   a. get much worse.
   b. remain about the same.
   c. develop a personality disorder.
   d. improve spontaneously.

2. The best predictor of recurrent depression is
   a. gender.
   b. age.
   c. depressed parents.
   d. past depression.

3. Marianne has been exposed to a number of stressors in her life beginning in childhood. As an adult it takes less and less stress to trigger her depressions. Her condition suggests the validity of the
   a. genetic marker theory.
   b. psychodynamic theory.
   c. existential/humanistic theory.
   d. behavioral sensitization theory.

4. Marilyn's psychiatrist diagnosed her condition as bipolar disorder and was reluctant to have her return to her family for fear that their high level of negativity might cause
   a. relapse.
   b. schizophrenia.
   c. major depression.
   d. cyclothymia.

APPLICATION MULTIPLE-CHOICE QUESTIONS

1. Jonathan was full of energy. He couldn't stop even for a moment in his athletic, academic, and social activities. His therapist diagnosed Jonathan as being in a _____ phase.
   a. cortisol
   b. manic
   c. unipolar
   d. depressive

2. Todd was pleased with the results of his lithium treatment, but wanted to know from his psychiatrist how long he would have to take the drug. Todd's doctor probably told him
   a. a few months.
   b. a few weeks.
   c. a few years.
   d. indefinitely.

3. Dr. Roberts is a counselor at a large, inner-city public hospital. The depressed patients she sees
   a. are almost exclusively women.
   b. are almost exclusively men.
   c. about equally distributed between women and men.
   d. are women twice as often as men.

4. Tom's depression began when he was a senior in high school. Recent research indicates that his condition
    a. is unusual for someone so young.
    b. is unusual for a male to be affected so young.
    c. reflects trends seen in national studies of depression.
    d. is probably just a temporary reaction to the problems of most teenagers.

5. Dr. Powell had seen Mr. Jameson twice and was convinced that unipolar depression was the primary problem. Yet he was concerned with other problems he knew were often comorbid with depression, such as
    a. obsessive-compulsive disorder.
    b. fugue.
    c. dissociative identity disorder.
    d. alcoholism.

6. Jane's psychiatrist prescribed Prozac. After about six months symptom-free, she discontinued the drug and her symptoms returned. Her psychiatrist would probably
    a. prescribe a more effective antidepressant.
    b. take her off the drug because it might make her suicidal.
    c. recommend psychoanalysis.
    d. put her on maintenance treatment with Prozac.

7. Murray had been on his antidepressant medication for over two years. His psychiatrist suggested a combination of medication and psychotherapy to reduce the chance of
    a. addiction.
    b. bipolar disorder.
    c. relapse.
    d. psychotic depression.

8. The psychiatric social worker at the retirement home was quite concerned about suicidal behavior from Mr. Miller because
    a. he had just been admitted to the home.
    b. his wife had recently died.
    c. he had been losing his memory.
    d. he had been diagnosed with a terminal illness.

9. Kurt Cobain, the lead singer for the hit rock band Nirvana, committed suicide. His death prompted other suicides. These are
    a. altruistic.
    b. cluster suicides.
    c. revenge type.
    d. murder-suicide.

10. Marlene attempted suicide, but was rescued by her husband. She refuses treatment. Her husband and psychiatrist agree that
    a. the danger is past.
    b. her attempt wasn't serious.
    c. Marlene was just feigning.
    d. she should be involuntarily hospitalized.

ANSWER KEY: KEY TERMS REVIEW

1. circadian rhythms (228)
2. norepinephrine (227)
3. sleep deprivation (237)
4. bipolar II (242)
5. cognitive triad (229)
6. mania (239)
7. syndrome (216)
8. major depressive disorder (219)
9. school-based prevention programs (254)
10. kindling (245)
11. depressive schemas (229)
12. unipolar depression (217)
13. cluster suicides (248)
14. cognitive appraisals (231)
15. mood disorders (216)
16. dopamine (244)
17. postpartum depression (228)
18. cortisol (227)
19. affective disorders (216)
20. postpartum blues (228)
21. cyclothymic disorder (242)
22. neuroendocrine systems (227)
23. melancholia (219)
24. serotonin (227)
25. seasonal affective disorder (219)
26. light therapy (237)
27. bipolar I (242)
28. psychotic depression (219)
29. attachment (232)
30. bipolar disorders (239)
31. crisis intervention (254)
32. hypomania (240)
33. premenstrual dysphoric disorder (220, 228)
34. interpersonal therapy (238)
35. reduced REM latency (228)
36. suicide prevention centers (254)
37. dysthymia or dysthymic disorder (220)
38. resilient (233)
39. recurrent brief depression (220)
40. hypothalamic-pituitary-adrenal (HPA) axis (227)
41. manic-depression (240)
42. anticonvulsants (246)
43. electroconvulsive therapy (ECT) (237)
44. monoamine oxidase inhibitors (MAOIs) (227)
45. behavioral sensitization (245)
46. dysregulation (227)
47. blind trials (236)
48. noncompliance (246)
49. hopelessness theory (230)
50. minor depression (220)
51. selective serotonin reuptake inhibitors (SSRIs) (235)
52. learned helplessness (230)
53. depressive disorder not otherwise specified (NOS) (220)
54. maintenance treatment (236)
55. lithium carbonate (246)
56. cognitive behavioral therapies (238)
57. continuation treatment (236)
58. tricyclic antidepressants (235)
59. monoamines (227)

ANSWER KEY: FACTUAL MULTIPLE-CHOICE QUESTIONS

1. *d. loss of pleasure (p. 223)
   a. Excitability is associated with mania.
   b. Hypomania is a milder form of mania.
   c. Depressed people have a difficult time finding the energy to go to work.

2. *d. psychotic depression (p. 227)
   a. Unlike schizophrenia, the depressed mood and other features of depression are present to a marked degree.
   b. Brief reactive psychosis is usually a response to a particular event or condition.
   c. Hypomania is a mild form of mania, the "up" of bipolar disorder.

3. *b. dysthymia (pp. 227–228)
   a. Cyclothymia is a milder form of bipolar disorder.
   c. Dysphoria is a general term for sadness, unhappiness.
   d. Melancholia is a term meaning profound loss of pleasure.

4. *b. increasing rates and earlier onset (p. 230)
   a. Rates and earlier onset have been increasing for many years.
   c. See b.
   d. See b.

5. *a. monoamines (p. 234)
   b. Hormones are not neurotransmitters.
   c. Tricyclics are antidepressant drugs.
   d. Neuroleptics are antipsychotic drugs.

6. *d. circadian rhythms (p. 236)
   a. Dysthymia is mild, prolonged depression.
   b. Cyclothymia is a mild form of bipolar disorder.
   c. Biofeedback is a technique to teach relaxation.

7. *a. light therapy (p. 248)
   b. The disorder is circadian rhythm dysfunction related to reduced light in winter, not cognitive distortion.
   c. Psychotherapy is less effective with this disorder.
   d. ECT is not used to treat SAD.

8. *d. rapid cyclers (p. 256)
   a. A diagnosis of psychotic depression is associated with delusions and hallucinations, not number of episodes per year.
   b. Bipolar II is bipolar disorder with hypomanic episodes, having to do with severity, not frequency of episodes.
   c. Comorbidity means the disorder coexists with other disorders.

9. *b. lithium carbonate (pp. 261–262)
   a. Dopamine is a neurotransmitter.
   c. Serotonin is another neurotransmitter.
   d. Norepinephrine is a neurotransmitter that plays a role in depression.

10. *d. have a diagnosable mental illness (pp. 270–271)
    a. Most suicides occur in the context of mental illness, not of criminal behavior.
    b. Suicide occurs in all socioeconomic groups.
    c. Young women actually commit suicide less often than other groups.

11. *d. men use more lethal methods (p. 274)
    a. Role differences and social isolation are more important differences.
    b. Reporting inaccuracies affects both men and women.
    c. Women may plan more, because less lethal methods (such as prescription drugs) require more preparation.

12. *b. psychiatric hospitalization (p. 284)
    a. Treatment for depression may take too long.
    c. Psychoanalytic therapy may also not have enough time before the person decides to act.
    d. Family therapy also takes time to get started.

ANSWER KEY: CONCEPTUAL MULTIPLE-CHOICE QUESTIONS

1. *d. improve spontaneously (p. 232)
   a. Even without treatment, many depressives will improve.
   b. Patients will usually improve.
   c. Depression is often comorbid with other psychological problems, but there is no direct connection between personality disorder and treatment of depression.

2. *d. past depression (p. 232)
   a. Women tend to develop depression earlier and more severely, but gender does not predict recurrence.
   b. Aging persons tend to be more depressed, but age is not predictive of recurrence.
   c. Depression in parents may be a causal factor, but it does not predict recurrence as well as past history of depression does.

3. *d. behavioral sensitization theory (p. 258)
   a. Nothing was said about her family's susceptibility to depression, and a genetic link to unipolar depression is weak.
   b. Psychodynamic theory would emphasize repressed conflicts.
   c. Existential/humanistic theory would emphasize crisis of meaning and freedom of choice.

4. *a. relapse (p. 261)
   b. Schizophrenics have relapse problems in families with high expressed emotion, but depressed people are unlikely to develop schizophrenia.
   c. The family interaction might cause a relapse of bipolar disorder, but not a major depression.
   d. This milder form of bipolar disorder is not as susceptible to such interactions as is the more serious form.

ANSWER KEY: APPLICATION MULTIPLE-CHOICE QUESTIONS

1. *b. manic (p. 253)
   a. Cortisol is a hormone that prepares the body for response to stress.
   c. Unipolar depression does not include the excitability phase.
   d. Depression is marked by the absence of energy.

2. *d. indefinitely (p. 262)
   a. The treatment must be maintained indefinitely. The drug takes effect almost immediately, but recurrence of symptoms occurs soon after reduction in dosage or cessation. Most patients require maintenance of the drug for a lifetime.
   b. See a.
   c. See a.

3. *d. are women twice as often as men (p. 233)
   a. The male-female ratio of depressed patients is 1:2.
   b. See a.
   c. See a.

4. *c. reflects trends seen in national studies of depression (p. 230)
   a. Recent studies indicate that depression is increasingly common among young people.
   b. The first major episode is most likely to occur between fifteen and nineteen for both men and women.
   d. Evidence of increased depression rates among the young are supported by increased hospitalization and suicide.

5. *d. alcoholism (p. 228)
   a. OCD is an anxiety disorder not usually associated with depression.
   b. Fugue is a dissociative disorder not usually associated with depression.
   c. DID is also a dissociative disorder not usually associated with depression.

6. *d. put her on maintenance treatment with Prozac (p. 246)
   a. The current antidepressant medications are about equally effective.
   b. Based on controlled studies it was determined that there was no evidence of a causal relationship between Prozac and suicidal behavior.
   d. The most effective psychotherapies for depression are cognitive-behavioral therapy and interpersonal therapy.

7. *c. relapse (p. 251)
   a. The new generation of antidepressants are not addictive.
   b. Antidepressants do not cause bipolar disorder.
   d. Psychotic depression would not be caused by antidepressant medication.

8. *b. his wife had recently died (p. 275)
   a. The home eased his social isolation.
   c. Memory loss does not account for suicidal behavior.
   d. A small percentage of suicides are related to terminal illness.

9. *b. cluster suicides (p. 269)
   a. There is no evidence that the suicides were motivated by concern for others.
   c. Revenge would not be a factor in a "copycat" type of suicide.
   d. Murder would not be part of this type of suicide.

10. *d. she should be involuntarily hospitalized (p. 284)
    a. She may be in great danger.
    b. Any attempted suicide is serious.
    c. Marlene's attempt may have been a cry for help, but that does not mean she was feigning.

CHAPTER 9
Schizophrenia

LEARNING OBJECTIVES

1. Define schizophrenia and the many terms that have been used for it over the years. (p. 260)

2. Explain the difference between schizophrenia and psychosis. (p. 260)

3. Discuss the contributions of Kraepelin and Bleuler to our understanding of schizophrenia. (p. 260)

4. Describe the clinical characteristics and major symptoms of schizophrenia. (pp. 260–265)

5. Distinguish between relatively normal experiences and those that would be considered schizophrenic. (pp. 263–264)

6. Explain the diagnostic requirements and subtypes of schizophrenia. (pp. 265–268)

7. Describe the positive and negative symptoms of schizophrenia. (pp. 267–268)

8. Discuss the prevalence of schizophrenia and the differences by culture and gender. (pp. 268–270)

9. Describe the course and predictors of schizophrenia. (pp. 271–272)

10. Describe the role of genetics in schizophrenia. (pp. 273–274)

11. Describe the abnormalities of the brain in schizophrenia. (pp. 274–276)

12. Discuss the abnormalities in neurocognitive functioning and neurodevelopmental factors that are associated with schizophrenia. (pp. 276–278)

13. Describe the biochemical abnormalities implicated in schizophrenia. (pp. 279–280)

14. Discuss the psychological causes of schizophrenia. (pp. 280–284)

15. Describe the role of expressed emotion as contributory to the course of schizophrenia. (pp. 282–283)

16. Explain the diathesis-stress approaches to schizophrenia. (p. 284)

17. Discuss antipsychotic medication as a treatment for schizophrenia. (pp. 285–287)

18. Describe the side effects of neuroleptic medications. (p. 287)

19. Describe the new antipsychotic clozapine and its advantages and limitations. (pp. 287–288)

20. Describe the psychosocial treatments for schizophrenia, including psychotherapy and cognitive therapy. (p. 289)

21. Discuss token economies and social skills training programs. (pp. 290–291)

22. Explain the difficulties for families living with a schizophrenic. (pp. 291–292)

23. Describe the efforts being made to help families cope with schizophrenia. (p. 292)

24. Discuss the goals of family and psychosocial treatments. (p. 292)

CHAPTER OUTLINE

I. Features of Schizophrenia

   A. Defining Schizophrenia

      1. Psychosis is the broad term that refers to all mental disorders characterized by major departures from reality.

      2. Schizophrenia is a type of psychosis marked by disturbances of thought, language, and behavior not due to a primary mood disorder or medical condition.

      3. May have different forms with different features and causes.

      4. Kraepelin used the term *dementia praecox* to describe progressive, irreversible mental deterioration that begins early in life.

      5. Bleuler introduced the term *schizophrenia* reflecting "splitting of the mind" (splitting of psychic functions, such as cognition and emotion).

      6. There is disagreement on the course of the disorder.

   B. Clinical Characteristics of Schizophrenia

      • Some experience terrifying alterations in perception, others withdraw into a private world.

      • Communication is difficult.

      • May be emotionally flat, depressed, anxious, scared, or angry with disrupted sense of a coherent self.

      • Marked by fundamental disturbances of thought, speech, and perceptual processes.

      • Schizophrenia disrupts all areas that are essential to human adaptation.

      1. Disturbances of thought and language

         a. Loose associations are a common speech characteristic of people with schizophrenia, consisting of unusual and idiosyncratic meanings of words or movement from one idea to another in ways that are hard to understand.

      b.   Speech may include clang associations, words that are related by sound, not meaning.

      c.   Can deteriorate to use of neologisms, made-up words.

      d.   Word salad: Highly disorganized speech seen in schizophrenia.

      e.   Poverty of speech conveys little information.

      f.   Concrete thinking reflects reduced ability to deal with abstractions.

2. Delusional thinking

      a.   Delusions are false beliefs held by individuals that have no basis in reality and are resistant to change despite evidence.

      b.   Common types of delusions:

            (1)   Delusions of grandeur: Belief that one has special powers or characteristics.

            (2)   Delusions of persecution: Belief that others are plotting against and mistrusting one.

            (3)   Delusions of reference: Belief that other people are making secret reference to one.

            (4)   Thought insertion: Belief that other people can put thoughts in one's head.

            (5)   Thought broadcasting: Belief that one's thoughts are being broadcast out loud.

            (6)   Nihilistic delusions: Belief that one is dead, that nothing exists, or people are only vapors.

      c.   People with delusional thought processes do not respond to objective evidence in the environment.

      d.   Lack of awareness of having a disorder is common.

3. Perceptual disturbances

      a.   Perceptual disorder involved in accurate perceptions and making cognitive sense of the perceptions.

      b.   The most characteristic perceptual disturbances are hallucinations, or reports of sensory stimulation when no such stimulation is present.

      c.   The most common hallucinations are auditory and visual hallucinations. Others include tactile, taste, and somatic hallucinations.

4. What's normal? When hallucinations are not symptoms: Research shows that normal people may have psychotic-like experiences under certain conditions.

5. Affective disturbances

      a.   Flat affect is evidenced by showing no facial expression and speaking in a monotone.

b.   Emotional responses may be inappropriate.

6.   Behavioral and psychomotor dysfunction

a.   Peculiar mannerisms, gestures, grimaces.

b.   Little spontaneity of movement.

7.   Impairment in interpersonal relationships

a.   Frequently unable to relate to others.

b.   May socially withdraw into a private fantasy world.

c.   May act socially inappropriately.

d.   May demonstrate decreasing interest in relationships.

8.   Lack of pleasure and motivation

a.   Anhedonia, lack of pleasure in any activity, is characteristic.

b.   Difficulty in self-initiated activity may also be evident.

C.   Diagnosing Schizophrenia

- To be diagnosed, a person must show two of the specified symptoms for at least one month and display major impairment in functioning.

1.   Diagnostic subtypes of schizophrenia

a.   Catatonic schizophrenia is marked by psychomotor disturbances ranging from rigid posture or stuporous inactivity to excited, excessive activity.

b.   Paranoid schizophrenia is marked by preoccupation with delusions or hallucinations that have an organized theme of persecution. Compared with other subtypes, paranoid schizophrenics have a later onset, better cognitive and social functioning, and more favorable outcomes.

c.   Disorganized schizophrenia is marked by severe disintegration of personality, incoherent speech, fragmentary delusions and hallucinations, extreme social impairment, and flat or inappropriate affect. Tend to have an earlier onset and a chronic, deteriorating course.

d.   Undifferentiated schizophrenia includes symptoms that do not clearly fit into other categories.

e.   Residual schizophrenia describes persons who have had at least one past episode and continuing evidence of the disorder but are currently free of the psychotic symptoms.

2.   Positive and negative-symptom schizophrenia

a.   Positive symptoms refer to the presence of bizarre behaviors and symptoms such as delusions, hallucinations, and thought disorder.

(1)   Psychotic symptoms (delusions and hallucinations).

(2)   Disorganized symptoms (inappropriate affect, bizarre behavior, and thought disorder).

    b.   Negative or deficit symptoms describe the absence of behaviors, including poor adjustment before onset, flat affect, lack of enjoyment and self-directed activity, apathy, social-relatedness disturbances.

    c.   Negative symptoms generally reveal a more serious impairment with poor response to treatment.

    d.   Positive-symptom schizophrenia shows good adjustment before onset, normal brain structures, and good response to treatment.

3.   Comorbidity of schizophrenia and other disorders

    a.   Depression and substance-use disorders are common in people with schizophrenia.

    b.   Any abuse may hasten the age of onset as well as relapse.

    c.   Alcohol-use disorders associated with poor outcomes and psychotic symptoms.

D. Who Is Affected with Schizophrenia?

1.   Occurs in every culture with a prevalence of 1 percent.

2.   Equal rates in men and women, though less severe among women.

3.   Age of onset 14 to 25 for men, 24 to 35 for women.

E. Course of Schizophrenia

•   Considerable variability. Starts in adolescence and is lifelong.

1.   Onset of symptoms

    a.   Early adolescent onset can be either gradual or acute.

    b.   Gradual onset schizophrenia is typified by poor functioning throughout childhood.

2.   Episodes and outcomes

    a.   Course varies from acute onset followed by complete recovery to gradual onset with *chronic* symptoms.

    b.   Many schizophrenic patients, even chronic schizophrenic patients, those who had a history of frequent episodes and multiple hospitalizations, improve rather than deteriorate over time.

    c.   Aging and corresponding reduction in dopamine function may be a factor in the improvement of older schizophrenic patients.

    d.   The majority of schizophrenic patients suffer relapses and multiple episodes.

    e.   Typical schizophrenic person experiences deteriorating phase for five to ten years, followed by a lengthy period of stable symptoms. Improvement comes in fifties and sixties.

3.   Predictors of the course of schizophrenia

     a.   Premorbid adjustment (person's level of functioning before apparent onset of the disorder) is important.

        (1)   Good premorbid adjustment reflects good physical health, friendships and romantic relationships, adequate performance at school and work.

        (2)   Poor adjustment reflects inadequacies in work, social, personal life. Onset is insidious, gradually worsening until psychotic symptoms are apparent.

     b.   There is evidence of greater social competence of female schizophrenics; women have significantly later age of onset.

     c.   Positive supportive relationships play a role in the course of schizophrenia.

     d.   Negative-positive symptom distinction is important.

        (1)   Negative symptom sufferers tend to have chronic course schizophrenia, poor personal resources, and poor coping capabilities.

        (2)   Likelihood of relapse greater.

II. Causes of Schizophrenia

   A. Biological Contributors to Schizophrenia

     1. The role of genetics in schizophrenia

        a.   Schizophrenia is possibly genetically transmitted, but what is transmitted and the mechanisms involved are unclear. A single gene for schizophrenia is unlikely.

        b.   Concordance rate suggests inherited tendency with environmental or personal stressors that activate gene's effects. Concordance: Comparison of diagnostic similarity between those with identical genes to those with less shared make-up.

        c.   Adoption studies confirm genetic influence on schizophrenia.

        d.   Quality of family life, however, affects the outcome of an underlying genetic predisposition.

        e.   One genetic marker for schizophrenia is *eye movement dysfunction*, related to defective frontal lobe functioning.

        f.   Neurocognitive deficits (difficulty in abstracting, verbal memory, and attention) are associated with schizophrenia.

     2. Abnormalities of the brain in schizophrenia

        a.   Two anatomical differences have been noted in some schizophrenics: enlargement of ventricles (fluid-filled spaces in the brain) and hypofrontality, or reduced flow of blood in the frontal regions of the brain. These abnormalities are apt to be found in patients with negative, more severe symptoms and in men.

        b.   Discordance of hypofrontality in identical twins indicates that it must be due to nongenetic factors.

3. Abnormalities in neurocognitive functioning

   a. Poor sustained attention (a function of the frontal lobe area) represents a stable liability marker for schizophrenia. These attention problems are associated with school, behavioral, and social adjustment difficulties in adolescence.

   b. Cognitive and social difficulties in high-risk children can lead to further stresses that contribute to schizophrenia.

4. Neurodevelopmental abnormalities: Patterns of abnormal mental or motor functioning, may be genetically transmitted, potentially leading to schizophrenia.

5. Focus on Research: Flu, famine, and films: How are scientists trying to crack the mystery of schizophrenia?

   a. Several factors contribute to neurological abnormalities and may produce schizophrenia:

      (1) Birth complications, low birth weight, pre- or postnatal brain injury or exposure to environmental toxins.

      (2) Children born during winter months to mothers who were exposed to influenza virus while pregnant.

      (3) Nutritional deficiency.

      (4) Neuromotor abnormalities and behavioral difficulties.

      (5) Mother-infant Rh blood incompatibility.

   b. Research suggests that some forms of schizophrenia, particularly early-onset and negative-symptom schizophrenia, involve damage to areas of brain associated with emotional and cognitive functioning.

6. Biochemical abnormalities in schizophrenia

   a. Dopamine processes associated with schizophrenic symptoms, but researchers are unclear whether dysfunctional dopamine processes play a role in the fundamental cause of schizophrenia.

   b. Neuroleptic medications seem to reduce positive symptoms, but have less effect on negative symptoms or can even make them worse.

B. Psychological Approaches to the Causes of Schizophrenia

   • Evidence that stressful circumstances can trigger schizophrenia in those who are biologically predisposed.

   1. Disturbed family interactions

      a. Family context as source of internal conflict: schizophrenogenic mother, a schizophrenia-inducing mother, theory lacked credibility (poor research methods).

      b. Later research was better designed and focused on disturbed role relationships within the family.

   c. *Family process theories* focus on communication that is unclear and inconsistent, creates problems in thinking, perceiving, and communicating that result in schizophrenia.

   d. *Double-bind communication* creates conflicting messages involving verbal and nonverbal content, which may lead to children's selectively ignoring aspects of communication and disturbed relationships and information processing.

   e. Communication deviance (CD) is problems in creating and maintaining a shared focus of attention generally found in families of schizophrenics.

   f. No causal link has been established between communication deviance and schizophrenia.

  2. Expressed emotion and schizophrenia

   a. Expressed emotion (EE) concerns the degree to which family members are either critical, overinvolved, or overprotective toward a schizophrenia patient.

   b. High levels of EE increase the likelihood of a relapse.

   c. Symptomatic behavior, particularly negative symptoms, may elicit negative reactions from families.

   d. The effect of EE and symptoms is probably mutual.

 C. The Diathesis-Stress Approach to Schizophrenia

  1. Combinations of ingredients are needed to produce schizophrenia, not just a genetic predisposition or environmental factors.

  2. The *diatheses* is a kind of vulnerability, possibly a genetically transmitted biological predisposition.

   a. May include structural alterations of the brain, cognitive processing deficits, and dysregulation of neurotransmitter systems.

   b. Vulnerability is a *necessary* but not *sufficient* cause of schizophrenia.

  3. The *stress* is some event or circumstance that shapes the developing organism.

   a. Can be biological environment (injury or virus).

   b. Can be psychological environment (negative life events).

   c. Low socioeconomic conditions can contribute.

III. Treatments for Schizophrenia

  • Early treatment was limited to hospital confinement and milieu therapy.

  • Deinstitutionalization in the 1960s.

 A. Antipsychotic Medication for Schizophrenia

  • Phenothiazines, a class of psychotropic medications such as Thorazine, found to have antipsychotic properties: Did not just sedate, but reduced intensity and frequency of hallucinations, delusions, and other psychotic behaviors.

- Other antipsychotic medications, or neuroleptics, were soon developed.

1. Serious limitations of neuroleptics:

    a. Require continuing use.

    b. Major side effects.

    c. Many patients do not improve with use of medications.

2. Effects of neuroleptics

    a. Block postsynaptic dopamine receptors.

    b. Reduce acute symptoms, especially positive symptoms.

    c. Have little effect on negative symptoms (may intensify them).

    d. It is recommended that patients take the medication indefinitely.

3. Side effects of neuroleptic medications

    a. Vary in severity and must be monitored carefully.

    b. Common side effects include muscle tightening, stiffness, reduced emotional spontaneity, and *akathisia* (motor restlessness).

    c. Neuroleptic malignant syndrome is rare, but sometimes fatal.

    d. Tardive dyskinesia (TD) is irreversible and includes involuntary grimacing, tongue thrusting, lip smacking, and eye blinking.

4. Clozapine: New wonder drug?

    a. New neuroleptic with fewer of the common side effects such as TD.

    b. Reduced symptoms in formerly unresponsive patients.

    c. Drawbacks include

       (1) Extremely expensive.

       (2) Can cause agranulocytosis, a potentially fatal blood disease. Weekly blood monitoring essential.

5. Gender and ethnic differences in the use of antipsychotic medication

    a. Women respond better to neuroleptics than men.

    b. Antipsychotics, in general, act similarly on different ethnic groups.

    c. Asians require lower dosages and show side effects at lower dosage levels.

B. Psychosocial Treatments of Schizophrenia

- Interest in psychological interventions has increased in recent years.

1. Psychotherapy for schizophrenia

    a. Various psychotherapeutic approaches have been used with limited success with schizophrenia.

b. Psychotherapy does provide a supportive, safe environment which can be helpful to the schizophrenic patient.

2. Cognitive rehabilitation and cognitive therapy

a. Because cognitive deficits are central to schizophrenia, treatment of cognitive problems has received some attention.

b. The effectiveness of such treatments remains unclear.

C. Combining Psychosocial Treatments and Medications

•   Combining these treatment approaches has resulted in improved functioning and resistance to relapse.

1. Token economies

a. Learning principles were used to reduce dysfunctional behaviors and increase adaptive behaviors.

b. Desirable behaviors reinforced by tokens, which can be exchanged for privileges or candy.

c. A "step" program promotes patients to higher steps for desirable behaviors and gives privileges and money.

d. These programs require tremendous effort on the part of staff to make them work.

2. Social skills training programs

a. Recent behaviorally oriented programs have emphasized social skills and personal competence.

b. Patients taught to correctly identify someone's emotions, maintain eye contact, and speak at an appropriate volume.

c. Proven effective in modifying maladaptive behaviors.

d. Not a cure, but a part of a treatment package.

D. Family Matters: Families of Schizophrenics Need Help, Too

•   Families of schizophrenics experience anger, frustration, blaming attitudes of ill-informed others, inadequate mental health care, and confusion about the disorder itself.

•   There is increased lobbying for better public facilities, more research funding, and improved awareness that mothers are not to blame.

•   Support groups train and help share burdens.

•   Treatment programs address relations with family.

1. Family psychoeducational programs

a. Psychoeducation is a combination of information about the disorder and psychological strategies to help deal with it.

b. This approach must be ongoing if the benefit is to be sustained.

IV. **What Lies Ahead?**

   A. Emergence of integrated diathesis-stress models.

   B. New antipsychotic medications will be developed.

   C. Increasing study of family and psychosocial treatments.

KEY TERMS REVIEW

1. A made-up word, characteristic of the speech of some people with schizophrenia, is called a(n) _____.

2. False beliefs held by individuals with psychotic disorders that have no basis in reality and are not influenced by facts are called _____.

3. A class of psychotropic medications thought to have tranquilizing properties and later found to have antipsychotic properties and thus used to treat schizophrenia and other psychotic disorders are called _____.

4. A legal, not a psychological, term referring to the general concept of psychosis is _____.

5. Highly disorganized speech seen in schizophrenia is called _____.

6. The lack of facial expression and speaking in a monotone or difficulty in controlling emotions or the experience of inappropriate emotions, characteristic of some people with schizophrenia, is called _____.

7. A person's level of functioning before the apparent onset of the disorder is called _____.

8. Reports of sensory perceptions when no stimuli are present are called _____.

9. The principle, used in genetic studies with twin pairs, to compare diagnostic similarity between those with less shared make-up, such as monozygotic twins vs. dizygotic twins, is called _____.

10. Lack of pleasure in any activity is called _____.

11. Fluid-filled spaces in the brain, which are enlarged in some people with mental disorders such as schizophrenia, suggesting brain damage or dysfunction, are called _____.

12. The theory of schizophrenia-inducing mother, proposed by earlier models of the disorder but no longer considered valid, is said to be a(n) _____.

13. Motor restlessness in which the person shows fidgety movements, shifting constantly, is called _____.

14. Unwarranted beliefs that others are making secret reference to oneself are called _____.

15. Belief that others are plotting against and mistreating oneself is called _____.

16. The ability of psychotropic medications to reduce the intensity and frequency of hallucinations, delusions, and other psychotic thinking is called _____.

17. An irreversible, undesirable neurological side effect of antipsychotic medications marked by involuntary facial movements and motor activity in the hands and feet is called _____.

18. Schizophrenia characterized by a predominance of behavioral and emotional deficits, such as lack of motivation, enjoyment, emotional responsiveness, and self-initiated behavior, is called _____.

19. One genetic marker for schizophrenia that is associated with cognitive functioning is _____.

20. A subtype of schizophrenia characterized by a preoccupation with delusions or hallucinations that have an organized theme of persecution is called _____.

21. Visions of persons or objects perceived to be present but which are not, in fact, there are called _____.

22. A method of treatment that combines information about a disorder and the teaching of psychological strategies to help deal with it, as in work with schizophrenic patients and their families, is called _____.

23. A subtype of schizophrenia marked by psychomotor disturbances ranging from rigid posture or stuporous inactivity to excited, excessive activity is called _____.

24. A subtype marked by severe disintegration of personality, with incoherent and unintelligible speech, fragmentary delusions and hallucinations, extreme social impairment, disorganized behavior, and flat or inappropriate affect is called _____.

25. Schizophrenia characterized primarily by the presence of bizarre behaviors and symptoms such as delusions, hallucinations, and thought disorder is called _____.

26. The delusional belief that others may put thoughts in one's head is called _____.

27. A neuroleptic drug that appears to have fewer side effects than other neuroleptics and may be helpful in patients who did not respond to other drugs is called _____.

28. Patterns of abnormal mental or motor functioning arising during pre- or postnatal brain development are called _____.

29. The experience by an individual of hearing voices talking to or about him or her when no such voices exist is called _____.

30. One of several mental disorders characterized by *major* departures from reality, such as delusions and hallucinations, is called _____.

31. A subtype of schizophrenia in which symptoms do not clearly fit into the other categories of schizophrenia are called _____.

32. Reduced blood flow in the frontal regions, suggesting damage—a characteristic of many people with schizophrenia—is called _____.

33. The degree to which family members are either critical of a recently hospitalized schizophrenic person or express overinvolved and overprotective attitudes toward the patient is called _____.

34. The use of words that are associated merely because of the way they sound, not by their meaning, is called _____.

35. The delusional belief that one's thoughts are being broadcast aloud so that others may hear them is called _____.

36. Another term for medication with *antipsychotic* properties is _____.

37. A form of affect disturbance in schizophrenia characterized by lack of emotionality is _____.

38. A subtype defining persons who have had at least one past episode of schizophrenia and continuing evidence of the disorder, but are currently free of the psychotic symptoms are said to have _____.

39. The reduced ability to understand abstractions, observed in some people with schizophrenia or cognitive impairment through their literal interpretations, is called _____.

40. A type of psychosis marked by disturbances of thought, language, and behavior not due to a primary mood disorder or medical condition is called _____.

41. Experiencing touch, taste, or physical stimuli when no such stimuli are present are called _____.

42. Problems in creating and maintaining a shared focus of attention, a pattern observed in some families with a schizophrenic offspring, is called _____.

43. A common speech characteristic of people with schizophrenia, consisting of unusual and idiosyncratic meanings of words or movement from one idea to another in ways that are hard to understand, is called _____.

44. Beliefs that one has special powers or characteristics are called _____.

45. A psychotic experience often associated with depression, beliefs that one is dead, that nothing exists, or that people are only vapors rather than meaningful physical entities, or other delusional beliefs about nonexistence or destruction are called _____.

46. Conversation that is adequate in form but conveys little information because it is stereotyped, abstract, characteristic, or vague is called _____.

FACTUAL MULTIPLE-CHOICE QUESTIONS

1. Psychosis, a broad term for mental disorders, refers to
   a. minor departures from reality.
   b. major departures from reality.
   c. psychodynamic theory.
   d. psychotherapy.

2. False beliefs that have no basis in fact are called
   a. hallucinations.
   b. repressions.
   c. neologisms.
   d. delusions.

3. A patient who reports that his insides are rotting away is experiencing a
   a. hallucination.
   b. loose association.
   c. multiple personality disorder.
   d. bipolar depression.

4. A patient who laughs at news of the death of her mother is demonstrating a disturbance of
   a. psychomotor functioning.
   b. affect.
   c. expressed emotion.
   d. memory.

5. A patient who stands for hours at a time facing the same direction without moving could be diagnosed with
   a. paranoid schizophrenia.
   b. undifferentiated schizophrenia.
   c. disorganized schizophrenia.
   d. catatonic schizophrenia.

6. A neurotransmitter implicated in schizophrenia is
   a. dopamine.
   b. serotonin.
   c. testosterone.
   d. progesterone.

7. Phenothiazines were originally thought to have
   a. tranquilizing properties.
   b. antipsychotic properties.
   c. anticonvulsant properties.
   d. antidepressant properties.

8. The most feared common side effect of long-term use of antipsychotic medications is
   a. akathisia.
   b. tardive dyskinesia.
   c. reduced spontaneous movements.
   d. increased negative symptoms.

9. A successful treatment in schizophrenia using learning theory is called
   a. systematic desensitization.
   b. client-centered therapy.
   c. token economies.
   d. paradoxical intention.

10. Families who learn about schizophrenia and its treatment are engaging in
   a. cognitive therapy.
   b. concrete thinking.
   c. psychoeducation.
   d. group therapy.

CONCEPTUAL MULTIPLE-CHOICE QUESTIONS

1. Schizophrenia is a specific type of disorder marked primarily by disturbances of
   a. mood.
   b. memory.
   c. thought.
   d. medical condition.

2. After Margie watched the television program *Sybil*, she said, "That's the best movie I've ever seen on schizophrenia." Like many other people, she thought schizophrenia was the same as
   a. dissociative identity disorder.
   b. bipolar disorder.
   c. amnesia.
   d. dementia praecox.

3. Mr. Smith has been hospitalized with chronic schizophrenia for over twenty years. At age sixty-four he has shown increasing signs of improvement. An explanation for this improvement might be
   a. reduction in dopamine function.
   b. reduction in male hormones.
   c. death of members of his family.
   d. long-term confinement in a mental institution.

4. Juan's brother was diagnosed with schizophrenia and Juan has just gone through a painful divorce. His psychiatrist feels he is in danger of schizophrenia. She subscribes to which theory of causation?
   a. diathesis-stress
   b. schizophrenogenic mother
   c. excess dopamine
   d. hypofrontality

5. Michael is being treated for schizophrenia. His MRI revealed ventricular enlargement. His symptoms might be
   a. social withdrawal and isolation.
   b. waxy flexibility.
   c. hallucinations and delusions.
   d. revolving around a plot.

6. After nine months at home Rhonda stopped her medication and her group therapy. Her symptoms reappeared and she had to be rehospitalized for schizophrenia. This highlights that
   a. none of the treatments for schizophrenia are effective.
   b. women are more likely to suffer relapse.
   c. Rhonda should not have been released until her recovery was complete.
   d. medication and psychosocial treatments must be ongoing.

7. Dr. Benjamin, an expert in research on schizophrenia, is convinced that further research will discover
   a. that the disorder is completely biologically determined.
   b. that schizophrenia is one discrete disorder.
   c. that psychosocial treatments are ineffective.
   d. new antipsychotic drugs.

8. Jason is assessed by a mental health worker and is found to have serious problems with his thought, language, and behavior. The worker is uncertain whether to assign Jason a schizophrenic diagnosis or a dissociative identity disorder diagnosis. What characteristic would probably make the diagnostician give Jason a schizophrenic diagnosis rather than a dissociative identity disorder diagnosis?
   a. Jason shows signs of auditory hallucinations.
   b. Jason cannot remember his name or information about his past life circumstances.
   c. Jason shows different personalities, and these personalities do not appear to recognize each other.
   d. Jason is homeless and consumes large quantities of alcohol.

9. A primary distinction between the terms *psychosis* and *insanity* is that insanity
   a. is the most serious disturbance listed in the DSM-IV.
   b. is a mental disorder diagnosis marked by disturbances in thought, language, and behavior.
   c. can be diagnosed only by a psychologist after certification by a psychiatrist.
   d. is a legal term.

10. Which of the following illustrates the "stress" part of the diathesis-stress model?
   a. eye movement dysfunction
   b. phenothiazines
   c. an infant's exposure to influenza virus while the mother is pregnant
   d. enlarged ventricles

APPLICATION MULTIPLE-CHOICE QUESTIONS

1. Ben told Dr. Katzman that he had been reading newspapers and magazines and was convinced that all the stories were about him. Dr. Katzman accurately described Ben's comments as
   a. delusions of grandeur.
   b. thought broadcasting.
   c. delusions of reference.
   d. persecution delusions.

2. Dr. Miller was right to be concerned about Jonathan's diagnosis of negative-symptom schizophrenia because of Jonathan's
   a. resulting poor overall prognosis.
   b. hallucinations.
   c. delusions.
   d. good adjustment before the onset of symptoms.

3. Mrs. Miller was surprised to learn that her adolescent daughter was diagnosed with schizophrenia because she knew that the disorder was
   a. more often found in men.
   b. strictly genetically caused and there was no history of the disorder in her family.
   c. usually found in women at a later age of onset.
   d. usually found in lower socioeconomic African Americans.

4. Dr. Choe continued to ask questions about her new patient's family even though she already knew that the patient's mother had schizophrenia because
   a. genetic transmission of schizophrenia has not been studied extensively.
   b. quality of family life may affect the outcome of underlying genetic predisposition.
   c. of the strong evidence of the schizophrenogenic mother theory.
   d. of the lack of any evidence to support genetic transmission of the disorder.

5. Marion's performance on the Attentional Deviance Index was weak, which might indicate
   a. the presence of a cognitive marker for schizophrenia.
   b. early onset schizophrenia.
   c. paranoid schizophrenia.
   d. delusions of reference.

6. When William returned home from the mental hospital he encountered much hostility and negativity from his family because of the stress his illness had created. His psychiatrist called their reaction
   a. a brief psychotic reaction.
   b. cognitive distortion.
   c. double-bind communication.
   d. expressed emotion.

7. Marsha had developed severe grimacing and facial tics after several years in the state mental hospital. These symptoms are the result of
   a. electroconvulsive therapy.
   b. clozapine.
   c. benztropine.
   d. phenothiazine.

8. Todd improved his personal hygiene regimen so much that he was given three television passes for the weekend. This approach to therapy is based on
   a. learning and conditioning principles.
   b. cognitive therapy.
   c. client-centered therapy.
   d. psychoanalysis.

9. Jackie has been prescribed a neuroleptic drug to help control her hallucinations. What did her doctor tell Jackie about taking neuroleptic drugs?
   a. The drugs will make her sleepy because they work primarily on the serotonin neurotransmitter system.
   b. Neuroleptics have few side effects and can be taken for years without any significant problems.
   c. She should have regular medical checkups because of potential toxicity from the drug.
   d. These drugs have been researched for many years and have minimal side effects.

ANSWER KEY: KEY TERMS REVIEW

1. neologism (262)
2. delusions (262)
3. phenothiazines (285)
4. insanity (260)
5. word salad (262)
6. affect disturbance (264)
7. premorbid adjustment (272)
8. hallucinations (263)
9. concordance (273)
10. anhedonia (265)
11. ventricles (275)
12. schizophrenogenic mother (281)

13. akathisia (287)
14. delusions of reference (262)
15. persecution delusions (262)
16. antipsychotic properties (285)
17. tardive dyskinesia (287)
18. negative-symptom schizophrenia (267)
19. eye movement dysfunction (274)
20. paranoid schizophrenia (266)
21. visual hallucinations (263)
22. psychoeducation (292)
23. catatonic schizophrenia (265)
24. disorganized schizophrenia (267)
25. positive-symptom schizophrenia (267)
26. thought insertion (262)
27. clozapine (287)
28. neurodevelopmental abnormalities (278)
29. auditory hallucinations (263)
30. psychosis (260)

31. undifferentiated schizophrenia (267)
32. hypofrontality (276)
33. expressed emotion (EE) (282)
34. clang association (262)
35. thought broadcasting (262)
36. neuroleptic (286)
37. flat affect (264)
38. residual schizophrenia (267)
39. concrete thinking (262)
40. schizophrenia (260)
41. tactile, taste, and somatic hallucinations (263)
42. communication deviance (CD) (282)
43. loose associations (262)
44. delusions of grandeur (262)
45. nihilistic delusions (262)
46. poverty of speech (262)

ANSWER KEY: FACTUAL MULTIPLE-CHOICE QUESTIONS

1. *b. major departures from reality (p. 260)
   a. Psychosis can be any mental disorder where there is a major departure from reality.
   c. Psychodynamic theory relates to cause and treatment of mental disorders.
   d. Psychotherapy deals with the treatment of mental disorders.

2. *d. delusions (p. 262)
   a. Hallucinations are reports of sensory perception when no stimuli are present.
   b. Repressions are thoughts pushed out of consciousness as a defense of the ego.
   c. Neologisms are the made-up words of some schizophrenics.

3. *a. hallucination (p. 263)
   b. Loose association is an idiosyncratic speech pattern not related to unrealistic perceptions.
   c. Multiple personality disorder involves the presence of several distinct personalities in the same person.
   d. Bipolar depression is characterized by alternating bouts of depression and mania.

4. *b. affect (p. 264)
   a. Psychomotor dysfunction, characteristic of catatonic schizophrenia, is unrelated to inappropriate communication.
   c. Expressed emotion is a critical or overinvolved or overprotective attitude toward a schizophrenic individual by family members.
   d. The patient is not demonstrating a disturbance of memory.

5. *d. catatonic schizophrenia (p. 265)
   a. Paranoid schizophrenia is characterized by delusions of persecution, and is unrelated to the catatonic state.
   b. Undifferentiated schizophrenia is given as a diagnosis when the symptoms do not fit any other type of the disorder and is not characterized by physical rigidity.
   c. Disorganized schizophrenia is marked by severe personality disintegration and not by lack of movement.

6. *a. dopamine (p. 280)
   b. Serotonin is a factor in the causation of depression, not schizophrenia.
   c. Testosterone is the male hormone responsible for sexual desire and is not associated with schizophrenia.
   d. Progesterone is the hormone associated with female characteristics.

7. *a. tranquilizing properties (p. 285)
   b. It was not until after their use as tranquilizers that their antipsychotic effects were discovered.
   c. They did not demonstrate any autoconvulsant effects.
   d. They did not demonstrate any antidepressant effects.

8. *b. tardive dyskinesia (p. 287)
   a. Akathisia is a side effect of fidgety movements and constant shifting, but is not irreversible as is tardive dyskinesia.
   c. Reduced spontaneous movements are side effects, but not as problematic as TD.
   d. Increased negative symptoms may be a side effect, but are ameliorated with lower dosages.

9. *c. token economies (p. 290)
   a. Systematic desensitization is used to treat phobias, not schizophrenia.
   b. Client-centered was proven to be relatively ineffective in treating schizophrenics.
   d. Paradoxical intention is used to treat obsessive-compulsive disorder, not schizophrenia.

10. *c. psychoeducation (p. 292)
    a. Cognitive therapy is used to treat schizophrenia directly.
    b. Concrete thinking is a reduced ability to understand abstractions observed in some schizophrenic patients and is unrelated to helping families cope with schizophrenia.
    d. Group therapy is aimed at improving a patient's behavior through a therapeutic experience; psychoeducation helps by educating the families.

ANSWER KEY: CONCEPTUAL MULTIPLE-CHOICE QUESTIONS

1. *c. thought (pp. 261–262)
   a. The definition of schizophrenia specifically excludes primary mood disorder as cause of the disturbed behaviors.
   b. Schizophrenia is a disturbance of thought, language, and behavior, not memory.
   d. Medical condition is also excluded as a causation of schizophrenic behaviors.

2. *a. dissociative identity disorder (p. 260)
   b. Bipolar disorder involves alternating episodes of mania and depression and would not be mistaken for schizophrenia in this example.
   c. Schizophrenia does not involve problems of memory of the amnesia-type.
   d. Dementia praecox, the early name for schizophrenia, is not in common use.

3. *a. reduction in dopamine function (p. 271)
   b. Male hormones do not play a role in schizophrenia.
   c. Since he has been hospitalized for so long the loss of support of family members would be less influential.
   d. Long-term hospitalization would probably worsen symptoms rather than cause improvement.

4. *a. Diathesis-stress (p. 284)
   b. The mother is not referred to here and the schizophrenogenic mother theory has been discounted.
   c. Excess dopamine is one of the neurological explanations of schizophrenia and would not be directly related to Juan's current distress.
   d. Hypofrontality is reduced blood flow to the frontal regions of the brain and is associated with biological rather than psychological causation.

5. *a. social withdrawal and isolation (p. 275)
   b. Waxy flexibility is a positive symptom not associated with ventricular enlargement, which causes negative symptoms.
   c. Hallucinations and delusions are positive symptoms less apt to be experienced with ventricular enlargement.
   d. Paranoid schizophrenia is a positive type not often associated with ventricular enlargement.

6. *d. medication and psychosocial treatments must be ongoing (p. 287)
   a. Many of the treatments for schizophrenia are effective, but they cannot be effective when they are refused.
   b. Women are less likely to suffer relapse.
   c. Schizophrenics are rarely completely cured, but must learn to live with the level of functioning they are able to attain and must stay on their therapeutic maintenance.

7. *d. new antipsychotic drugs (pp. 292–293)
   a. Research has already shown that the diathesis-stress model best explains the etiology of the disorder.
   b. Evidence continues to appear that schizophrenia is a heterogeneous disorder with many causes and forms.
   c. Psychosocial treatments have been proven effective, particularly in combination with medication.

8. *a. Jason shows signs of auditory hallucinations. (p. 260)
   b. Dissociative amnesia is one of the dissociative disorders, not a schizophrenic disorder.
   c. Dissociative identity disorder and schizophrenia are not the same.
   d. About 13 percent of homeless people are schizophrenic, and there exists comorbidity with substance use disorders; however, this is not the primary defining feature of schizophrenia.

9. *d. is a legal term. (p. 260)
   a. Insanity is not listed in the DSM-IV because it is a legal, not a psychiatric, term.
   b. Insanity is not a diagnostic category.
   c. Insanity is a legal determination made by the courts.

10. *c. an infant's exposure to influenza virus while the mother is pregnant. (p. 278)
    a. Eye movement dysfunction is a genetic marker for schizophrenia.
    b. Phenothiazines are a class of antipsychotic drugs.
    d. Enlarged ventricles are nonspecific; they appear in the brains of persons with other disorders and may be due to either brain injury or damage or a failure of the brain to mature and develop normally.

ANSWER KEY: APPLICATION MULTIPLE-CHOICE QUESTIONS

1. *c. delusions of reference (p. 262)
   a. Delusions of grandeur are beliefs that one has special powers or characteristics and are unrelated to what others say.
   b. Thought broadcasting is the belief that others can hear your thoughts, not that they are referring to you.
   d. Persecution delusions are beliefs that others are plotting against one.

2. *a. resulting poor overall prognosis (pp. 267–268)
   b. Overt symptoms like hallucinations are associated with positive-symptom schizophrenia and tend to reflect a better prognosis than negative-symptom schizophrenia.
   c. Delusions are also associated with positive-symptom schizophrenia.
   d. The doctor would have been relieved, not concerned, if Jonathan had had a good premorbid adjustment.

3. *c. usually found in women at a later age of onset (pp. 269–270)
   a. The prevalence of schizophrenia is about the same for men and women.
   b. Studies have shown that environmental as well as genetic factors are implicated in the development of schizophrenia.
   d. Schizophrenia is found in all social classes, with some weight toward the stressors of socioeconomic struggle.

4. *b. quality of family life may affect the outcome of underlying genetic predisposition (p. 275)
   a. Genetic transmission of schizophrenia has been studied extensively.
   c. The schizophrenogenic mother theory has been largely debunked.
   d. There is much evidence to support the genetic transmission theory, but it doesn't account for all the variability of disease etiology.

5. *a. the presence of a cognitive marker for schizophrenia (pp. 276–278)
   b. Women ordinarily have later onset schizophrenia.
   c. Attentional Deviance does not indicate what type of schizophrenia might develop.
   d. Delusions of reference are related to paranoid schizophrenia, not attention span.

6. *d. expressed emotion (p. 282)
   a. The family's reaction would be considered normal, not psychotic.
   b. Their reaction was probably an accurate evaluation of the stress of having a schizophrenic in the family and not a distortion.
   c. Double-bind communication is thought to play a role in the development of the disorder and is usually expressed, at least in part, positively.

7. *d. phenothiazine (p. 287)
   a. ECT may cause short-term memory loss but not involuntary muscle spasms.
   b. Clozapine has relatively few side effects, except agranulocytosis, a potentially fatal blood disorder.
   c. Benztropine is a drug used to control the side effects of the neuroleptics. It doesn't have an effect on TD.

8. *a. learning and conditioning principles (p. 290)
   b. Cognitive therapy deals with distortions of thought.
   c. Client-centered therapy is an insight-based psychotherapy.
   d. Psychoanalysis is based on the principles of psychodynamics.

9. *c. She should have regular medical checkups because of potential toxicity from the drug. (pp. 287–288)
   a. These drugs work on the dopamine neurotransmitter systems.
   b. Side effects may be seen with some neuroleptic drugs, including nonreversible neurological problems.
   d. Tardive dyskinesia (TD) is estimated to affect 20 percent of patients on neuroleptics after six months to one year.

CHAPTER 10

Psychophysiological Disorders and Behavioral Medicine

LEARNING OBJECTIVES

1. Define psychophysiological disorders. (p. 298)

2. Describe the role psychological factors play in causing physical symptoms and actual tissue damage. (pp. 298–300)

3. Explain the difference in approach to these disorders taken by the DSM-IV. (pp. 298–300)

4. Describe how Western medicine and psychology define the relationship between mind and body. (pp. 298–299)

5. Describe different approaches to the relationship between mind and body. (p. 299)

6. Discuss the development of behavioral medicine. (p. 299)

7. Discuss the emergence of health psychology from the ongoing study of the relationship between illness and behavior. (p. 299)

8. Explain the psychophysiologic model and the recognition of stressors as contributory to physical illness. (pp. 299–300)

9. Describe the effect of constitutional vulnerability and stress. (pp. 299–300)

10. Define stress according to the stimulus, response, and transactional definitions. (pp. 300–301)

11. Discuss different individual coping responses to stress. (p. 301)

12. Discuss the measurement of life changes in terms of the degree of change or stress in one's life. (p. 301)

13. Describe the importance of daily hassles as sources of stress. (pp. 301–302)

14. Discuss the importance of cognitive appraisal of events which might cause stress. (p. 302)

15. Describe how the sympathetic nervous system stimulates the fight-or-flight response. (pp. 302–303)

16. Describe the response to stress called the general adaptation syndrome. (p. 303)

17. Discuss Schwartz's disregulation model. (p. 304)

18. Describe emotion-focused coping as part of the cognitive and emotional responses to stress. (p. 305)

19. Discuss the importance of social support as a protection against stress reactions. (pp. 305–306)

20. Describe procedures for reducing stress. (pp. 306–307)

21. Discuss the effect of stress on coronary heart disease (CHD). (pp. 307–309)

22. Discuss the relationship among personality, family interactional style, and CHD. (pp. 309–313)

23. Describe methods of identifying and modifying Type A behavior. (pp. 309–310)

24. Discuss factors that contribute to essential hypertension. (pp. 313–314)

25. Discuss reasons that may account for the differences between African Americans and white Americans regarding hypertension. (pp. 315–317)

26. Describe the functioning of the immune system and psychoneuroimmunology. (pp. 317–319)

27. Discuss the effect of stress on the immune system and on cancer. (pp. 319–321)

28. Discuss other stress-related disorders, such as ulcers and headaches. (pp. 321–325)

29. Describe the "biopsychosocial audit." (pp. 326–327)

30. Describe the health-beliefs model of the cognitive approach to health behavior. (pp. 326–327)

CHAPTER OUTLINE

I. Mind, Body, and Stress

- Psychophysiological disorders are medical conditions, once referred to as psychosomatic, influenced by stress.

- Tissue damage occurs in these disorders.

A. Contemporary Psychophysiological Models

1. Modern Western medicine assumed the mind and body were separate.

2. In the 1940s and 1950s a psychoanalytic approach to psychosomatic illness became popular.

3. Behavioral factors emerged in the 1970s as important for the prevention, diagnosis, and treatment of disease.

4. Behavioral medicine, integrating behavioral and biomedical science and applying this knowledge to disease, was created.

5. Health psychology, the effort to understand the relationship between risky behaviors and illness, as well as between stress, cognitive factors, and susceptibility to disease, developed.

6. The psychophysiologic model describes the interaction of stressors with constitutional vulnerability and cognitive factors to produce disorders.

B. What Is Stress?

1. Stimulus definition: a demand or threat.

2. Response definition: the organism's reaction to a threat or demand.

3. Transactional definition: a particular relationship between the individual and the situation.

4. Stress occurs when an individual perceives an imbalance between demand and the individual's ability to meet that demand.

5. Coping responses have different effects on health.

C. What's Normal? Is Your Life Dangerously Stressful?

1. The Social Readjustment Rating Scale measures stress by rating the Life Change Units (LCUs) a person has experienced.

2. Stressful events influence unhealthful behaviors.

3. The scale now includes time proximity and specific events for special populations.

4. Daily hassles, the "little things" that go wrong, can be a source of stress.

5. Cognitive appraisal of the environment is also an important factor on the effect of stress.

D. Physiological Arousal and Stress

1. The sympathetic nervous system (SNS) produces the fight-or-flight response.

2. A wide range of physiological responses are triggered by the SNS response to stress: epinephrine, norepinephrine, corticosteroids, and endorphins are released into the bloodstream.

3. The parasympathetic nervous system (PNS) calms the arousal of the SNS.

4. Selye proposed a three-stage set of responses to stress, the general adaptation syndrome (GAS): (1) alarm reaction, (2) resistance, and (3) exhaustion.

5. Another model is Schwartz's disregulation model: When proper feedback is disrupted without corrective action, physical dysfunction may follow.

6. Stress affects the body as well as the mind.

E. Moderators of the Stress Response

• Interaction among types of stressors, cognitive appraisals of stressors, and the pattern of stress responses.

1. Coping response

   a. Active coping is an effort to escape or avoid exposure to the stressor.

   b. Passive coping is toleration of stress.

   c.   Problem-focused coping involves attempts to escape, control, or avoid the threatening event.

   d.   Response-focused coping involves efforts to minimize the effects of an event.

2.   Cognitive and emotional responses

   a.   Cognitive processing or appraisal of an event helps determine its stressfulness.

   b.   Events perceived as out of control produce higher stress.

   c.   Emotion-focused coping attempts to regulate the emotional consequences of a stressful event.

3.   Social support

   a.   Social support networks can buffer or protect against the health-damaging effects of stress.

   b.   Social networks must be emotionally supportive.

4.   Individual differences

   a.   Reactions to stress vary by gender (women have a more ruminative response style).

   b.   May be individual differences in autonomic reactivity.

F.   Procedures for Reducing Stress

   a.   Relaxation training, meditation, biofeedback, and cognitive restructuring are some techniques for reducing stress.

   b.   Stress management includes self-monitoring and time management.

II.   Cardiovascular Diseases

A.   Coronary Heart Disease (CHD)

   •   CHD is caused by reduced blood flow to the heart.

   •   CHD refers to (1) angina pectoris, (2) myocardial infarction, and (3) sudden coronary death.

   •   Coronary atherosclerosis (CHD) is the narrowing of the arteries by fatty deposits on the walls.

   •   CHD is more common among men, older people, Caucasians, Africans, smokers, and those with high blood pressure and high LDL cholesterol.

1.   Stress and CHD

   a.   Animal studies suggest that stress can produce CHD.

   b.   Links between significant job changes, bereavement, and CHD in humans.

2.   Personality and CHD: The Type A pattern

   a.   The Type A pattern is characterized by competitiveness, impatience, overcommitment to work, hostility, and loud rapid speech.

b. Type B is characterized by a relatively relaxed and easygoing attitude.

c. Type A persons display greater physiological reactivity to the environment that could produce greater vulnerability to CHD.

d. Cynical hostility is the most damaging component of the Type A pattern.

e. The causal relationship among behavior, negative emotional states, and CHD is uncertain.

3. Focus on the family: Can your family cause Type A behavior?

a. Characteristics of wives affect CHD risk for Type A men: highly educated, active, and dominant wives increase men's CHD risk.

b. Married persons who are both Type A produce heightened hostile dominance behaviors.

c. Children may be influenced by Type A parents.

4. Are you a Type A?

a. Self-diagnosis is frequently inaccurate.

b. The best diagnostic technique is the personal interview, where behaviors such as impatience can be observed.

5. Reducing risk for CHD: Modifying the Type A pattern

a. Stress management programs combining behavior skills training and cognitive restructuring have shown promise for men.

b. No evidence for women or non-whites.

B. Essential Hypertension

- Blood pressure (BP), or hypertension, is the force with which blood presses against the artery walls.

- Untreated high blood pressure can lead to heart disease or stroke.

- 35 million Americans have high blood pressure.

- Only 10 to 15 percent of hypertension cases are due to disease.

- The other cases are of unknown origin and are referred to as essential hypertension.

1. Predisposing factors in hypertension

a. A clear-cut biological cause has not been identified.

b. Biological and environmental factors influence hypertension.

2. Psychological factors in hypertension

a. Social and occupational stress can contribute to hypertension.

b. Suppressed anger may cause physiological consequences related to essential hypertension.

3. Links between stress and hypertension

   a. Stressors produce transient high blood pressure.

   b. Permanent alteration of physiological factors controlling BP can occur through peripheral resistance in the capillaries and arterioles.

   c. Stress may alter organ functioning such as kidney output, thereby increasing BP.

4. Focus on research: Are there racial differences in essential hypertension?

   a. Higher incidence of essential hypertension in Africans than in white populations is confirmed by epidemiological studies.

   b. Biologically, blacks are more susceptible to the negative effects of sodium.

   c. Behavior patterns such as "John Henryism," the self-perception that an individual can succeed through hard work and determination may contribute to hypertension.

   d. Low socioeconomic status and living in high-stress urban neighborhoods as well as suppressed hostility may contribute to higher rates of BP for blacks.

   e. These findings support the diathesis-stress model.

5. Treating hypertension

   a. Medication is the primary treatment.

   b. Stress management, exercise, low sodium diets, weight loss, improved marital communication also help control high BP.

III. Stress and the Immune System: Cancer and the Common Cold

   • The immune system is the body's defense against microbial invasion.

   • Psychoneuroimmunology is the study of psychological influences on the immune system.

   • Research has demonstrated the possibility of decreased immunological efficiency with increased stress.

   A. An Overview of the Immune System: The immune system is a complex interaction among lymphocytes, T-cells, and killer cells that attack invading antigens to protect the organism.

   B. The Effects of Stress on Immune Function

      1. A variety of stressors reduce immune functioning and increase risk for illness.

      2. The psychological energy needed to adjust to stressful events may activate parts of the brain that affect immune functioning.

      3. There is evidence that stress reduction can improve immune functioning.

   C. Stress and Cancer

      1. Cancer is a dysfunction of the controls for growth and reproduction within the cells.

2. Stress may impair the functioning of the cells of the immune system which attack and control cancerous cells.

3. Stress may also affect behaviors such as smoking and drinking as well as the body's ability to repair DNA damage, thus increasing the likelihood of cancer.

D. Psychological Interventions for Cancer Patients: Psychological interventions have been shown to extend survival times and alter risk behaviors.

IV. Other Stress-Related Disorders

A. Ulcers

1. Peptic ulcers, disruptions of the lining of the stomach or duodenum resulting from excess pepsin and acid cause pain and bleeding.

2. Causal influences of ulcers

a. Stress may be implicated in the oversecretion of stomach acid.

b. Animal studies have shown that control over and predictability of stressors provide some protection against developing ulcers.

c. Genetics: Some people have an inherited biological vulnerability (see diathesis-stress model).

3. Treatment for ulcers

a. Psychological treatment is usually directed toward reducing stress.

b. Medication.

B. Headaches

1. Causal influences of headaches

a. Tension headaches include an ache or sensation of tightness or pressure in the neck or back of the head.

b. Migraine headaches typically involve pain on one side of the head of a throbbing or pulsing type.

c. Both types are associated with muscular and vascular stress responses.

d. Cognitive factors may influence the onset and treatment of headaches.

2. Treatments for headaches

a. Medications and psychological interventions can be effective.

b. Relaxation training and biofeedback have proven to be effective.

V. Targeting Health-Related Behavior

A. Targets for Assessment

1. The physical disorders discussed in this chapter are influenced by psychological forces, but are not psychological abnormalities.

2. A complete health assessment includes a "biopsychosocial audit" to assess psychological and social assets and liabilities.

B.   Health-Behavior Relationships

1.   Perceiving one's locus of control as internal rather than external facilitates health intervention.

2.   Perceptions of threat and behavioral efficacy influence a person's health behavior.

3.   The health-beliefs model predicts that health protective behaviors occur when the individual recognizes a health risk and believes that a specific behavior will reduce that risk.

VI.   What Lies Ahead?

A.   Women's health issues will receive equal time with men's.

B.   Psychological aspects of AIDS will be expanded both for prevention and treatment.

C.   Interest will continue in the roles of stress, social support, and individual appraisals of situations and their interaction with medical health.

KEY TERMS REVIEW

1.   The body's defense against infections is called the _____.

2.   The disease causing CHD, in which the arteries carrying blood to the heart muscle are narrowed by fatty deposits in their walls, is called _____.

3.   High blood pressure that is not due to a known biological cause is called _____.

4.   Responding to stress by exerting an effort to minimize exposure to the stressor is called _____.

5.   Referring to psychological origins of physical symptoms is called _____.

6.   An interdisciplinary field concerned with the integration of behavioral and biomedical science relevant to health and illness and the application of this knowledge for prevention, diagnosis, and treatment is called _____.

7.   The aggregate of the specific contributions of psychology to the promotion and maintenance of health, the prevention and treatment of illness, and an understanding of the cause and correlates of health and related behaviors is called _____.

8.   A more relaxed and easygoing as well as less competitive pattern of behavior than the Type A pattern is called _____.

9.   Defining stress in terms of an organism's reaction to the environmental threat or demand is called the _____.

10.   Measuring stress in terms of the accumulation of little things that can go wrong and cause distress is called _____.

11.   Responding to stress by tolerating it is called _____.

12.   The force with which the blood presses against artery walls is called _____.

13. Physical conditions in which tissue damage has occurred and psychological factors are believed to play a role in the onset or exacerbation of the physical condition are called _____.

14. A pattern of behavior characterized by hard-driving competitiveness, impatience, easily provoked hostility, overcommitment to work, and a loud, rapid speaking style is called _____.

15. A stronger or more frequent fight-or-flight response, associated with people who show the Type A pattern of personality, is called _____.

16. The first stage of the GAS, another term for fight-or-flight response, is _____.

17. Responding to stress by directing efforts toward regulating the emotional consequences of the stressful event is called _____.

18. Defining stress not in terms of the environmental stimuli or the organism's response but in the particular relationship that exists between the individual and the situation is called the _____.

19. A disease caused by decreased blood flow to the heart and associated with angina pectoris (chest pain), myocardial infarction (death of the heart muscle from lack of oxygen), and sudden coronary death (death caused by interruption in the heart's blood-pumping) is called _____.

20. Headache pain that is typically experienced on one side of the head, described as "throbbing" or "pulsing," and often associated with nausea and even vomiting is called _____.

21. The third stage of the GAS, in which the organism's physiological resources to contend with stress are depleted and the organism may show signs of physical deterioration or illness, is called _____.

22. Discomfort that begins as an ache or sensation of tightness in the neck or back of the head and worsens and spreads until it is a dull, steady pain on both sides of the head is called a(n) _____.

23. Any of more than one hundred diseases caused by a dysfunction of the controls for growth and reproduction within cells is called _____.

24. Defining stress in terms of an external event or situation that represents a demand or threat is called _____.

25. Responding to stress characterized by escaping, avoiding, or controlling the threatening event itself is called _____.

26. Responses made to manage stress are called _____.

27. The part of the autonomic nervous system that mediates the body's response to stress, speeding up the heart rate, increasing blood pressure, and generally preparing for action, is the _____.

28. The interaction of environmental, psychological, and physical domains in the production of illness is called the _____.

29. The bodily reactions to a stressful situation, controlled by the sympathetic system, consisting of increased heart rate, greater blood flow, and increased oxygen supply to the major muscles and the release of glucose and hormones into the bloodstream, is called the _____.

30. The second stage of the GAS, in which the organism maintains and enhances the bodily responses mobilized in the first phase, is called _____.

31. The study of psychological influences on the immune system is called _____.

32. A view of stress stating that when proper feedback is disrupted and a corrective action to return to normal functioning does not occur, physical dysfunction may result is called the _____.

33. Environmental challenges, threats, or demands are called _____.

34. A cognitive approach to health behavior suggesting that the practice of health behaviors is determined by the degree to which the individual perceives a personal health threat and the perception that a particular behavior will reduce the threat is called the _____.

35. The feeling of unease that occurs when an important environmental demand is seen by the individual as taxing or exceeding his or her ability to meet that demand is called _____.

36. Responding to stress by dealing with the causes and consequences of the negative event is called _____.

37. A three-stage set of physiological reactions to stress is called the _____.

FACTUAL MULTIPLE-CHOICE QUESTIONS

1. Psychophysiological disorders were at one time called
   a. somatoform.
   b. psychosomatic.
   c. psychoanalytic.
   d. psychodynamic.

2. The way a person appraises a stressor and takes action to alter the situation or change its effect is called a
   a. diathesis-stress model.
   b. life change unit.
   c. transactional definition.
   d. coping response.

3. Under stress, the sympathetic nervous system releases epinephrine into the bloodstream. This powerful hormone is also known as
   a. adrenaline.
   b. HPA.
   c. endorphin.
   d. corticosteroid.

4. A technique that allows a person to monitor changes in his or her levels of physiological arousal in order to alter it is called
   a. cognitive restructuring.
   b. biofeedback.
   c. systematic desensitization.
   d. the autonomic nervous system.

5. Research into Type A behavior has determined that the most dangerous type of negative emotional state for risk of CHD is
    a. depression.
    b. mania.
    c. obsessive-compulsive disorder.
    d. cynical hostility.

6. The reason cancer cells are not controlled by normal bodily processes is
    a. due almost entirely to genetics.
    b. related to gender.
    c. related to race.
    d. not yet understood.

7. Psychological interventions for patients with cancer are intended to
    a. enhance the quality of life.
    b. reverse the progress of the disease.
    c. assist with diagnosis.
    d. prevent patients from discovering the true extent of their illness.

8. Recent findings suggest that ulcers may be caused by
    a. smoking.
    b. excessive secretion of mucus.
    c. a bacterial process.
    d. depression.

9. A headache experienced on one side of the head is described as a
    a. tension headache.
    b. migraine headache.
    c. muscular headache.
    d. pressure headache.

10. It would be advisable for a psychologist involved in health care to administer a
    a. personality inventory.
    b. series of intelligence tests.
    c. biopsychosocial audit.
    d. TAT.

CONCEPTUAL MULTIPLE-CHOICE QUESTIONS

1. Essential hypertension is caused by
    a. some form of disease.
    b. unknown factors.
    c. hypertension medication.
    d. amount of dietary sodium.

2. Persons who believe that illness is something that happens to them are said to have
    a. an internal locus of control.
    b. an external locus of control.
    c. paranoid schizophrenia.
    d. obsessive-compulsive disorder.

3. Dr. Miller heads a program that helps patients develop psychological coping resources in order to meet excessive environmental demands. She subscribes to the
   a. medical model.
   b. psychophysiologic model.
   c. somatic weakness model.
   d. psychodynamic model.

4. Ron's reaction to problems at the office was to fly into a rage and ceaselessly plan how to get back at those who had caused the problem. His likelihood of cardiac heart disease as a result of his response patterns is
   a. less than normal.
   b. about the same as normal.
   c. greater than normal.
   d. unrelated to his response patterns.

5. Jeanne had formed her own company. She was a hard-driving worker who had contempt for most of her clients and spent much of her time talking about how she hated having to be nice to them for the business. Jeanne's therapist is concerned about her health because of Jeanne's
   a. paranoia.
   b. obsessive-compulsive tendencies.
   c. Type B personality.
   d. cynical hostility.

6. Terry believed that anger should never be shown but should be kept inside to avoid unpleasant displays. His physician is concerned because of the link between suppressed anger and
   a. the fight-or-flight response.
   b. hypertension.
   c. somatizing disorders.
   d. Type B personality.

7. Zack is the head Resident Adviser in the freshman dormitory. During final exams he observed that the number of students contracting colds and flu rises dramatically. He is seeing an example of
   a. Type A personality.
   b. Type B personality.
   c. the effect of late night studying.
   d. the effect of stress on the immune system.

8. Mark's job was dependent on factors that he could not control, such as waiting for potential clients to return his calls. He responded badly to the lack of control in his job and went to his physician, who told him that this set of circumstances might increase his risk for
   a. migraine headaches.
   b. cancer.
   c. peptic ulcers.
   d. tension headaches.

9. One difference between problem-focused coping and response-focused coping is that
   a. problem-focused coping addresses the problem directly and actively.
   b. problem-focused coping minimizes the effects of the event.
   c. response-focused coping is aimed at escaping or avoiding the threatening event.
   d. response-focused coping occurs following the occurrence of the stressful event, while problem-focused coping attempts to prevent the event from occurring.

10. The relationship between stress and the development of various psychophysiological disorders is best understood by understanding the effect of stress on
    a. HPA dysregulation.
    b. passive coping.
    c. the immune system.
    d. somatization disorders.

APPLICATION MULTIPLE-CHOICE QUESTIONS

1. John's wife died after a brief, unexpected illness. He understands the process that led to his wife's illness and death and realizes he did everything possible to help her. His psychiatrist feels John has
    a. low risk of developing stress-related health problems.
    b. an unknown risk of developing stress-related health problems.
    c. high risk of developing stress-related health problems.
    d. no chance of avoiding stress-related health problems.

2. Jane's day had gone badly, with one minor mishap after another. She felt close to a breaking point even though these stressful events were not catastrophic. Her therapist described her experiences under the label
    a. compulsions.
    b. manic depression.
    c. panic attack.
    d. daily hassles.

3. On the freeway driving home Jonathan was cut off by a large truck. His physical reaction of increased heart rate and hormones pouring into his bloodstream could be described as
    a. a fight-or-flight response.
    b. panic reaction.
    c. agoraphobia.
    d. misappraisal.

4. Barbara's new job was not going well. She did not get along well with her new boss and had become ill and despondent as a result of the continual confrontations. In which phase of the GAS was she?
    a. alarm reaction
    b. resistance
    c. denial
    d. exhaustion

5. Jeremy was scheduled to make a major presentation at his company's annual conference. In order to reduce his stress he carefully wrote and rewrote the speech and rehearsed constantly. His response is
    a. passive coping.
    b. problem-focused coping.
    c. response-focused coping.
    d. emotion-focused coping.

6. Dr. Karlsberg was concerned that the death of Amy's husband would result in serious physical and emotional problems for her because her family and friends were either dead or unavailable to her. Dr. Karlsberg subscribes to the theory of coping with stress that emphasizes the importance of
   a. social support.
   b. medication.
   c. physiological influences.
   d. genetic influences.

7. Mary Ann lost her job and began to suffer severe stress as a result of trying to find a new one. Her therapist encouraged her to think of the situation as an opportunity to try a new career rather than as a loss. This approach to stress management could be called
   a. cognitive restructuring.
   b. relaxation training.
   c. biofeedback.
   d. meditation.

8. Many of Dr. Perry's patients are African American. Which of the following factors is *not* likely to contribute to hypertension among her patients?
   a. biological
   b. behavioral
   c. social
   d. genetic

9. Jill's recurring headaches did not respond to medication and caused her to lose time from her job. Her psychologist recommended
   a. psychodynamic therapy.
   b. that she change her medication.
   c. biofeedback.
   d. that she change her job.

10. A health psychologist plans to give a lecture on stress and coping to employees at a large electronics manufacturing company. Whom should she highlight as particularly prone to developing CHD?
    a. Type A men who are married to Type B women
    b. Middle managers who are responsible for production outcomes of a department.
    c. Type A men who have essential hypertension.
    d. Type B men who pursue pleasurable hobbies with friends outside the work situation.

ANSWER KEY: KEY TERMS REVIEW

1. immune system (317)
2. coronary atherosclerosis (CAD) (308)
3. essential hypertension (314)
4. active coping (304)
5. psychosomatic (298)
6. behavioral medicine (299)
7. health psychology (299)
8. Type B pattern (309)
9. response definition (300)
10. daily hassles (301)
11. passive coping (304)
12. blood pressure (313)
13. psychophysiological disorders (298)
14. Type A pattern (309)
15. physiological reactivity (309)
16. alarm reaction (303)
17. emotional-focused coping (305)
18. transactional definition (300)
19. coronary heart disease (CHD) (308)
20. migraine headaches (323)

21. exhaustion (303)
22. tension headache (323)
23. cancer (319)
24. stimulus definition (300)
25. problem-focused coping (304)
26. coping responses (301)
27. sympathetic nervous system (302)
28. psychophysiologic model (299)
29. fight-or-flight response (302)

30. resistance (303)
31. psychoneuroimmunology (317)
32. disregulation model (304)
33. stressors (299)
34. health-beliefs model (326)
35. stress (300–301)
36. response-focused coping (304)
37. general adaptation syndrome (GAS) (303)

ANSWER KEY: FACTUAL MULTIPLE-CHOICE QUESTIONS

1. *b. psychosomatic (p. 298)
   a. Somatoform disorders involve complaints of physical symptoms that have *no* organic basis.
   c. Psychoanalysis is the therapy developed by Freud based on his psychodynamic theory.
   d. Psychodynamics is Freud's theory of personality and abnormal behavior.

2. *d. coping response (p. 301)
   a. The diathesis-stress model illustrates interaction between preexisting physical and psychological domains in the production of illness.
   b. Life change units measure the amount of effort required to adapt to major life events.
   c. A transactional definition of stress deals with the relationship that exists between the individual and the situation.

3. *a. adrenaline (p. 303)
   b. HPA is the hypothalamic-pituitary-adrenocortical axis.
   c. Endorphins are opiatelike substances produced by the body.
   d. Corticosteroids are also hormones involved in the fight-or-flight response.

4. *b. biofeedback (p. 306)
   a. Cognitive restructuring is used to alter the way a person appraises threat, using visual imagery.
   c. Systematic desensitization is a technique used to treat anxiety disorders.
   d. The autonomic nervous system regulates the body's internal environment.

5. *d. cynical hostility (p. 310)
   a. Depression is not linked to Type A pattern of behavior.
   b. Mania is associated with manic-depressive or bipolar disorder, not Type A behavior.
   c. Obsessive-compulsive disorder is associated with anxiety, intrusive thoughts, or ritualistic acts, not Type A behavior.

6. *d. not yet understood (pp. 319–320)
   a. Genetics does not account for all the variability in the etiology of cancer.
   b. The cancer process does not differ by gender.
   c. The cancer process does not differ by race.

7. *a. enhance the quality of life (p. 321)
    b. Cancer patients have been given much longer lives with the effects of psychological interventions, but no reversal of the progress of the disease.
    c. The cancer has already been diagnosed when psychological intervention is begun.
    d. Psychological interventions are usually designed to help people deal with the reality of their illness.

8. *c. a bacterial process (p. 322)
    a. Smoking and ulcers have not been associated.
    b. Ulcers are caused by excess secretion of gastric acid. The mucus protects the stomach lining from the acid.
    d. Stress, rather than depression, is likely to be the cause of an ulcer.

9. *b. migraine headache (p. 323)
    a. Tension headaches begin in the neck or back of the head.
    c. Muscular headaches are similar to tension headaches.
    d. Pressure is often a symptom of the tension headache.

10. *c. biopsychosocial audit (p. 326)
    a. Personality inventories have little to do with physical health.
    b. Intelligence tests are not relevant to health care issues.
    d. The Thematic Apperception Test is a projective test used to measure personality and adjustment, not physiological matters.

ANSWER KEY: CONCEPTUAL MULTIPLE-CHOICE QUESTIONS

1. *b. unknown factors (p. 314)
    a. Only about 15 percent of hypertension is attributed to some form of disease.
    c. Medications prescribed to control hypertension do not exacerbate the condition, they do help reduce blood pressure.
    d. Sodium processing by the body, not the amount ingested, is linked with essential hypertension, particularly among African Americans.

2. *b. an external locus of control (p. 326)
    a. People with an internal locus of control believe their own behavior can affect their health.
    c. Paranoid schizophrenics believe that others are actively plotting to endanger them.
    d. Obsessive-compulsive disorder is an anxiety disorder unrelated to beliefs about the cause of illness or disease.

3. *b. psychophysiologic model (p. 299)
    a. The medical model sees mental disorders the same way as physical disorders.
    c. The somatic weakness model suggests that illness will strike at the part of the body that has been weakened in some way before exposure to an environmental stressor.
    d. The psychodynamic model is Freud's theory of behavior, which addresses internal conflicts from childhood.

4. *c. greater than normal (p. 310)
    a. Ron's response demonstrates hostility, which correlates with greater risk of CHD.
    b. His pattern of behavior is typical of Type A, which has a greater likelihood of CHD.
    d. This response pattern is recognized as a risk factor for CHD.

5. *d. cynical hostility (p. 310)
   a. Paranoia, or a delusion of persecution, is not seen as a risk factor for CHD.
   b. Obsessive-compulsive tendencies are related to anxiety disorders, not to angry behavior.
   c. Type B personality, characterized by an easygoing attitude, does not create a health risk.

6. *b. hypertension (pp. 313–315)
   a. The fight-or-flight response is caused by stressors and may cause stress-related problems.
   c. Somatization disorders involve complaints of a number of physical symptoms for which no physiological basis can be found.
   d. Type B personality is unrelated to physiological disorders.

7. *d. the effect of stress on the immune system (pp. 317, 319)
   a. Type A personality is not known to effect the immune system, but creates greater risk for CHD.
   b. Type B personality is unconnected to physiological reactions to stress.
   c. Late night studying happens at other times during the year as well as during final exams.

8. *c. peptic ulcers (p. 322)
   a. Migraine headaches are caused by a combination of vascular and muscular conditions.
   b. Stress may increase the types of behaviors that cause cancer such as smoking.
   d. Tension headaches are often related to a number of life stressors.

9. *d. response-focused coping occurs following the occurrence of the stressful event, while problem-focused coping attempts to prevent the event from occurring. (p. 304)
   a. Problem-focused coping attempts to escape, avoid, or control the threatening event itself.
   b. Response-focused coping minimizes the effects of the event.
   c. This is problem-focused coping.

10. *c. the immune system. (p. 317)
    a. Stress may activate the hypothalamic-pituitary-adrenocortical (HPA) axis, which mobilizes energy, but this effect may be positive or negative.
    b. Passive coping occurs when the individual cannot attempt to minimize exposure to the stressor and must tolerate it.
    d. Somatization disorder occurs when a person has a long-standing history of physical complaints for which medical tests indicate the person is normal.

ANSWER KEY: APPLICATION MULTIPLE-CHOICE QUESTIONS

1. *a. low risk of developing stress-related health problems (pp. 300–301)
   b. The set of circumstances surrounding a major life change such as death of a spouse has been studied extensively to give us reasonably accurate methods of assessing possible danger in such cases.
   c. He appears to be using effecting coping strategies.
   d. John may develop stress-related problems if he has no social supports or uses ineffective coping responses to deal with the loss.

2. *d. daily hassles (p. 301)
    a. Compulsions are ritualistic acts performed by a sufferer of OCD.
    b. Manic depression or bipolar disorder is a mood disorder.
    c. A panic attack is a disorder related to anxiety in which physical symptoms are exhibited that have no basis in physiology.

3. *a. a fight-or-flight response (p. 302)
    b. Panic reactions are often unrelated to anything frightening in the environment.
    c. Agoraphobia is a fear of being in public places.
    d. Misappraisal is when a person is incorrect in evaluating the seriousness of a stressful event.

4. *d. exhaustion (p. 303)
    a. Alarm reaction, the first stage of the GAS, rapidly prepares the body to meet a threat or demand.
    b. Resistance, the second stage of the GAS, attempts to maintain the responses from the alarm reaction.
    c. Denial is not one of the stages of the GAS.

5. *c. response-focused coping (p. 304)
    a. In passive coping the person tolerates the stressor without attempting to minimize it.
    b. Problem-focused coping involves attempts to escape, avoid, or control the stressor.
    d. Emotion-focused coping is directed toward regulating the emotional consequences of a stressful event.

6. *a. social support (pp. 305–306)
    b. Her doctor emphasized the social factors in stress control, not the medical.
    c. Physiological influences are biological. The doctor's concern is with the lack of a social support system.
    d. Genetic influences are not a factor in a case where the friends and family have provided support and are now gone.

7. *a. cognitive restructuring (p. 306)
    b. Her therapist did not suggest one of the relaxation training programs.
    c. Biofeedback is designed to help a person relax by means of visual and auditory signals.
    d. Meditation is a relaxation technique designed to reduce physiological arousal.

8. *d. genetic (pp. 315–316)
    a. Biological factors such as sodium retention may increase risk for African Americans.
    b. Behaviors such as "John Henryism" may place African Americans at greater risk for hypertension.
    c. Social factors such as lower socioeconomic status could be a factor.

9. *c. biofeedback (p. 325)
    a. Psychodynamic therapy deals with repressed material, not the world of everyday stressors.
    b. Since Jill's headaches did not respond to one type of medication, a different type of treatment might prove to be effective.
    d. All jobs have stress and a new one might have even more.

10. *c. Type A men who have essential hypertension. (pp. 307–311)
   a. A husband's Type A status alone is not sufficient to produce the heightened hostile dominance pattern between spouses. It also requires a Type A spouse.
   b. Recurrent, uncontrollable stressors are related to CHD. This may be a risk factor if the manager is not given appropriate tools or resources to do a high-demand job.
   d. Relaxation, meditation, and social support are effective buffers to stress.

CHAPTER 11

Substance-Related Disorders

LEARNING OBJECTIVES

1. Describe the widespread use of psychoactive substances and the extent of the problems arising from their abuse. (p. 332)

2. Define *addiction* and distinguish among addiction, dependence, tolerance, and withdrawal. (p. 332)

3. Describe the process of psychological dependence on drugs. (pp. 332–333)

4. Define the cultural context of drug use. (pp. 333–334)

5. Describe the role of expectancies on the psychological and behavioral effects of drugs and how researchers study the role that expectancies play. (pp. 334–335)

6. Describe the effects of alcohol on behavior and its patterns of use. (pp. 335–338)

7. Describe the epidemiology of alcohol use and the differential use of alcohol by gender and ethnic groups. (pp. 337–338)

8. Describe the effects and epidemiology of cannabis. (pp. 338–340)

9. Discuss the effects and epidemiology of amphetamines. (pp. 340–341)

10. Discuss the effects and epidemiology of cocaine. (pp. 341–342)

11. Describe the effects and epidemiology of hallucinogens. (pp. 342–343)

12. Discuss the effects and epidemiology of nicotine. (pp. 343–344)

13. Describe the effects and epidemiology of opioids. (pp. 344–345)

14. Describe the effects and epidemiology of sedatives, hypnotics, and anxiolytics. (p. 345)

15. Discuss the addictive process. (pp. 345–346)

16. Describe the various theories about alcohol use and the controversy over whether or not there is a genetic predisposition to alcoholism. (pp. 346–352)

17. Describe the personality factors that may influence substance abuse. (p. 358)

18. Explain the theory of alcoholism as a learned behavior. (pp. 348–349)

19. Discuss the effects of social learning processes on substance abuse. (p. 349)

20. Explain the cognitive expectancy theory and the perceived effects theory. (p. 350)

21. Discuss the effects of the family on substance-use disorders. (p. 351)

22. Describe how genetic and environmental effects may combine to produce vulnerability. (pp. 351–352)

23. Describe the course of substance-use disorders including remission, relapse, and recovery. (pp. 352–356)

24. Summarize the research on smoking-cessation programs. (pp. 353–355)

25. Discuss the various treatments for addictions. (pp. 356–364)

26. Discuss the controversy surrounding abstinence versus controlled drinking as a goal of addiction treatment. (p. 358)

27. Describe the formats and settings for treating substance abuse. (pp. 358–359)

28. Describe the cognitive-behavioral and family approaches to treating addictions. (pp. 359–361)

29. Explain the need for differential and culture-specific treatments for substance abuse. (p. 361)

30. Describe the use of medication and peer-support programs in treating addiction. (pp. 361–363)

31. Discuss the effectiveness of early prevention programs. (pp. 363–364)

32. Describe what lies ahead in the understanding of substance abuse and its treatment. (pp. 364–365)

CHAPTER OUTLINE

    I. Defining the Problem of Addiction

- One-fourth of the population aged fifteen to fifty-four have a history of substance-use disorder.

- An addiction is the use of a psychoactive substance characterized behaviorally by a subjective compulsion to use the drug and progressive compromise of activities that are not drug related, and physically by tolerance and withdrawal.

        A. Physical Processes of Addiction

           1. Physical dependence is the physiological need for a drug, characterized by tolerance and withdrawal.

           2. Tolerance is the need for increased dosages of drugs or alcohol to experience the same effect.

           3. Withdrawal is the effect on the body when the substance is not given.

        B. Behavioral and Psychological Aspects of Addiction

1. Psychological dependence is a major hazard of drug use.

2. Diagnoses of substance dependence are made on a psychological concept of dependency.

3. Substance dependence can be with or without physiological dependence.

C. What's Normal? Consider Cultural Context

1. The "relative" definition of normal use suggests that normal use is based on the individual, family, peer group, and cultural background.

2. Since normal substance use is found in almost every culture throughout history, the important question is what is healthy?

D. The Role of Expectancies in Substance Use

1. Expectancies are beliefs about what an individual anticipates will occur; can exert greater control over functioning than the pharmacological effects.

2. The balanced placebo design is a research strategy in which four groups are used in an effort to separate the pharmacological from the expectancy effects of drugs.

II. The Addictive Agents and Their Effects

- There is much misinformation about drug use among youths.

- Active use of most agents is concentrated among the young.

- Youths show the most promise for prevention and early intervention.

A. Alcohol

- Classified as a sedative-hypnotic agent.

- Depresses the central nervous system, first the inhibitory centers of the brain, then the arousal centers, then coordination and respiration.

- Patterns of use vary. They include alcoholic subtypes: chronic daily use, chronic regular use, and binge or spree use.

1. Unwanted effects of alcohol

a. Medical crises: injuries and accidents, fetal alcohol syndrome (FAS), liver diseases, brain damage.

b. Psychological effects: depression, anxiety, paranoia, violence (including explosive disorder).

c. Co-occurrence with other psychological disorders, including schizophrenia and affective disorder.

d. Withdrawal usually lasts a few days with headache, nausea, and mood disturbances.

e. Delirium tremens (DTs) may accompany withdrawal.

2. Epidemiology of alcohol use

a. High continuation rate (percentage of first-time users who persist in taking a drug).

b. Russia has the highest concentration of drinking problems in the world.

c. Alcohol is by far the most widely used substance among American youth, especially college students.

d. More males have problems with alcohol than females.

e. More Native Americans and white adolescents are heavy drinkers than Asian, African American, and Hispanics.

B. Cannabis

- Includes marijuana, hashish, cannabis resin, and THC.

- Is usually classified as a *hallucinogenic agent.*

- Users frequently abuse other substances concurrently.

- Has varied effect on users.

1. Unwanted effects of cannabis

    a. Lung disease, because of the method of smoking cannabis (inhaling deeply and holding smoke in lungs).

    b. Cannabis amotivational syndrome: lethargy, unpleasant mood, impaired judgment, loss of interest in personal appearance or conventional goals.

    c. May negatively affect attention and memory functions.

2. Epidemiology of cannabis use

    a. In the United States, cannabis is the most widely used substance other than alcohol.

    b. Males are much heavier users than females.

C. Amphetamines or Similarly Acting Drugs

- Available as stimulants or appetite suppressants.

- Classified as *stimulant-euphoriant agents.*

- Produce excitatory effect.

- Effects include decreased fatigue, increased alertness, heightened feelings of esteem and sexual potency.

- Mimic the stimulation of the sympathetic nervous system.

1. Unwanted effects of amphetamines

    a. Rapid elevation in blood pressure and pulse rate may cause cardiac malfunction.

    b. Delirium and delusional disorders, intense agitation and paranoia

    c. Depression, irritability, anger, anxiety, sexual dysfunction, and loss of concentration and memory

2. Epidemiology of amphetamine use

      a.   Use is common, but continuation rate is low.

      b.   Second most widely used illicit drug among youths.

      c.   Increased use among females.

D.   Cocaine

- Available as coca leaf, cocaine hydrochloride powder ("snow"), and smokable cocaine alkaloid forms ("freebase" or "crack").

- Classified as stimulant-euphoriant agent.

- Produces powerful temporary excitatory effect.

   1. Unwanted effects of cocaine

      a.   Rapid elevation in blood pressure and pulse rate may cause cardiac problems and sudden death.

      b.   Delirium and delusional disorders, irritability, anger, anxiety, sexual dysfunction, and loss of concentration and memory.

   2. Epidemiology of cocaine use

      a.   High continuation rate.

      b.   Most dangerous in smokable form, "crack."

      c.   Use increases after completion of high school (40 percent of young adults have used it).

      d.   Use of cocaine has recently declined.

      e.   Greater use of the concentrated form of the drug ("crack") by African Americans and inner-city underclass youth.

E.   Hallucinogens

- Occur naturally as peyote, mescaline, and psilocybin.

- Occur synthetically as lysergic and diethylamide (LSD).

- Produce varied powerful perceptual alterations (*hallucinations*) and excitation of the central nervous system.

   1. Unwanted effects of hallucinogens

      a.   Delusional thinking and severe mood disorders.

      b.   Panic attacks, psychotic disorders, and flashbacks.

   2. Epidemiology of hallucinogen use

      a.   Use peaked in 1970s.

      b.   White males, non-college-bound, urban dwellers most likely users.

F.   Nicotine

- Widely available in tobacco products.

- Classified as a stimulant-euphoriant.

- Alters behavior, mood, and physical sensation.

- Stimulates respiration.

- Affects the peripheral nervous system (increased heart rate and blood pressure).

- Very high continuation rate.

1. Unwanted effects of nicotine

   a. Constricted blood pathways, high blood pressure, and coronary artery disease.

   b. Carcinogenic effects: lung cancer, emphysema, oral and gastric cancers.

   c. Withdrawal symptoms include irritability, loss of concentration, decreased metabolic rate, hunger, restlessness, and anxiety.

2. Epidemiology of nicotine use

   a. Declined use in the United States recently, but at high levels in other parts of the world.

   b. High continuation rate (83 percent).

   c. More people dependent on nicotine than any other drug.

   d. Implicated in over 300,000 deaths in the United States per year (25 percent, or 53 million American users).

G. Opioids

   1. Occur naturally as opium, morphine, heroin, and codeine.

   2. Occur synthetically as methadone and dilaudid.

   3. Produce sedative, anesthetic, and euphoriant effect on the central nervous system.

   4. Overdose a major risk.

   5. Hepatitis and AIDS passed through shared needles.

   6. Produce depression and anxiety.

   7. Intense withdrawal symptoms encourage daily use.

   8. Rapid pronounced tolerance.

   9. Use is rare, with the exception of Vietnam veterans.

H. Sedatives, Hypnotics, and Anxiolytics

   1. Include barbiturates ("downers"), benzodiazepines (Valium, Librium, and Xanax), and analgesics (chloral hydrate or methaqualone).

   2. Produce a temporary nonspecific depressant effect, similar to alcohol.

   3. Produce relaxation and light-headedness, poor coordination, slurred speech, and sleep.

4. Can produce fatal overdoses, particularly when used with alcohol which leads to respiratory suppression and death.

5. Promote rapid tolerance and severe, abiding withdrawal.

6. More "legitimate" prescription users than illegal users.

7. Use of these agents among youth declining.

III. Addictive Processes

- Explanation for substance-use disorders include genetic factors, environmental forces, family factors, and peer influences.

A. Alcoholism as a Disease

1. Dr. Benjamin Rush (1814) hypothesized an addictive illness, *intemperance*, with causal agent (liquor), symptoms (compulsive drinking), a predictable course (progressive deterioration), a common outcome (insanity or death), and an effective cure (total abstinence).

2. The unitary disease model holds that alcoholics

   a. Have a psychological predisposition and sensitivity to alcohol.

   b. Experience irreversible physical and psychological changes

      (1) Craving

      (2) Loss of control regarding alcohol

   c. Alcoholism can be remedied only through lifelong abstinence.

3. Jellinek developed the stage theory of alcoholism

   a. *Prealcoholic symptomatic phase:* Social drinking becomes habituated.

   b. *Prodromal phase:* Guilt, denial, secretiveness, and blackouts occur.

   c. *Crucial phase:* Loss of control and beginnings of social damage.

   d. *Chronic phase:* Drinking wholly obsessive and sustained, deterioration leads to insanity or death.

4. Critics of the disease model say that it suppresses the psychological and contextual features of substance abuse, removes responsibility from user, and functions as a self-fulfilling prophecy and contradicts available data on controlled drinking.

5. Substance-use disorders, including alcoholism, are a heterogeneous class of problems in living. "Disease" concept is a metaphor.

B. Heredity and Alcoholism

1. The theory that alcoholism is genetically transmitted has long had its advocates.

2. The role of genetics seems to vary with the type of alcoholism:

   a. Type 1 alcoholism: Biological sons raised by foster parents twice as likely to develop alcoholism.

      b.   Type 2 alcoholism: Biological sons raised by foster parents nine times as likely to develop alcoholism.

   3.   Genetic influence is greater in males than in females.

   4.   There is general acceptance of genetic contributions to the risk of alcoholism.

C.   Personality Factors and Substance Abuse

   1.   The psychodynamic model suggested regression to the oral stage of psychosexual development resulting in an oral-dependent personality.

   2.   Recent research shows that personalities characterized by difficulties with interpersonal relationships, weak impulse control, and subjective distress appear to be associated with frequent drug use at age eighteen.

   3.   Psychopathy is strongly associated with alcohol and other drug abuse.

   4.   There are multiple personality traits that, combined, are associated with substance abuse.

D.   Alcoholism as Learned Behavior

   1.   The tension reduction hypothesis (John Conger) holds that people learn to use alcohol and other drugs to relieve tension, fear, or for social avoidance.

   2.   Other cognitive factors, including attention allocation and expectations, have been found to be important in understanding tension reduction.

E.   Social Learning Processes and Substance Abuse

   1.   Reinforcement and modeling may contribute to substance abuse.

   2.   Peer pressure, the influence of one's friends, is often cited as a cause for drug use among adolescents.

F.   Cognitive Influences and Alcoholism

   1.   The cognitive expectancy theory states that people learn from family, friends, the media, and other models to expect that drinking will have positive consequences.

   2.   Brown et al. found that drinkers expect alcohol to

      a.   Help experience events in a pleasurable way.

      b.   Increase social and physical pleasure.

      c.   Enhance sexual experience.

      d.   Increase feelings of personal dominance.

      e.   Increase assertiveness in social situations.

      f.   Relieve subjective tension.

   3.   The perceived effects theory states that the perceived benefits of substance use outweigh the perceived costs or negative consequences.

   4.   Drinking can serve as a tranquilizer even in highly stressful circumstances.

5. Drinking may provide a self-handicap for the un-self-confident person who survives a stressful situation by attributing the failure to alcohol rather than to personal inadequacy.

G. Family Matters: Are There Alcoholic Families?

1. The family can play a part in alcohol and other drug problems by modeling substance use and by influencing attitudes and expectations.

2. Ethnic influences play a role in determining personal attitudes toward alcohol.

3. Parental influences are almost as potent as peer influences in initiating alcohol use by adolescents.

H. Vulnerability: Synthesizing Genetic and Environmental Factors

1. Vulnerability refers to how likely a person is to respond maladaptively to a situation.

2. Stressful disruptions to life contribute to vulnerability.

3. Multiple-risk-factor model relies on the number of risks to predict adolescent alcohol and other drug use.

IV. The Course of Disorder

A. Remission

1. Remission is a state of health in which a previously active disorder or illness has receded or disappeared entirely.

2. Remission is common in addictive disorders.

3. All substance-use disorders decline with age.

4. Reasons for decline include

a. Death.

b. Active treatment.

c. Natural remission.

d. Loss of desire.

e. Fear of consequences.

f. Family influences.

B. Focus on Research: Can You Kick the Cigarette Habit?

1. Success rate for self-quitting is 10 to 20 percent, lower than reported in early studies.

2. Recent research demonstrates the difficulty of quitting a nicotine habit, with less than 25 percent of participants nicotine-free following treatment.

C. Relapse

1. Relapse is the reappearance of substance-use or other disorders following a period of remission.

2. Relapse is common in alcohol and other drug-use disorders.

3. High-risk situations are circumstances that may lead a former substance abuser to begin drinking or taking drugs again. They include

    a. A negative emotional state.

    b. Social pressure.

    c. Interpersonal conflict.

4. The abstinence violation effect (AVE) is a person's reaction to an initial relapse into drug use, usually creating

    a. Increased consumption.

    b. Conflict and guilt.

    c. Increased drug use to relieve unpleasant feelings.

    d. Negative spiral.

5. Mood and cognition are important factors in prediction of abstinence.

D. Recovery

1. Recovery is the return to and maintenance of a healthy state following relapse.

2. A majority of alcohol and drug abusers achieve recovery.

3. Recovery is initiated for the following reasons:

    a. Reaching a personal low point.

    b. Developing a serious illness as a result of drinking.

    c. Developing an aversion to alcohol.

    d. Deciding to make a serious life change.

    e. Undergoing a spiritual experience.

V. Getting Clean and Sober: Treating the Addictions

*   Few addicts volunteer for treatment: denial is a common symptom of addiction.

*   Coerced clients are required by the courts to receive treatment for substance abuse.

*   Treatments include

1. Medication

2. Counseling

3. Group therapy

4. Halfway houses

5. Hospital stays

A. Goals of Addiction Treatments

1. Abstinence versus controlled drinking is a debate about the proper treatment goals for alcohol dependence disorders.

2. Controlled drinking is an option for subjects who

   a. Are not severely dependent.

   b. Believe controlled drinking is possible.

3. Abstinence is considered by many to be the best treatment goal for alcoholism.

B. Formats and Settings for Treating Substance Use

1. Outpatient treatment is the primary setting for substance abuse therapy in the United States.

2. Hospitals provide

   a. Inpatient services.

   b. Outpatient services.

   c. Partial hospitalization.

3. Detoxification (usually involving only physical care during withdrawal) requires three to five days in a hospital.

4. Halfway houses (residential treatment facilities or group homes) employ several forms of treatment, particularly group therapy.

C. A Cognitive-Behavioral Approach to Treatment

1. According to this model relapse represents failure at a choice point.

2. Relapse prevention training is a combination of cognitive and behavioral skills taught to clients who are trying to gain control over their drinking.

   a. Based on the idea that excessive drinking represents a sacrifice of long-term goals for near-term gratifications.

   b. Patients taught to differentiate between minor and major lapses and to recognize high-risk situations.

D. Family Approaches to Treating Addictions

1. Structural-strategic family therapy is a therapy for clients and their families that includes designing specific strategies that the families can use to solve problems, and changing the relationships among individual pairs within the family.

2. More research is needed in this area.

E. The Need for Culture-Specific Treatment Programs

1. Risk factors vary from culture to culture.

2. Treatments must be sensitive to and incorporate cultural differences.

F. Treating Addictions with Medication

1. Medications are widely available to treat drug problems.

2. *Antabuse* deters impulsive drinkers by causing severe unpleasant physical reactions when they drink.

3. Methadone reduces the craving for heroin.

4. These medications are usually given with other forms of treatment.

G. "Anonymous" Peer-Support Programs

1. "The Program" includes Alcoholics Anonymous (AA), Narcotics Anonymous, Cocaine Anonymous, and other similar organizations.

2. AA is a huge, worldwide organization based on a twelve-step program of recovery.

3. Rigorous scientific evaluation of the effectiveness of AA is lacking.

H. Prevention Programs

1. Prevention, intervention to reduce the likelihood of future pathology, is best aimed at early adolescence.

2. Successful prevention programs demonstrate the need for continued support.

    a. Botvin et al.'s cognitive-behavioral intervention included life skills training and substance-specific information.

    b. Johnson et al.'s prevention program, directed at entire community, taught "resistance" skills and encouraged parent-child interactions.

VI. What Lies Ahead?

A. Increased recognition of the negative effects of substance abuse has led to an increase in preventive efforts.

B. Greater recognition of cultural changes needed to prevent substance-use disorders.

C. Additional research is required to discover

1. Biochemical processes underlying addiction.

2. Cognitive and social learning factors.

3. Components of treatment needed to correct abuse.

4. Most effective treatment strategies.

5. Vulnerability.

6. Comorbidity of substance use with other disorders.

D. Attention to individuals with comorbid diagnoses.

KEY TERMS REVIEW

1. Part of the unitary disease model of alcoholism suggesting that a person develops alcoholism after going through a series of mutually exclusive, invariable phases is called the _____.

2. The view that people learn from models to expect that drinking will have positive consequences for them, including being socially stimulating and helping them forget aversive events or unpleasant memories, is called _____.

3. Circumstances that may lead a former substance abuser to begin drinking or taking drugs again are called _____.

4. A set of symptoms, usually opposite in nature to the effects of the drug itself, that result when prolonged use of a substance has altered the body to such an extent that it is affected when the substance is not taken is called _____.

5. The need for increased dosages of psychotropic medications to experience the same effects is called _____.

6. The debate over whether treatment for alcoholism should be total cessation of drinking or moderately controlled drinking refers to _____.

7. A combination of cognitive and behavioral skills taught to clients who are trying to gain self-control over their drinking is called _____.

8. The term used in psychodynamic theories to describe individuals who are prone to alcoholism because their need for oral gratification was not satisfied early in life is _____.

9. A set of behaviors including lethargy, an inability to derive pleasure, unpleasant mood, impaired judgment, lack of interest in conventional goals, and perhaps some deterioration of attention and memory which may result from long-term use of cannabis is called _____.

10. Drugs, including alcohol, that exercise temporary and nonspecific depressant effects on the central nervous system are called _____.

11. Physiological need for a drug, characterized by tolerance and withdrawal, is called _____.

12. A synthetic drug administered orally, the actions of which are similar to those of the opioids, used in some programs to treat opiate dependence is called _____.

13. The likelihood that a person will respond maladaptively to a situation is called _____.

14. A person's reaction to an initial relapse into drug use is called _____.

15. The view that alcohol and other drugs are used excessively because the user perceives that they will have positive effects and that those effects are desired to repair defects of character or to achieve subjective sensations is called the _____.

16. A type of study in which four groups are used in an effort to separate the pharmacological from the expectancy effects of drugs is called a(n) _____.

17. A learning theory view that people learn to use alcohol and other drugs because such use relieves tension, whether from anxiety, depression, fear, or social avoidance, is called the _____.

18. The percentage of first-time users who persist in the use of a drug is called _____.

19. The influence of one's friends is called _____.

20. Subgroups of alcohol users are called _____.

21. A system that predicts adolescent alcohol and other drug use that relies on the sheer *number* of risks involved is called _____.

22. A therapy for substance abusers and their families that includes designing specific strategies the families can use to solve problems and changing the relationships among individual pairs within the family is called _____.

23. Use of a psychoactive substance characterized behaviorally by a subjective compulsion to use the drug and by a progressive compromise of activities that are not drug related and physically by tolerance and withdrawal is called _____.

24. Reappearance of substance abuse following a period of remission is called _____.

25. A model of addiction suggesting that alcoholics differ from normal persons in terms of psychological predisposition and an "allergic" sensitivity to alcohol which lead to a craving for alcohol and loss of control regarding alcohol is called the _____.

26. Interventions to reduce the likelihood of substance abuse are called _____.

27. Individuals receiving treatment for substance abuse who are required by courts to receive the treatment are called _____.

28. A state of health in which a previously active disorder or illness has receded or disappeared entirely is called _____.

29. A collection of symptoms—including low weight and small size at birth, some facial and limb irregularities, and mental and motor retardation—exhibited by some children born of women who drank heavily while pregnant is called _____.

30. A class of alcoholism in parents characterized by beginning to drink in early adulthood and showing health effects in middle age is called _____.

31. An individual's beliefs about the effects a drug will have, which can sometimes exert greater control over psychological and behavioral functioning than the pharmacological effects of the drug itself, are called _____.

32. A class of alcoholism in parents characterized by few medical problems but severe social, interpersonal, and occupational disruptions of life in which their sons are far more likely than sons of normal parents to become alcoholic is called _____.

33. The return to and maintenance of a healthy state following relapse is called _____.

FACTUAL MULTIPLE-CHOICE QUESTIONS

1. The role of expectancies in substance use is tested by using
   a. biofeedback.
   b. personality inventories.
   c. balanced placebo design experiments.
   d. double blind design experiments.

2. Alcohol has an effect on the central nervous system similar to
   a. nicotine.
   b. the hallucinogens.
   c. cocaine.
   d. the barbiturates.

3. One potential effect of the use of amphetamines is
   a. weight gain.
   b. increased fatigue.
   c. increased sleep.
   d. cardiac dysfunction.

4. The use of LSD would produce an effect which most closely resembles
   a. schizophrenia.
   b. dissociative identity disorder.
   c. obsessive-compulsive disorder.
   d. amnesia.

5. A drug whose use is dropping in the United States but rising in other parts of the world is
   a. cocaine.
   b. nicotine.
   c. LSD.
   d. benzodiazepine.

6. The learning theory explanation for the development of alcoholism is based on the
   a. tension reduction hypothesis.
   b. oral-dependent personality theory.
   c. genetic predisposition theory.
   d. peer pressure hypothesis.

7. For the development of alcoholism, gender is a risk factor for
   a. women.
   b. men.
   c. neither men nor women.
   d. about the same risk for both.

8. Over a period of many years most alcohol and drug abusers will
   a. become steadily worse.
   b. remain about the same.
   c. give up their addictive patterns.
   d. move on to stronger drugs.

9. The substance that has been called the most addictive of all drugs is
   a. heroin.
   b. cocaine.
   c. nicotine.
   d. alcohol.

10. Most candidates for alcohol and drug treatment
    a. check themselves in for detoxification.
    b. volunteer for family therapy.
    c. go without any undue pressure.
    d. rarely volunteer for treatment.

CONCEPTUAL MULTIPLE-CHOICE QUESTIONS

1. Which of the following is *not* part of the definition of addiction?
   a. physical dependence
   b. psychological dependence
   c. relapse
   d. tolerance

2. If children consume large quantities of alcohol it is
   a. always illegal.
   b. always legal.
   c. never culturally condoned.
   d. occasionally culturally condoned.

3. Caroline had been in recovery for several months. After a particularly stressful day at the office she had a drink with a friend. Her therapist told her to think of this event as
   a. evidence that she isn't fully committed to recovery.
   b. the need for more intensive psychotherapy.
   c. a minor relapse that shouldn't stop her self-control efforts.
   d. the beginning of a major relapse.

4. Todd is a high school senior with a long series of bouts with drugs and alcohol. Bruce is a successful businessman with a serious cocaine and alcohol problem. The treatment for Todd and Bruce
   a. should be different because of their different life circumstances.
   b. should be the same and not show favoritism.
   c. should focus on the similarities in their lifestyles.
   d. should focus on the family interaction with their problems.

5. Dr. Webster was concerned because Janet was drinking an increasing amount of alcohol to get relief from anxieties. Dr. Webster's observation was of what part of the addictive process?
   a. withdrawal
   b. tolerance
   c. relapse
   d. remission

6. Mike was convinced that his father's alcoholism was responsible for his own drinking problem. The real cause of his problem is
   a. peer influences.
   b. environmental forces.
   c. family factors.
   d. impossible to know because there is no single cause.

7. Kate lost her job and was required to move to try to find another one. In addition, her parents were both alcoholics and were in ill health. Her doctor felt she was in danger of drinking too much to relieve the stress. The doctor probably subscribes to the
   a. unitary disease model.
   b. vulnerability model.
   c. genetics model.
   d. cognitive expectancy theory.

8. Which of the following concepts would be advanced by a cognitive therapist as a primary cause of relapse among former substance users?
   a. tension reduction
   b. environmental cues
   c. oral fixations
   d. remission.

9. Which of the following illustrates the concept of "self-handicapping"?
   a. Damien drinks a couple of beers in order to ease his anxiety before going on a first date.
   b. After failing an important exam, Jim attributes the failure to a wild drinking party he attended the evening prior to the exam.
   c. Lupe believes that by drinking a couple of shots of tequila she will feel more adept in a new social situation.
   d. Candy feels guilty about her failure to stop smoking and blames herself for having weak willpower and an inability to overcome the severe withdrawal symptoms.

10. Which statement best characterizes the research on the heritability of alcoholism?
    a. There is a substantial genetic influence for women born to alcoholic parents.
    b. There is a substantial genetic influence for both men and women born to alcoholic parents.
    c. In general, there is a modest genetic influence for men and women born to alcoholic parents but increasing risk for males whose parents show early-onset alcoholism.
    d. Genetics plays almost no role in the development of alcoholism.

APPLICATION MULTIPLE-CHOICE QUESTIONS

1. Sean had struggled with his drinking problem for several years. The best course for him to follow is
   a. controlled drinking.
   b. total abstinence.
   c. planned relapse.
   d. peer support.

2. Miriam was put on a program of Antabuse to help her control her drinking. The success of this program is in doubt because
   a. the drug makes Miriam nauseous.
   b. the drug is hard to find.
   c. the drug is self-administered.
   d. this program substitutes one addiction for another.

3. Joe decided to join AA, but wanted to get some research on the effectiveness of the program. He found that
   a. the research demonstrated a solid record of improvement for AA members.
   b. the therapeutic content of the program was quite good.
   c. more than 50 percent of AA members are over age 50.
   d. AA does not open itself to scientific evaluation.

4. Sally and Jeff wanted to form a chapter of SADD (Students Against Drunk Driving) on their high school campus. This is a good idea, because
   a. most high school students haven't had experience with drinking.
   b. the program will reinforce the good information students are already getting from other sources.
   c. dissemination of preventive information is needed during early years.
   d. there are no other programs to help teenagers deal with drinking.

5. Tommy's parents were concerned about his behavior. He had dropped out of his activities at school and was spending most of his time in his unkempt room, sleeping or listening to rock music. These behaviors could be symptoms of
   a. cocaine use.
   b. LSD use.
   c. cannabis use.
   d. amphetamine use.

6. Dr. Willis was treating Martha for severe depression. After a brief, angry exchange with her boyfriend, Martha seemed so devastated by this depression that the doctor suspected she was also using
   a. cannabis.
   b. cocaine.
   c. LSD.
   d. benzodiazepines.

7. Bill told his friends that he would have no trouble kicking his pack-and-a-half nicotine habit. He underestimated the effect of
   a. tolerance.
   b. withdrawal.
   c. low dosages of the drug.
   d. slow to act nature of the drug.

8. Hal drifted from job to job and lost each one because of his drinking. He said he only used alcohol to help him overcome his shyness and felt powerless to prevent recurrence. His attitude reflects the
   a. perceived effects theory.
   b. psychodynamic model.
   c. heredity model.
   d. tension reduction hypothesis.

9. Martin had just made his presentation at the office. The boss was critical and made him feel inadequate. That afternoon Martin had a terrible craving for a drink. He was facing
   a. peer pressure.
   b. remission.
   c. a high-risk situation.
   d. withdrawal.

10. Marnie had her first night of sleep in three days. The sweats and tremors had subsided. She was going through
    a. relapse.
    b. remission.
    c. tolerance.
    d. detoxification.

ANSWER KEY: KEY TERMS REVIEW

1. stage theory (346)
2. cognitive expectancy theory (350)
3. high risk situations (359)
4. withdrawal (332)
5. tolerance (332)
6. abstinence versus controlled drinking (358)
7. relapse prevention training (359)
8. oral-dependent personality (348)
9. cannabis amotivational syndrome (339)
10. sedative-hypnotic-anxiolytic agents (345)
11. physical dependence (332)
12. methadone (361)
13. vulnerability (351)
14. abstinence violation effect (AVE) (355, 359)
15. perceived effects theory (350)
16. balanced placebo design (334)
17. tension reduction hypothesis (349)
18. continuation rates (337)
19. peer pressure (349)
20. alcoholic subtypes (347)
21. multiple-risk-factor model (352)
22. structural-strategic family therapy (360)
23. addiction (332)
24. relapse (355)
25. unitary disease model (346)
26. prevention (363)
27. coerced clients (357)
28. remission (352)
29. fetal alcohol syndrome (FAS) (336)
30. type 1 alcoholism (347)
31. expectancies (334)
32. type 2 alcoholism (347)
33. recovery (356)

ANSWER KEY: FACTUAL MULTIPLE-CHOICE QUESTIONS

1. *c. balanced placebo design experiments (p. 334)
   a. Biofeedback is used to reduce stress.
   b. Personality inventories are designed to provide information on a person's attitudes and feelings.
   d. Double blind design experiments are a less sophisticated approach to control the placebo effect.

2. *d. the barbiturates (p. 336)
   a. Nicotine increases arousal.
   b. The hallucinogens produce powerful perceptual alterations.
   c. Cocaine has an excitatory effect on the central nervous system.

3. *d. cardiac dysfunction (p. 340)
   a. Amphetamines are often used to lose weight.
   b. Amphetamines have a powerful excitatory effect and decrease fatigue.
   c. Amphetamines may reduce the need for sleep. In withdrawal the patient may experience sleep disorders.

4. *a. schizophrenia (p. 342)
   b. Dissociative identity disorder is not associated with hallucinations but is a disturbance of identity.
   c. Obsessive-compulsive disorder is related to anxiety with intrusive thoughts and ritualistic acts.
   d. Amnesia is a disturbance of memory.

5. *b. nicotine (p. 343)
   a. Cocaine use peaked in the mid-1980s in the United States, but is concentrated in American cities.
   c. LSD use is down worldwide.
   d. Amphetamine use is increasing among females.

6. *a. tension reduction hypothesis (p. 349)
   b. The oral-dependent personality theory is based on psychodynamic principles of regression to the oral stage of psychosexual development.
   c. Genetic predisposition theory states that a person inherits a characteristic that makes him or her prone to abuse of alcohol.
   d. Peer pressure is part of the social learning process.

7. *b. men (p. 347)
   a. Women are less likely to become problem drinkers than men.
   c. Men are at greater risk for developing alcoholism.
   d. Gender is just one of many factors, such as other mental health problems which cause increased risk.

8. *c. give up their addictive patterns (pp. 352–353)
   a. Many alcoholics recover spontaneously without any intervention.
   b. Most drug abusers will improve with the passage of time for a variety of factors.
   d. Moving to stronger drugs may be a pattern for younger abusers, but older drug users tend to give up their addictive patterns.

9. *c. nicotine (pp. 343, 353–355)
   a. Heroin is relatively rarely used.
   b. Cocaine use has declined overall, but is concentrated in certain locations and among certain populations.
   d. Alcohol is widely used, but is not as pervasive as nicotine.

10. *d. rarely volunteer for treatment (p. 357)
    a. Denial is common among alcohol and drug abusers.
    b. Often family problems are what precipitate a person seeking treatment.
    c. Many abusers who seek treatment are required to do so by the courts and are called coerced clients.

ANSWER KEY: CONCEPTUAL MULTIPLE-CHOICE QUESTIONS

1. *c. relapse (p. 330)
   a. Physical dependence is part of the addiction process, which results in physical changes to the body.
   b. Psychological dependence causes people to continue with drugs despite adverse social and medical consequences.
   d. Tolerance is the body's decreased response to the drug, which means more of the drug is required for the same effect.

2. *d. occasionally culturally condoned (pp. 333–334)
   a. Children consuming alcohol is legal in some countries.
   b. It is illegal in many countries.
   c. In France and parts of the U.S. childhood drinking is condoned.

3. *c. a minor relapse that shouldn't stop her self-control efforts (p. 359)
   a. Avoiding abstinence violation effect is a goal of treatment to prevent relapse.
   b. Terry was in a high-risk situation and may need additional assistance in identifying these times, but not necessarily more intense therapy.
   d. Her therapist will use all possible means to avoid this episode from becoming a major relapse.

4. *a. should be different because of their different life circumstances (p. 356)
   b. Their circumstances are so different that the same treatment may not have the desired effect.
   c. There appear to be very few similarities in their lives.
   d. Because of Todd's age, family interactions may be more pertinent for him than for Bruce.

5. *b. tolerance (p. 332)
   a. Withdrawal is the condition associated with removal of the drug from the patient's system.
   c. Relapse is the reappearance of substance abuse after a period of remission.
   d. Remission is the state of health following reduction or disappearance of the drug from the patient.

6. *d. impossible to know because there is no single cause (p. 346)
   a. Peer influences are only one of many factors contributing to alcohol abuse.
   b. Environmental forces play a role in substance abuse, but only partially explain the cause.
   c. Family factors are only one among many contributing elements that help us understand the cause of drug abuse.

7. *b. vulnerability model (p. 351)
   a. The unitary disease model holds that alcoholics differ from normal persons in terms of psychological predisposition and sensitivity to the drug.
   c. Genetics seems to contribute to the risk of developing alcoholism, but doesn't fully explain it.
   d. The cognitive expectancy theory relates to those who typically cope with stress by avoidance and expected positive effects from alcohol.

8. *b. environmental cues (p. 355)
   a. Tension-reduction hypothesis would be supported by behavioral therapists.
   c. Oral fixation is a psychodynamic concept.
   d. *Remission* is a term that describes a state of health in which a previously active disorder or illness has receded or disappeared entirely.

9. *b. After failing an important exam, Jim attributes the failure to a wild drinking party he attended the evening prior to the exam. (p. 351)
   a. Damien's actions reflect the tension-reduction hypothesis.
   c. By removing an aversive emotional state, Lupe is reducing tension, not setting up a situation where poor performance can be covered up.
   d. Withdrawal symptoms are a realistic occurrence associated with smoking cessation, and Candy's feelings are indicative of the abstinence violation effect (AVE).

10. *c. In general, there is a modest genetic influence for men and women born to alcoholic parents but increasing risk for males whose parents show early-onset alcoholism. (p. 347)
    a. Research shows greater heritability for men than for women and depends on the parents' alcoholic history.
    b. There is a modest genetic influence.
    d. The role of genetic factors seems to vary with the type of alcoholism.

ANSWER KEY: APPLICATION MULTIPLE-CHOICE QUESTIONS

1. *b. total abstinence (p. 358)
    a. Controlled drinking is a controversial aspect of treatment for alcoholism. The consensus is that it will not work for most alcoholics.
    c. Planned relapse is a controversial part of relapse prevention training.
    d. Peer support groups, such as AA, require abstinence as one of their goals.

2. *c. the drug is self-administered (p. 361)
    a. The drug is supposed to make Miriam nauseous when alcohol is in her system.
    b. The drug is available in treatment programs nationwide.
    d. Antabuse is not addictive; methadone is, and for this reason is controversial.

3. *d. AA does not open itself to scientific evaluation (pp. 362–363)
    a. There is no research record on the success of AA. The results reported are anecdotal.
    b. AA consistently contends that its programs are not therapy.
    c. More than one half of the members of AA are between the ages of 31 and 50.

4. *c. dissemination of preventive information is needed during the early years (p. 363)
    a. Up to 90 percent of high school students have had experience with drinking.
    b. Most high school students receive misinformation about alcohol and drugs.
    d. There are now many programs to help adolescents deal with drinking, but many more are needed.

5. *c. cannabis use (pp. 338–340)
    a. Cocaine causes feelings of euphoria and excitation.
    b. Hallucinogens have the effect of creating sensory distortions.
    d. Amphetamines have a powerful excitatory effect, alertness, and heightened feelings of self-esteem.

6. *b. cocaine (p. 341)
    a. Use of cannabis ordinarily does not cause a depression such as that experienced by users of cocaine.
    c. LSD produces the sensory distortion effect, but not a severe depression.
    d. Benzodiazepines produce a sense of relaxation, but not the severe depression of cocaine use.

7. *b. withdrawal (p. 332)
    a. Tolerance is the need for larger amounts of a substance to achieve the effect.
    c. Nicotine is taken in very high, precise dosages, more than 200 a day in Bill's case.
    d. Nicotine is a fast-acting drug.

8. *a. perceived effects theory (p. 350)
    b. The psychodynamic model suggests regression to the oral stage as a result of conflicts as the reason for alcoholism.
    c. Heredity is only one of many possible causative factors in alcohol abuse.
    d. The tension reduction hypothesis has to do with learning theory and doesn't account for expectations and coping styles.

9. *c. a high-risk situation (pp. 351–352)
 a. Peer pressure is usually not associated with a single incidence of stress but with socialization with alcohol-approving peers.
 b. Remission is the disappearance or reduction of an illness or disorder.
 d. Withdrawal is the set of symptoms that result when a substance is taken away after body-altering long-term use.

10. *d. detoxification (p. 358)
 a. Relapse is the reappearance of substance abuse following remission.
 b. Remission is the reduction or disappearance of an active disorder or illness.
 c. Tolerance is the need for increased dosages of a drug to experience the same effects.

CHAPTER 12
Sexual Dysfunctions and Disorders

LEARNING OBJECTIVES

1. Describe how human sexual functioning is affected by mental processes. (pp. 370–371)

2. Describe how internal and external stimuli may trigger or inhibit sexual responses. (pp. 370–371)

3. Explain how the mental processes interact with the biological aspects of sexual behavior. (pp. 370–371)

4. Discuss the differences in how male and female sexual desire is linked to androgens. (p. 371)

5. Describe the physiological changes that take place during the stages of the sexual response cycle. (pp. 371–373)

6. Discuss the importance of communication between partners because of the variability in the sexual response cycle. (pp. 371–372)

7. Describe recent changes in what is accepted as normal sexual behavior. (pp. 372–375)

8. Discuss how the view of homosexuality has changed in the mental health field. (pp. 375–376)

9. Describe current research regarding the causes of homosexuality, including genetic studies supporting biological factors in homosexuality. (pp. 375–376)

10. Describe the effects of aging on sexual behavior. (pp. 376–377)

11. Identify factors that predict safer sexual practices among youth at risk for AIDS. (pp. 377–378)

12. Define sexual dysfunction. (p. 378)

13. Describe the features and causes of sexual desire disorders. (pp. 378–380)

14. Describe the features and causes of male and female sexual arousal disorders. (pp. 380–382)

15. Describe the features of male and female orgasm disorders. (pp. 382–383)

16. Discuss sexual pain disorders. (p. 383)

17. Describe the methods of treatment for sexual dysfunction. (pp. 383–386)

18. Distinguish between the features of paraphilias and sex crimes. (pp. 386–387)

19. Identify common paraphilias and describe the characteristics of persons engaged in these behaviors. (pp. 387–393)

20. Describe the features of incest and the characteristics of fathers who commit incest. (pp. 393–394)

21. Discuss the causes of sexual paraphilias and sexual violence, including biological and social approaches. (pp. 394–396)

22. Describe the various treatments and successes of sex disorders. (pp. 396–397)

23. Describe the features of gender identity disorder. (pp. 397–399)

24. Discuss the causes of gender identity disorder. (pp. 399–400)

25. Explain the treatment approaches for gender identity disorders. (pp. 400–401)

CHAPTER OUTLINE

- *Sexual dysfunctions:* Difficulties in normal sexual activity related to arousal and performance.

- *Paraphilias:* Atypical forms of sexual behavior or desire, legal or illegal.

- *Gender identity disorders:* Identification with and desire to be the gender different from one's biological sex.

I. Normal Sexual Functioning

   A. Mental and Biological Processes in Sexual Functioning

      1. Mental processes in sexual functioning

         a. Human sexuality is greatly affected by mental processes.

         b. Sexual cognitions are strongly influenced by learning.

         c. The ability to enjoy and function in a sexual relationship depends on many factors, such as

            (1) Attitudes

            (2) Beliefs

            (3) Emotions

            (4) Personal experiences

            (5) Cultural and historical sexual mores

            (6) Nature of the relationship itself

            (7) Family relationships

      2. Hormonal factors and sexual desire

a. Hormones regulate sexual response.

b. Hypothalamic hormones produce sex steroid hormones such as estrogen and androgens that affect sexual characteristics and desire.

c. In males, androgens (such as testosterone) are related to sexual desire.

d. In females, estrogen and progesterone as well as mood and energy level contribute to sexual desire.

B. Sexual Response Cycle

1. Human sexual response occurs in stages:

a. *Desire:* the usual beginning point, a state of interest or motivation for sexual activity.

b. *Excitement:* vasocongestion of various areas of the body including sexual organs, producing erection (men) and vaginal lubrication (women).

c. *Plateau:* sexual tension mounts to a peak leading to orgasm.

d. *Orgasm:* involuntary muscle spasms including uterine contraction in women and ejaculation in men.

e. *Resolution:* return to the normal physical state.

f. *Refractory (for men only):* a time during which no amount of stimulation will result in orgasm.

2. Because of the variability of the response cycle, communication is important between partners.

C. Normal Sexual Behaviors and Variations

1. The definition of deviant sexual behavior has shifted over the years.

2. What's Normal: Normality changes over time

a. Masturbation is widely practiced by men and women.

b. Premarital sexual intercourse has increased considerably by both men and women, with some ethnic/racial differences in frequency.

c. From a psychological and scientific standpoint, homosexuality, once considered a disorder, is now considered a normal variation in sexual behavior. New conclusion based on

(1) Similarity of personalities of homosexuals and heterosexuals.

(2) No evidence of greater psychiatric impairment.

(3) Growing emphasis on human rights.

(4) Prevalence of homosexuality.

d. Homosexuality more than sexual behavior: includes a psychological, emotional, and social preference for the same sex.

e. Continuum of sexual orientation ranges from exclusive heterosexuals to exclusive homosexuals.

    f.   Sexual orientation reflects interaction of biological, cultural, experiential, and socialization history.

    g.   Gender nonconformity, the rejection of traditional masculine or feminine roles, is seen as one of best predictors of adult homosexuality.

    h.   Biological factors have emerged as a cause of homosexuality.

3.   Sex and normal aging

    a.   Studies show a decline in sexual activity as people age.

    b.   Physiological changes of aging partially account for this decline:

        (1)   Decreased androgen and testosterone levels in men (reduced sexual desire and activity)

        (2)   Decreased estrogen in women (reduced vaginal lubrication and thinning of vaginal wall create discomfort)

    c.   Negative attitudes accompanying aging are a greater obstacle to sexual enjoyment than physical effects of aging.

4.   Focus on Research: What predicts safer sex among youth at risk for AIDS?

    a.   The factors that distinguish youth who practice safer sex from youth who relapse into unprotected sex include higher self-esteem, lower anxiety, and lower alcohol use.

    b.   Youths also need comprehensive health care to combat depression and other emotional problems.

II.   Sexual Dysfunction

- Sexual dysfunction is the general term for problems in sexual interest or performance that cause distress.

- Not a clinically diagnosable problem unless persistent and disturbing to individual

- Disorders categorized according to the phase of sexual response cycle in which they occur.

A.   Sexual Desire Disorders

- Hypoactive sexual desire is characterized by low or absent desire for sexual activities.

1.   Features of sexual desire disorders

    a.   Imbalanced sexual desire between a man and a woman common.

    b.   Sex dysfunction creates relationship difficulties.

    c.   Sexual aversion disorder is a rare and severe form of sexual desire disorder involving extreme aversion to sexual contact and total avoidance of sexual activity.

2.   Causes of sexual desire disorders

    a.   Relationship and psychological factors:

         (1)   Family and cultural prohibitions.

         (2)   Fear of psychosexual closeness and vulnerability.

         (3)   Unacceptable sexual preferences.

         (4)   Stress.

    b.   Biological and medical issues:

         (1)   Aging

         (2)   Clinical depression

         (3)   Medical illnesses

         (4)   Some medications

         (5)   Alcohol and drug use and abuse

B.   Sexual Arousal Disorders

    1.   Features of sexual arousal disorders

        a.   Female arousal disorder, refers to difficulties in attaining or maintaining physical arousal.

        b.   Male erectile disorder, once referred to as impotence, is difficulty in attaining or sustaining adequate erection for sexual activity.

    2.   Causes of sexual arousal disorders

        a.   Psychological factors including personal conflicts and relationship conflicts.

        b.   Spectator role is the adoption of a role as a critical observer of oneself rather than a participant.

        c.   Because 50 percent of erectile problems are caused by physiological problems, it is important to determine whether physical problems are the source of the difficulty.

        d.   Aging and changes in testosterone levels.

        e.   Medical illnesses, psychotropic drugs, alcohol and other drugs.

C.   Orgasm Disorders

    1.   Female orgasmic disorder (anorgasmia): Once called *frigidity*, refers to a women's inability to sustain arousal or achieve orgasm, which causes personal distress or interpersonal difficulties.

    2.   Premature ejaculation: Man reaches orgasm so quickly that his own enjoyment or that of his partner is reduced, causing great distress or interpersonal difficulties. Occurs most often in young men.

    3.   Male orgasmic disorder (inhibited male orgasm).

    4.   Causes of orgasm disorders

        a.   Relationship factors and attitudes about sex are important.

b.   Premature ejaculation is affected by learning, conditioning, anxiety, and infrequency of orgasm.

D. Sexual Pain Disorders

1.   Dyspareunia is genital pain during or after intercourse in men or women.

2.   Vaginismus is involuntary muscular spasm of the outer portion of the vagina interfering with entry and the penis.

3.   Causes of sexual pain disorders

a.   Vaginismus caused by conditioned sexual fear response.

b.   Dyspareunia has physical causes, such as inadequate lubrication, vaginal infections, or damage during childbirth.

E. Treatment of Sexual Dysfunction

•   Sex therapy, brief behaviorally oriented therapy with techniques aimed specifically at sexual problems of couples, was developed by Masters and Johnson in the 1970s.

•   Now sex therapy is multimodal; therapies use a variety of techniques.

1.   Shared components of sex therapies

a.   Treatment for both members of a couple.

b.   Education involving explicit information about sexual functioning.

c.   Identification and correction of maladaptive cognitions about sexual functioning.

d.   Learning about one's body and communication with the partner.

e.   Sensate focus: a technique to improve exploration and communication.

f.   Various techniques to deal with arousal and orgasm disorders, including sensate focusing, pause and squeeze techniques, and directed masturbation.

g.   Psychodynamically oriented therapies for aversion dysfunction; combine cognitive-behavioral procedures and insight-oriented therapy.

h.   Success predicted on quality of relationship.

i.   Vaginismus treated by exercise of pubococcygeal muscle and use of dilators.

2.   Medical treatments for sexual dysfunctions

a.   Penile prostheses: surgically implanted artificial means of achieving erections.

b.   Drug injection or oral medication for erectile dysfunction.

c.   Surgery.

d.   Psychotropic medications.

e.   Hormone replacement.

III. Paraphilias and Sex Crimes

    A. Features of Paraphilias and Sex Crimes

        1. *Paraphilia* means "beyond usual love"; refers to recurrent, intense, sexual urges about an atypical choice.

            a. Telephone scatologia (obscene phone calls).

            b. Necrophilia (having sex with corpses).

            c. Bestiality (having sex with animals).

            d. Having sex with amputees or elderly persons.

            e. Frotteurism (rubbing up against strangers).

        2. Sexual urges involve

            a. Nonhuman objects.

            b. Suffering or humiliation.

            c. Children or other nonconsenting persons.

        3. Many persons with marked paraphilias lack intimate relationships, have more than one paraphilia, and have additional psychiatric disorders.

        4. The extent of these disorders is unknown.

        5. They occur virtually always in men.

    B. Some Common Paraphilias

        1. Exhibitionism and voyeurism

            a. Exhibitionism: the display of genitals to an involuntary observer.

            b. Goal: to obtain an extreme emotional reaction, a desire for power and control over women.

            c. Voyeurism: a paraphilia characterized by the desire to watch unsuspecting people, usually strangers, who are nude, undressing, or engaging in sexual activity.

            d. May begin in adolescence and become chronic.

            e. Characterized by insecurity and poorly developed social skills.

        2. Fetishes

            a. Fetishism: intense sexual urges involving nonsexual items, such as clothing or a part of the body.

            b. Transvestic fetishism: a fetish involving a male wearing women's clothing, cross-dressing for sexual purposes.

        3. Sexual sadism and masochism

            a. Central element is the experience or infliction of pain

b.   Sexual masochism: recurrent intense sexually arousing fantasies involving being humiliated, beaten, bound, or made to suffer.

c.   Sexual sadism: sexually arousing urges and fantasies involving acts that cause physical or psychological suffering to another person.

d.   Hypoxyphilia: a dangerous form of sexual masochism that involves sexual arousal by oxygen deprivation. Occasionally leads to death by suffocation.

e.   Severe and dangerous forms of sexual sadism involve rape, assault, and murder.

f.   Lust murders: an example of severe sexual sadism accompanied by antisocial personality disorder. Often are serial murders involving mutilations.

4. Pedophilia

a.   Pedophilia: recurrent intense sexual urges and fantasies about sexual activity with a child by persons aged sixteen or older and where a five-year age difference exists.

b.   Child molestation: the legal concept describing sexual activities perpetrated by an older person on a child.

c.   Incest: sexual molestation involving sexual contact between family members.

d.   Course of pedophilia usually chronic; might be precipitated by stress or unavailability of a preferred partner.

e.   Characteristics of pedophiles:

(1)   Majority are males.

(2)   Less socially competent.

(3)   Passive.

(4)   Less apt to have conduct problems in school.

(5)   Lower intelligence.

(6)   Dysfunctional family backgrounds including physical abuse and neglect.

(7)   Had been victims of sexual assaults themselves.

5. Family Matters: Incest

a.   A significant amount of all sexual molestation of children occurs in the family.

b.   Father-child incest is very serious (in terms of harm to families).

c.   Children who are sexually victimized may have long-term consequences; the distortion of normal relationship bonds violates trust.

d.   Incest occurs

(1)   In families at all socioeconomic levels.

(2)   In the context of poor marital relationships.

           (3)   Father may have alcoholism or other mental disorders.

           (4)   In families with economic hardships.

   e.   Incestuous fathers often

           (1)   Are not empathic or nurturing.

           (2)   Lack social skills.

           (3)   May have been sexually abused themselves.

           (4)   Believe their children desire the sexual contact.

6.   Rape: Most rapes are not sex disorders in the clinical diagnostic sense.

C.   Causes of Sexual Paraphilias and Sexual Violence

- Causes are biological and psychological, shaped by cultural norms and learned values.

1.   Biological approaches

   a.   Genetic studies are rare and inconclusive because of small sample sizes.

   b.   There is some (inconclusive) evidence to support the possible effect of chromosomal anomalies on paraphilias.

   c.   Some types of brain dysfunction such as temporal lobe epilepsy may be involved.

2.   Psychological approaches

   a.   Psychodynamic explanations (symbolic meanings representing unresolved, unconscious conflicts) are largely untestable.

   b.   Learning experiences are important in variant sexual preferences.

   c.   Lack of acceptable outlets, perhaps due to underdeveloped social skills, may promote fantasies or experiences of sexual encounters with inappropriate partners.

   d.   Problem with conditioning and learning approach is that the disorder is extremely rare in women.

   e.   *Imprinting* is the critical period of learning during which a particular stimulus acquires major significance. Males might have biologically based targeting for sexual arousal that females do not have.

   f.   Most available research is limited: based on incarcerated populations, which represent an extreme sample of the population, retrospective studies, and correlational data.

D.   Treatment of Sex Disorders

- Rehabilitative efforts are not particularly effective with men convicted of sex crimes.

- Many are also suffering from personality and substance-use disorders.

- Many are receiving treatment involuntarily.

- Measure of effectiveness of treatment is recidivism, or likelihood that after release from prison offender is later convicted of another crime. It is high for sex offenders.

1. Cognitive-behavioral treatments of sex disorders

   a. Altering sexual preferences: reducing arousal to inappropriate stimuli, encouraging arousal to appropriate stimuli.

   b. Modifying social incompetence: *social skills training* procedures and problem-solving techniques strongly emphasized.

   c. Changing distorted cognitions: *cognitive strategies* identify and challenge distorted beliefs, attitudes, and expectations.

   d. Treatment is promising for certain types of sexual disorders (child molesters and exhibitionists lower recidivism with treatment than rapists).

2. Physical treatments of sex disorders

   a. Psychosurgery and castration have been used in some countries, but effectiveness has not been demonstrated. Also, ethical concerns.

   b. Antiandrogen medications, drugs that suppress testosterone and thus reduce sex drive in males, have also been used.

   c. Many men drop out of treatment.

IV. Gender Identity Disorder

   A. Features of Gender Identity Disorder

   - Gender identity disorder: A condition in which a person persistently experiences discomfort with his or her biological sex and expresses profound identification with the other sex.

   - Transsexuals have an intense desire to be transformed through hormonal and surgical means into the opposite sex.

   - Gender dysphoria is dissatisfaction with one's biological identity.

   - Transsexualism differs from transvestic fetishism in that transsexuals do not obtain sexual gratification by cross-dressing.

   1. Course of gender identity disorder

      a. Childhood gender identity disorder is early experiences of wishing to be (or believing that one truly is) the opposite sex.

      b. Gender-atypical behaviors fairly common in childhood; unclear how many children who display this behavior become transsexuals.

   2. Epidemiology of gender identity disorder

      a. Data unavailable.

      b. Estimates indicate higher rates among men than women.

   B. Causes of Gender Identity Disorder

1. Sexual identity evolves from a complex set of biological and psychological factors (John Money).

    a. Biological differences have not been found.

    b. Psychological factors are involved, including cognitive social-learning processes.

2. Some evidence of reinforcement as a mechanism in gender identity disorder.

3. Cultural and societal values also may play a role.

C. Treating Gender Identity Disorders

1. Psychotherapy ineffective in resolving gender conflict.

2. Surgery and hormonal alterations to alter sexual anatomy successful.

3. Sex reassignment treatment involves careful evaluation. Four stages:

    a. Counseling and psychological evaluation to determine acceptability for this arduous treatment.

    b. Hormonal treatment.

    c. Living the life of the desired gender for a year before surgery.

    d. Surgery.

V. What Lies Ahead?

A. The specter of AIDS dominates sexual behavior research.

B. Sexual victimization has been increasingly brought to light with increasing efforts to change unwanted behaviors.

KEY TERMS REVIEW

1. Feelings of dissatisfaction with one's biological identity is called _____.

2. A technique used in sex therapy to improve both physical exploration and communication, in which partners progress through various types of touching to learn more about what gives pleasure to each other, is called _____.

3. A paraphilia characterized by the desire to watch unsuspecting people, usually strangers, who are nude, undressing, or engaging in sexual activity, is called _____.

4. Early experiences of wishing to be (or believing that one truly is) the opposite sex is called _____.

5. Low or absent desire for sexual activities or lack of sexual fantasies is called _____.

6. The legal definition of sexual activity perpetrated by an older person on a child is called _____.

7. In sex dysfunctions, the adoption of a role as a critical observer of oneself rather than a participant, which grows out of performance anxiety and can impair further erectile disorder, is called the _____.

8. Increased worry about personal sexual performance by a male who experienced erectile disorder in the past; paired with the *spectator role* is called _____.

9. A form of sexual molestation involving sexual contact between family members is called _____.

10. A female sex hormone, the levels of which affect the development and maintenance of secondary sex characteristics in women, is called _____.

11. Hormones such as testosterone, which are related in males to sexual desire and motivation, are called _____.

12. Involuntary muscle spasms of the outer portion of the vagina that interfere with entry of the penis is called _____.

13. A term applied to therapies that use a variety of techniques and commonly include extensive assessment, communications skills training, and cognitive-behavioral and behavioral components is called _____.

14. A stage of the sexual response cycle during which sexual tension mounts to a peak, usually leading to orgasm, is called the _____.

15. Genital pain during or after intercourse in either males of females is called _____.

16. The likelihood that after release from prison an offender is later convicted of another crime is called _____.

17. A more severe and infrequent form of sexual desire disorder, involving extreme aversion to sexual contact and total avoidance of sexual activity, is called _____.

18. A stage of the sexual response cycle during which various areas of the body, including sexual organs, experience vasocongestion (swelling) and muscle tension, heart rate, and blood pressure increase is called the _____.

19. Drugs that suppress testosterone and thus reduce the sex drive are called _____.

20. A female sex hormone that varies in level throughout the menstrual cycle is called _____.

21. A form of sexual masochism that involves sexual arousal by oxygen deprivation is called _____.

22. The first stage of the sexual response cycle; a state of interest in or motivation for sexual activity is called the _____.

23. The final stage of the sexual response cycle, consisting of a return to the normal physical state after orgasm, is called the _____.

24. The displaying of genitals to an involuntary observer is called _____.

25. Another term for a person with gender identity disorder is _____.

26. The rejection of traditional masculine or feminine roles is called _____.

27. Difficulties experienced by females in attaining or maintaining sexual arousal is called _____.

28. Brief, behaviorally oriented treatments with techniques aimed specifically at sexual problems and typically treated in the context of a couple relationship is called _____.

29. Intense sexual urges involving nonsexual items or a part of the body is called _____.

30. A fetish in men involving the wearing of women's clothing as a means of increasing sexual pleasure is called _____.

31. A female's inability to sustain sexual arousal or achieve orgasm is called _____.

32. The general term for problems in sexual interest or performance that cause distress to individuals or difficulties in their relationships is called _____.

33. A condition in which a person persistently experiences discomfort with his or her biological sex and expresses profound identification with the other sex is called _____.

34. Sexually arousing urges and fantasies involving acts that cause physical or psychological suffering to another person is called _____.

35. Inhibited male orgasm is called _____.

36. Recurrent, intense sexual urges and fantasies about an atypical choice that may be acted on or cause marked distress for at least six months is called a _____.

37. Difficulties experienced by males in attaining or sustaining adequate erection until completion of sexual activity is called _____.

38. Recurrent intense sexually arousing fantasies and urges involving being humiliated, beaten, bound, or otherwise made to suffer is called _____.

39. A cause of treatment that includes careful psychological screening and counseling, hormonal treatment, and sex-change surgery, all aimed at enabling an individual to alter lifestyle and physical characteristics to match gender identify, is called _____.

40. A stage of the sexual response cycle characterized by involuntary muscle spasms and the release of tension is called the _____.

41. Surgically implanted artificial means of achieving erections are called _____.

42. Recurrent intense sexual urges and fantasies about sexual activity with a child by persons at least sixteen years old and at least five years older than the child is called _____.

43. A male's reaching orgasm so quickly that his own enjoyment or that of his partner is reduced is called _____.

FACTUAL MULTIPLE-CHOICE QUESTIONS

1. In males, the substances responsible for sexual desire and motivation are called
   a. androgens.
   b. antiandrogens.
   c. estrogen.
   d. progesterone.

2. Which of the following is not part of the human sexual response cycle?
   a. desire
   b. excitement
   c. plateau
   d. transference

3. An essential ingredient in resolving problems with the sexual response cycle is
   a. medication.
   b. surgery.
   c. psychoanalysis.
   d. communication.

4. Surveys of sexual activity have indicated that
   a. the majority of males masturbate.
   b. masturbation is considered taboo by males and females.
   c. few males masturbate.
   d. virtually no females masturbate.

5. Same-sex sexual contact
   a. is common among the majority of adults.
   b. is common during childhood.
   c. is rare during childhood.
   d. is rare during adolescence.

6. Sex researchers have noted that the greatest obstacle to sexual enjoyment for older males is
   a. increased androgen levels for men.
   b. inevitable decline in interest.
   c. hormonal decreases.
   d. negative attitudes.

7. Masters and Johnson developed a sex therapy technique for couples that is called
   a. multimodal.
   b. sensate focus.
   c. multiple orgasms.
   d. the spectator role.

8. Which of the following characteristics would *not* be typical of an exhibitionist?
   a. shy
   b. unassertive
   c. masculinity
   d. sexually experienced

9. A child who expresses that he or she is really of the opposite sex is experiencing
   a. pedophilia.
   b. incest.
   c. transvestism.
   d. childhood gender identity disorder.

10. The final step in sex reassignment treatment is
    a. hormone treatment.
    b. counseling.
    c. surgery.
    d. psychological evaluation.

CONCEPTUAL MULTIPLE-CHOICE QUESTIONS

1. Of the following, which one has the least effect on sexual functioning?
   a. the brain
   b. cognitions
   c. hormones
   d. age

2. Recent studies of genetics indicate that homosexuality is
   a. definitely transmitted genetically.
   b. caused by a dominant mother.
   c. caused by a passive father.
   d. in some cases genetically transmitted.

3. Don began therapy in 1972 and admitted he was gay to his therapist. Two years later he returned to therapy. What would have changed about Don's diagnosis in those intervening years?
   a. Homosexuality was discovered to be genetically determined.
   b. Homosexuality was designated a more serious disorder.
   c. Homosexuality was removed from the DSM.
   d. Homosexuality was designated a less serious disorder.

4. Mike worked sixty-hour weeks for several months to complete a project suddenly given to him. His inability to maintain an erection during this time would be diagnosed as
   a. hypoactive sexual desire.
   b. sexual aversion disorder.
   c. a normal reaction to stress and fatigue.
   d. male erectile disorder.

5. Joanne had orgasms infrequently even though she had been married happily for twelve years. She enjoyed her sex life, but asked her doctor what she would recommend. Her doctor recommended
   a. psychoanalysis.
   b. sensate focus therapy.
   c. hormone treatment.
   d. no treatment at all.

6. Mary is disturbed by her husband's insistence that she wear a certain pair of shoes during sexual intercourse. He insists that there is nothing wrong with his request. If Mary refused to wear the shoes the likely outcome would be
   a. her husband would develop a transvestic fetish.
   b. she would lose her desire for sex.
   c. her husband would not be able to experience sexual arousal.
   d. her husband would become a sexual sadist.

7. Although his sexual anatomy and hormonal functioning are normal, Roger insists on dressing in women's clothing to help him achieve sexual satisfaction. His diagnosis would be
   a. gender dysphoria.
   b. transvestism.
   c. male erectile disorder.
   d. sexual masochism.

8. Paraphilias differ from sexual dysfunctions in that paraphilias
    a. typically are of no harm to others, only to the individual with the paraphilia.
    b. are likely to affect men and women equally, while sexual dysfunctions predominantly affect women.
    c. are often illegal, while sexual dysfunctions are not.
    d. involve problems of sexual arousal while sexual dysfunctions do not.

9. Research on child molesters suggests that they
    a. become sexually aroused even in the face of a child's expression of distress compared with normal men.
    b. have abnormally high levels of hormonal imbalances and male erectile problems.
    c. are of high intelligence and are socially sophisticated, thus permitting them to pass as well-adjusted individuals.
    d. are motivated by pedophilic urges.

10. Premature ejaculation and male erectile disorder are similar in that they
    a. are disorders of the arousal phase of the sexual response cycle.
    b. are disturbances in the orgasm phase of the sexual response cycle.
    c. cause distress to men and impair interpersonal relationships.
    d. are best treated by the use of anti-androgen medications.

APPLICATION MULTIPLE-CHOICE QUESTIONS

1. Marcia and John lost interest in becoming intimate even though they had been married more than ten years. Their therapist diagnosed their problem as
    a. sexual aversion disorder.
    b. sexual desire disorder.
    c. female orgasmic disorder.
    d. dyspareunia.

2. Dianne was sexually assaulted six weeks ago. She sought help for a painful condition which her therapist felt was the result of her fear response to the rape. The condition is
    a. dyspareunia.
    b. vaginismus.
    c. female orgasmic disorder.
    d. performance anxiety.

3. John's fantasies include displaying his genitals to the women who ride on the bus with him. He hasn't acted on his fantasies, but he feels an increasing need to do so. He is in danger of committing
    a. exhibitionism.
    b. voyeurism.
    c. frotteurism.
    d. sexual sadism.

4. Janet has severe difficulties dealing with her sexuality. She has difficulty trusting men and forming relationships. She may be suffering from
    a. adult consequences of incest.
    b. anorgasmia.
    c. sexual masochism.
    d. sexual arousal disorder.

5. Lyle was given a prescription for antiandrogen medication. Lyle's diagnosis would probably be
   a. male erectile disorder.
   b. premature ejaculation.
   c. fetishism.
   d. sexual sadism.

6. Rhonda refuses to date and is virtually panic-stricken at the thought of sexual contact. Her psychiatrist considers Rhonda to be suffering from
   a. female orgasmic disorder.
   b. hypoactive sexual desire.
   c. female arousal disorder.
   d. sexual aversion disorder.

7. Jay is in his early twenties and after his first sexual encounter went to his doctor with a sexual performance problem that he was embarrassed to discuss. The problem is
   a. male erectile disorder.
   b. hypoactive sexual desire.
   c. premature ejaculation.
   d. male orgasmic disorder.

8. Mildred found sexual intercourse painful because of lack of vaginal lubrication. The treatment for this condition is
   a. surgery.
   b. hormone therapy.
   c. sensate focus.
   d. psychotherapy.

9. Jerome's fantasies included being bound and beaten by a woman in a mask who made him ask for punishment. His diagnosis is
   a. transvestism.
   b. sexual sadism.
   c. sexual masochism.
   d. transsexualism.

10. Your friend mentioned that she saw a television program that included a transvestite. Although she did not watch the entire program, she believes that transvestites must be severely psychologically disturbed for wanting to have a sex-change operation. What response would be appropriate?
    a. Agree that the transvestite has severe psychological difficulties for wanting to have a sex-change operation.
    b. Tell your friend that transvestites typically do not like to wear women's clothing.
    c. Inform your friend that transvestites differ from those individuals feeling uncomfortable with their gender.
    d. Indicate that most transvestites probably suffered from hypoactive sexual desire disorder.

ANSWER KEY: KEY TERMS REVIEW

1. gender dysphoria (398)
2. sensate focus (384)
3. voyeurism (388)
4. childhood gender identity disorder (399)
5. hypoactive sexual desire (378)
6. child molestation (392)
7. spectator role (381)
8. performance anxiety (381)
9. incest (392)
10. estrogen (371)
11. androgens (371)
12. vaginismus (383)
13. multimodal (384)
14. plateau phase (371)
15. dyspareunia (383)
16. recidivism (396)
17. sexual aversion disorder (379)
18. excitement phase (371)
19. antiandrogen medications (397)
20. progesterone (371)
21. hypoxyphilia (391)
22. desire phase (371)
23. resolution phase (371)
24. exhibitionism (387)
25. transsexual (397)
26. gender nonconformity (375)
27. female arousal disorder (380)
28. sex therapy (383)
29. fetishism (388)
30. transvestic fetishism (390)
31. female orgasmic disorder (382)
32. sexual dysfunction (378)
33. gender identity disorder (397)
34. sexual sadism (390)
35. male orgasmic disorder (382)
36. paraphilia (370, 386)
37. male erectile disorder (380)
38. sexual masochism (390)
39. sex reassignment treatment (401)
40. orgasm phase (371)
41. penile prostheses (386)
42. pedophilia (392)
43. premature ejaculation (382)

ANSWER KEY: FACTUAL MULTIPLE-CHOICE QUESTIONS

1. *a. androgens (p. 371)
   b. Antiandrogens are used to reduce sexual drive in sex offenders.
   c. Estrogen is the female sex hormone.
   d. Progesterone is another female sex hormone.

2. *d. transference (p. 371)
   a. The desire phase is the first stage of the sexual response cycle.
   b. Excitement is the stage in the sexual response cycle during which there are changes in various parts of the body.
   c. The plateau is the phase leading to orgasm.

3. *d. communication (p. 372)
   a. Medication is sometimes used to control anxiety or depression, which may interfere with sexual functioning.
   b. Surgery is occasionally used to repair damage done during childbirth.
   c. Psychoanalysis is not usually recommended for problems with sexual functioning.

4. *a. the majority of males masturbate (p. 373)
   b. Masturbation is no longer generally taboo for either males or females.
   c. The majority of males masturbate.
   d. Recent studies have shown that the majority of young women masturbate.

5. *b. is common during childhood (p. 374)
   a. Most adults do not have same-sex sexual contact.
   c. Such contact is common during childhood.
   d. Such contact is common during adolescence.

6. *d. negative attitudes (p. 377)
   a. Androgens are associated with male sexual drive; androgen levels decrease with age.
   b. Research has shown that there does not have to be a decline in interest in sexual behavior.
   c. Hormonal decreases account for only a small percentage of decline in sexual interest.

7. *b. sensate focus (p. 384)
   a. Multimodal approaches incorporate a variety of assessment and treatment techniques.
   c. Multiple orgasms, possible for females but not necessary for normal sexual functioning, are not a sex therapy technique.
   d. The spectator role figures in male erectile disorder along with performance anxiety.

8. *c. masculinity (pp. 387–388)
   a. Exhibitionists are often shy, particularly with women.
   b. They are also unassertive.
   d. Exhibitionists tend to be relatively inexperienced sexually.

9. *d. childhood gender identity disorder (pp. 397–398)
   a. Pedophilia is the direction of sexual attention toward children.
   b. Incest is sexual activity with members of one's family.
   c. Transvestism is a fetish involving males wearing women's clothing.

10. *c. surgery (p. 399)
    a. Hormone treatment is one of the preparative steps in the treatment.
    b. Counseling takes place early in the process and continues throughout.
    d. Psychological evaluation is done at the beginning of the process to determine if the individual is a good candidate for this rigorous procedure.

ANSWER KEY: CONCEPTUAL MULTIPLE-CHOICE QUESTIONS

1. *d. age (p. 376)
   a. The brain is one of the most potent sexual organs affecting physiological and cognitive responses.
   b. Cognitions have a powerful effect on how stimuli are interpreted.
   c. Hormones control sexual response.

2. *d. in some cases transmitted genetically (pp. 375–376)
   a. It is not definitely transmitted genetically in every case.
   b. The dominant mother theory has been debunked.
   c. The passive father theory has also been discredited.

3. *c. Homosexuality was removed from the DSM. (p. 374)
   a. Research has determined that some forms of homosexuality may be genetically transferred.
   b. Homosexuality was determined not to be a disorder at all.
   d. Don's diagnosis after 1973 would not have turned on his sexual orientation.

4. *c. a normal reaction to stress and fatigue (pp. 380–381)
   a. Hypoactive sexual desire is low or absent sexual desire, regardless of circumstances. Mike's desire is unaffected.
   b. Sexual aversion disorder involves extreme aversion to sexual contact.
   d. Mike's problem is not persistent or recurrent enough to meet the diagnostic criteria for male erectile disorder.

5. *d. no treatment at all (p. 382)
   a. Psychoanalysis is not recommended for sexual disorders.
   b. Sensate focus therapy is recommended for couples who have more severe forms of sexual disorders.
   c. Hormone treatment would be recommended for women who have reduced hormones that may interfere with sexual functioning.

6. *c. her husband would not be able to experience sexual arousal. (pp. 388–390)
   a. Transvestic fetishism involves a man wearing women's clothing to increase sexual pleasure.
   b. Mary has shown no desire to wear the shoes. Her desire for sex would be unaffected.
   d. If sadomasochism was not already part of Mary's behavior, there is little evidence that he might turn to that.

7. *b. transvestism (p. 390)
   a. Gender dysphoria is feelings of dissatisfaction with one's biological identity, not episodic like transvestism.
   c. Male erectile disorder is not a factor for fetishists, who are able to realize their fetishistic urges.
   d. Sexual masochism involves being made to suffer.

8. *c. are often illegal, while sexual dysfunctions are not. (p. 391)
   a. Paraphilias such as exhibitionism, sadism, and pedophilia do harm others.
   b. There is a higher frequency of paraphilias among men than women.
   d. Individuals showing paraphilias may not have problems with sexual arousal, but the target of their arousal is abnormal. Some sexual dysfunctions are defined by disturbances in sexual arousal.

9. *a. become sexually aroused even in the face of a child's expression of distress compared with normal men. (p. 392)
   b. Research has not concluded that there are hormonal imbalances or erectile problems among child molesters.
   c. Child molesters tend to be less socially active and competent and of lower intelligence.
   d. Most incest is probably not motivated by pedophilic urges.

10. *c. cause distress to men and impair interpersonal relationships. (pp. 380, 382–383)
    a. Premature ejaculation is a disturbance of the orgasm phase.
    b. Male erectile disorder is a disturbance of the arousal phase.
    d. Antiandrogen medications such as depo-provera suppress testosterone and would tend to lower sexual drive.

ANSWER KEY: APPLICATION MULTIPLE-CHOICE QUESTIONS

1. *b. sexual desire disorder (pp. 378–379)
   a. Sexual aversion disorder is a more severe and rare form of sexual desire disorder.
   c. Female orgasmic disorder is the inability to achieve an orgasm.
   d. Dyspareunia is genital pain during or after intercourse.

2. *b. vaginismus (p. 383)
   a. Dyspareunia commonly has a physical rather than a traumatic psychological cause.
   c. Female orgasmic disorder is a problem of arousal, not of pain.
   d. Performance anxiety is most often associated with males.

3. *a. exhibitionism (p. 387)
   b. Voyeurism has to do with watching others undress or engage in sexual activity.
   c. Frotteurism is rubbing against strangers to achieve sexual gratification.
   d. Sexual sadism is inflicting suffering upon another person for sexual gratification.

4. *a. adult consequences of incest (pp. 393–394)
   b. Anorgasmia is the inability to sustain arousal or achieve orgasm.
   c. Sexual masochism is urges involving being humiliated or made to suffer.
   d. Sexual arousal disorder includes difficulties that occur in the excitement phase of the sexual response cycle.

5. *d. sexual sadism (p. 397)
   a. Antiandrogens would only aggravate male erectile disorder.
   b. Premature ejaculation is an orgasmic disorder usually affecting younger men; it would not be helped by antiandrogens.
   c. Fetishism involves nonsexual items or a part of the body and would not be helped by antiandrogens.

6. *d. sexual aversion disorder (p. 379)
   a. Female orgasmic disorder might be a problem if Rhonda agreed to any sexual contact.
   b. Hypoactive sexual desire is low or absent sexual desire, not complete aversion.
   c. Female arousal disorder is a less severe form of arousal disorder than the one Rhonda is suffering.

7. *c. premature ejaculation (p. 382)
   a. Male erectile disorder is not usually associated with young men and their first sexual encounters.
   b. Hypoactive sexual desire is usually not a problem for young men.
   d. Male orgasmic disorder would be the opposite problem from the one presented here.

8. *b. hormone therapy (p. 386)
   a. Surgery is occasionally used to repair damage from childbirth which might later cause pain to the woman, but it does not affect vaginal lubrication.
   c. Sensate focus is therapy for couples and would only be a treatment in a case such as this if Mildred's complaint were accompanied by arousal disorder.
   d. Psychotherapy would not be the treatment of choice for a physiological problem such as this.

9. *c.   sexual masochism (p. 390)
   a.   Transvestism is not usually part of the sadomasochistic paraphilia.
   b.   Sexual sadism involves giving rather than receiving punishment or pain.
   d.   Transsexualism is the desire to have one's biological sex altered to conform with the subjective view of one's gender identification.

10. *c.   Inform your friend that transvestites differ from those individuals feeling uncomfortable with their gender. (pp. 397–398)
   a.   Transvestic fetishism is a fetish involving the wearing of women's clothing.
   b.   This is the definition of transvestic fetishism.
   d.   Hypoactive sexual desire disorder is a lack of interest in sexual activity.

CHAPTER 13
Personality Disorders

LEARNING OBJECTIVES

1. Distinguish the merely eccentric from personality disorders. (pp. 406–407)

2. Describe the features of personality disorders. (pp. 406–413)

3. Discuss the difficulties in defining personality disorders. (pp. 406–407)

4. Describe the importance of rigid traits, maladaptive lifestyles, and interpersonal relations in defining personality disorders. (pp. 406–407)

5. Describe the diagnostic categories and characteristics of Cluster A personality disorders, the eccentric/odd. (pp. 407–408)

6. Describe the diagnostic categories and characteristics of Cluster B personality disorders, the dramatic/erratic. (pp. 408–412)

7. Describe the diagnostic categories and characteristics of Cluster C personality disorders, the anxious/fearful. (pp. 412–413)

8. Discuss the problems involved in estimating the prevalence of personality disorders. (pp. 413–414)

9. Explain the problems involved with the classification and diagnosis of personality disorders. (pp. 414–417)

10. Describe the problems with diagnostic overlap and comorbidity of personality disorders with other disorders and how coexistent diagnoses may be forms of the same disorder. (pp. 416–417)

11. Describe the debate over personality dimensions versus discrete categories in defining personality disorders. (pp. 417–419)

12. Discuss the use of the five key personality dimensions to define personality disorders. (pp. 418–419)

13. Describe the causal factors involved in personality disorders using a biological perspective. (pp. 419–421)

14. Discuss Jerome Kagan's research and its implications for personality traits marked by inhibition. (pp. 421–422)

15. Describe the various psychological explanations of personality disorders. (pp. 422–424)

16. Discuss research on the link between personality disorders and early childhood experiences. (pp. 424–425)

17. Describe how various causes of personality disorders may be viewed as interactive in causation. (pp. 424–426)

18. Evaluate the effectiveness of treatment for personality disorders and some of the obstacles to the successful treatment. (pp. 426–427)

19. Describe promising new approaches to treatment for personality disorders. (pp. 427–429)

CHAPTER OUTLINE

* Traits are characteristic attitudes, beliefs, behaviors, reactions, and ways of thinking about oneself and the world.

* Extreme traits that produce notable impairment are linked to personality disorders.

I. Features of Personality Disorders

   * There is no consistent viewpoint about the nature of personality disorders or the utility of these diagnoses.

   A. Defining Personality Disorders

      1. Ten constellations of personality traits diagnosed in the DSM-IV are grouped in three broad clusters: A, B, and C.

      2. Personality disorder: a continuing pattern of perceiving and relating to the world that is maladaptive across a variety of contexts and results in notable impairment or distress.

      3. Nonpsychotic.

      4. Difficult to treat.

      5. Marked by dysfunctional interpersonal relations.

      6. Personality-disordered persons are frequently more disturbing to others rather than disturbed themselves.

   B. Cluster A: The Eccentric/Odd Personality Disorders

      1. Paranoid personality disorder

         a. Marked by pervasive suspicion of others and distrust of their motives.

         b. Sensitive to perceived slights, respond angrily, hold grudges.

         c. Perceived as hostile, stubborn, needing to be in control, and preoccupied with power.

         d. Delusions, hallucinations, or thought disorders associated with schizophrenia are not present in paranoid personality disorders.

2. Schizoid personality disorder

   a. Marked by aloofness from relationships and emotional coldness.

   b. Classic "loner."

3. Schizotypal personality disorder

   a. Marked by difficulties in interpersonal relationships as well as by abnormalities of thought, behavior, and appearance.

   b. May include unusual speech or beliefs, strange perceptual experiences, and eccentricities.

C. Cluster B: The Dramatic/Erratic Personality Disorders

1. Histrionic personality disorder

   a. Characterized by excessive overemotionality, flamboyance, and attention seeking.

   b. Seductive, excitable, overreactive, and highly suggestible.

   c. Appear emotionally shallow and self-centered.

2. Borderline personality disorder

   a. Characterized by pervasive instability of mood, chaotic relationships, and uncertain self-definition.

   b. Mood disturbances include rapid shifts into depression, anxiety, and anger.

   c. Intense unstable personal relationships.

   d. Fear of being alone.

   e. Occasional self-destructive activity, impulsive suicidal threats, or temporary dissociative reactions.

3. Narcissistic personality disorder

   a. Marked by grandiosity—an inflated sense of self-importance, accompanied by the expectation of special treatment or exemption from the rules others must follow.

   b. May be exploitative and lacking in sympathy.

   c. This category is controversial, with some clinicians believing it doesn't exist.

4. Antisocial personality disorder

   a. Characterized by a history of callousness, disregard for social conventions and others' rights and feelings, and illegal conduct.

   b. For diagnosis, there must be a conduct disorder, a childhood or adolescent problem consisting of a repetitive and persistent problem of behavior that involves violation of the basic rights of others.

   c. Marked by aggressiveness, deceit, irresponsibility, impulsivity, reckless disregard for safety, lack of remorse.

D.   Cluster C: The Anxious/Fearful Personality Disorders

   1.   Obsessive-compulsive personality disorder

      a.   Marked by perfectionism, orderliness, and control over the self and others to the point of rigidity and inefficiency.

      b.   Focus on details, rules, form, organization, and schedules.

      c.   Tend to be moralistic and judgmental.

   2.   Avoidant personality disorder

      a.   Marked by social discomfort, timidity, and fear of negative evaluation.

      b.   Desire for social interaction hampered by fear of negative reactions or criticism.

   3.   Dependent personality disorder

      a.   Marked by pervasive patterns of dependent and submissive behavior, leaving the person seemingly unable to make even everyday decisions for himself or herself.

      b.   Appear helpless; require much reassurance.

      c.   Desperate to maintain close relationships; fear abandonment.

E.   Who Is Affected with Personality Disorders?

   1.   Although difficult to estimate, studies have shown 6 to 9 percent of the total population in North America and Europe manifests some symptoms of personality disorder.

   2.   Personality disorder is associated with urban populations, lower socioeconomic status, and gender.

   3.   There is a striking presence of personality disorders among treated populations, especially borderline personality disorder.

F.   Problems with Classification of Personality Disorders

   •   Personality disorders are beset with problems of validity and reliability of diagnosis.

   1.   Selection and definition of Axis II disorders

      a.   Choice of ten pathological manifestations of personality is arbitrary.

      b.   Some categories came from psychoanalytic theory and practice, others from clinical observation.

      c.   There is potential for *sex or cultural bias* in the diagnostic criteria themselves or by clinicians.

      d.   Gender bias may occur with clinicians reluctant to label women antisocial or men as histrionic.

   2.   Diagnostic overlap and comorbidity

      a. DSM method of characterizing disorders of personality based on assumption of separate, distinct categories, but this assumption is problematic, calling into question validity of separate diagnostic categories.

      b. High levels of Axis II comorbidity may exist because of considerable overlap of symptoms.

      c. Co-occurrence of Axis I and II diagnoses may arise from shared risk and causal factors (one disorder may cause the other) or simply from shared symptoms.

      d. There may be overlap because of imprecise or arbitrary diagnostic boundaries.

      e. Borderline personality disorders may be a subtype of depression.

      f. Schizotypal personality disorder may be a prodromal phase of schizophrenia and not a distinct disorder.

      g. Social phobia and avoidant personality disorder may differ only in severity.

   3. Categories versus dimensions

      a. One solution to the classification problem is to characterize personality disorders not as specific entities but as personality dimensions, a continuum from low to none to extreme on which personality traits may be measured.

      b. Patients would be described by the degree to which they display specific characteristics, not by presence of a specific diagnostic category.

G. What's Normal? Using the Dimensions of Normal Personality to Define Personality Disorders

   1. Five key dimensions ("big five") underlie all human traits:

      a. Extroversion/introversion.

      b. Friendliness/hostility (or agreeableness).

      c. Conscientiousness (or will).

      d. Neuroticism/emotional stability.

      e. Intellect (or openness to experience).

   2. Studies have shown that using these dimensions one can describe the personality disorders.

   3. Other researchers have found that more dimensions may be needed, making diagnosis considerably more complex.

II. Causes of Personality Disorders: Some Research Findings

A. Biological Perspectives on Personality Disorders

   1. The lack of clear boundaries between disorders makes interpretation of genetic research difficult.

2. Dimensions of personality, such as impulsive aggressiveness, rather than diagnostic categories, such as antisocial personality disorder, may be a better approach.

3. Biological mechanisms such as neurotransmitter serotonin may be specific to certain core personality dimensions.

4. There is evidence that certain traits, such as outgoingness and sociability, may have a *genetic* basis.

5. Temperaments, or behavior tendencies believed to be biologically based and present from birth, may persist into adulthood, becoming a risk factor for development of personality disorders.

B. Focus on Research: Do infant traits portend personality disorder?

1. Kagan and colleagues tested the theory that shy children might be at risk for developing avoidant or dependent personality disorders.

2. To test the persistence of this trait, Kagan studied children at various ages and in different settings.

3. Most children remained inhibited (shy, quiet, and timid) or uninhibited (sociable, talkative, and spontaneous) over time.

4. Physiological reactions to novelty or change were found to correlate with differences in behavioral inhibition.

5. Inhibited children were relatively more aroused or had lower thresholds for response to change or challenge.

6. Children of parents with anxiety disorders were significantly more likely to display behavioral inhibition.

C. Psychological Contributions to Personality Disorders

- Research is constrained by methodological problems, such as *retrospective reports.*

- *Prospective (longitudinal) studies* are needed.

1. Psychodynamic explanations

   a. Borderline personality disorder seen as the product of disturbed object relations.

   b. Failure to develop a coherent sense of self and of positive relations with others from an early age contributes to borderline or narcissistic psychological disorder.

   c. Disturbed family relationships and evidence of childhood trauma are common in borderline patients.

D. Family Matters: Borderline Personality Disorder and Malevolent Object Relations

- Object relations models propose disturbances in *the object world*, how patients construe and feel about the self and others.

- Borderline personality sufferers may reflect object representations, viewing others as *malevolent,* hurtful, dangerous, uncaring, and untrustworthy.

- This theory was tested by Westen and colleagues, using the TAT responses of borderline patients.

- Borderline patients reported stories of people as malevolent, with grossly illogical explanations of behavior.

- Early childhood experiences of trauma may contribute to later life anxiety, rage, and depression.

- Those results are consistent with evidence of childhood abuse in patients with borderline personality disorders.

- The causal relationship between early family experiences and borderline personality disorder has not been established.

1. Cognitive-behavioral explanations

    a. Personality disorders may arise from maladaptive *schemas:* assumptions, beliefs, and attitudes that guide the selection and interpretation of information. Schemas are resistant to change.

        (1) Core schema for paranoid personality disorder might be *suspicion.*

        (2) Core schema for obsessive-compulsive personality might be the belief that certainty is essential.

    b. Maladaptive schemas are acquired in the earliest years and exert a pervasive influence.

    c. Understanding the family environment is essential to understanding the cause of personality disorder.

    d. Behaviorists emphasize the client's failure to develop adaptive skills, or learning dysfunctional behaviors.

2. Toward integrative models of causality

    a. Million's *biosocial* approach starts with the proposition that constitutional differences and neuropsychological maturation stages in the child set the stage for further learning.

    b. These dispositions are further accentuated by caretakers who respond to and reward, punish, and shape the child's behavior.

    c. At present, Million's hypotheses lack empirical support.

III. Treatment of Personality Disorders

A. Obstacles to Successful Treatment

1. Personality disorders are difficult to treat successfully: Problems are lifelong, patterns entrenched and pervasive, no relatively healthier baseline condition to which to return, few social supports.

2. Therapeutic success depends on traits these patients don't have:

    a. Motivation.

b.   Acceptance of responsibility.

c.   Ability to work cooperatively.

d.   Ability to retain sense of self between therapy sessions.

e.   Ability for objective appraisal of reality.

3.   Relationship between therapist and patient may be marked by excessive dependency, mistrust, or resistance.

4.   There is little research on treatments for these disorders.

5.   If other disorders occur, personality disorders interfere in treatment for them.

B.   New Therapies and Research on Treatments for Personality Disorders

1.   Object relations approaches

a.   Object relations: a psychodynamic theory of psychotherapy that deemphasizes impersonal forces and counterforces and focuses on the influences of interpersonal relationships stemming from early mother-child relationships.

b.   Aimed at repairing the defects of the self resulting from maladaptive formative experiences in early childhood.

c.   Supportive environment given where the defenses and distortions are confronted.

d.   Results with this approach encouraging.

2.   Cognitive-behavioral and behavioral approaches

a.   Therapy seeks to identify fundamental maladaptive schemas and challenge them with cognitive restructuring techniques and systematic behavioral assignments.

b.   Some success obtained with borderline patients.

3.   Medications

a.   No drug has been specifically proven to be successful for personality disorders.

b.   Neuroleptic, or antipsychotic, medication may help borderline patients reduce some of their maladaptive behaviors, while antidepressants may alleviate mood symptoms or compulsive behaviors.

IV.   What Lies Ahead?

A.   Diagnostic systems will be studied along with normal personality and functioning.

B.   More attention will be paid to treatment for these intractable disorders, including psychodynamic methods and family influences.

KEY TERMS REVIEW

1. A personality disorder marked by difficulties in interpersonal relationships as well as by abnormalities of thought, behavior, and appearance that are similar to, but not severe enough to be considered, schizophrenia is called _____.

2. A personality disorder marked by pervasive suspicion of others and distrust of their motives is called _____.

3. A personality disorder characterized by a history of callousness, disregard for social conventions and others' rights and feelings, and illegal conduct is called _____.

4. A trait indicated by a person's being sociable, talkative, and outgoing is called being _____.

5. A personality disorder marked by aloofness from relationships and emotional coldness is called _____.

6. A trait indicated by a person's being shy, quiet, and timid is called _____.

7. A personality disorder characterized by social discomfort—timidity and fear of negative evaluation—is called _____.

8. A personality disorder characterized by pervasive patterns of dependent and submissive behavior, leaving the person seemingly unable to make even everyday decisions for himself or herself, is called _____.

9. Behavior tendencies believed to be biologically based and present from birth; disposition is called _____.

10. A personality disorder characterized by pervasive instability of mood, chaotic relationships, and uncertain self-image is called _____.

11. A personality disorder characterized by traits such as excessive emotionality, flamboyance, and attention seeking is called _____.

12. A childhood or adolescent problem, consisting of a repetitive and persistent pattern of behavior that involves violation of the basic rights of others is _____.

13. A continuum from low or none to extreme on which personality traits may be scaled; a proposed alternative view of personality disorders is called _____.

14. A disorder marked by an overall pervasive preoccupation with perfectionism, orderliness, and control over the self and others to the point of rigidity and inefficiency, is called _____.

15. A personality disorder characterized by grandiosity—an inflated sense of self-importance, accompanied by the expectation of being treated as special and being entitled to favorable treatment or exemption from the rules others must follow—is called _____.

16. A continuing pattern of perceiving and relating to the world, usually present since childhood or adolescence, that is maladaptive across a variety of contexts and results in notable impairment or distress, is called a(n) _____.

FACTUAL MULTIPLE-CHOICE QUESTIONS

1. A person who is aloof, solitary, and seemingly unable to enjoy things would be diagnosed with
   a. schizoid personality disorder.
   b. antisocial personality disorder.
   c. avoidant personality disorder.
   d. borderline personality disorder.

2. A person who is socially anxious, talks with vague or abstract speech, and dresses inappropriately would be diagnosed with
   a. dependent personality disorder.
   b. antisocial personality disorder.
   c. avoidant personality disorder.
   d. schizotypal personality disorder.

3. A person who is seductive, desires attention, and seems excitable and overreactive would be diagnosed with
   a. borderline personality disorder.
   b. narcissistic personality disorder.
   c. obsessive-compulsive personality disorder.
   d. histrionic personality disorder.

4. A person who is unstable in mood and relationships and subject to bouts of depression, anxiety, and anger would be diagnosed with
   a. borderline personality disorder.
   b. histrionic personality disorder.
   c. antisocial personality disorder.
   d. paranoid personality disorder.

5. A patient who has an inflated sense of self-importance, expects to be specially treated, and feels no need to follow established rules would be diagnosed with
   a. narcissistic personality disorder.
   b. histrionic personality disorder.
   c. borderline personality disorder.
   d. paranoid personality disorder.

6. A patient who had difficulties as a child and is now irresponsible, deceitful, and impulsive would be diagnosed with
   a. paranoid personality disorder.
   b. borderline personality disorder.
   c. schizotypal personality disorder.
   d. antisocial personality disorder.

7. A patient who is preoccupied in many areas of his or her life with perfectionism, orderliness, and control over others would be diagnosed with
   a. narcissistic personality disorder.
   b. avoidant personality disorder.
   c. obsessive-compulsive personality disorder.
   d. dependent personality disorder.

8. A patient who is submissive, unable to make decisions, and in need of constant reassurance would be diagnosed with
    a. dependent personality disorder.
    b. avoidant personality disorder.
    c. passive-aggressive personality disorder.
    d. antisocial personality disorder.

9. A patient who suffers greatly from social discomfort, timidity, and fear of negative social reactions would be diagnosed with
    a. schizoid personality disorder.
    b. avoidant personality disorder.
    c. obsessive-compulsive personality disorder.
    d. borderline personality disorder.

10. The most prevalent personality disorder among populations of patients with other psychological disorders is
    a. antisocial personality disorder.
    b. paranoid personality disorder.
    c. obsessive-compulsive personality disorder.
    d. borderline personality disorder.

CONCEPTUAL MULTIPLE-CHOICE QUESTIONS

1. Which of the following is *not* true of individuals with personality disorders?
    a. They have difficulty with interpersonal relationships.
    b. They are difficult to diagnose.
    c. They recognize that they have a problem.
    d. They have a maladaptive pattern of dealing with the world.

2. The presence of a personality disorder implies that an Axis I disorder will be
    a. easier to treat.
    b. more difficult to treat.
    c. composed of fewer symptoms.
    d. less likely to recur.

3. Joan was amazed at how different her two children's personalities were. Even though born only eighteen months apart, one was outgoing and active, the other timid and passive. These different characteristics could be labeled
    a. disorders.
    b. categories.
    c. diagnostic overlap.
    d. temperaments.

4. Dr. Johnson's prognosis for her new patient with narcissistic personality is
    a. good, because personality disorder patients respond well to therapy.
    b. good, because narcissistic personality disorder patients are willing to listen to others.
    c. bad, because narcissistic personality disorder patients are shy and timid.
    d. bad, because personality disorders are based on entrenched, lifelong patterns.

5. Sue has been arrested for shoplifting three times. She has been diagnosed with antisocial personality disorder. Her case is unusual because
   a. she was apprehended by the law.
   b. most antisocial personality disordered patients would not repeat the same crime.
   c. antisocial personality patients are too timid to be in scrapes with law enforcement.
   d. most antisocial personality disorder patients are male.

6. What primarily distinguishes avoidant personality disorder from schizoid personality disorder?
   a. the degree of introversion expressed between the two disorders
   b. differences in treatment success following use of antipsychotic medications
   c. the motivation that underlies social distance for the two disorders
   d. ethnic and culture differences between the two disorders

7. The diagnostic overlap between the personality disorders raises questions about
   a. the temperaments of those individuals diagnosed with personality disorders.
   b. individual reactivity to external stimuli.
   c. the lack of successful object relations.
   d. the validity of these diagnoses.

8. One limitation associated with the DSM-IV and reflected in personality disorder diagnoses is that
   a. traits cannot be reliably identified because they are frequently unstable, changing from moment to moment.
   b. gross categories are used rather than specific trait dimensions along which people may be measured.
   c. personality disorders may be diagnosed based on clearly defined biological markers.
   d. early childhood factors are ignored in the treatment of personality disorders.

9. Jerome Kagan would be likely to agree with which of the following statements?
   a. Most behavioral tendencies observed in children are the result of learning from the environment.
   b. Temperament plays little role in influencing the behavior of children or adults.
   c. Inhibition in children may reflect a biological, genetically transmitted risk factor for anxiety disorders and perhaps personality disorders.
   d. Children who are inhibited can easily learn to become more sociable with experience from the environment.

10. How are object relations therapy and cognitive-behavioral therapy similar?
    a. They both emphasize reinforcement, punishment, and shaping of behavior as the cause of personality disorders.
    b. They both stress unconscious personality processes as the cause of personality disorders.
    c. Both theories stress the importance of understanding the family environment as the cause of personality disorders.
    d. Both were rejected completely by Sigmund Freud.

11. Dr. Cantor has been invited to give a presentation on the topic "assessment and diagnosis of personality disorders." What should Dr. Cantor say about diagnostic bias and the classification of personality disorders?
    a. Traits that reflect conformity to sex-role stereotypes traditionally urged for women may be diagnosed as dependent personality disorder, yet there is no corresponding diagnostic category to reflect men's conformity to sex-role-stereotyped behavior.
    b. Because the DSM-IV lists specific criteria required to diagnose a disorder, clinicians are rarely biased in their diagnoses of personality disorders.
    c. Biological tests have been developed that make it relatively easy to reliably detect a personality disorder.
    d. Sex-role stereotypes rarely play a role in what types of behavior come to be viewed as disorders of personality.

APPLICATION MULTIPLE-CHOICE QUESTIONS

1. Dr. Fairbanks had a long interview with Jonathan regarding his family's role in Jonathan's personality disorder. The doctor is somewhat skeptical about the information he has received because
    a. personality-disordered patients tend to be compulsive liars.
    b. personality disorders are often comorbid with dissociative disorders.
    c. retrospective information is limited.
    d. the etiological models for personality disorder have been scientifically validated.

2. Clark's parents were constantly demeaning him and embarrassing him for the slightest fault. The schema that develops from such treatment could result in
    a. paranoid personality disorder.
    b. borderline personality disorder.
    c. depressive personality disorder.
    d. avoidant personality disorder.

3. Pamela's therapist challenged her on her statement that she couldn't do anything right. Pamela was given techniques to change her perspective. Her therapist is using
    a. psychoanalysis.
    b. a cognitive-behavior approach.
    c. an object relations approach.
    d. a humanistic approach.

4. Diane was diagnosed with severe borderline personality disorder. Her psychiatrist
    a. prescribed antipsychotic medication.
    b. said the symptoms for borderline were of little danger or concern.
    c. suggested just waiting for the symptoms to subside.
    d. said nothing helped with this type of disorder.

5. Sam never left his office until everyone had gone for fear that someone would break into his desk and look for incriminating material to use against him. Sam's diagnosis would be
    a. avoidant personality disorder.
    b. histrionic personality disorder.
    c. borderline personality disorder.
    d. paranoid personality disorder.

6. Every time Marie entered the doctor's office she did her impression of Loretta Young, moving through the door with a flourish. Her actions typified the behavior of
   a. borderline personality disorder.
   b. histrionic personality disorder.
   c. avoidant personality disorder.
   d. obsessive-compulsive personality disorder.

7. Marcia made her office colleagues nervous. Her moods were difficult to predict and she could fly into sudden rages over seeming trifles. She would spend hours talking about her latest romantic adventures, which always seemed to end in disaster. Marcia is typical of
   a. schizotypal personality disorder.
   b. antisocial personality disorder.
   c. histrionic personality disorder.
   d. borderline personality disorder.

8. Rich was considered the most knowledgeable professional in his field. But he made it his goal to always go "by the book." He was so intent on protecting the process that he was inefficient. Rich is typical of
   a. obsessive-compulsive personality disorder.
   b. borderline personality disorder.
   c. histrionic personality disorder.
   d. narcissistic personality disorder.

9. Sonny made it a point to bring work home with him every night and on weekends. He rarely took a vacation and when he did he longed to get back to his job. He hated waiting for anything and got into several fights over breaking into lines and pushing people. He would be diagnosed with which personality disorder?
   a. obsessive-compulsive
   b. borderline
   c. paranoid
   d. not descriptive of any current DSM personality disorder

10. Dieter was diagnosed with avoidant personality disorder. Which of the "big five" trait dimensions would best fit his diagnosis?
    a. conscientiousness
    b. friendliness/hostility
    c. intellect
    d. extroversion/introversion

ANSWER KEY: KEY TERMS REVIEW

1. schizotypal personality disorder (408)
2. paranoid personality disorder (407)
3. antisocial personality disorder (APD) (411)
4. uninhibited (421)
5. schizoid personality disorder (408)
6. inhibited (421)
7. avoidant personality disorder (413)
8. dependent personality disorder (413)
9. temperament (420)
10. borderline personality disorder (410)
11. histrionic personality disorder (409)
12. conduct disorder (411)
13. dimensions (418)
14. obsessive-compulsive personality disorder (412)
15. narcissistic personality disorder (410)
16. personality disorder (407)

ANSWER KEY: FACTUAL MULTIPLE-CHOICE QUESTIONS

1. *a. schizoid personality disorder (p. 408)
   b. Antisocial personality disordered patients have a history of disregard for others' rights and feelings.
   c. Avoidant personality disorder is characterized by timidity and fear of negative evaluation.
   d. Borderline personality disorder is marked by instability of mood, relationship, and self-image.

2. *d. schizotypal personality disorder (p. 408)
   a. Dependent personality disorder is characterized by patterns of submissive behavior.
   b. Antisocial personality disorder is marked by callous disregard for others' rights and feelings.
   c. Avoidant personality disorder is marked by timidity and fear.

3. *d. histrionic personality disorder (p. 409)
   a. Borderline personality disorder is characterized by instability of mood, relationship, and self-image.
   b. Narcissistic personality disorder is characterized by an inflated sense of self-importance.
   c. Obsessive-compulsive personality disorder is marked by a preoccupation with perfectionism.

4. *a. borderline personality disorder (p. 410)
   b. Histrionic personality disorders are marked by excessive emotionality and flamboyance.
   c. Antisocial personality disorder is a condition characterized by a history of callousness.
   d. Paranoid personality disorder is characterized by pervasive suspicion and distrust.

5. *a. narcissistic personality disorder (p. 410)
   b. Histrionic personality disorder is characterized by excessive emotionality and flamboyance.
   c. Borderline personality disorder is characterized by instability of mood, relationships, and self-image.
   d. Paranoid personality disorder is marked by suspicion and distrust of others.

6. *d. antisocial personality disorder (p. 411)
   a. Paranoid personality disorder is marked by suspicion and distrust of others.
   b. Borderline personality disorder is characterized by instability of mood, relationships, and self-image.
   c. Schizotypal personality disorder is marked by disturbed interpersonal relationships and abnormalities of thought and behavior.

7. *c. obsessive-compulsive personality disorder (p. 412)
   a. Narcissistic personality disorder is marked by an inflated sense of self-importance.
   b. Avoidant personality disorder is characterized by social discomfort, timidity, and fear.
   d. Dependent personality disorder is characterized by submissive, indecisive behavior.

8. *a. dependent personality disorder (p. 413)
   b. Avoidant personality disorder is in the same cluster as dependent, but marked by social discomfort and fear rather than submissiveness.
   c. Passive-aggressive personality disorder was removed from the DSM-IV; when it was in the DSM, it was not described by submission.
   d. Antisocial personality disorder is more aggressive than the anxious/fearful cluster disorders.

9. *b. avoidant personality disorder (p. 413)
   a. Schizoid personality disorder is characterized by aloofness and is more serious in its symptomatology than the anxious/fearful cluster disorders.
   c. Obsessive-compulsive disorder is similar to the anxiety disorder of the same name, but lacks the compulsions of the Axis I diagnosis and is not preoccupied with rejection.
   d. Borderline personality disorder is characterized by much more aggressive and volatile symptoms than the anxious/fearful cluster.

10. *d. borderline personality disorder (p. 410)
    a. Antisocial personality disorder is in the same dramatic/erratic cluster, but is marked by callous disregard of others, and illegal conduct, less typical of borderline.
    b. Paranoid personality disorder is marked by suspicion, and not by the instability of mood characteristic of borderline.
    c. Obsessive-compulsive personality disorder is preoccupation with perfectionism, not a quality noted with borderline patients.

ANSWER KEY: CONCEPTUAL MULTIPLE-CHOICE QUESTIONS

1. *c. They recognize that they have a problem. These patients typically do *not* recognize that the problem lies with themselves. (p. 407)
   a. Relationship problems are characteristic of most personality disorders.
   b. Because of overlapping symptoms and other problems, these disorders are among the most difficult to diagnose.
   d. Characteristic of these disorders is a continuing pattern of relating to the world that is maladaptive.

2. *b. more difficult to treat (p. 407)
   a. Personality disorders make treatment of other disorders much more difficult.
   c. Symptoms will be compounded with the presence of both types of disorders.
   d. There is a greater risk of recurrence.

3. *d. temperaments (p. 420)
   a. It is too early to tell if either child will develop a disorder.
   b. Categories do not fit these children, since their behavior would not be classified as extreme.
   c. Diagnostic overlap is a problem with personality disorders, making clear distinctions among them difficult.

4. *d. bad, because personality disorders are based on entrenched, lifelong patterns. (p. 407)
   a. Personality disorder patients traditionally do not respond well to most therapies.
   b. Narcissistic patients want others to listen to them, and rarely have the time or interest to listen to someone else.
   c. Narcissistic patients are at the other of the spectrum from shy and timid.

5. *d. most antisocial personality disorder patients are male (p. 414)
 a. Many antisocial patients have scrapes with the law.
 b. Antisocial patterns include the inability to learn from past mistakes or punishments.
 c. Antisocial patients are often described as "fearless."

6. *c. the motivation that underlies social distance for the two disorders. (p. 413)
 a. Both avoidant and schizoid personality disorders appear aloof, but for different reasons.
 b. Antipsychotic medications may be useful in treating borderline and schizotypal personality disorders.
 d. There are limited epidemiological data on personality disorders, and none on ethnic and cultural differences.

7. *d. the validity of the diagnoses. (p. 416)
 a. *Temperament* is the term for behavioral tendencies believed to be biologically based and present from birth.
 b. Individuals with some personality disorders (e.g., avoidant) show differences in reactivity patterns.
 c. Object relations theory is a psychodynamic theory of psychotherapy that deemphasizes impersonal forces and counterforces and focuses on the influences of interpersonal relationships stemming from early mother-child interactions.

8. *b. gross categories are used rather than specific trait dimensions along which people may be measured. (pp. 417–418)
 a. Traits such as the "big five" are reliably measured and are relatively consistent over the lifespan.
 c. There are no accepted biological markers for personality disorders.
 d. Early childhood factors are a primary focus of object relations therapy.

9. *c. Inhibition in children may reflect a biological, genetically transmitted risk factor for anxiety disorders and perhaps personality disorders. (p. 422)
 a. Kagan and colleagues emphasize the idea that important behaviors are a function of temperament.
 b. Kagan thinks that temperament, such as extraversion/introversion, has an important influence on the expression of behavior.
 d. There is a correlation between being a shy child and being a shy adult, although this trait is not unchangeable.

10. *c. Both theories stress the importance of understanding the family environment as the cause of personality disorders. (p. 426)
 a. Behaviorists tend to emphasize these concepts and the failure to acquire adaptive skills (or learning dysfunctional behaviors) as the cause of personality disorders.
 b. Unconscious processes are emphasized in psychodynamic theory, from which object relations is derived.
 d. Cognitive therapy was developed following the decline of Freudian theory.

11. *a. Traits that reflect conformity to sex-role stereotypes traditionally urged for women may be diagnosed as dependent personality disorder, yet there is no corresponding diagnostic category to reflect men's conformity to sex-role-stereotyped behavior. (p. 416)
 b. Although specific diagnostic criteria are available, the application of these criteria may differ depending on the clinician's judgment.
 c. There are no biological tests to detect personality disorders.
 d. Sex-role stereotypes may influence the identification of personality disorders.

ANSWER KEY: APPLICATION MULTIPLE-CHOICE QUESTIONS

1. *c. retrospective information is limited (p. 423)
   a. Not all personality disorder patients are compulsive liars; antisocial personality disorder patients are most likely to fit this description, though.
   b. Dissociative disorders are less likely to be comorbid than schizophrenia or depression.
   d. Scientific validation is sorely lacking in the etiologic models for personality disorders.

2. *d. avoidant personality disorder (p. 413)
   a. It is not clear that there is a particular type of family trauma that contributes to paranoid personality disorder.
   b. There is increasing evidence that childhood sexual abuse, not embarrassment, may influence the development of borderline personality disorder.
   c. Depressive personality disorder is not currently in the DSM but has been proposed for future inclusion.

3. *b. a cognitive-behavior approach (pp. 425, 428–429)
   a. Psychoanalysis is not confrontational in the manner described.
   c. An object relations approach would deal with early memories of relations with significant persons such as parents.
   d. A humanistic approach would emphasize the role of meaning and responsibility in the life of the patient.

4. *a. prescribed antipsychotic medication (p. 429)
   b. Borderline symptoms are often highly aggressive and even dangerous.
   c. Borderline symptoms may not subside, but may increase in intensity.
   d. Antipsychotic medication does improve functioning of borderline patients.

5. *d. paranoid personality disorder (p. 443)
   a. Avoidant personality behavior types have less suspicion and more fear and timidity.
   b. Histrionic patients would not arrive early and leave late. They would want to be the center of attention.
   c. Borderline patients would not be furtive about their demands and suspicions. They might take direct hostile action.

6. *b. histrionic personality disorder (p. 409)
   a. Borderline patients are not noted for their dramatic flair, but for instability of mood.
   c. Avoidant personality patients would be totally uncomfortable "making an entrance" anywhere.
   d. Obsessive-compulsive types would be focused on perfectionism.

7. *d. borderline personality disorder (p. 410)
   a. Schizotypal patients exhibit abnormalities of thought, behavior, and appearance.
   b. Antisocial patients would be callous and uninterested in anyone's feelings about their life.
   c. Histrionic patients would be more flamboyant and attention seeking.

8. *a. obsessive-compulsive disorder (p. 412)
   b. Borderline sufferers are unconcerned with rules.
   c. Histrionic personality disorder is characterized by flamboyance, not rule obsession.
   d. Narcissistic patients are only concerned about themselves and their treatment.

9. *d. not descriptive of any current DSM personality disorder (pp. 414–418)
   a. Obsessive-compulsives would be concerned about perfectionism.
   b. Borderline patients probably would not be concerned about work.
   c. Paranoid personality disorder is characterized by suspicion and distrust, not hostility.

10. *d. extroversion/introversion (pp. 418, 422)
   a. Avoidant personality types are not known for conscientiousness.
   b. Avoidant types are not particularly friendly or hostile, but frightened.
   c. Avoidant types are not particularly open to new experiences or intellectual curiosity.

CHAPTER 14
Antisocial Personality and Violent Conduct

LEARNING OBJECTIVES

1. Discuss the connection between mental illness and violent and antisocial behavior. (pp. 434ff)

2. Define antisocial personality disorder (APD). (pp. 434–435)

3. Define psychopathy and explain the differences and similarities among APD, psychopathy, and criminality. (pp. 435–436)

4. Discuss the relationship of violence to APD and psychopathy. (pp. 436–437)

5. Describe how violence has been accepted as a means of conflict resolution. (pp. 437–438)

6. Explain who is affected with APD (including gender, cultural, and ethnic differences), and discuss the effects of poverty and disadvantaged backgrounds on the development of criminality and APD. (pp. 439–440)

7. Discuss the course of APD (including childhood deviance, the stability of aggression, and adult patterns of APD). (pp. 440–442)

8. Discuss the possible causes of APD and violent conduct from a biological perspective. (pp. 442–446)

9. Describe the possible relationship between violence and neurotransmitters and hormones, particularly serotonin and testosterone. (pp. 443–445)

10. Discuss the possibility of deficient emotional arousal as a causative factor in APD. (pp. 445–446)

11. Discuss the connection between learning deficits and APD. (pp. 446–447)

12. Describe the evidence for information processing deficits in APD. (pp. 446–447)

13. Discuss the role of learning and cognition in understanding aggression and antisocial behavior. (pp. 446–449)

14. Discuss the effects of the family environment on aggression and violent behavior. (pp. 447–448)

15. Explain how distorted cognitions may contribute to social learning or antisocial traits and conduct. (p. 448)

16. Discuss the effect of observational learning from violent models, particularly television, on aggressive and antisocial behavior. (pp. 448–449)

17. Describe the difficult tasks of treatment and prevention of antisocial behaviors. (pp. 449–451)

18. Discuss the characteristics, predictors, and consequences of violence. (pp. 451ff)

19. Discuss physical child abuse and its consequences. (pp. 451–452)

20. Describe the effects of intergenerational transmission of abuse. (pp. 452–453)

21. Describe the effects of spousal abuse on the children as well as the parents. (pp. 454–455)

22. Discuss the responses to spouse abuse and the patterns that tend to perpetuate it. (pp. 454–455)

23. Describe the features of sexual assault, including frequency and consequences. (pp. 455–457)

24. Discuss the causes and predictors of sexual assault. (pp. 457–458)

25. Discuss the treatment of victims and prevention of violence. (pp. 459–461)

26. Discuss the continued interest in attempting to find answers to the questions of how to prevent violence and antisocial behavior. (pp. 461–462)

CHAPTER OUTLINE

I. Features of Antisocial Personality Disorder

    A. Defining Antisocial Personality Disorder

- Antisocial personality disorder (APD): a personality disorder characterized by a history of callousness, disregard for social conventions and others' rights and feelings, and illegal conduct.

- An enduring pattern of irresponsible behaviors recognizable by adolescence or earlier.

- Characterized by aggressiveness, financial irresponsibility, recklessness, lying, and showing little regard for others' welfare, and rarely expressing remorse.

        1. Psychopathy

            a. Refers to a kind of personality with prominent traits of selfishness, deceitfulness, and callousness that may be reflected in various illegal ways.

            b. Cleckley noted psychopaths are often intelligent and likable but are manipulative and egocentric, feeling no guilt over injuries to others.

        2. APD, psychopathy, and criminality

            a. APD is commonly found in criminal populations.

b. Criminality: a legal rather than a mental health concept, which refers to violations of the law owing to any cause.

c. Most criminals are not psychopaths, and most psychopaths are not criminals.

3. The relationship of violence to APD and psychopathy

   a. Violence refers to lawful and unlawful acts of destruction.

   b. Most violence results from situational factors, such as stress, conflict, or diminished control, not psychological abnormality.

4. What's Normal? Violence in U.S. Society

   a. Violence is legitimized in U.S. culture to the point that it has become "normal."

   b. Violence is an everyday experience for the youth of America.

   c. Violence is an accepted method of dealing with interpersonal conflict.

   d. Southerners tend to condone the use of violence more than people from other parts of the United States.

   e. Extensive exposure to violence and permissive attitudes toward the use of violence tend to normalize it.

5. Mental illness, violence, and criminality

   a. People diagnosed with major mental disorders commit more crimes and violent acts than those without such diagnoses.

   b. Studies show that substance-use disorders are frequently diagnosed among these offenders.

B. Who Is Affected with Antisocial Personality Disorder?

   • APD predominantly affects young, low-income, poorly educated males.

   1. Gender differences in APD

      a. APD appears far more frequently and starts earlier in men than in women.

      b. Symptoms differ by gender.

      c. Gender bias may partially account for low diagnosis level of women as APD.

   2. Cultural and ethnic differences in APD

      a. Rates differ by the type of sociocultural variations.

      b. Much higher rates in inner-city areas.

      c. APD and criminality both linked to poverty and disadvantaged backgrounds.

C. The Development and Course of Antisocial Personality Disorder

   1. The course of childhood deviance

      a. Problems of youth associated with adult conduct problems.

b. Elevated risk of *criminal* behavior with childhood hyperactivity and poor impulse control or a difficulty in delaying or suppressing an immediate urge or response when a careful or controlled response might produce more desirable or appropriate results.

2. The stability of aggression

   a. Childhood aggressiveness is a strong predictor of adult aggressiveness and antisocial conduct.

   b. Pattern occurs for both males and females, although it is stronger among males.

3. Adult patterns of APD

   a. Highest diagnosis rate for APD between ages of twenty-five and forty-four.

   b. Mellowing process occurs around middle age, where rates of conviction drop.

II. Causes of Antisocial Personality and Violent Conduct

   • Data are based on heterogeneous samples of individuals with criminal records, antisocial behaviors, violent offenses, and other crimes.

   • Few studies on individuals who actually meet DSM criteria for APD.

   A. Biological Perspectives on Antisocial Personality Disorder

      1. Genetics: Is there a bad seed?

         a. Studies demonstrate a portion of criminality is consistent with genetic vulnerability.

         b. Environmental factors are more important predictors of antisocial conduct than genetics.

      2. Neurochemical abnormalities and APD

         a. There is a correlation between monoamine neurotransmitter functioning and impulsive, aggressive behavior.

         b. Testosterone also may play a role in violent behavior, but research is inconsistent.

      3. Focus on Research: Is a brain chemical responsible for violence?

         a. Early research saw relationship between violent suicide attempts in unipolar patients and low levels of serotonin.

         b. Virkkunen speculated that impulsive aggressiveness, aggressiveness that erupts suddenly, might be associated with low serotonin, but not with planned violence.

         c. Alcohol use is a factor in virtually all recidivism.

         d. Children in treatment for disruptive behavior disorders (behavioral excuses or poorly controlled behaviors that are bothersome to others) found to have low serotonin levels, which indicated later aggression.

e.   Psychosocial factors, such as socioeconomic status, race, and IQ scores, were neglected in these studies.

f.   Aggressiveness ratings and loss of impulse control in rhesus monkeys correlated significantly with low serotonin metabolite levels.

g.   Some forms of violence may be linked to genetic abnormalities: absence of *monoamine oxidase A* (metabolism of serotonin).

4.   Deficiencies in emotional arousal

a.   Psychophysiological arousal: body signs of awareness such as heart and respiration rate and electrodermal activity.

b.   Deficient emotional arousal, no or low levels of physical reactions to fearful or aversive conditions, are typical of psychopaths or people with ADP.

c.   Sensation seeking, a desire for exciting, stimulating, or even dangerous experiences, may be one explanation of antisocial behavior.

5.   Learning and neurocognitive deficits

a.   Psychopaths may learn from rewards, but not punishment. They tend to show deficient avoidance learning.

b.   Some theorists say psychopaths are disinhibited, lack the ability to inhibit responses even in the face of punishment.

c.   Other theorists stress neurocognitive dysfunction (impaired executive functions associated with frontal cortex), perhaps caused by poor maternal prenatal care, substance exposure, neurotoxic substances, injuries, and genetic factors.

d.   Biosocial model (interaction of biological and psychological factors) may best explain antisocial behavior and violence.

B.   Cognitive Social Learning Perspectives on Antisocial Personality Disorder

•   Social learning theorists say children acquire behavioral tendencies and cognitive schemas through learning.

•   Exposure to deviant role models may lead to antisocial conduct.

•   Higher intelligence and problem-solving and social competence skills may protect children from the effects of a difficult environment.

•   Once these problem behaviors are learned, they tend to be stable.

1.   The family environment

a.   Dysfunctional family experiences in childhood are a powerful predictor of later APD and aggressive conduct.

b.   Persons with APD often marry one another (assortative mating), increasing the risk for disorder in the children.

2.   Distorted cognitions

a.   Hostile attribution biases are the tendencies to believe that negative events are caused by other people intending harm.

      b.   This cognitive style increases the chances of aggressive responses.

    3.   Exposure to violent models

      a.   Observational learning, the acquisition of behaviors and attitudes from watching others, takes place on three levels:

          (1)   Culture-wide attitudes (tolerance of violence).

          (2)   Exposure to abusive parents.

          (3)   Violence on television, in films and musical lyrics.

      b.   Modest but significant associations exist between viewing violence on television and aggressive behavior.

      c.   Exposure to television violence leads to emotional desensitization, an unresponsiveness or callousness toward victims.

    4.   Multiple roots of risk for antisocial conduct and violence

      a.   Antisocial and aggressive conduct is caused by multiple factors.

      b.   Researchers understand a lot about the causal factors but little about their relative importance.

III.   Treatment and Prevention of Antisocial Conduct

   A.   Treatment of These Disorders Difficult

    1.   Individuals who need the treatment rarely seek it. Sometimes may seek treatment under court mandate.

    2.   Intervention often takes the form of incarceration, imprisonment as punishment for a crime, which is usually unsuccessful as rehabilitation.

    3.   Juvenile diversion programs provide an alternative to incarceration.

    4.   Multisystemic treatment involving a cognitive, school, family, and peer treatment focus shows some promise.

    5.   Prevention programs involving high-risk persons may reduce antisocial behavior and violent conduct.

IV.   Violence: Characteristics, Predictors, and Consequences

   •   Domestic violence is considered to be the most common form of violence.

   A.   Physical Abuse of Children

    •   Physical abuse is the infliction of damage to another person.

    •   Neglect is failure to provide proper care for children (nutritional, emotional, medical, and physical needs).

    1.   Consequences to the abused child

      a.   Abused children

          (1)   Are more aggressive.

      (2)   Show more behavioral conduct problems.

      (3)   Show increased depression.

      (4)   Show increased emotional symptoms.

      (5)   Have lower intellectual functioning.

      (6)   Are less compliant.

      (7)   Are less socially competent.

   b.   The effect of abuse varies depending on severity, duration, and overall social context.

  2. Does violence beget violence?

     a.   Although the majority of abused children do not commit crimes, there is a correlation between child abuse and later abusive behavior.

     b.   The relationship between abuse and later criminality is stronger for men than women and for African Americans than for whites.

B. Family Matters: Intergenerational Transmission of Abuse

- Families tend to transmit abuse from one generation to the next.

- Many abusive parents deny that they were abused, making research difficult.

- Maladaptive interpersonal schemas (negative beliefs and expectations about other people's values, trustworthiness, and caring) may be acquired, which limit the ability to relate effectively to others.

- Attachment theory states maladaptive attachment caused by abuse is likely to result in damaged attachment in the next generation.

- Being abused as a child increases risk for being an abusive parent.

  1. Are abusive parents mentally ill?

     a.   The majority do not have diagnosable disorders.

     b.   There are shared characteristics:

      (1)   Deficient ability to deal with stress.

      (2)   Deficient social competence.

      (3)   Deficient relationship and parenting skills.

      (4)   Inability to control angry impulses.

      (5)   Social isolation.

      (6)   Marital problems.

      (7)   Rigid and domineering interpersonal style.

      (8)   Alcohol and substance abuse.

      (9)   Distorted cognitions.

        (10)   Inappropriate expectations.

        (11)   Misinterpretation of misbehavior as intentional.

C.   Marital Violence

- Marital violence is high.

- Women suffer more extreme consequences of abuse than men.

- Children witnessing abuse also suffer.

1.   Causes of spousal abuse

    a.   Occurs at all levels of society, but more frequently with younger and poorer populations.

    b.   Marital unhappiness is contributory.

    c.   Good predictor is whether aggression occurred in relationship before marriage.

    d.   *Psychological aggressiveness* (insulting the partner, stomping out of the house, etc.) is predictive of physical aggressiveness.

    e.   Tied to inability to control underlying hostility.

    f.   Excessive use of alcohol frequently involved.

    g.   Cultural differences exist.

2.   Responses to spousal abuse

    a.   Tolerance of the violence by a spouse may perpetuate it.

    b.   Battered women (women who have been physically beaten by their domestic partners) display certain characteristics:

        (1)   Difficulty making appropriate decisions.

        (2)   Flashbacks, numbing, withdrawal, other PTSD symptoms.

        (3)   Learned helplessness.

        (4)   Report financial difficulties, no place to turn.

        (5)   Often misinterpret the event (deny the violence).

    c.   There are now many community intervention programs to help abused spouses.

D.   Sexual Assault

- Sexual assault is defined in many ways but generally refers to the use of psychological pressure or physical force to engage in sexual contact.

- Rape is sexual assault that involves sexual penetration and with physical coercion or threat of harm.

- Childhood sexual assault specifies that the assailant be several years older than the child.

1. Frequency and characteristics of sexual assault

   a. Estimates are that between one in seven and one in four women is raped at some time in her life.

   b. Sexual molestation is sexual contact with a minor child by someone several years older, frequently occurs in the family, but more commonly with acquaintances.

   c. Perpetrators of childhood sexual molestation are predominantly males and acquaintances.

   d. Victims of rape most commonly young, college-age women.

   e. Perpetrators of rape are predominantly acquaintances or friends.

2. Consequences of sexual assault

   a. Outcomes are more severe when

      (1) Abuse is repeated.

      (2) The perpetrator has a close relationship with the victim.

      (3) Victim's background is troubled.

   b. Immediate problems include:

      (1) Behavioral difficulties.

      (2) Learning problems.

      (3) Depressed mood.

      (4) Guilt.

      (5) Sleep disturbances.

      (6) Occasional heightened sexual preoccupation and precocity.

   c. Many rape victims experience PTSD (posttraumatic stress disorder) as well as serious later psychological difficulties.

3. Causes and predictors of sexual assault

   a. Rape may be viewed as sexual aggression, yet such characterization oversimplifies the many varieties of rapes and the theories explaining rape behavior.

   b. One of the best predictors of sexual aggression is past sexual offending.

   c. Biological and learning deficits are both factors.

   d. Many men are aroused by sexually aggressive behavior, but normal individuals control their urges.

   e. Some societies are rape-free, characterized by equality of the sexes and low levels of violence.

   f. Sexually aggressive men often have negative relationships with women, are impulsive, lose control with alcohol, and value sexual prowess.

g. Five motives for rape:

   (1) Opportunistic.

   (2) Pervasively angry.

   (3) Sadistic.

   (4) Nonsadistic sexual.

   (5) Vindictive.

V. Treating Victims and Preventing Violence

   A. Treating and Preventing Child Abuse

      1. Treating child abuse

         a. A national emergency

         b. Three types of treatment programs:

            (1) Child-focused interventions.

            (2) Parent-focused treatments.

            (3) Multiservice programs.

         c. Behavioral and cognitive-behavioral programs teach child management, anger and stress control.

         d. Programs do not change personality deficits.

         e. More multiservice programs needed to stabilize dysfunctional situations.

      2. Preventing child abuse

         a. Goal: to identify high-risk parental situations for intervention before abuse occurs.

         b. Low-income and teenage mothers with small children have high rates of child abuse and are targeted for preventive treatments.

         c. Programs use home visits and group educational sessions on parenting and are effective.

         d. Limitation of programs is that many only include mothers, not fathers, who are major factors in abuse.

   B. Treating Spousal Violence

      1. Psychological services to battered women and their children are limited.

      2. Limited research exists on program efficacy.

      3. Legal reforms are being pursued to arrest violent spouses even if the victim does not bring charges.

   C. Treating Sexual Assault

      1. Most victims do not seek treatment.

2. The most effective programs include

    a.   Avoidance of victim blame.

    b.   Providing a nonstigmatizing view of rape.

    c.   Establishing an environment encouraging the overcoming of social avoidance and withdrawal.

    d.   Giving positive information about trauma reactions.

D.   Treating Childhood Sexual Abuse

1. Treatment programs for adult survivors of childhood sexual abuse exist, but research establishing the effectiveness of such programs is lacking.

2. Memory restoration of repressed childhood abuse is quite controversial, with no data to support claims.

E.   Preventing Child Molestation

1. Little evidence that prevention programs work, and some suggest the programs may be harmful.

2. Some feel these efforts may be harmful.

VI.   What Lies Ahead?

A.   Antisocial conduct and violence are on the rise.

B.   Topic polarizes political, religious, and philosophical viewpoints.

C.   Much of the emphasis will be on the *family*.

D.   Trying to find the best, most affordable treatments will be a high priority.

E.   Research will focus on scientific understanding and practical, cost-effective solutions.

KEY TERMS REVIEW

1. A treatment program for young juvenile offenders that has a cognitive, school, and family focus is called _____.

2. Behavioral excesses or poorly controlled behaviors that are bothersome to others are called _____.

3. Failure to respond to punishment is called _____.

4. Lawful and unlawful acts of destruction are called _____.

5. Another term for *childhood sexual assault* is called _____.

6. A personality disorder characterized by a history of callousness, disregard for social conventions and others' rights and feelings, and illegal conduct is called _____.

7. Beliefs and expectations about other persons' availability, trustworthiness, and caring, which can be positive or negative, are called a _____.

8. A tendency to be numb, unresponsive, or even callous is called _____.

9. Difficulty in delaying or suppressing an immediate urge or response when a careful or controlled response might produce more desirable or appropriate results is called _____.

10. A model that emphasizes the interaction of biological and psychological factors in the development of antisocial conduct and violent behavior is the _____.

11. A person who lacks the ability to inhibit responses in the face of possible punishment is called _____.

12. Aggressiveness that erupts suddenly is called _____.

13. Women who have been physically beaten by their domestic partners are called _____.

14. The type of rapist motivated by the experience of sexual pleasure from the pain, suffering, and humiliation of women is called _____.

15. A hormone associated with male characteristics that has been studied in regard to a possible role in aggressiveness and sexual behaviors is called _____.

16. A marriage between persons with similar psychological disorders or who both have some psychological disorder is called _____.

17. A kind of personality with prominent traits of selfishness, deceitfulness, and callousness that can be reflected—although not necessarily demonstrated—in various illegal ways is called _____.

18. Acquisition of behaviors and attitudes from watching others is called _____.

19. A framework holding that the quality of the parent-infant bond guides fundamental aspects of the child's social, intellectual, and self-esteem development by shaping how the child views the self and other people is called _____.

20. Desire for exciting, stimulating, or even dangerous experiences, hypothesized to be related to antisocial behavior, is called _____.

21. Sexual assault that involves sexual penetration in the context of physical coercion or the threat of harm is called _____.

22. A legal rather than a mental health concept, which refers to violations of the law owing to any cause, is called _____.

23. Imprisonment as punishment for a crime is called _____.

24. The use of psychological pressure or physical force to engage in sexual contact with a child in which the assailant is at least several years older than the child is called _____.

25. Body signs of awareness such as heart and respiration rate and electrodermal activity are called _____.

26. The use of psychological pressure or physical force to engage in unwanted sexual contact that involves genital touching or intercourse is called _____.

27. The infliction of damage sufficient to cause injury and even death, as well as psychological scars, is called _____.

28. The failure to provide proper care for children or to meet their nutritional, emotional, medical, and physical needs is called _____.

29. Violence that occurs in the home between intimates is called _____.

30. Efforts of public agencies to provide counseling and community and school programs as alternatives to incarceration for youths found guilty of criminal or antisocial behavior are called _____.

31. The tendency to believe erroneously that negative events are caused by other people who intend harm is called _____.

32. Absent or low levels of physical reactions to fearful or aversive conditions is called _____.

FACTUAL MULTIPLE-CHOICE QUESTIONS

1. Antisocial personality disorder criteria evolved from the earlier concept of
   a. sociopathy.
   b. psychopathy.
   c. criminality.
   d. conduct disorder.

2. Childhood aggressiveness is a strong predictor of
   a. schizophrenia.
   b. adult phobias.
   c. adult aggressiveness.
   d. good social and adaptive skills.

3. Excessive violence and antisocial behavior can be predicted by low levels of
   a. testosterone.
   b. serotonin
   c. dopamine.
   d. progesterone.

4. The most common form of intervention for antisocial conduct is
   a. psychoanalysis.
   b. electro convulsive therapy.
   c. incarceration.
   d. testosterone replacement therapy.

5. A child who witnesses parental violence most likely will be
   a. harmed as if he or she had experienced physical abuse.
   b. unaffected by the experience.
   c. turned over to the juvenile authorities.
   d. a better parent because of the trauma witnessed.

6. At least one-half of the acts of rape are committed by
   a. known sexual offenders.
   b. complete strangers.
   c. acquaintances or friends.
   d. alcoholics.

7. Which of the following is *not* one of Knight and Prentky's major motives for rape?
   a. psychotic
   b. opportunistic
   c. sadistic
   d. vindictive

8. The institution which is now recognized to be the source of danger and violence in today's society is
   a. the schools.
   b. the prisons.
   c. law enforcement.
   d. the family.

9. Children who are physically or sexually abused may develop negative beliefs and expectations about other people's values and the trustworthiness and caring of these individuals. These maladaptive beliefs are known as
   a. deficient avoidance learning.
   b. hostile attributional biases.
   c. assortative mating.
   d. maladaptive interpersonal schemas.

10. Some researchers believe that an underlying cause of antisocial behavior may be
    a. the desire for sensation seeking.
    b. imbalances with the neurotransmitter dopamine.
    c. dysfunction in the occipital cortex.
    d. high levels of psychophysiological arousal.

CONCEPTUAL MULTIPLE-CHOICE QUESTIONS

1. Which of the following is *not* a personality disorder?
   a. schizotypal
   b. psychopathy
   c. antisocial
   d. borderline

2. In order for an individual to meet the criteria for antisocial personality disorder (APD), he or she must
   a. be a criminal.
   b. meet the criteria for psychopathy.
   c. meet the criteria for criminality.
   d. meet the criteria for childhood conduct disorder.

3. There is ample evidence that violence is
   a. sometimes used for constructive purposes.
   b. declining in American culture.
   c. frequently used to solve interpersonal disputes.
   d. isolated in the inner cities of America.

4. The connection between underarousal and antisocial behavior is
   a. neurotransmitters.
   b. sensation-seeking.
   c. information processing.
   d. testosterone.

5. A child who has experienced parental conflict, parental illness, and neglect is at risk for criminality because of
   a. new legislation aimed at young criminals.
   b. poor education.
   c. passive-avoidance error.
   d. multiple deprivation experiences.

6. Most studies evaluating the success of child abuse preventive treatment programs are limited because they do *not* include
   a. young parents.
   b. low-income mothers.
   c. fathers and male partners.
   d. high-risk situations.

7. Johnny had been a problem for his teachers for years. In preschool he hit and taunted his classmates and was caught more than once stealing. His likelihood for developing APD is
   a. high because problems that start young tend to continue.
   b. low because he will probably outgrow the problems.
   c. low because there is little correlation between childhood conduct disorders and APD.
   d. high because all youngsters with conduct disorders develop an adult antisocial personality disorder.

8. Harry had been diagnosed with APD and been in and out of prison since he was eighteen. Now, at age forty-eight he is being paroled again. Studies have shown that Harry
   a. might not return because of mellowing that takes place with middle-age APD.
   b. will return because conviction rates for psychopaths remain constant.
   c. will probably die from homicide or drug overdose.
   d. will return because psychopaths never learn the skills they need to stay out of prison.

9. Jerry rode his motorcycle recklessly and was always ready for anything dangerous. His arrest for robbery supports the
   a. low serotonin theory.
   b. testosterone theory.
   c. deficient emotional arousal theory.
   d. the deficient avoidance learning theory.

10. Which of the following reasons would be used by a social learning theorist to explain the causes of antisocial behavior and violence?
    a. Defects in impulse-control by the Id
    b. Poor modeling and inconsistent reinforcement contingencies from family members
    c. Neurotransmitter irregularities caused by assortative mating
    d. Inadequate development of positive attachment between the parent and child

APPLICATION MULTIPLE-CHOICE QUESTIONS

1. Mark was able to charm everyone. He lied to his coworkers about his background and places he had traveled. He also stole infrequently from his office workers and fixed the blame on his colleagues. He rarely got into trouble because of his ability to manipulate others. Mark would be diagnosed
   a. with APD.
   b. as a criminal.
   c. with borderline personality disorder.
   d. as a psychopath.

2. Reginald is a fifteen-year-old high school student who lives in a large inner-city community. As a young African American male, he is at risk for
   a. death by homicide.
   b. death by accident.
   c. death by suicide.
   d. death by natural causes.

3. Marshall lives in Tupelo, Mississippi. Late one night he hears a knock on the door and sees a young Asian man dressed in what appears to be a disguise. According to research findings on the likelihood of the use of violence, Marshall's reaction might be
   a. to call 911.
   b. to ask for identification from the caller.
   c. to turn off the lights and ignore the situation hoping the caller will go away.
   d. to get one of his many guns and challenge the caller.

4. Diane repeatedly lied and cheated in her daily activities. She had constant battles with her spouse and had left him many times. Her diagnosis of APD reflects
   a. an accurate diagnosis.
   b. a diagnosis that is often made for women.
   c. higher vulnerability for women to develop APD.
   d. earlier onset of problems for women who develop APD.

5. Maurice was in a lab test study while in prison. It was determined that he had a low level of serotonin. He has just been paroled. He is likely to
   a. be able to control his impulse aggressiveness.
   b. be able to have a successful career in the military.
   c. be able to control his self-destructive tendencies.
   d. return to jail because low serotonin levels predict repeat offending.

6. Michael's family was in constant conflict. His father had been imprisoned several times and his mother was a drug user and pusher. Because Michael's scores on intelligence tests were well above average, his chances of succeeding are
   a. good, because many children are unaffected by parental aggression.
   b. good, because children exposed to antisocial behaviors tend to stay in school.
   c. good, because if he drops out of school he can probably find a good job to help him get started.
   d. good, because his higher intelligence may allow him to resist an antisocial lifestyle.

7. Janet and her brothers watch a lot of violent television and videos. When she witnesses one of the frequent scenes of violence in her neighborhood she pays little attention. She may be experiencing
   a. cognitive distortion.
   b. hostile attributional biases.
   c. a dysfunctional family.
   d. emotional desensitization.

8. When Susan, a college student, reported she had been raped by her date, the volunteer at the rape crisis center was
   a. shocked that the rapist was known to Susan.
   b. surprised that a college student had reported the rape.
   c. not surprised since at least one-half of the acts of rape are committed by acquaintances.
   d. surprised that a college woman would allow herself to be raped.

9. Margaret had been raped six months ago and suffered posttraumatic stress disorder (PTSD). She went to her therapist for help. Margaret's case is unusual because
   a. psychological reaction to rape is rare.
   b. most persons with histories of sexual assault do not seek treatment.
   c. unless the rape is violent it usually isn't traumatizing.
   d. it is rare for the reaction to take the form of PTSD.

10. Margot has a six-month-old. She is sixteen, and unwed. Her best chance to avoid abusing her child is
   a. for her to find a program to enhance her competency as a parent.
   b. to find one of the many programs available for her child's father.
   c. to try to make it on her own.
   d. not to even try because the programs that are available don't make any difference.

ANSWER KEY: KEY TERMS REVIEW

1. multisystemic treatment (MST) (450–451)
2. disruptive behavior disorders (444)
3. deficient avoidance learning (446)
4. violence (444)
5. sexual molestation (456)
6. antisocial personality disorder (APD) (434)
7. interpersonal schemas (453)
8. emotional desensitization (449)
9. poor impulse control (440)
10. biosocial model (447)
11. disinhibited (446)
12. impulsive aggressiveness (444)
13. battered women (455)
14. sadistic rapists (458)
15. testosterone (445)
16. assortative mating (447)
17. psychopathy (435)
18. observational learning (449)
19. attachment theory (453)
20. sensation-seeking (446)
21. rape (456)
22. criminality (436)
23. incarceration (450)
24. childhood sexual assault (456)
25. psychophysiological arousal (445)
26. sexual assault (456)
27. physical abuse (451)
28. neglect (452)
29. domestic violence (451)
30. juvenile diversion programs (450)
31. hostile attributional biases (448)
32. deficient emotional arousal (445)

ANSWER KEY: FACTUAL MULTIPLE-CHOICE QUESTIONS

1. *a. sociopathy (p. 435)
   b. Psychopathy is not a disorder, although it is similar to APD.
   c. Criminality is a legal concept.
   d. Conduct disorder must be present in childhood in order to meet the criteria for APD.

2. *c. adult aggressiveness (p. 440)
   a. Schizophrenia usually has onset during adolescence and is not related to childhood aggressiveness.
   b. Adult phobias are usually unrelated to violent symptoms in childhood.
   d. Aggressive children are at greater risk for developing many later problems.

3. *b. serotonin (pp. 443–444)
   a. Testosterone studies have not shown consistent results regarding predicting behavior.
   c. High levels of dopamine are associated with schizophrenia.
   d. Progesterone is a hormone associated with female characteristics.

4. *c. incarceration (p. 450)
   a. Psychoanalysis would not be the treatment of choice for manipulative APD patients.
   b. Electro convulsive therapy would be used in cases of chronic depression.
   d. Testosterone is a male hormone possibly implicated in APD, but not used in treatment.

5. *a. harmed as if he or she had experienced physical abuse (pp. 454–455)
   b. A child witnessing such violence is usually affected.
   c. A child who does not suffer direct abuse will probably not be turned over to the authorities.
   d. Research has shown that children exposed to domestic violence often become abusers themselves.

6. *c. acquaintances or friends (p. 456)
   a. Many rapes are committed by friends who are not known criminals.
   b. Complete strangers commit a smaller percentage of rapes than acquaintances.
   d. Alcohol is a factor in some rapes, but studies do not mention it as a major consideration.

7. *a. Psychotic (p. 458)
   b. Opportunistic rapes are unplanned.
   c. Sadistic rapists take pleasure from the suffering of their victims.
   d. Vindictive rapists focus on anger toward women.

8. *d. the family (p. 462)
   a. The schools are, in many ways, a haven for children who are victims of violence.
   b. The prisons have long been recognized as sources of violence.
   c. Law enforcement can be a source of violence, but should be the protector of society from violence.

9. *d. maladaptive interpersonal schemas. (p. 453)
   a. Deficient avoidance learning refers to the tendency not to learn from punishment.
   b. Hostile attributional bias is the tendency to believe that others are intentionally causing negative events.
   c. Assortative mating is the tendency for others with mental disorders to marry individuals with similar problems.

10. *a. the desire for sensation seeking. (p. 446)
    b. Low levels of serotonin are associated with impulsive antisocial behavior.
    c. There appears to be some neurocognitive dysfunction in the brain's frontal cortex, which involves our ability to plan, reason, and evaluate consequences (i.e., the "executive" functions of the brain).
    d. Researchers have found that persons with APD and conduct disorder show low levels of psychophysiological reactions to fearful or aversive conditions.

ANSWER KEY: CONCEPTUAL MULTIPLE-CHOICE QUESTIONS

1. *b. psychopathy (p. 435)
   a. Schizotypal is one of the ten personality disorders.
   c. Antisocial personality disorder is closely connected to psychopathy, which is a personality type, not a disorder.
   d. Borderline personality disorder is of the dramatic/erratic cluster of personality disorders.

2. *d. must meet the criteria for childhood conduct disorder (p. 435)
   a. Many persons with APD are not criminals and vice versa.
   b. Psychopathy, unlike antisocial personality disorder, is not a DSM-IV disorder.
   c. Criminality is a legal, not a mental health term.

3. *c. frequently used to solve interpersonal disputes (p. 437)
   a. Violence has become such a part of American life that it is accepted, but not constructive.
   b. Most of the evidence suggests increasing violence.
   d. Violence occurs frequently in the inner cities, but is part of American life everywhere.

4. *b. sensation-seeking (p. 446)
   a. Neurotransmitters are responsible for synaptic transmission of electrical impulses.
   c. Information processing is part of the learning deficits theory of APD.
   d. The link between testosterone and antisocial behavior is unclear.

5. *d. multiple deprivation experiences (p. 447)
   a. Legislation is aimed at offenders after they have committed their crimes.
   b. Poor education is often associated with lower socioeconomic groups, but is less traumatic than other violent experiences.
   c. Passive-avoidance error is a typical response of psychopaths, not a result of child neglect.

6. *c. fathers and male partners (p. 460)
   a. Young parents are considered a high-risk population.
   b. Low-income mothers are also considered a high-risk group.
   d. The studies focus on the populations which are in high-risk situations.

7. *a. high because problems that start young tend to continue (pp. 440–441)
   b. The problems tend to diversify rather than go away.
   c. Childhood conduct disorder is a requirement for diagnosis with APD.
   d. Only about 40 percent of males with conduct disorders develop APD.

8. *a. might not return because of mellowing that takes place with middle age (p. 442)
    b. Conviction rates drop after APD patients reach age forty.
    c. Death from homicide or overdose is reduced if an APD reaches middle age.
    d. Recidivism rates drop because some APD inmates learn positive life skills.

9. *c. deficient emotional arousal theory (pp. 445–446)
    a. Low serotonin correlates with impulse aggressiveness.
    b. Testosterone levels do not correlate with thrill-seeking behavior.
    d. The deficient avoidance learning theory does not deal with sensation-seeking activity.

10. *b. Poor modeling and inconsistent reinforcement contingencies from family members. (p. 447)
    a. This answer reflects a psychodynamic perspective.
    c. Assortative mating and neurotransmitter concepts are part of the biological perspective.
    d. Attachment theory is associated with psychodynamic models, especially object relations theory.

ANSWER KEY: APPLICATION MULTIPLE-CHOICE QUESTIONS

1. *d. as a psychopath (p. 435)
    a. APD criteria tend to emphasize criminal behavior.
    b. Most psychopaths are not criminals.
    c. Borderline personality disorder patients are more dramatic and erratic compared to the outward calm of the psychopath.

2. *a. death by homicide (p. 437)
    b. Whites have higher rates for accidents.
    c. Whites also have higher rates for suicide than African Americans.
    d. Death by natural causes is becoming increasingly unusual for African American males from the inner cities.

3. *d. to get one of his many guns and challenge the caller (pp. 437–438)
    a. Calling 911 would not be consistent with the level of violence accepted in the southern United States.
    b. Asking for identification would also be inconsistent with southern attitudes.
    c. Turning off the lights would not be consistent with what Marshall might perceive as a threat to his family or property.

4. *a. an accurate diagnosis (p. 439)
    b. APD is a diagnosis not often made for women.
    c. Women apparently have a lower vulnerability to APD.
    d. Women who develop APD tend to have later onset of problems.

5. *d. return to jail because low serotonin levels predict repeat offending (p. 444)
    a. Low serotonin level correlates with impulse aggressiveness; he may tend to have trouble controlling his aggressiveness.
    b. Low serotonin levels predicted discharge from the military because of excessive violence.
    c. Self-directed aggression also correlates with low serotonin levels.

6. *d. good, because his higher intelligence may allow him to resist an antisocial lifestyle (p. 448)
   a. Most children are negatively affected by family violence.
   b. Children exposed to such violence are at greater risk for dropping out.
   c. Students who drop out of school often find low-level employment, with little chance of advancement.

7. *d. emotional desensitization (p. 449)
   a. Cognitive distortions take the form of believing that negative events are caused by people intending harm.
   b. Hostile attribution biases are a form of cognitive distortion.
   c. Janet's family situation may be unrelated to her exposure to media violence.

8. *c. not surprised, since at least one-half of the acts of rape are committed by acquaintances (p. 456)
   a. Acquaintance/date rape is quite common.
   b. Educated women are more willing to report rape.
   d. Rape can happen to anyone.

9. *b. most persons with histories of sexual assault do not seek treatment (p. 460)
   a. Psychological reaction to rape is common.
   c. All rapes are traumatizing to the victim.
   d. Often rape victims suffer from PTSD.

10. *a. for her to find a program to enhance her competency as a parent (pp. 459–460)
    b. There are very few programs that focus on fathers or male partners.
    c. Margot has few resources to help her make it on her own.
    d. Many of the programs have shown significant positive results with at-risk populations of young, low-income mothers.

CHAPTER 15

Behavioral and Emotional Disorders of Childhood and Adolescence

LEARNING OBJECTIVES

1. Describe the differences between the mental disorders of children and adolescents and those of adults. (p. 466)

2. Discuss the importance of identifying and treating the mental disorders of childhood and adolescence. (p. 466)

3. Discuss the emphasis of developmental psychopathology on the interaction between the child and her or his context. (p. 466)

4. Describe how the disorders of childhood and adolescence are assessed and some commonly used assessment instruments. (pp. 467–468)

5. Discuss how the disorders of childhood and adolescence are classified and the difference between internalizing and externalizing disorders. (pp. 468–470)

6. Describe the treatment of youth disorders. (p. 470)

7. Describe the features of attention-deficit hyperactivity disorder (ADHD). Discuss who is affected by ADHD, the course of ADHD, and how ADHD is assessed and diagnosed. (pp. 470–472)

8. Describe the presumed causes and treatment of ADHD. (pp. 474–477)

9. Describe the features of conduct disorders. Discuss who is affected by and the course of conduct disorders. (pp. 477–480)

10. Discuss the presumed causes and treatments for conduct disorder. (pp. 480–483)

11. Describe the features of emotional disorders. (pp. 483–484)

12. Discuss anxiety disorders in youth. (pp. 484–486)

13. Discuss the features of depression in youth. (pp. 486–488)

14. Discuss the effects of divorce on childhood development. (p. 480)

15. Describe the treatments for youthful depression. (p. 489)

16. Describe the features of eating disorders anorexia and bulimia. (pp. 489–493)

17. Describe the treatment for anorexia and bulimia. (pp. 493–494)

18. Discuss the features and treatments of tic disorders such as Tourette's disorder and coprolalia. (pp. 494–495)

19. Describe the features and treatments of enuresis and encopresis. (pp. 495–496)

CHAPTER OUTLINE

I.   Understanding the Disorders of Youth

- Children and adolescents differ from adults in their problems, their responses to treatments, and the course of their disorders.

- Untreated problems may persist into adulthood.

A. Developmental Psychopathology

1. Views psychological maladjustment in relation to major changes across the life cycle.

2. Recognizes the important interaction between the child and the context.

3. Emphasizes the importance of acknowledging what is normal for a given age.

B. Assessing Childhood and Adolescent Disorders

1. Child Behavior Checklist used to assess children. It is a rigorously developed and standardized rating scale, available for both parents and teachers, for assessing the most common dimensions of psychological disorder in childhood.

2. The Diagnostic Interview for Children and Adolescents, a structured diagnostic interview form, also helps in diagnosis.

3. The Response Class Matrix is used to observe and assess parent-child interactions.

C. Classifying Childhood and Adolescent Disorders

1. The DSM is the most widely used diagnostic system.

2. DSM-IV has a separate section for disorders usually first diagnosed in infancy, childhood, or adolescence.

3. Multivariate statistical taxometric system classifies disorders using statistical procedures to determine what symptoms occur together with other symptoms.

4. Childhood disorders fall into two categories:

a. Internalizing disorders:

(1) Inner-directed psychological difficulties.

(2) Core symptoms associated with overcontrolled behaviors, such as anxiety, depression, isolation, and the eating disorders.

           (3)   More females identified with internalizing disorders.

      b. Externalizing disorders:

          (1)   Maladaptive behavior patterns that create problems for others.

          (2)   Also called *uncontrolled disorders* or *behavioral disorders.*

          (3)   More males identified with undercontrolled disorders.

          (4)   Although problems displayed outwardly, there is still considerable inner turmoil.

D. Treating Disorders of Youth

    1. Children do not seek treatment but rather are sent for it.

    2. Behavioral or cognitive-behavioral approaches are the most effective.

    3. Important differences exist between adult and child therapy:

      a. The role of the parents.

      b. The use of play in therapy.

      c. The use of medications. Few controlled studies exist regarding medications for children.

II. Behavior Disorders

A. Attention-Deficit Hyperactivity Disorder (ADHD)

    1. *Hyperactivity* is the popular designation, has been widely studied.

    2. The DSM-IV provides diagnostic criteria for different types of ADHD:

      a. Predominantly inattentive.

      b. Predominantly hyperactive.

      c. Combined type.

    3. A controversial disorder in its definition and its treatment

    4. Clinical characteristics of ADHD

      a. Attention-deficit hyperactivity disorder is a disruptive behavior disorder with three essential features:

          (1)   Developmentally inappropriate levels of inattention

          (2)   Impulsivity

          (3)   Hyperactivity

      b. Inattention: unable to listen or complete tasks; rapid shift of activity

      c. Impulsivity: acting without thinking (e.g., interrupting, failure to wait for turn, trouble organizing schoolwork).

      d. Overactivity: fidgety, restless, unable to sit still.

      e.   Difficulties with peer relationships central to ADHD: rule violations and aggression, social rejection.

      f.   High degree of comorbidity with other disorders: learning disabilities and aggression are common.

  2.   Who is affected with ADHD?

      a.   Male-to-female ratio of between 4 to 1 and 8 to 1 is typical.

      b.   Boys show more aggression and girls more anxiety and withdrawal.

      c.   Somewhat greater frequency among lower socioeconomic classes.

      d.   Cross-cultural differences emerging, although may be due to inconsistent diagnostic practices.

  3.   The course of ADHD

      a.   Developmental appropriateness determines a diagnosis of ADHD.

      b.   Some symptoms, excessive motor activity, may improve with age, but attentional focus and social difficulties persist.

B.   Focus on Research: Are there ADHD adolescents? Adults?

- ADHD children have more numerous and intense family conflicts.

- Difficulty in conducting longitudinal studies on this topic.

- Persistence of ADHD partly explained by comorbidity of other behavior problems

- Whether ADHD children have continued problems into early adulthood cannot be clearly answered at present.

  1.   Assessing and diagnosing ADHD

      a.   Ratings of the child's behavior by parents and teachers (e.g., CBCL).

      b.   Interviews with the child, parents, and teachers.

      c.   Direct observation of behavior and task performance (e.g., Matching Familiar Figures Test).

      d.   Assessments are used in combination.

  2.   Causes of ADHD

      a.   *Genetic factors* may create a predisposition to develop ADHD in response to environmental agents.

      b.   The hypothesis that *brain damage* causes ADHD has not been supported.

      c.   The hypothesis that *brain dysfunction* or *neurological immaturity* partially cause ADHD has received some support, although the data are correlational.

      d.   *Diet* does not appear to be related. Sugar does not cause hyperactivity.

     e.   *Social and environmental* factors more significant in course and outcome than in cause of ADHD.

     f.   *Multiple pathways model,* similar to the diathesis-stress model, is probably the best explanation for ADHD.

   3.   Treatments for ADHD: medications and psychosocial programs

     a.   *Medications* typically involve stimulants for a "focusing" effect: psycho-stimulant medications methylphenidate (Ritalin), pemdine (Cylert), or dextroamphetamine (Dexedrine).

         (1)   Increase attention span.

         (2)   Decrease impulsiveness.

         (3)   Improve fine motor skills.

         (4)   Improve cognitive performance.

     b.   Paradoxical effect: stimulant medications have a quieting and focusing effect on ADHD *and* non-ADHD children. (Earlier belief that quieting proved the presence of ADHD is false.)

     c.   Medication use effective for about 70 percent of children diagnosed with ADHD.

     d.   There are unwanted side effects; not all children respond positively.

     e.   *Psychological approaches* emphasize teaching skills to improve attention, self-control, reduce excessive motor activity, and manage anger.

     f.   Parent-training programs teach behavior management skills to reduce child's noncompliance and encourage self-control.

     g.   Classroom management programs develop child's ability to benefit from classroom instruction.

     h.   Both parent-training programs and classroom management programs have diminished effect after program is discontinued.

     i.   Combination of medication and behavior programs have shown promise.

C.   Conduct Disorders

   1.   Clinical characteristics and diagnosis of conduct disorder

     a.   Repetitive and persistent pattern of behavior involving violation of the rights of others and of age-inappropriate social norms.

     b.   Common features: physical aggression, cruelty, property damage, arson, stealing, lying, cheating.

     c.   Oppositional defiant disorder: a pattern of negativistic, hostile, and defiant behavior that has lasted at least six months.

     d.   Behaviors: losing temper, arguing, defying rules, intentionally annoying others, temper tantrums, etc.

     e.   Conduct disorders: a heterogeneous grouping—not all aggressive.

    f.   Some persons with conduct disorders display overt behaviors: confrontational

    g.   Others show covert behaviors: concealed actions, such as stealing, truancy, and lying

2.   Who is affected with conduct disorder?

    a.   4 to 10 percent of children.

    b.   Male to female ratio between 3 to 1 and 7 to 1.

    c.   Age of onset is earlier for boys, before the age of ten.

    d.   More prevalent in low socioeconomic status families and in urban settings.

3.   The course of conduct disorder

    a.   Aggressive behavior is stable over time.

    b.   Conduct disorders related to later aggression, antisocial behavior, and other adult problems.

4.   Cognitive factors in conduct disorder

    a.   Academic and intellectual difficulties predict conduct disorder.

    b.   Aggressive youth lack problem-solving skills and the ability to generate multiple solutions to problems.

    c.   Display cognitive distortions when thinking about social interactions.

    d.   Aggressive children show hostile attributional bias: attribute negative motivation to others in ambiguous situations.

5.   Genetic factors

    a.   Studies have been obfuscated by use of different labels.

    b.   Genetic contributions to aggressive behavior may exist, but specific causal factors are unknown.

6.   The role of the family

    a.   Family is a major factor in the cause of conduct disorders.

    b.   Four alternative patterns are common in families with conduct disorder children:

        (1)   Parental deviance (e.g., criminal behavior and alcoholism).

        (2)   Parental rejection and coerciveness (e.g., physical abuse).

        (3)   Lack of discipline or supervision (e.g., reinforce children's use of coercive behaviors).

        (4)   Marital conflict and divorce.

7.   Treatments for conduct disorder

    a. Systemwide programs in schools or behaviorally oriented parent training is effective.

    b. Prevention programs may help reduce the emergence of conduct disorder.

    c. *Parent training:* action-oriented family therapy teaches parents skills for managing their children.

    d. These programs may lead to improved functioning and less antisocial behaviors.

    e. *Cognitive processing* approaches target deficient and distorted thinking and teaches children to think and engage in problem solving.

    f. Work with younger children shows promise of positive intervention before patterns are ingrained.

III. Emotional Disorders

  A. What's Normal? Facing Emotional Challenges

    1. Fears and anxieties in childhood are common. Only when fears and anxieties in childhood are intense and prolonged do they signal psychological disorder.

    2. Fears change according to age.

    3. For adolescents, conflicts or emerging independence and challenges posed by autonomy can trigger fears.

  B. Anxiety Disorders

    1. Symptoms associated with anxiety in youth resemble those found in adults, including physiological, behavioral, and cognitive symptoms.

    2. Symptoms include stomachaches, headaches, muscle tension, sweating, jittery behavior, or feelings of suffocation or choking.

    3. Separation anxiety disorder (SAD) is specific to children and is manifested by obvious distress from excessive concern about being separated from those to whom the child is attached.

      a. In early childhood separation anxiety appears and recedes as part of normal development.

      b. In an older child it can signal maladaptive adjustment.

    4. Who is affected with anxiety disorders?

      a. In childhood, boys and girls show comparable rates of disorder.

      b. Adolescent girls report more fears than boys.

    5. Causal forces and treatment approaches in anxiety disorders

      a. Psychosocial treatment of anxiety includes skill in management of arousal and exposure to the feared situation.

      b. Different approaches are used to treat school phobia, including behavioral treatment (most successful), hospitalization with medication, and psychotherapy with home tutoring (least successful).

C.   Depression: Does It Exist in Children and Adolescents?

- Adult criteria for depression can be applied to children.

- Depressive symptoms relatively rare in early childhood, but become more common with increasing age; by adolescence the number is comparable to adults.

- Gender differences = none in childhood, 1 to 2 (male-female) ratio in adolescence.

- Depression in youth may be increasing.

1.   Assessing depression in youth

   a.   Measuring depression is complex, and different measurement strategies show little convergent validity.

   b.   Child's self-report important in assessing emotional distress.

2.   Do depressed children become depressed adults?

   a.   Insufficient longitudinal data exist, so no conclusions possible.

   b.   Episodes of depression in childhood may predict future depression.

3.   What causes depression in youth?

   a.   Biological and genetic predispositions interact with family distress.

   b.   Depression tends to run in families.

   c.   Likely to occur when the child feels bad about self or has a poor relationship with parents or when family disruption occurs.

4.   Family Matters: The effects of divorce

   a.   Half of marriages in the United States do not last, and 40 percent of children grow up in a divorced family.

   b.   Younger children adjust after a few years of disorders:

      (1)   Boys' problems are more intense and enduring.

      (2)   Children in custody of parent of same gender show healthier adjustment.

   c.   Early adolescents show acting-out behaviors, difficulty in school, and withdrawal.

   d.   Conditions before the separation predict much of the effect of divorce.

5.   Treating depression in youth

   a.   Antidepressant medication (major treatment for adult depression) is not effective with children.

   b.   Cognitive-behavioral therapy is promising.

   c.   Teaching self-management skills, self-monitoring, and social problem solving produced gains.

IV.   Eating Disorders

- Eating disorders are comorbid with a wide variety of other disorders.

A. Anorexia Nervosa

1. "Nervous loss of appetite" is a misnomer, since persons with the diagnosis do experience hunger.

2. An eating disorder characterized by an intense fear of becoming obese, distorted self-perception of body image, refusal to maintain minimal normal body weight, cessation of menstruation.

3. Patient is persistent in desire for additional weight loss.

4. Risk of onset high between ages 14 and 18.

5. Eight to eleven times more common in females than in males.

6. Although identified worldwide, there are wide cross-cultural differences: rare in China, common in Japan.

7. One-third of patients are chronically ill, less than 5 percent die.

8. Patients described as obsessional, neurotic, controlling, depressive, negative attitudes about sexuality, and rarely engage in sexual activity.

9. Psychological explanations for anorexia nervosa

    a. Differing viewpoints exist as to causes. Female increase in body fat with adolescence associated with concerns about increased weight.

    b. Not eating gives the patient a false sense of control.

    c. Personality traits linked to anorexia: compliance, perfectionism, and dependence, and no school problems.

    d. Minuchin describes the family of the anorectic as *enmeshed*, each member lacking distinct identity; the patient, by not eating, is rebelling against the enmeshment.

    e. Families also marked by rigidity and a failure to resolve conflicts.

    f. Also described as an avoidance response, reinforced by attention received.

    g. Cultural pressure to be thin.

    h. Patients may feel they "must" be thin, making continued weight loss evidence of power and control.

    i. Inaccurate cognitive evaluations (distortions) made about weight.

10. Biological factors in anorexia nervosa

    a. Genetic factors may predispose some people to the onset of the disorder, but limited by use of twin studies and causal mechanisms are unclear.

    b. Cause is interaction between biological predisposition and adverse environmental forces.

B. Bulimia

1. An eating disorder characterized by binge eating, rapid consumption of a large amount of food in a discrete period of time, and the feeling of a lack of control over eating, plus inappropriate behaviors to prevent weight gain, such as self-induced vomiting or use of laxatives.

2. Also includes diuretics, fasting, vigorous exercise, and a persistent concern about weight and shape.

3. Diagnosis requires three months of two binges per week.

4. Bulimia is also referred to as the *binge-purge syndrome.*

5. Occurs primarily in females, with onset in late adolescence.

6. 50 percent of anorexics show some signs of bulimia.

7. Problematic family interactions one factor.

8. Difference between normal eaters, who stop when they are full, and restrained eaters, who ignore biological signals and eat when they "should," might be a factor in bulimia.

C. Treating Eating Disorders

    1. Psychodynamic treatments have not been rigorously evaluated.

    2. Behavior modification, cognitive therapy, and family systems approaches have all shown positive results.

V. Other Disorders

  A. Tic Disorders

    1. Tics are involuntary, rapid, recurrent, and stereotyped motor movement or vocalizations.

    2. Motor and verbal tics classified as chronic or transient.

      a. Chronic: last more than a year.

      b. Transient: less than a year.

    3. Include neck-jerking, rapid eye-blinking, facial grimacing, grunting, throat-clearing, repeating sounds made by others.

    4. Tourette's disorder involves multiple motor and one or more verbal tics.

    5. Coprolalia occurs in about one-third of Tourette's patients. Individual utters, calls, or screams obscenities.

    6. Average age of onset of Tourette's disorder is seven.

    7. Children with Tourette's disorder have difficulty maintaining age-appropriate social skills.

    8. Discipline problems are often evident in children with Tourette's.

    9. Disruptive behaviors and ADHD and OCD may be comorbid with Tourette's.

    10. A genetic factor may be implicated, but the causal mechanism is unclear.

11. Medications may show some benefit, but associated with unwanted side effects.

   B. Enuresis and Encopresis

     1. Enuresis is wetting in the absence of a urologic or neurologic pathology.

     2. Common in five-year-olds; 20 percent qualify as enuretic.

     3. Gender differences exist for enuresis: No difference until age five; by age eleven, 2 to 1 male-female ratio.

     4. Encopresis is the fecal parallel to enuresis but much less prevalent than enuresis.

     5. Gender differences exist for encopresis, with a 3 to 1 male-female ratio.

     6. It appears there are multiple causes for enuresis, including genetic factors, response to arousal during sleep, emotional conflicts, smaller bladder capacity, and failure to learn an adaptive response to a full bladder.

     7. Psychological treatment was reported superior to medication such as imipramine.

     8. Psychological treatment superior to medication.

     9. Bell and pad urine-sensing devices are used to awaken the child in time to use the toilet.

VI. What Lies Ahead?

   A. Research will broaden our understanding of the causes of and treatments for child and adolescent psychological disorders.

   B. Focus will be on cognitive processing and behavioral patterns of youth with disorders.

   C. Increased experimental focus on the family, parent and child interactions, and parenting styles.

KEY TERMS REVIEW

1. A characteristic of ADHD, the tendency to take action suddenly, without considering the consequences, is called _____.

2. The inappropriate elimination of feces in the absence of a physical disorder: fecal parallel to enuresis is called _____.

3. A condition manifested in a pattern of negativistic, hostile, and defiant behavior that has lasted a minimum of six months is called _____.

4. Psychological difficulties that are considered inner-directed, core symptoms associated with overcontrolled behaviors, are called _____.

5. A treatment applied to the families of children with conduct disorder in which parents are taught skills for better managing their children with the aim of undermining detrimental family interactions is called _____.

6. Maladaptive behavior patterns in children, across several situations, that create problems for others are called _____.

7. Another term for bulimia is _____.

8. Another term for externalizing disorders is _____.

9. A tic disorder that involves multiple motor tics, usually involving the head and that consists of one or more verbal tics is called _____.

10. Applied to a child with a conduct disorder to describe antisocial behaviors that are confrontive, such as fighting, arguing, and temper tantrums, is the term _____.

11. An eating disorder characterized by an intense fear of becoming obese, a distorted self-perception of body image, refusal to maintain normal body weight, and, in females, cessation of menstruation is called _____.

12. A childhood or adolescent problem consisting of a repetitive and persistent pattern of behavior that involves violation of the basic rights of others and of the major age-appropriate social norms is called _____.

13. The tendency to believe erroneously that negative events are caused by other people who intend harm is called _____.

14. An eating disorder characterized by binge eating: the rapid consumption of a large quantity of food in a discrete period of time and the feeling of a lack of control over eating is called _____.

15. A disruptive behavior disorder of children that has three essential features—developmentally inappropriate levels of inattention, impulsivity, and hyperactivity—with onset before age seven, is called _____.

16. Involuntary, rapid, recurrent, and stereotyped motor movements or vocalizations are called _____.

17. A urine-sensing device that rests between the child and the mattress during sleeping hours and that sounds an alarm if the child urinates in bed; used to treat enuresis is called _____.

18. The calming and focusing effect on ADHD children after administering stimulant medications is called the _____.

19. A characteristic of ADHD, in which children are, relative to peers and developmental level, fidgety, restless, and unable to sit still, is called _____.

20. A rigorously developed and standardized rating scale completed by parents and teachers to assess the most common dimensions of psychological disorders in children is called the _____.

21. A structured interview instrument that assesses symptoms of psychological disorders in children is called _____.

22. In the case of a child with a conduct disorder, applied to describe antisocial behaviors that are concealed, such as stealing, truancy, and lying, is called _____.

23. A childhood condition manifested by obvious distress from and excessive concern about being apart from those to whom the child is attached is called _____.

24. A plan for classifying disorders by using statistical procedures to determine what symptoms occur together with what other symptoms is called _____.

25. The inappropriate occurrence of urinating in the absence of a urologic or neurologic disorder is called _____.

26. A characteristic of ADHD, a child's seeming inability to pay sustained attention and failure to complete tasks, is called _____.

27. The suitableness of a child's behavior to his or her stage of development. With regard to ADHD, the suitableness of attention, impulsivity, and level of activity, is called _____.

28. A method for observing and recording the behavior of both the parent and the child while in parent-child interactions is called a(n) _____.

29. The study of maladjustment and its interface with normal development, which views that maladjustment in relation to the major changes that occur throughout the life cycle, is called _____.

30. Medicines administered to children with ADHD to increase their ability to sustain attention, decrease impulsiveness, and improve performance on tasks are called _____.

FACTUAL MULTIPLE-CHOICE QUESTIONS

1. An important feature of developmental psychopathology is that it places child disorders against
    a.   the DSM-IV.
    b.   what is normal for adults.
    c.   disorders of adults.
    d.   what is normal for a given age.

2. Psychological disorders of childhood such as anxiety and depression would be classified as
    a.   internalizing disorders.
    b.   externalizing disorders.
    c.   behavioral disorders.
    d.   undercontrolled disorders.

3. Which of the following is *not* one of the differences between adult and child therapy?
    a.   the role of parents
    b.   the use of play
    c.   the use of medications
    d.   the effectiveness of therapy

4. Which of the following is *not* one of the essential features of ADHD?
    a.   depression
    b.   inattention
    c.   impulsivity
    d.   overactivity

5. When ADHD children grow up, the symptom which seems to subside is
    a.   attentional focus problems.
    b.   excessive motor activity.
    c.   academic difficulties.
    d.   social difficulties.

6. A diagnosis of conduct disorder
   a. is preempted by a diagnosis of oppositional defiant disorder.
   b. preempts a diagnosis of oppositional defiant disorder.
   c. is not possible in the DSM-IV.
   d. is not affected by physical aggression.

7. The following are all overt conduct behavior problems *except*
   a. fighting.
   b. arguing.
   c. temper tantrums.
   d. lying.

8. Childhood depression
   a. has been identified for generations.
   b. is completely different from adult depression.
   c. reaches adult rates when the child reaches puberty.
   d. is much higher in boys than in girls.

9. Anorexia nervosa patients
   a. rarely think about food.
   b. experience intense hunger pangs.
   c. rarely think about their body shape.
   d. know when they have reached their ideal weight.

10. Which of the following is *not* typical of an anorexia patient?
    a. compliance
    b. perfectionism
    c. stable family situation
    d. dependence

CONCEPTUAL MULTIPLE-CHOICE QUESTIONS

1. Stimulant medications have a focusing and quieting effect
   a. only on ADHD children.
   b. with only one administration per day.
   c. on children with or without an ADHD diagnosis.
   d. on nearly 100 percent of the children taking them.

2. One of the most important factors in determining the effect of divorce on children is
   a. the age of the parents.
   b. the small percentage of marriages which end in divorce.
   c. conditions before the separation.
   d. conditions after the separation.

3. Maria, a first-grader, was a constant problem for her parents and teachers. She was always fighting with her classmates and throwing temper tantrums. Maria's case is unusual because
   a. externalizing disorders are unusual for girls.
   b. her symptoms indicate that she has little internal distress.
   c. these problems usually don't show up in school.
   d. girls rarely have childhood disorders.

4. Dewayne, aged nine, was depressed. His doctor would probably prescribe
   a. antidepressant medication.
   b. no treatment because Dewayne is too young.
   c. further observation until the real problem surfaced.
   d. behavioral or cognitive therapy to prevent worsening of the condition.

5. Tommy's psychiatrist considered all but which of the following as a possible source for Tommy's ADHD?
   a. x-rays emitted from fluorescent lighting
   b. genetic factors
   c. brain function
   d. social and environmental factors

6. Dr. Henry did right in recommending that treatment for José's hyperactivity include
   a. medication alone.
   b. cognitive-behavioral treatment alone.
   c. parent-training programs.
   d. a combination of medication and behavior therapy.

7. Ms. Brendan suspected Justin of stealing lunch money and pencils from his fellow first-graders. When she saw him take something from another student's backpack and confronted him he lied, saying the money really belonged to him. His behavior may warrant a diagnosis of
   a. ADHD-combined type.
   b. oppositional defiant disorder.
   c. antisocial personality disorder.
   d. conduct disorder.

8. At age seven Jennifer cried every day and all day at school. Putting her in another room and trying to integrate her into the class did not help. She would wail until one of her parents came to get her. Her problem is
   a. generalized anxiety disorder.
   b. separation anxiety disorder.
   c. social phobia.
   d. agoraphobia.

9. Dr. Gormley was unsure what course of action to take with Jeanne's school phobia. This was because
   a. none of the treatments available are effective.
   b. after extensive study few effective interventions have been found.
   c. there are several good antidepressant medications to be used for school phobia.
   d. anxiety disorders have been studied much less than disruptive behavior problems.

10. Julie had good days and bad days. On her bad days she would pull into her shell and not speak to anyone. Occasionally she would complain of headache or stomachache. Julie has
   a. ADHD—predominantly inattentive type.
   b. conduct disorder—covert type.
   c. depression.
   d. conduct disorder—overt type.

APPLICATION MULTIPLE-CHOICE QUESTIONS

1. Joey, aged five, hated to sleep alone. He would call to his parents repeatedly to bring him water and check for monsters. Once he went to sleep, he rarely woke up until morning. He would be diagnosed with
   a. externalizing disorder.
   b. conduct disorder.
   c. normal childhood development.
   d. enuresis.

2. Forest hated to wait for recess or for anything else. His teacher was frustrated because she could rarely get him to sit still. His parents refused to allow medication, saying they couldn't afford it. The medication that might help Forest is a(n)
   a. antiandrogen.
   b. neuroleptic.
   c. antidepressant.
   d. psychostimulant.

3. Corey was repeatedly in fights with other children at school. Even an accidental touch by another student would send him into a rage. His psychologist suggested this response resulted from
   a. the psychostimulant medication he was taking.
   b. the aggressiveness of the other students.
   c. cognitive distortion of ambiguous actions.
   d. his mother's overprotectiveness.

4. Estella's parents went through their divorce amicably and had good relationships before their separation. Her acting out in class and other problems are
   a. probably a result of the divorce.
   b. a result of the parents not getting the divorce sooner.
   c. probably not related to the divorce since conditions were good before the separation.
   d. because girls tend to find family breakups more distressing.

5. Margaret had always been a perfectionist. In the last year she had lost over 25 percent of her body weight through strict dieting and vigorous exercise, yet she felt she still had not reached her goal of slimness. She would be diagnosed with
   a. obsessive-compulsive disorder.
   b. anorexia.
   c. borderline personality disorder.
   d. narcissistic personality disorder.

6. Diane, of an average weight, loved to eat and would fix huge meals which she would devour in one sitting. She would then spend a long time in the bathroom, where she said she was "freshening up." In reality, she was vomiting. Diane did not gain or lose weight because she was
   a. bulimic.
   b. depressed.
   c. anorexic.
   d. always dieting.

7. Mac had a difficult time controlling his neck-jerking and grimacing behaviors. He disconcerts his friends in public restaurants because he sometimes suddenly shouts an obscenity. Mac's condition could be
   a. schizophrenia.
   b. obsessive-compulsive disorder.
   c. Korsakoff's psychosis.
   d. Tourette's disorder with coprolalia.

8. One advantage of using an instrument such as the CBCL is that
   a. the decision of whether or not the child's behavior is developmentally appropriate is aided by comparisons of the child's behavior with a normative sample.
   b. parent-child interactions are objectively assessed by the instrument.
   c. the client's projection onto the ambiguous drawings reveals the underlying reasons for the child's psychopathology.
   d. face-to-face interviews are the only reliable way to detect disorders such as bulimia and anorexia nervosa.

9. Lawrence plans to give a speech to his abnormal psychology class about ADHD. Which of the following should Lawrence say best explains the causes of ADHD?
   a. Anatomical brain differences caused by minimal brain dysfunction.
   b. Allergic reactions caused by an oversensitivity to dietetic factors, especially sugar sensitivity.
   c. ADHD is probably caused by multiple pathways.
   d. Reactions to lighting conditions, especially x-rays emitted from fluorescent lights.

10. Which of the following situations would Salvador Minuchin say may be the cause of Claudia's anorexia?
    a. Claudia is an independent teenager, looking forward to attending college out of state. Her parents support her college choice.
    b. Claudia is very popular in high school and participates in several campus clubs. She also has a challenging job and spends a lot of time working, saving her earnings so she can pay for her upcoming college expenses.
    c. Claudia's mother and father frequently fight and are on the verge of divorce. They spend many hours at their respective jobs, leaving Claudia and the other children alone to care for themselves.
    d. Claudia's parents do not permit her have many outside interests or to hold a job for fear that she will meet a boy, get sexually involved, and become pregnant.

ANSWER KEY: KEY TERMS REVIEW

1. impulsivity (473)
2. encopresis (487)
3. oppositional defiant disorder (480)
4. internalizing disorders (471)
5. action-oriented family therapy (484)
6. externalizing disorders (471)
7. binge-purge syndrome (497)
8. behavioral disorders (470)
9. Tourette's disorder (496)
10. overt behaviors (479)
11. anorexia nervosa (492)
12. conduct disorder (479)
13. hostile attributional biases (482)
14. bulimia (494)
15. attention-deficit hyperactivity disorder (ADHD) (473)
16. tics (496)
17. bell and pad (496)
18. paradoxical effect (476)
19. overactivity (473)
20. Child Behavior Checklist (CBCL) (467)

21. Diagnostic Interview for Children and Adolescents (DICA) (467)
22. covert behaviors (479)
23. separation anxiety disorder (486)
24. multivariate statistical taxometric system (469)
25. enuresis (497)
26. inattention (473)
27. developmental appropriateness (474)
28. Response Class Matrix (467)
29. developmental psychopathology (468)
30. psychostimulant medications (476)

ANSWER KEY: FACTUAL MULTIPLE-CHOICE QUESTIONS

1. *d. what is normal for a given age (p. 466)
   a. The DSM-IV provides the diagnostic criteria.
   b. What is normal for adults may have little relevance for child disorders.
   c. Disorders of adults are recognized as not being appropriate as measures for child disorders.

2. *a. internalizing disorders (p. 469)
   b. Externalizing disorders are behavioral disorders that create problems for others.
   c. Behavioral disorders is another term for externalizing disorders.
   d. Undercontrolled disorders is another term for externalizing disorders.

3. *d. the effectiveness of therapy (p. 470)
   a. The role of parents is important in child therapy.
   b. Play is often used in dynamically oriented therapies for children.
   c. Medications used for adult disorders often do not work with children or have negative side effects.

4. *a. depression (p. 471)
   b. Inattention affects listening and task completion and is definitely a feature of ADHD.
   c. Impulsivity, acting without thinking, is characteristic of ADHD.
   d. Overactivity is seen in fidgeting, restlessness, and inability to sit still, a key feature of ADHD.

5. *b. excessive motor activity (p. 472)
   a. Attentional focus problems may persist into adulthood.
   c. Academic difficulties continue to be a problem.
   d. Social difficulties continue to interfere with the lives of ADHD adolescents and adults.

6. *b. preempts a diagnosis of oppositional defiant disorder (p. 478)
   a. Oppositional defiant disorders is usually part of conduct disorder.
   c. This diagnosis is in the DSM-IV.
   d. Physical aggression is a common feature of conduct disorder.

7. *d. lying (p. 479)
   a. Fighting is a common overt behavior problem.
   b. Arguing is also an overt behavior problem.
   c. Temper tantrums, usually displayed in public, are an overt behavior problem.

8. *c. reaches adult rates when the child reaches puberty (p. 487)
   a. Until recently it was believed that children did not suffer from depression.
   b. Adult criteria for depression are applied to children, with some differences.
   d. Is much higher in girls than boys.

9. *b.   experience intense hunger pangs (p. 490)
   a.   Anorexics often spend hours preparing and serving food that they never eat.
   c.   Anorexics have a distorted self-perception of body image and are obsessed with their body shape.
   d.   Anorexics fail to recognize successful weight loss.

10. *c.   stable family situation (p. 491)
   a.   Compliance is a typical personality trait of anorexics.
   b.   Perfectionism is another personality trait often observed in anorexics.
   d.   Dependence is also characteristic of the personality of an anorectic.

ANSWER KEY: CONCEPTUAL MULTIPLE-CHOICE QUESTIONS

1. *c.   on all children (p. 476)
   a.   The medication works well with ADHD patients and normal children as well.
   b.   Medications often are given three times a day.
   d.   Stimulant medication works on about 70 percent of children with ADHD.

2. *c.   conditions before the separation (p. 488)
   a.   Age of the parents has relatively little to do with the quality of the marriage or the effect of the divorce on children.
   b.   Half of marriage contracts do not last.
   d.   Conditions after separation are not as important as prior conditions.

3. *a.   externalizing disorders are unusual for girls (p. 470)
   b.   Externalizers may also be suffering from inner turmoil that takes an outward form.
   c.   Often the place where problems become acute is in school.
   d.   Girls have many forms of childhood disorders, but less of the overt type.

4. *d.   behavioral or cognitive therapy to prevent worsening of the condition (p. 489)
   a.   Many medications that work for adults do not work for children.
   b.   Dewayne needs help if the symptoms are to be prevented from worsening.
   c.   Dewayne has a real problem with depression that needs treatment.

5. *a.   X-rays emitted from fluorescent lighting (p. 475)
   b.   Genetic factors may play a role in the disorder.
   c.   Some studies have indicated that brain function may be impaired in children with ADHD, but differences may be due to other influences.
   d.   Failure to learn adequate cognitive and behavioral skills can be a factor, as can a child's environment.

6. *d.   a combination of medication and behavior therapy (p. 477)
   a.   There are shortcomings when medication is used alone.
   b.   Cognitive-behavioral treatment doesn't work as well alone as it does in combination with medication.
   c.   Parent-training programs help give children the skills they need, but symptom control is best with medication in combination with other therapy.

7. *d. conduct disorder (p. 479)
   a. Justin's behavior would not qualify for a diagnosis of ADHD. Nothing is said about his level of activity or attention.
   b. Oppositional defiant disorder is more related to defiant behavior than to violations of the rights of others.
   c. Antisocial personality disorder is an adult diagnosis that requires conduct disorder in childhood.

8. *b. separation anxiety disorder (p. 486)
   a. Generalized anxiety disorder would not find such a specific focus.
   c. Social phobia is a more general fear of being in the public and fear of doing something embarrassing.
   d. Agoraphobia is fear of being in public places with no way to escape.

9. *d. anxiety disorders have been studied much less than disruptive behavior problems (p. 486)
   a. There are effective treatments available, both medication and psychosocial therapies.
   b. These problems have not been studied as extensively as the conduct disorders.
   c. Antidepressant medication has not proven to be effective with children.

10. *c. depression (pp. 486–487)
   a. Julie's condition would not warrant a diagnosis of ADHD.
   b. Julie does not have a conduct problem, either overt or covert.
   d. Julie's problem is not a conduct problem. It is an affective problem.

ANSWER KEY: APPLICATION MULTIPLE-CHOICE QUESTIONS

1. *c. normal childhood development (p. 466)
   a. Externalizing disorders have to do with overt aggressive behaviors, not fears.
   b. Joey's symptoms have little conduct disorder relation.
   d. Enuresis is bedwetting, which is not mentioned in Joey's case.

2. *d. psychostimulant (p. 476)
   a. Antiandrogen medications are used to control violence in adults.
   b. Neuroleptics are used to treat adult psychotic disorders and cause serious side effects in children.
   c. Antidepressants used for adults often do not work with children. It is also unclear that Forest is depressed.

3. *c. cognitive distortion of ambiguous acts (p. 480)
   a. Psychostimulant medication would have had a calming effect on Corey.
   b. The other students were probably minding their own business when Corey misinterpreted a neutral act.
   d. Parental overprotectiveness is not correlated with conduct disorder; difficulties with appropriate discipline have been found to be a problem.

4. *c. probably not related to the divorce since conditions were good before the separation (p. 488)
   a. Studies have shown that conditions prior to the divorce are more predictive of the effect on children than the divorce itself.
   b. If conditions were good before the separation, there is no indication that an earlier divorce would have made a difference in her condition.
   d. Girls tend to find breakups less distressing; they are likely to live with their mothers, which appears to ease the adjustment for girls.

5. *b. anorexia (p. 492)
   a. Obsessive-compulsive disorder is an anxiety disorder that does not usually have somatic elements such as those found in anorexia.
   c. Borderline personality disorder is an adult disorder marked by serious instability of relationships.
   d. Narcissistic personality disorder is when a person has a grandiose sense of his or her own importance.

6. *a. bulimic (p. 494)
   b. Depression is not the most salient feature reflected in the bingeing described in this case.
   c. Anorexics often binge/purge, but their weight is drastically below normal minimum.
   d. Bulimics are not always dieting, because they can use the binge/purge cycle to eat as much as they want without gaining.

7. *d. Tourette's disorder with coprolalia (p. 496)
   a. Some forms of schizophrenia have somatic elements, but not of this type.
   b. Obsessive-compulsive disorder does not include such physical manifestations.
   c. Korsakoff's psychosis is related to chronic alcohol abuse.

8. *a. the decision of whether or not the child's behavior is developmentally appropriate is aided by comparisons of the child's behavior with a normative sample. (p. 467)
   b. The Response Class Matrix assesses parent-child interactions.
   c. The CBCL is not a projective test. It measures behavior problems and social competence.
   d. The CBCL is completed by parents and teachers and assesses social problems, aggressive behavior, anxiety, and depression.

9. *c. ADHD is probably caused by multiple pathways. (p. 476)
   a. CT scans do not reveal anatomical brain differences between ADHD and normal individuals.
   b. Sugar does not cause hyperactivity.
   d. Lighting conditions have no effect on hyperactivity.

10. *d. Claudia's parents do not permit her to have many outside interests or to hold a job for fear that she will meet a boy, get sexually involved, and become pregnant. (p. 491)
    a. Independence is not a characteristic of an enmeshed family.
    b. There is nothing in the response that suggests that Claudia's identity is weak or that she is enmeshed with her family.
    c. Although marital discord may contribute to stress for Claudia, there is no indication of enmeshment.

CHAPTER 16
Mental Retardation and Developmental Disorders

LEARNING OBJECTIVES

1. Define mental retardation. (p. 500)

2. Discus the fairness of IQ tests in determining mental retardation. (pp. 501–502)

3. Discuss the prevalence of mental retardation. (pp. 502–503)

4. Describe the incidence of other disorders with mental retardation. (p. 503)

5. Describe the causes of mental retardation. (pp. 503–506)

6. Describe the characteristics of Down syndrome and other forms of mental retardation. (pp. 503–504)

7. Discuss the treatment, placement, and education of the mentally retarded. (pp. 506–508)

8. Discuss the use of medications with the mentally retarded. (p. 508)

9. Identify the features of learning disabilities. (pp. 508–509)

10. Discuss the possible causes of learning disabilities. (pp. 509–510)

11. Describe the treatments for learning disabilities. (p. 510)

12. Describe the characteristics and possible causes of autism. (pp. 510–515)

13. Describe the treatment programs for autistic persons, including DRO, electric shock, and intensive behavior modification. (pp. 515–518)

14. Discuss the programs for training parents of autistic children. (pp. 518–519)

15. Discuss the trends in the research and treatment of mental retardation and pervasive disorders. (p. 520)

CHAPTER OUTLINE

I. Mental Retardation

- Mental retardation is significantly subaverage general intellectual functioning with deficits in adaptive behavior, identified before eighteenth birthday.

- Adaptive behavior is the self-care skills needed to live independently.

    A. What's Normal? Are IQ Test Scores "Fair"?

        1. IQ score equal to or greater than two standard deviations below the mean is required for diagnosis of mental retardation.

        2. Distribution of "normal" IQ scores is based solely on a chosen criterion.

        3. Not all persons scoring in the retarded range lack adaptive behavior.

        4. Interpretation of test results is subject to bias.

    B. Who Is Affected with Mental Retardation?

        1. Range between 1 to 3 percent of worldwide population.

        2. Degree of severity varies.

        3. Prevalence affected by gender, socioeconomic status, and race.

            a. Male-female ratio is 2 to 1.

            b. Higher frequency in blacks than in whites.

            c. Higher frequency in low socioeconomic groups.

        4. Other problems, usually physical, frequently accompany mental retardation: ambulatory problems, speech, hearing, visual, epilepsy, cerebral palsy.

        5. Psychiatric disorders more common among mentally retarded than general population.

    C. Causes of Mental Retardation

        1. Biological factors in mental retardation

            a. Down syndrome is a form of mental retardation, caused by the presence of an extra set of genes in the twenty-first chromosome.

                (1) Physical characteristics include short broad neck, below average height, small head, poor muscle tone.

                (2) Age of mother at time of child's birth related to risk of Down syndrome.

            b. Fragile X syndrome is a form of mental retardation named for a constricted region at the end of the X chromosome.

                (1) More common in males than females.

                (2) Distinctive physical features include short stature, prominent forehead, prominent mandible, and large ears, hands, and feet.

    c. Phenylketonuria (PKU) is a hereditary error of metabolism resulting from an inactive liver enzyme, which can, if untreated in the first year of life, produce mental retardation.

        (1) PKU can be prevented with early dietary modifications.

        (2) Carriers of PKU pass on a recessive gene to their children.

  2. Prenatal environment and mental retardation

    a. Maternal conditions such as malnutrition, tobacco, alcohol consumption, infections, drugs, radiation, and a lack of oxygen can affect the fetus.

        (1) Alcohol can cause *fetal alcohol syndrome,* which affects intellectual functioning and physical growth.

        (2) Unclear how much alcohol consumption causes FAS.

  3. Social environment and mental retardation

    a. Extreme psychological and social deprivation can cause mental retardation.

    b. Individuals from culturally deprived and economically disadvantaged environments are likely to show lower IQ scores.

D. Placement, Treatment, and Education in Mental Retardation

  1. Placement refers to the living arrangements that must be organized for the person.

    a. Custodial care in large institutions on the decline in the United States.

    b. Alternative arrangements provide more homelike atmosphere.

    c. More mentally retarded children are remaining at home, with help for parents.

  2. Treatment refers to interventions aimed at the remediation of the associated emotional and behavioral problems.

    a. Treatments tend to follow behavioral orientation, such as teaching specific adaptive skills.

    b. Family members increasingly involved in treatment.

    c. Treatments do not cure the disorder, but produce specific gains in behavior problems.

    d. Public education is guaranteed to all mentally retarded persons.

        (1) In the least restrictive environment.

        (2) Educational interventions include specific teaching strategies to facilitate learning.

        (3) Mainstreaming is the policy of placing once-separated children with disabilities in regular classrooms. Has not provided convincing evidence of improved academic or social skills functioning.

E. Use of Medications with Mentally Retarded Persons

  1. Drug therapy is aimed at reducing psychopathological conditions.

      a.   Disruptive behaviors, psychotic symptoms, or attentional problems are treated.

      b.   Anticonvulsant medications are used for seizures and stimulant medications for attentional problems.

   2.   The effect of medications is not well documented.

II. Learning Disabilities

   A.   Identifying Learning Disabilities

      1.   Estimates of prevalence range from 5 to 15 percent.

      2.   Male to female ratios range between 2 to 1 and 5 to 1.

      3.   Definitional problems make reliability and validity of learning disorders questionable.

      4.   Learning disorders: a condition in which academic achievement is below that expected given a person's chronological age, measured intelligence, and age-appropriate education, as measured by an individually administered standardized test.

         a.   DSM-IV uses a combination of IQ and below age and grade level.

         b.   Diagnoses include reading disorder, mathematics disorder, and disorder of written expression.

         c.   The condition must interfere with academic achievement or activities in daily living.

         d.   There are often emotional and behavioral problems associated with learning disabilities, particularly ADHD.

   B.   Possible Causes of Learning Disabilities

      1.   Exact causes are unknown.

         a.   Genetic factors, brain functioning, cognitive and motivational influences have all been considered.

         b.   Learning disabled children do not use effective problem-solving strategies.

   C.   Treatments for Learning Disabilities: Cognitive-processing strategies help improve reading comprehension.

III. Pervasive Developmental Disorders: Autism

   •   Pervasive developmental disorders involve severe upset in the child's cognitive social, behavioral, and emotional growth that produces widespread distortion of the developmental process.

   •   Autism affects basic human qualities: interpersonal socialization and complex communication.

   A.   Characteristics of Autistic Disorder

      1.   Kanner's definition: "The children's inability to relate themselves in the ordinary way to people and situations from the beginning of life."

2. Early symptoms: Baby is indifferent to being held, flaccid muscle tone, cries infrequently, fails to notice the mother, delayed or absent smiling, lacks interest in toys.

3. Unresponsive socially.

4. Obsessive desire for sameness in the environment, self-stimulatory behavior, lack of eye contact, fascination with inanimate objects.

5. DSM identifies three key features:

   a. Qualitative impairment in social interaction.

   b. Severe impairments in communication.

   c. Restricted, repetitive, and stereotyped patterns of behavior.

6. Echolalia, the repetition or echoing back of speech, is one form of communication difficulty typical of autistic children.

7. Stimulus overselectivity: responding to only select aspects of stimulus materials.

8. Difficulty processing and integrating information.

9. Three-fourths of autistic persons show some intellectual deficits.

10. Some display remarkable skills, such as in mathematical or artistic fields.

B. Who Is Affected with Autistic Disorder?

1. Prevalence rate is 0.05 to 0.10 percent.

2. Male-female ratio is 3 to 1 to 4 to 1.

3. Rates differ by country (China low, Japan high); methodological and diagnostic variations might explain the differences.

C. Course of Autistic Disorder

1. Most autistic disorders continue into adulthood.

2. Language and IQ scores are the best prognostic indicators.

3. Only 50 percent develop useful speech.

4. 75 percent are moderately retarded.

5. During adolescence, behavior and emotional problems emerge.

D. Possible Causes of Autism

1. Bettelheim proposed the cold and unloving "refrigerator" parent (not upheld by later research).

2. No strong evidence of genetic linkage.

3. Possibly an inherited abnormality of language and sociability.

4. Tiny minority of cases result from diseases such as congenital rubella (measles at birth).

5. Possible prenatal damage or disrupted development cause autism.

6. Central nervous system disorder and neurological abnormalities are evident.

E. Programs for Autistic Persons

1. Some language ability and a normal score on nonverbal intelligence tests predict better long-term prognosis.

2. Very few autistic children live independent lives.

3. Traditional psychotherapy is ineffective.

4. Medications are not effective.

5. Behavior modification, parent training, and highly structured environments have shown positive effects.

F. Focus on Research: What Can Be Done about Self-Injury?

1. Self-injurious behavior frequent in severely handicapped children; includes head-banging, hair-pulling, and self-biting.

2. Physical restraints and medication can prevent physical injury, but also hinder other treatments.

3. Differential reinforcement of other behavior (DRO) is a behavioral procedure that provides reinforcement after periods of time when no self-injury occurs.

4. Other procedures include extinction and time-out.

5. Averse procedures such as mild electric shock is effective, but controversial.

6. Reinforcers used on a contingency basis to shape behaviors with rewards have shown some success.

7. Many behavioral programs focus on language development.

8. Lovaas initiated intensive behavior modification to reduce aggression and encourage language growth, emotional expression, and preacademic skills.

9. Highest successes are with intensive intervention of very young, select patients.

G. Family Matters: Training Parents of Autistic Children

1. Parents are involved in language training as well as disruptive and dangerous behavior modification.

2. Treatment includes lectures, readings, demonstrations and role playing, home visits and telephone contacts.

3. Treatment is valuable to improve home and general family environment and prevent parental burnout and distress.

H. Other Pervasive Developmental Disorders

1. Rhett's disorder.

2. Asperger's disorder.

3. Childhood disintegrative disorder.

IV. What Lies Ahead?

    A.   Increased involvement of the family.

    B.   Treatment will continue to use behavioral interventions.

    C.   Early identification of fetal Down syndrome and autism raise important ethical issues.

KEY TERMS REVIEW

1.   A dated and discarded notion that a cold and unloving parent caused a child to withdraw into autism is called a(n) _____.

2.   A form of mental retardation named for a constricted region at the end of the X chromosome that is more common in males than females is called _____.

3.   A condition measured by academic achievement, as measured on an individually administered standardized test that is below that expected given a person's chronological age, measured intelligence, and age-appropriate education, is called _____.

4.   The self-care skills (such as the ability to dress appropriately and groom oneself and hold a simple job) needed to live independently are called _____.

5.   An inability to read, dyslexia, a type of learning disorder defined by DSM-IV, is a(n) _____.

6.   Intervention aimed at the remediation of the emotional and behavioral problems associated with retardation is called _____.

7.   Significantly subaverage general intellectual functioning that exists concurrently with deficits in adaptive behavior, which, for a diagnosis, must begin to be displayed before the person's eighteenth birthday, is called _____.

8.   A behavioral procedure for treating self-injurious behavior that involves providing reinforcement after periods of time when no self-injury took place is called _____.

9.   Such personally harmful actions as head-banging, hair-pulling, self-biting, and eating nonedible substances, which some severely handicapped children may engage in, is called _____.

10.   The idea that children with disabilities should be placed in classrooms with nondisabled children whenever possible is called the _____.

11.   A program of treatment for autism that lasts two years or more and involves more than forty hours of one-on-one treatment per week is called _____.

12.   A pervasive developmental disorder that affects basic human qualities and has three features, qualitative impairment in social interaction, severe impairments in communication, and restricted, repetitive, and stereotyped patterns of behavior, is called _____.

13.   Responding to only select aspects of stimulus materials, which is typical of autistic children, is called _____.

14.   A social and familial milieu that lacks learning opportunities is called a(n) _____.

15. An approach to treating mental retardation that includes specific teaching strategies to facilitate learning is called _____.

16. The living arrangements that must be organized for a mentally retarded person are called _____.

17. Measles present in an infant at birth is called _____.

18. The policy of placing once-separated children with disabilities in classrooms with nondisturbed students is called _____.

19. Suffering the reduced opportunities associated with poverty is called _____.

20. Severe upset in a child's cognitive, social, behavioral, and emotional growth that produces widespread distortion of the developmental process, for example, childhood autism, is called _____.

21. A type of learning disorder, involving numeric calculations, defined by DSM-IV, is _____.

22. The repetition or echoing back of speech sometimes seen in autistic children is called _____.

23. A hereditary error of metabolism resulting from an inactive liver enzyme, which can, if untreated in the first year of life, produce mental retardation is called _____.

24. A form of mental retardation caused by the presence of an extra set of genes in the twenty-first chromosome is called _____.

FACTUAL MULTIPLE-CHOICE QUESTIONS

1. A person who is able to care for him or herself is said to have
   a. mental retardation.
   b. adaptive skills.
   c. self-abusive behavior.
   d. stereotyped behavior.

2. The average score on the WISC-III is
   a. 15.
   b. 70.
   c. 130.
   d. 100.

3. Individuals with mental retardation often have other problems, such as
   a. hypochondriasis.
   b. Type A personality.
   c. dissociative identity disorder.
   d. speech, hearing, and visual impairments.

4. A form of retardation caused by the presence of an extra twenty-first chromosome is called
   a. fragile X syndrome.
   b. Down syndrome.
   c. subaverage intellectual functioning.
   d. low intellectual functioning.

5. Infants who are born with a hereditary error of metabolism will develop mental retardation if left untreated. This disorder is known as
   a. fragile X syndrome.
   b. fetal alcohol syndrome.
   c. cerebral palsy.
   d. phenylketonuria.

6. A trend that is on the rise with regard to the treatment of mentally retarded children is
   a. custodial care.
   b. stay at home care.
   c. community centers.
   d. separation from the family.

7. Which of the following is *not* considered a possible cause of learning disabilities?
   a. neurotransmitter dysfunction
   b. genetic factors
   c. brain dysfunction
   d. motivational and cognitive factors

8. Parents of autistic children report that
   a. autistic children, at first, seem normal.
   b. autistic children are quite responsive to their parents.
   c. the baby seems different from other babies.
   d. autistic babies demand much attention.

9. On IQ tests, most autistic children
   a. show remarkably high intelligence.
   b. show some intellectual deficits.
   c. show the ability to perform almost magical feats of intellectual power.
   d. are uniform in their intellectual functioning.

10. Bruno Bettelheim popularized the theory of the causation of autism which was related to
    a. learning theory.
    b. the "refrigerator" parent.
    c. the overprotective parent.
    d. the too permissive parent.

CONCEPTUAL MULTIPLE-CHOICE QUESTIONS

1. The effect of medications in treating the mentally retarded
   a. has been proven through carefully controlled studies.
   b. has been demonstrated by the successful use of stimulants with severe retardation.
   c. has been demonstrated by the control of seizures, which are part of all mental retardation.
   d. has not been proven because of lack of proper methodology.

2. Variations in the estimates of the number of children with learning disabilities are a result of
   a. the inconsistency in the definition used to identify learning disabled children.
   b. the relative rarity of the condition.
   c. the fact that the disorder strikes girls more often than boys.
   d. the minor effect these disorders have on the life of a child.

3. The learning disabled student has been described as
   a. an eager attentive learner.
   b. an inactive maladaptive learner.
   c. one who employs effective problem-solving techniques.
   d. one who uses memory strategies.

4. The primary difference between autism and childhood schizophrenia is
   a. that children outgrow autism, but not schizophrenia.
   b. childhood schizophrenia is characterized by extreme sociability and autism by severe withdrawal.
   c. children with schizophrenia are diagnosed at an earlier age than those with autism.
   d. children with schizophrenia have a period of normal adjustment followed by onset of symptoms.

5. Mikey had a positive prognosis for improvement of his autism because
   a. he was older than the other kids in his group.
   b. the program would take a relaxed approach to treatment.
   c. his mental ability was above average for an autistic child.
   d. his parents would stay away from any involvement in his treatment.

6. Dr. Roberts has suggested a full psychiatric evaluation of Judy after she was diagnosed with mild mental retardation because
   a. all persons with mental retardation have psychiatric disorders.
   b. mentally retarded persons are likely to become suddenly violent at unexpected times.
   c. psychiatric disorders are three to four times more common in persons with mental retardation.
   d. the mentally retarded should be institutionalized.

7. Janice and Jerry want to have a child. Janice will be forty-one in a few months and Jerry will be fifty-one. They have been told by their physician that
   a. they have nothing to worry about regarding having a baby at their age.
   b. Jerry's age should not be a factor in their decision about having a baby.
   c. there is no relationship between a mother's age and the likelihood of genetic problems with a baby.
   d. there is an increased likelihood of genetic problems with a baby as the mother's age increases.

8. Bill was mildly mentally retarded. The program he was in was designed to
   a. teach him specific skills for more successful functioning.
   b. cure his mental retardation.
   c. improve his intellectual functioning.
   d. ignore emotional problems, because the mentally retarded have few such disorders.

9. Because José was not a good reader, his parents were fearful that he might have a learning disability. They will find that
   a. the number of children identified as learning disabled has been declining.
   b. there is uniform agreement on the definition of learning disability.
   c. the classification system for learning disability is empirically valid and reliable.
   d. there is inconsistency in the definition used to identify children with a learning disability.

10. Max was constantly out of his seat and had difficulty following the teacher's instructions. His academic record was erratic. He might be suffering from a learning disorder, because
    a. all students with behavioral problems have learning disorders.
    b. learning disabled youth are usually very social.
    c. learning disabled students are never able to sit still.
    d. emotional and behavioral complications are often found with learning disorders.

APPLICATION MULTIPLE-CHOICE QUESTIONS

1. John and Mary were convinced that their autistic son was in danger because of
    a. the lack of interest in finding effective treatments for autism.
    b. his complete recovery and entry into a normal yet potentially threatening lifestyle.
    c. the peer pressure from his friends.
    d. his self-injurious behaviors.

2. John and Mary were concerned about electric shock to reduce the self-injurious behavior of their son because
    a. of its lack of effectiveness.
    b. they didn't consider his case to be that extreme.
    c. the lack of research interest in this treatment.
    d. it is given sometimes in harmful amounts.

3. Marie and Donald have just been told that their eighteen-month-old son is autistic. They must consider
    a. how to manage the considerable community resources available to them.
    b. how having an autistic child will probably bring them closer together.
    c. how to best devote their entire lives to the support of their child.
    d. facing the lifelong task of managing a severely handicapped child.

4. Johnny is an African American from an inner-city area. He just took an IQ test because he has been having difficulties in school. His parents are
    a. concerned that Johnny will be unfairly evaluated because of a racial stereotype.
    b. concerned that students in the class who speak Spanish as their first language will have an advantage.
    c. concerned that students from the inaccessible parts of the state will be evaluated more fairly than Johnny.
    d. unconcerned because these tests are always evaluated fairly.

5. Debbie and Rob were trying to conceive their first child. Regarding alcohol, Debbie should
    a. not worry about drinking since this is her first child.
    b. refrain entirely from drinking because a small amount can affect the fetus.
    c. reduce her consumption to protect the baby.
    d. not worry, since the amount of alcohol consumption necessary to hurt the fetus is not known.

6. Dr. Murdoch prescribes psychotropic medications for her mentally retarded patients
    a. to cure the retardation.
    b. to improve intellectual abilities.
    c. because of their proven effect with mentally retarded individuals.
    d. to reduce psychopathological conditions.

7. Ralph had great difficulty with reading when he was a child. He is worried about his newborn son because
   a. children of parents with reading difficulties always develop the same patterns.
   b. genetics has more to do with reading difficulty than the environment.
   c. there would be no constructive treatment in reading difficulty.
   d. children of parents with a reading difficulty have a greater chance of having reading problems.

8. Bobby was struggling in school and had been diagnosed with a learning disability. His psychologist recommended
   a. psychodynamic therapy.
   b. differential reinforcement of other behavior.
   c. aversive shock therapy.
   d. cognitive-processing strategies.

9. Yvonne and Dan disagreed with the doctor's diagnosis of autism for their son because
   a. his IQ scores were average.
   b. he could calculate the day of anyone's birthday instantaneously.
   c. he could focus on his mathematics with remarkable intensity.
   d. his ability to communicate was quite good.

10. Beth and Louis attended a school board meeting, where the topic "mainstreaming severely mentally disordered children" was discussed. Most parents in the room advocated that the school should use mainstreaming strategies in order to increase children's academic and social skills. Based on their knowledge of the research on this topic, Beth and Louis should say that
    a. mainstreaming children has been proven very effective in raising achievement scores and in developing social skills among severely mentally disordered children.
    b. mainstreaming has been very effective in improving social skills, but not achievement, among severely mentally disordered children.
    c. mainstreaming has not been very effective in developing either social or academic skills among severely mentally disordered children.
    d. DRO has been found to be more effective than mainstreaming in improving social and academic skills among severely mentally disordered children.

ANSWER KEY: KEY TERMS REVIEW

1. "refrigerator" parent (514)
2. fragile X syndrome (504)
3. learning disorders (508)
4. adaptive behavior (500)
5. disorder of written expression (508)
6. treatment (506)
7. mental retardation (500)
8. differential reinforcement of other behavior (DRO) (517)
9. self-injurious behavior (516)
10. least restrictive environment (mainstreaming) (507)
11. intensive behavior modification (517)
12. autism (510)
13. stimulus overselectivity (513)
14. culturally deprived environment (506)
15. educational intervention (507)
16. placement (506)
17. congenital rubella (514)
18. mainstreaming (507)
19. economically disadvantaged (506)
20. pervasive developmental disorders (510)
21. mathematics disorder (508)
22. echolalia (512)
23. phenylketonuria (PKU) (504)
24. Down syndrome (503)

ANSWER KEY: FACTUAL MULTIPLE-CHOICE QUESTIONS

1. *b. adaptive skills (p. 500)
   a. A diagnosis of mental retardation is only made if the person has a significantly subaverage general intellectual functioning and is unable to care for him or her self.
   c. Self-abusive behavior is an area of maladaptive behavior contrasted with self-direction.
   d. Stereotyped behavior is the restricted repetitive behavior characteristic of autistic people.

2. *d. 100 (p. 501)
   a. The standard deviation is 15.
   b. A person with a score of 70 or less would meet one of the criteria for a diagnosis of mental retardation. Two percent of the population of the United States meet the less than 70 IQ score criterion.

3. *d. speech, hearing, and visual impairments (p. 503)
   a. *Hypochondriasis* is a somatoform disorder characterized by excessive concern over minor physical ills and is not related to mental retardation.
   b. Type A personality is characterized by urgency and competitiveness and is not associated with mental retardation.
   c. Dissociative identity disorder is a disorder in which the individual has two or more separate personalities; it is not associated with mental retardation.

4. *b. Down syndrome (p. 503)
   a. Fragile X syndrome is a form of mental retardation named for a constricted region at the end of the X chromosome.
   c. Subaverage intellectual functioning is common in all forms of mental retardation.
   d. Low intellectual functioning is another term associated with the diagnosis of mental retardation.

5. *d. phenylketonuria (p. 504)
   a. Fragile X syndrome involves the X chromosome and is more common in males than females.
   b. Fetal alcohol syndrome involves the ingestion of alcohol by a pregnant woman, possibly resulting in mental retardation.
   c. Cerebral palsy is impaired muscular power and coordination resulting from brain damage which usually occurs before birth.

6. *b. stay at home care (pp. 506–507)
   a. Custodial care is losing favor to care provided by the parents at home.
   c. Mainstreaming, rather than special education classes, has been on the rise.
   d. A return to family care is the trend.

7. *a. neurotransmitter dysfunction (pp. 509–510)
   b. Children of parents with reading difficulties have a greater chance of reading problems than children of parents who read normally.
   c. Brain dysfunction has been suggested as a possible cause of learning disabilities.
   d. Motivational and cognitive factors are emphasized as part of psychological explanations of these disorders.

8. *c. the baby seems different from other babies (p. 512)
    a. Autistic infants seem different almost from birth.
    b. Autistic children are not responsive to their parents or to other people.
    d. Autistic babies are very undemanding.

9. *b. show some intellectual deficits (p. 513)
    a. Some autistic children do achieve normal scores but none have high scores on IQ tests.
    c. A few autistic persons show remarkable skills, but their number is very small.
    d. There is variability in the intelligence level of autistic persons.

10. *b. the "refrigerator" parent (p. 514)
    a. Bettelheim's theory was based on psychodynamic principles, not learning theory.
    c. The theory was based on a cold, distant parent/child relationship, not on an overprotective parent.
    d. Parents were seen as distant and cold, not as too permissive.

ANSWER KEY: CONCEPTUAL MULTIPLE-CHOICE QUESTIONS

1. *d. has not been proven because of lack of proper research methodology (p. 508)
    a. Carefully controlled studies have not been done on the effects of psychotropic medications on the mentally retarded.
    b. Stimulants do not work well with severe retardation.
    c. Seizures are not part of all forms of mental retardation.

2. *a. the inconsistency in the definition used to identify learning disabled children (p. 508)
    b. The prevalence of learning disabilities appears to be on the rise.
    c. Learning disabilities are found more often in boys.
    d. These disorders have major disruptive effects on the lives of the child and of the family.

3. *b. an inactive maladaptive learner (p. 510)
    a. Learning disabled students are not attentive learners.
    c. Learning disabled students do not employ problem-solving techniques.
    d. Learning disabled students do not use memory strategies, such as rehearsal or clustering.

4. *d. children with schizophrenia have a period of normal adjustment followed by onset of symptoms (p. 511)
    a. Children do not outgrow either autism or childhood schizophrenia.
    b. They are both characterized by severe withdrawal.
    c. Autism is usually detected much earlier than schizophrenia.

5. *c. his mental ability was above average for an autistic child (p. 518)
    a. The older the child the less likely that intervention will be effective.
    b. Effective treatments are intensively applied.
    d. Effective treatments usually involve the parents as active participants.

6. *c. psychiatric disorders are three to four times more common in persons with mental retardation (p. 503)
    a. Not all mentally retarded persons have psychiatric disorders.
    b. There is no evidence that mentally retarded persons will become violent.
    d. The mentally retarded are increasingly being treated in their homes, living with their families.

7. *d. there is an increased likelihood of genetic problems with a baby as the mother's age increases (pp. 503–504)
   a. The likelihood of a genetic problem increases with age.
   b. Some researchers believe that the age of the father is also a factor in determining genetic anomalies.
   c. The age of the mother at the time of the child's birth is related to the incidence of Down syndrome.

8. *a. teach him specific skills for more successful functioning (p. 506)
   b. There is no cure for mental retardation.
   c. Intellectual functioning cannot be improved; adaptive skills, however, do respond to training.
   d. The mentally retarded often have psychiatric problems.

9. *d. there is inconsistency in the definition used to identify children with a learning disability (p. 508)
   a. The number of children identified as learning disabled is increasing.
   b. There is disagreement on the definition of learning disability.
   c. The definitions of learning disabled children do not meet basic empirical criteria for reliability and validity.

10. *d. emotional and behavioral complications are often found with learning disorders (p. 509)
    a. Behavioral problems and learning disorders do not always coexist.
    b. Learning disabled children often have difficulties with socialization.
    c. Learning disabled children do not necessarily have ADHD symptoms.

ANSWER KEY: APPLICATION MULTIPLE-CHOICE QUESTIONS

1. *d. his self-injurious behavior (pp. 516–517)
   a. There is a great deal of interest in finding effective treatments for autism.
   b. Most autistic persons continue into adulthood severely handicapped and unable to live a normal life.
   c. Autistic persons have few friends.

2. *b. they didn't consider his case to be that extreme (p. 517)
   a. Shock is the most generally effective method of reducing self-injurious behavior.
   c. Shock is the most widely researched and widely used treatment for self-injurious behavior.
   d. The electrical stimulus is physically harmless.

3. *d. facing the lifelong task of managing a severely handicapped child (p. 519)
   a. There are usually scarce community resources available to help severely handicapped children.
   b. Having an autistic child will undoubtedly put great strain on their relationship.
   c. In order to provide the best care for their child, they need to provide for some time for themselves to avoid burnout.

4. *a. concerned that Johnny will be unfairly evaluated because of a racial stereotype (p. 501)
   b. Bilingual students are also likely to receive unfair evaluations.
   c. Very rural students are also subjected to unfair evaluation.
   d. There is the possibility that interpretations will be made unfairly of a fair test.

5. *b. refrain entirely from drinking, because a small amount can affect the fetus (pp. 505–506)
   a. Any child can be affected by alcohol consumed by the mother during pregnancy.
   c. Consumption should be completely stopped to prevent the possibility of damage.
   d. The exact amount is not known, but it is known that a small amount can have serious effects if at a critical period of fetal development.

6. *d. to reduce psychopathological conditions (p. 508)
   a. There is no cure for mental retardation.
   b. Intellectual abilities cannot be improved with medication or any other intervention currently available.
   c. The effects of psychotropic medications have not been well documented.

7. *d. children of parents with a reading difficulty have a greater chance of having reading problems (p. 509)
   a. There is a greater chance of developing a reading difficulty, but not a certainty.
   b. The environment has a great deal to do with the development of learning disabilities.
   c. Strategy training and other treatments are effective in helping learning disabled children improve their reading comprehension.

8. *d. cognitive-processing strategies (p. 510)
   a. Psychodynamic therapy will not address the learning deficits.
   b. DRO is prescribed for children suffering with autism.
   c. Aversive shock therapy is also used for intractable cases of self-injury in autism.

9. *d. his ability to communicate was quite good (p. 512)
   a. Some autistic children will score in the normal range on IQ tests.
   b. Special abilities are seen in persons with autism.
   c. Autistic children often focus intently on a single, sometime irrelevant stimulus.

10. *c. mainstreaming has not been very effective in developing either social or academic skills among severely mentally disordered children. (p. 507)
    a. Advocates of mainstreaming may tend to use ideological points rather than reliance on empirically based research outcomes.
    b. Neither social nor academic skills are greatly improved among individuals with severe disorders.
    d. Differential reinforcement of other behavior (DRO) is a behavioral procedure for treating self-injurious behavior, not social or academic skills.

CHAPTER 17
Cognitive and Neuropsychiatric Disorders

LEARNING OBJECTIVES

1. Describe why the term *organic mental disorders* is not consistent with current conceptualizations of mental disorders. (p. 524)

2. Discuss the difficulties involved in classifying psychological problems caused by brain dysfunctions. (pp. 524–526)

3. Explain the DSM-IV diagnostic system for disorders brought on by medical conditions. (p. 524)

4. Describe how certain parts of the brain control different functions. (pp. 524–525)

5. Describe the difficulties of, and advances made in, assessing brain damage and function. (p. 525)

6. Discuss the effects of aging on psychological adjustment and mental health. (pp. 526–528)

7. Describe the normal effects of aging on cognitive functioning. (pp. 527–528)

8. Discuss the cognitive impairment disorders delirium, amnestic disorders, and dementia. (pp. 528–531)

9. Describe the characteristics of degenerative brain diseases such as Alzheimer's disease. (pp. 531–534)

10. Describe the research done on beta-amyloid deposits and Alzheimer's disease. (pp. 533–535)

11. Discuss the characteristics of Parkinson's disease and Huntington's disease. (pp. 535–536)

12. Describe the effects of traumatic brain injury. (pp. 537–538)

13. Discuss the characteristics of cerebral vascular disorders such as vascular dementia and brain tumors. (pp. 539–540)

14. Describe the characteristics of endocrinological disorders such as hypothyroidism. (pp. 540–541)

15. Discuss the consequences of infectious diseases such as AIDS and untreated syphilis on mental functioning. (pp. 541–542)

16. Describe the effects of exposure to poisons, toxins, and drugs on mental functioning. (pp. 542–543)

17. Discuss the treatment of cognitive impairment disorders. (pp. 543–546)

18. Describe the demands on those who must care for persons suffering with dementia. (pp. 544–545)

19. Describe the new field of cognitive rehabilitation. (p. 546)

20. Discuss the future of research in such areas as brain functioning and dementia and the cures and prevention of these disorders. (p. 546)

CHAPTER OUTLINE

I. Assessing and Classifying Dysfunctions of the Brain

- Organic mental disorders is the pre-DSM-IV term for psychological conditions known or suspected to be caused by a medical problem.

- Problem with organic mental disorders terminology:

  1. Suggests that mind and body are separate entities

  2. Suggests that many disorders are nonorganic

- Cognitive disorders: The DSM-IV term for medically caused delirium, dementia, or amnesia.

A. Diagnosing Brain Dysfunctions

  1. Different functions are served by different lobes, structures, and hemispheres in the brain.

     a. Extensive intercommunication among the regions of the brain.

     b. Damaged brain tissue does not regenerate.

     c. Noninjured parts of the brain have limited capacity to take over functions of damaged areas.

  2. Ability to assess brain damage improved.

     a. Neuroimaging techniques to view living brain:

        (1) Positron emission tomography (PET) scans.

        (2) Magnetic imaging (MRI).

        (3) Computerized axial-tomography (CT) scans.

     b. Neuropsychological testing to locate lesions in the brain.

     c. Complications in diagnosing neuropsychiatric disorders:

        (1) Complex interconnection of regions and functions.

        (2) Gaps in scientific knowledge.

(3)   Many injuries not localized.

(4)   Human brains vary.

B.   Assessing the Aged

1.   *Dementia:* current term (not senility) to describe an abnormal pattern of mental deterioration involving deficits of memory, of information processing, of judgment, planning, etc.

a.   Not limited to any age group.

b.   Occurs more frequently in older adults.

2.   Mental health in older age related to earlier health and adjustment rather than aging itself.

C.   What's Normal? Aging and Intellectual Functions

1.   Intellectual abilities do not invariably decline with age.

2.   In normal aging

a.   People who worry the most about memory problems do not have the most memory loss.

b.   Changes in brain structure (shrinking is called *cortical atrophy*) do not necessarily reflect reduced cognitive capabilities.

c.   Generally slower mental activity may not mean mental deterioration.

II.   Cognitive Impairment Disorders

A.   Delirium

1.   Refers to changes in level of consciousness that may be accompanied by cognitive changes, such as memory or language deficit, disorientation, or hallucinations.

2.   Causes associated with temporary changes in brain activity include medically frail elderly patients, those with preexisting brain damage, burn victims, heart surgery patients, drug-dependent patients in withdrawal, AIDS patients.

B.   Amnestic Disorders

1.   Amnesia: impairment of short- or long-term memory.

2.   Psychogenic amnesia is memory disorders linked to dissociation rather than medical condition.

3.   Medical conditions or injuries to the head affecting the *hippocampus* and *amygdala*

4.   Injuries produce severe memory impairment, but leave language, judgment, personality unchanged

5.   Memory impairment shown as

a.   *Anterograde amnesia:* difficulty in learning new information

b.   *Retrograde amnesia:* inability to recall previously learned information

C. Dementia

- General, multiple cognitive deficits reflecting a decline from previously higher levels of functioning. Acquired, not born with the disorder.

- For diagnosis, a person must have a cognitive deficit (aphasia, aproxia, agnosia, or disturbance of execution function) with memory impairment.

- Symptoms include being forgetful, disoriented, showing reduced spontaneous speech, perseveration, impaired judgment, and personality changes.

1. Who is affected with dementia?

   a. More frequent among older people: affects 2 to 4 percent of persons under age sixty-five and 30 percent of those over eighty.

   b. Increasing elderly population suggests a fivefold increase in demented patients by 2050.

2. Racial and gender differences in dementia

   a. Higher rates of dementia among African American than white American elderly.

   b. Much higher for female than male African Americans.

   c. Chronic health problems contribute to these higher rates of dementia.

3. Causes of dementia

   a. Many medical conditions may cause dementia.

   b. Some are the results of progressive brain disease, such as Alzheimer's disease.

   c. Dementia in most patients is irreversible and progressive.

III. Some Degenerative Brain Diseases

A. Alzheimer's Dementia

1. Characteristics of Alzheimer's disease

   a. Alzheimer's dementia (AD) is a progressive disease, usually occurring in older ages, involving cognitive impairment due to brain changes, especially in the cortex and hippocampus.

   b. Plaques (extracellular protein deposits) and neurofibrillary tangles (nerve cell malformation) may cause damage to critical areas of the brain.

   c. Symptoms include intellectual changes, personality changes, apathy, passivity, loss of energy, delusions (paranoid, persecutory), and mood disorders.

2. Diagnosing Alzheimer's dementia

   a. Distinction between Alzheimer's and depression is important and occasionally difficult. Depression is treatable; Alzheimer's is not.

   b. A definitive diagnosis of Alzheimer's can only be done postmortem.

    c.   Diagnosis of AD requires ruling out any other possible factors.

3.   Course of Alzheimer's disease

    a.   A progressive disease, with onset usually after 55, that lasts for an average of ten years from diagnosis to death.

    b.   Forgetfulness and mild personality change are initial symptoms, followed by intellectual dysfunction, confusion, disorientation, and dramatic personality changes.

    c.   Symptoms are irreversible, with death the result of disorders associated with the physical decline of the patient.

    d.   AD may have different subtypes.

        (1)   Earlier onset progresses more rapidly than later onset.

        (2)   Familiar form (inherited) uncommon.

        (3)   Sporadic form common.

    e.   Men and women are equally affected.

    f.   Prevalence is estimated at more than 10 to 15 percent of adults over 65.

4.   Causes of Alzheimer's disease

    a.   Actual cause of the disease is still unknown.

        (1)   Aluminum toxicity hypothesis has been discredited.

        (2)   Virus, head trauma, and neuroendocrine abnormalities suggested as possible causes.

    b.   One form genetically transmitted.

    c.   Beta-amyloid protein, a major component of the plaques observed in brains of AD patients, may have a defective precursor gene, creating deposits that cause AD degeneration.

B.   Focus on Research: Have We Found the Predisposition for Common Alzheimer's Disease?

1.   Gene located on chromosome 19 linked to late-onset AD.

2.   The gene may be a predisposing factor, but not the cause of AD.

3.   Defective beta-amyloid may be involved in sporadic form of AD.

C.   Parkinson's Disease

1.   A degenerative brain disease that causes tremor, muscle rigidity, and difficulty initiating movement and may involve cognitive impairment.

2.   Symptoms appear between ages of fifty and sixty-nine.

3.   Other psychological symptoms:

    a.   Major depression, or dysthymia.

          b.   Dementia.

    4.   Prevalence

          a.   60 to 170 per 100,000.

          b.   Men may be at greater risk than women.

          c.   Four times as many whites as African Americans.

          d.   Greater in northern than southern states.

    5.   Causes may be drug-induced, postencephalitic (following brain inflammation), or idiopathic (causes unknown).

    6.   Cells of a brain nucleus (*substantia nigra*) which produces dopamine die, which causes motor control dysfunction.

    7.   Treatment: dopamine-enhancing drug helps.

D.   Huntington's Disease

    1.   A genetically caused degenerative brain disease of motor functioning that causes severe dementia and personality change as well as *chorea*—irregular jerks, grimaces, and twitches.

    2.   Relatively rare, 7 to 19 per 100,000.

    3.   First signs may be psychological: memory and concentration loss, depression.

    4.   Intellectual deficit pronounced with progression of disease

    5.   Death comes ten to twenty years after initial symptoms.

    6.   Always runs in families (transmitted by a dominant gene on chromosome 4).

    7.   The mechanism of its action and therefore a clue to cure remain unclear.

IV.   Other Sources of Brain Damage

    A.   Traumatic Brain Injury

        1.   Traumatic brain injuries: damage to the brain by

           a.   *Penetrating injuries* (e.g., gunshot wounds).

           b.   *Closed head injuries* (e.g., falls and motor vehicle accidents).

        2.   Common, a major public health problem.

        3.   Intellectual and personality changes typical after these injuries.

        4.   Severity and location of brain damage determines the form of the personality and other changes, such as *mood liability.*

           a.   Frontal lobe injuries:

               (1)   Social and behavioral changes.

               (2)   Affective changes.

               (3)   Intellectual changes.

   b.   *Anosognosia:* Brain-injured person's denial of change in abilities or potentials.

   c.   Postconcussion syndrome: mild symptoms following a blow to the head.

B.   Cerebral Vascular Disorders

1.   These are problems in the circulatory system feeding the brain, which may cause brain-damaging strokes.

2.   *Stroke:* Sudden and localized damage from blockage or hemorrhage of blood.

3.   Create neurological changes that affect movement, behavior, and cognition.

4.   Psychological symptoms include depression, anxiety, paranoia, and mania.

5.   Recovery sometimes occurs when other areas of the brain take over lost functions

6.   Vascular dementia

   a.   Accumulation of small strokes may destroy large areas of the brain and produce vascular dementia (*multi-infarct dementia*).

   b.   The extent of intellectual, motor, and personality changes depends on extent of tissue damage.

7.   Poststroke depression

   a.   A depressive episode associated with damage to certain areas of the cortex associated with stroke.

   b.   Recovery may take one to two years, depending on the location of the lesion.

C.   Brain Tumors

1.   Can cause numerous psychological symptoms, including anxiety disorders, psychoses, personality disorders, etc.

2.   Cause damage where they grow and create damage from an increase in intracranial pressure.

3.   Symptoms include headache and vomiting, personality, cognitive, and motor changes, depending on location.

4.   Treatment is problematic.

   a.   Surgery causes damage to healthy tissue.

   b.   Radiation sometimes helps.

   c.   Chemotherapy unsuccessful because chemicals may not cross the blood-brain barrier.

D.   Endocrinological Disorders

1.   Include an insufficiency or excess of thyroid, calcium, parathyroid, and insulin.

2.   May cause anxiety, mood disorders, psychotic symptoms, and medical problems.

3.   Severe cases can also cause coma, delirium, and dementia.

4. Hypothyroidism (too little thyroid) causes problems in memory and calculation. Severe cases can cause delirium, dementia, and psychosis.

5. Often seen in patients with mood disorders.

E. Infectious Diseases

   1. AIDS

      a. Virus damages immune system, leaving body vulnerable to disease.

      b. Thought to enter the brain at an early time in the illness.

      c. Cognitive impairment may occur early in the disease.

      d. Symptoms include apathy and depression, mental slowing, memory impairment, followed by psychosis, amnesia, and subcortical dementia.

   2. Syphilis

      a. An infectious, often sexually transmitted, disease that if left untreated, in later stages may cause general paresis: A severe mental disorder that produces memory problems, poor intellectual functioning, bad judgment, dementia, personality changes, and delusions on a deteriorating course leading to death.

      b. Blood test determines presence.

      c. Can be treated with penicillin in early stages.

F. Poisons, Toxins, and Drugs

   1. *Lead* may cause delirium, dementia, psychosis, irritability, depression, and seizures.

   2. Children absorb lead more readily than adults.

   3. Associated with impulsivity, hyperactivity, low tolerance for frustration, and deficits in intellectual functioning.

   4. Lead cannot be removed from the body.

   5. *Organic solvents*, such as paint thinner, glues, spot removers, may cause intellectual performance deterioration and motor abnormalities.

   6. Drugs and alcohol

      a. May cause delirium, amnesia, dementia, psychosis, depression, and anxiety.

      b. Korsakoff's syndrome (*alcohol amnestic disorder*) caused by deficiency in vitamin B_1 (thiamine) stemming from nutritional neglect during alcohol abuse.

      c. Symptoms include severe amnesia, generally irreversible.

      d. *Alcohol dementia* may also occur.

V. Treatment of Cognitive Impairment Disorders

   • *Tacrine,* a drug to improve intellectual functioning of people with Alzheimer's, being tested.

- Improved motor functioning in people with Parkinson's by brain implantation of fetal tissue.

A. Psychotropic Medications

1. Use of antidepressants for persons with Parkinson's and Alzheimer's.

2. Neuroleptics may reduce psychotic symptoms among patients with dementias.

B. Behavioral Change Programs

1. Most degenerative dementias can't be treated directly, so goal is frequently to reduce psychological distress and assist patients and families in coping with the disorder.

2. Behavior modification programs can help reduce the problems associated with dementia by rewarding desired behaviors.

C. Family Matters: Caregivers Have Their Own Problems

1. Caregiving is very demanding.

2. More than 50 percent of caregivers are diagnosably depressed.

3. Effects are particularly severe when the caregiver is a spouse. Physical as well as mental health of caregiver may decline.

4. Two main sources of distress to caregivers

a. depression, withdrawal, and apathy in the patient.

b. disruptive behaviors, such as assaultiveness, swearing, lack of cooperation, and social withdrawal.

5. Support groups are now generally available.

D. Cognitive Rehabilitation

1. A field of neuropsychology, the goals of which are to retrain or provide compensatory skills to counteract the effects of brain damage

2. Behavioral techniques used.

3. Other cognitive rehabilitation efforts focus on self-regulation skills.

VI. What Lies Ahead?

A. Advances expected in knowledge about memory, thinking, learning, emotion, and the effects of injury, disease, and stress on these processes.

B. Aging society and longer lifespans will require increased attention to these disorders.

C. Increased understanding of the dementias and development of treatments, cures, and preventive measures.

KEY TERMS REVIEW

1. A pattern of apparent heritability, as in one form of Alzheimer's dementia, is called _____.

2. Problems in the circulatory system feeding the brain, which may cause brain-damaging strokes, are called _____.

3. A form of dementia caused by the accumulated effect of many small strokes is called _____.

4. A depressive episode associated with damage to certain areas of the cortex associated with stroke is called _____.

5. A progressive disease, usually occurring in older ages, involving cognitive impairment due to brain changes, especially in the cortex and hippocampus, is called _____.

6. A problem of concentration, memory, and personality changes, usually mild, that follows a blow to the head causing little or no loss of consciousness is called _____.

7. *Alcohol amnestic disorder*, a condition caused by vitamin B_1 deficiency that produces severe retrograde and anterograde amnesia, is also called _____.

8. A field of neuropsychology, the goals of which are to retrain the individual or provide compensatory skills to counteract the effects of brain damage, is _____.

9. Damage to the brain, caused either by penetrating injuries (such as a gunshot) or closed head injuries (such as a blow to the head), is called _____.

10. A major component of the plaques observed in the brains of persons with Alzheimer's dementia is _____.

11. Diminished production of thyroid hormone, which can impair cognitive abilities and cause other psychological disorders, is called _____.

12. An infectious, often sexually transmitted, disease that if untreated may cause general paresis is _____.

13. Impairment of short- or long-term memory is called _____.

14. A severe mental disorder caused by syphilis that produces memory problems, poor intellectual functioning, bad judgment, dementia, personality changes, and delusions on a deteriorating course leading to death is called _____.

15. A degenerative brain disease that causes tremor, muscle rigidity, and difficulty initiating movement and may involve cognitive impairment is called _____.

16. Memory disorders linked to the psychological condition of dissociation are called _____.

17. The DSM-IV term for medically caused delirium, dementia, or amnesia is _____.

18. General, multiple cognitive deficits reflecting a decline in previously higher levels of functioning that are acquired (rather than being present at birth, as mental retardation) are called _____.

19. The form of Alzheimer's dementia with no apparent family pattern of transmission is called _____.

20. Nerve cell malformations in the brain, one of the kinds of damage brought on by Alzheimer's disease, are called _____.

21. Changes in level of consciousness that may be accompanied by cognitive changes; may be temporary or progressive are called _____.

22. The pre-DSM-IV term for psychological conditions known or suspected to be caused by a medical problem are called _____.

23. A genetically caused degenerative brain disease of motor functioning that causes severe dementia and personality change as well as *chorea*—irregular jerks, grimaces, and twitches—is called _____.

24. Damage to the anterior part of the brain that can cause impaired memory, concentration, reasoning, leaning, and possible personality changes is called _____.

25. Extracellular protein deposits that damage the brain as part of Alzheimer's disease are called _____.

FACTUAL MULTIPLE-CHOICE QUESTIONS

1. Before DSM-IV, conditions that were known or suspected to be due to a medical problem were classified as
   a. the schizophrenias.
   b. somatoform disorders.
   c. psychogenic.
   d. organic mental disorders.

2. Which of the following is *not* considered a cognitive disorder?
   a. mania
   b. delirium
   c. dementia
   d. amnesia

3. Long-term memory and the ability to reason and to draw from experience
   a. do not decline with age.
   b. virtually disappear in the elderly.
   c. are lost as part of the general deterioration associated with aging.
   d. stay the same because there are not changes in cognitive functioning for the elderly.

4. The term *dementia* refers to
   a. schizophrenia.
   b. acquired cognitive deficits.
   c. psychosis.
   d. mental retardation.

5. By far the leading cause of dementia is
   a. stroke.
   b. Parkinson's disease.
   c. Alzheimer's disease.
   d. Korsakoff's syndrome.

6. Which of the following is *not* true of Alzheimer's disease?
   a. It is a disease.
   b. It is degeneration of the brain from aging.
   c. A definitive diagnosis can only be made postmortem.
   d. Depression rarely occurs with Alzheimer's patients.

7. The biological factor being intensively studied as a possible cause of Alzheimer's is
   a. cerebrospinal fluid.
   b. beta-amyloid precursor protein.
   c. dopamine.
   d. serotonin.

8. A person who suffers intellectual and personality changes following several small strokes is suffering from
   a. Type A personality.
   b. vascular dementia.
   c. Huntington's chorea.
   d. myocardial infarction.

9. The AIDS virus causes cognitive impairment
   a. rarely.
   b. only in the later stages of the illness.
   c. before AIDS-related symptoms occur.
   d. but not depression.

10. Children exposed to lead
    a. absorb the lead more readily than adults.
    b. are protected by a natural immunity.
    c. are probably safe if the levels are low.
    d. will fully recover once the lead has been removed.

CONCEPTUAL MULTIPLE-CHOICE QUESTIONS

1. The extent and permanence of brain function changes depend on
   a. the skill of the therapist.
   b. the skill of the surgeon.
   c. the severity of damage to the brain tissue and its location.
   d. how quickly the brain tissue regenerates.

2. A decline in mental functioning for the elderly is
   a. inevitable.
   b. related to adjustment earlier in life.
   c. always irreversible.
   d. always related to Alzheimer's disease.

3. Mr. Ford's wife had been deteriorating badly for three years as a result of Alzheimer's disease. Once he made the decision not to have her institutionalized, his doctor
   a. felt that Mr. Ford would recover from his depression.
   b. was worried that his depression would worsen.
   c. felt sure that Mr. Ford would not have any physical symptoms.
   d. felt Mr. Ford could handle the situation without any outside help.

4. Dr. Riordan had completed an evaluation of Mr. Ramirez. She hesitated to make a diagnosis of Alzheimer's disease because
   a. Alzheimer's rarely strikes nonwhites.
   b. she wanted to wait until she could make a definitive diagnosis.
   c. a definitive diagnosis can only be made postmortem.
   d. Mr. Ramirez had no history of depression.

5. When Julie and Jon heard from their father's doctor that the probable cause of the disturbing changes in his behavior was due to Alzheimer's disease, they
   a. were hopeful that their father would improve.
   b. were dismayed because they knew the disease was progressive and irreversible.
   c. realized that death would probably come quickly.
   d. realized that Alzheimer's would be the direct cause of death.

6. Margaret had always led an active life as a professional photographer and adventurer. When she developed symptoms of Parkinson's disease her doctor was concerned because
   a. of the likelihood of major cognitive impairment.
   b. women are at much greater risk than men for developing the disease.
   c. the physical symptoms of tremors and muscular rigidity would preclude her photography and adventuring.
   d. of the likelihood of early onset dementia.

7. Arlo was concerned about his own future health, because his father suffers from Huntington's disease. Arlo will have to wait before he knows his fate because
   a. onset of the disease may not happen until he is close to fifty years old.
   b. a definitive diagnosis can't be made until his dad has died.
   c. it is not known if Huntington's is inheritable.
   d. genetic analysis does not reveal if a person carries the defective gene.

8. Ray's doctor told him that the tingling sensation he felt in his hands was probably the result of a small stroke. Ray should
   a. not be worried because small strokes don't do much damage.
   b. be concerned because small strokes can cause major brain damage.
   c. not be worried because small strokes may cause some motor damage and nothing else.
   d. not worry because there is no way to tell if he is actually having a stroke.

9. Mrs. Lee is a seventy-year-old woman whose children brought her to the doctor because she suddenly lost the ability to speak, was confused and had memory loss, and could not move the right side of her body. The doctors disagreed over Mrs. Lee's diagnosis. Dr. Chin believes that Mrs. Lee has a somatoform disorder, but Dr. Lau thinks that Mrs. Lee has a cognitive disorder. You are called in to give an opinion. What would you say?
   a. Agree with Dr. Chin that Mrs. Lee has a somatoform disorder, most probably conversion disorder.
   b. Agree with Dr. Lau that Mrs. Lee has a cognitive disorder.
   c. Disagree with both Drs. Lau and Chin, because Mrs. Lee shows signs of a dissociative disorder, most likely dissociative amnesia.
   d. Disagree with both Drs. Lau and Chin, because Mrs. Lee is showing signs of Korsakoff's syndrome.

10. Which of the following situations suggests a link to cognitive disorders?
    a. Kathy, a sixteen-year-old, who is diagnosed with mental retardation
    b. Paul, a seven-year-old with Down syndrome
    c. Jon, a fourteen-year-old chronic glue sniffer
    d. Mary, who has been taking antidepressant medications to treat her Parkinson's disease

APPLICATION MULTIPLE-CHOICE QUESTIONS

1. Marty had spent over fifteen years in the Army, but he couldn't remember either his last duty station or the name of his commanding officer. Marty's heavy drinking may have caused
   a. Parkinson's disease.
   b. Huntington's disease.
   c. Korsakoff's syndrome.
   d. Alzheimer's disease.

2. Marianne's car had been rear-ended in a multi-car accident on the highway. She was unconscious for some time after hitting her head. Her doctor made arrangements for
   a. psychotherapy.
   b. neuroimaging to determine any damage.
   c. her to return to her home.
   d. an x-ray examination.

3. Polly, at age 77, had some difficulty moving about as well as occasional difficulty remembering where she had left things in her apartment. Otherwise, she did well, with a circle of friends and an active social and volunteer schedule. Her doctor saw these symptoms as
   a. signs of inevitable dementia.
   b. a natural part of the aging process.
   c. a serious problem because Polly complained about her memory loss.
   d. evidence of early stage Alzheimer's disease.

4. John was recovering from a serious surgical procedure and had been in intensive care for several days. His children and grandchildren were looking forward to his return home, but his doctor was concerned that he might develop
   a. amnesia.
   b. Alzheimer's disease.
   c. Huntington's disease.
   d. delirium.

5. Mr. Baker was having difficulties remembering where he was as well as trouble speaking with the attendants at the home where he lived. His doctor made a diagnosis of
   a. dementia.
   b. schizophrenia.
   c. Parkinson's disease.
   d. Korsakoff's syndrome.

6. Mrs. Johnson, an African American, and Mrs. Smith, a white American, were both in the same retirement home. Mrs. Johnson has
   a. lower risk for developing dementia.
   b. higher risk for developing dementia.
   c. equal risk for developing dementia.
   d. fewer chronic health problems.

7. Mrs. Pickering was convinced that the phone calls her husband received were part of a plot to have her kidnapped. She became increasingly hostile and often refused to speak. Her doctor characterized these symptoms as signs of
   a. Huntington's disease.
   b. Parkinson's disease.
   c. schizophrenia.
   d. Alzheimer's disease.

8. Pauline's mother was suffering from Alzheimer's disease. Pauline and her husband discussed whether or not they should have children because
   a. there is no chance that Alzheimer's can be genetically transmitted.
   b. there is a slight chance that Alzheimer's can be transmitted.
   c. there is a 50 percent chance that some form of Alzheimer's can be genetically transmitted.
   d. research has not established that there is any genetic transmission of AD.

9. Ryan suffered a mild head injury during a baseball game. His mother
   a. has nothing to worry about since mild injuries don't cause problems.
   b. should be concerned about personality changes but not cognitive changes.
   c. should be concerned because even mild injuries can cause problems some time later.
   d. should be concerned because Ryan has always been a good student and well adjusted.

10. Following a car accident, Jennifer remained in the hospital for several weeks because she had trouble in concentration, planning, reasoning, and making decisions. The doctors examined a PET scan, which showed Jennifer having
    a. hypothyroidism.
    b. problems with her limbic system.
    c. abnormalities in functioning of the cerebellum.
    d. frontal lobe injuries.

ANSWER KEY: KEY TERMS REVIEW

1. familial (533)
2. cerebral vascular disorders (539)
3. vascular dementia or multifarct dementia (539)
4. poststroke depression (540)
5. Alzheimer's dementia (AD) (531)
6. postconcussion syndrome (538)
7. Korsakoff's syndrome (543)
8. cognitive rehabilitation (546)
9. traumatic brain injuries (537)
10. beta-amyloid protein (534)
11. hypothyroidism (541)
12. syphilis (542)
13. amnesia (529)
14. general paresis (542)
15. Parkinson's disease (535)
16. psychogenic amnesia (529)
17. cognitive disorders (524)
18. dementia (529)
19. sporadic (533)
20. neurofibrillary tangles (532)
21. delirium (528)
22. organic mental disorders (524)
23. Huntington's disease (HD) (536)
24. frontal lobe injuries (538)
25. plaques (532)

ANSWER KEY: FACTUAL MULTIPLE-CHOICE QUESTIONS

1. *d. organic mental disorders (p. 524)
   a. Schizophrenia is a serious disorder involving a decline in function, hallucinations, and delusions. It was not suspected to be caused by a medical problem.
   b. Somatoform disorders include hypochondriasis and conversion disorders, which are not caused by medical problems.
   c. Psychogenic disorders are thought to have their causes in the mind, not the body.

2. *a. mania (p. 524)
   b. Delirium is a cognitive disorder that involves changes in levels of consciousness.
   c. Dementia is general, multiple cognitive deficits.
   d. Amnestic disorders are cognitive disorders that involve impairment of short- or long-term memory.

3. *a. do not decline with age (p. 528)
   b. These abilities do not disappear as a natural result of aging.
   c. There are changes in cognitive functioning, but not general deterioration.
   d. There are changes in cognitive functioning, but not of a general nature.

4. *b. acquired cognitive defects (p. 529)
   a. Dementia is characterized by language and thought disturbances, not the unusual content of schizophrenia.
   c. Psychosis is marked by a withdrawal from reality.
   d. Dementia is acquired later in life, mental retardation is related to deficits that begin before the age of eighteen.

5. *c. Alzheimer's disease (p. 531)
   a. Stroke is the second leading cause of dementia.
   b. Parkinson's disease accounts for about 8 percent of dementia cases.
   d. Korsakoff's syndrome is severe amnesia as a result of long-term abuse of alcohol.

6. *b. It is a degeneration of the brain from aging (pp. 531–532)
   a. Alzheimer's is a disease with a disease process. It is not the result of aging.
   c. Improvements in neuroimaging have increased the accuracy of diagnosis, but it is still a matter of eliminating all other possibilities before making the diagnosis.
   d. Depressive symptoms occur in 30 to 40 percent of cases of AD.

7. *b. beta-amyloid precursor protein (pp. 534–535)
   a. Cerebrospinal fluid is examined to determine if AD is present, but is not a cause.
   c. Dopamine is implicated in Parkinson's disease, not Alzheimer's.
   d. Serotonin is implicated in depression and is not a cause of Alzheimer's.

8. *b. vascular dementia (p. 539)
   a. Type A personality is associated with cardiovascular illness, and not with strokes or dementia.
   c. Huntington's chorea is a rare disorder involving involuntary jerking and twisting movements. It is not associated with strokes.
   d. Myocardial infarction is the term for a heart attack in which the heart muscle dies from lack of blood. It is not connected to strokes.

9. *c. before AIDS-related symptoms occur. (p. 541)
   a. The AIDS virus always causes cognitive impairment when it enters the brain.
   b. Mild cognitive symptoms may develop early, long before full AIDS symptoms appear.
   d. AIDS patients often suffer from depression.

10. *a. absorb the lead more readily than adults (p. 542)
   b. There is no immunity from lead exposure.
   c. Even low levels of lead may be toxic.
   d. The lead cannot be removed from the body.

ANSWER KEY: CONCEPTUAL MULTIPLE-CHOICE QUESTIONS

1. *c. the severity of damage to the brain tissue and its location. (p. 525)
   a. Therapists can help patients cope with the problems resulting from tissue damage, but cannot influence actual brain function.
   b. A skilled surgeon can often help, but surgical techniques to relieve conditions such as tumors often result in significant brain tissue damage.
   d. Brain tissue does not regenerate.

2. *b. related to adjustment earlier in life (p. 527)
   a. Declines in mental functioning and dementia are far from inevitable.
   c. Approximately 10 percent of dementias are treatable.
   d. Approximately 55 percent of dementias are related to AD.

3. *b. was worried that his depression would worsen (p. 545)
   a. 50 percent of caregivers of dementia patients meet criteria for diagnosable depression.
   c. Caregivers also have significantly higher rates of chronic medical disorders.
   d. Support groups and self-help organizations are crucial in helping caregivers cope with the demands.

4. *c. a definitive diagnosis can only be made postmortem (p. 533)
   a. AD strikes all ethnic groups.
   b. Definitive diagnosis is not possible until autopsy.
   d. Depression and AD can be unrelated conditions.

5. *b. were dismayed because they knew the disease was progressive and irreversible (p. 533)
   a. AD is irreversible; there is presently no improvement possible.
   c. Death may take as long as ten years from onset of symptoms.
   d. AD is often not the direct cause of death; rather it is from the physical decline or age-related diseases such as pneumonia.

6. *c. the physical symptoms of tremors and muscular rigidity would preclude her photography and adventuring (pp. 535–536)
   a. Many Parkinson's patients show little or no cognitive impairment.
   b. Men are at greater risk than women.
   d. Dementia is most likely in the advanced stages of the disorder.

7. *a. onset of the disease may not happen until he is close to fifty years old (p. 536)
   b. Huntington's disease can be diagnosed definitively while the patient is alive.
   c. It is definitely known that Huntington's is genetically transmittable.
   d. Genetic analysis will tell if a person carries the defective gene.

8. *b. be concerned because small strokes can cause major brain damage (p. 539)
   a. Accumulated small strokes may cause as much damage as a major stroke.
   c. Small strokes may cause the same types of damage as a major stroke.
   d. There are many techniques to determine if a patient is having a stroke.

9. *b. Agree with Dr. Lau that Mrs. Lee has a cognitive disorder. (pp. 524–528, 539)
   a. Her age and the rapid onset would suggest that Mrs. Lee may have a vascular disease and has perhaps suffered a stroke.
   c. Dissociative amnesia would not cause paralysis. The symptoms suggest a real physical problem.
   d. No mention is made of alcohol use by Mrs. Lee.

10. *c. Jon, a fourteen-year-old chronic glue sniffer. (p. 524–526, 542–543)
   a. Mental retardation is not considered to be a cognitive disorder since it is diagnosed before one's eighteenth birthday, and cognitive disorders suggest a decline in ability from a previously higher level.
   b. Down syndrome is a congenital birth defect, and cognitive disorders suggest a decline in ability from a previously higher level.
   d. Antidepressant medications are not known to cause cognitive disorders.

ANSWER KEY: APPLICATION MULTIPLE-CHOICE QUESTIONS

1. *c. Korsakoff's syndrome (p. 543)
   a. Parkinson's disease is not related to alcohol consumption.
   b. Huntington's disease is caused by one dominant gene, not by drinking.
   d. Alzheimer's disease is unrelated to alcohol consumption.

2. *b. neuroimaging to determine any damage (p. 525)
   a. Psychotherapy is not necessarily called for at all.
   c. Head injuries should be carefully examined to determine the extent of neurological damage.
   d. X-ray technology has given way to the new generation of neuroimaging techniques in diagnosing head injuries.

3. *b. a natural part of the aging process (pp. 527–528)
   a. Dementia is not an inevitable part of aging.
   c. Those who complain about memory loss are probably the ones least needy of assistance.
   d. These symptoms are not as pervasive as those associated with AD.

4. *d. delirium (p. 528)
   a. Amnesia is not associated with surgery.
   b. Alzheimer's symptoms would probably have been noticed long before the surgery and would not develop as a result of surgery.
   c. Huntington's disease is caused by a dominant gene, not by trauma such as surgery.

5. *a. dementia (pp. 529–531)
   b. Schizophrenia is marked by hallucinations and delusions, not by memory problems.
   c. Parkinson's is characterized by tremors, not by memory loss.
   d. Korsakoff's is related to long-term abuse of alcohol and massive amnesia.

6. *b. higher risk for developing dementia (pp. 530–531)
   a. African Americans have a significantly higher rate of dementia than white Americans.
   c. The difference in rates is 16 percent to 3 percent.
   d. African Americans, especially women, have higher rates of chronic health problems such as high blood pressure.

7. *d. Alzheimer's disease (p. 532)
   a. Huntington's disease is characterized by motoric problems and declines in memory and intellectual functioning, not by hostility and paranoia.
   b. Parkinson's disease is characterized by a loss of muscle control, not by hostility and paranoia.
   c. Schizophrenia is marked by disturbed thought processes and unusual content, not defective cognitive processes as in AD.

8. *c. there is a 50 percent chance that some form of AD can be genetically transmitted (pp. 533–535)
   a. The familial form of the illness is genetically transmittable.
   b. There is a 50 percent chance the disorder will be transmitted.
   d. Research has established the genetic transmission of AD.

9. *c. should be concerned because even mild head injuries can cause problems some time later (p. 537)
   a. Even mild injuries can cause serious problems.
   b. Cognitive as well as personality changes can occur even in mild injuries.
   d. Previous adjustment and educational level predict better functioning after a head injury.

10. *d. frontal lobe injuries. (p. 538)
    a. Hypothyroidism is not detectable by brain imaging and would not cause these symptoms.
    b. The limbic system is involved in emotional regulation and memory processes, not "executive" functions.
    c. The cerebellum is involved in balance and fine motor coordination.

CHAPTER 18
Legal, Ethical, and Social Issues in Mental Health

LEARNING OBJECTIVES

1. Discuss how abnormal psychology raises important legal, ethical, and social issues. (pp. 550–555)

2. Describe the tension between protecting the community and protecting the rights of individuals. (p. 550)

3. Describe legal issues pertaining to the mentally ill, including competency to stand trial, and the various standards for the insanity defense. (pp. 550–553)

4. Discuss involuntary hospitalization and the procedures used and the limitations involved with such procedures. (pp. 553–554)

5. Describe the legal rights of patients, including the right to treatment, to the least restrictive alternative, to refuse treatment, and to confidentiality. (pp. 554–555)

6. Discuss the responsibilities of therapists in providing psychotherapy services and the rights of consumers receiving these services. (pp. 555–560)

7. Compare and contrast the similarities and differences between social support systems and formal therapy. (pp. 556–557)

8. Discuss how to choose a therapist. (p. 558)

9. Discuss desirable ethical conduct of therapists in the protection of the client's welfare. (pp. 558–560)

10. Describe various barriers affecting access to psychological treatment, including the negative effects of privatization of health care on the mentally ill. (pp. 560–561)

11. Discuss the effects of deinstitutionalization of the mentally ill. (pp. 561–563)

12. Describe the problems of the mentally ill homeless and the potential negative effects of homelessness on children. (pp. 563–564)

13. Discuss the relationship between ethnicity and the availability of, utilization of, and responsiveness to mental health treatment. (pp. 564–567)

14. Describe some of the alternatives to traditional mental health services, such as self-help groups and the use of nonprofessionals. (pp. 567–569)

15. Discuss the potential negative effects resulting from the marketing of mental health services. (pp. 569–570)

16. Discuss the benefits and limitations of prevention programs, particularly with potentially troubled youth. (pp. 570–572)

17. Describe prevention efforts to address the conditions that contribute to mental health problems. (pp. 572–575)

18. Discuss the linkage between poverty and family dysfunction and mental disorders and health. (pp. 571–572)

19. Describe some current preventive efforts and the controversy surrounding their costs and effectiveness. (pp. 572–575)

20. Discuss future trends in the efforts to meet the enormous problems of mental disorders. (p. 575)

CHAPTER OUTLINE

I. The Law and Mental Illness

- Balance needed between protecting community and protecting rights of individual.

- Currently, balance is tipped toward protection of individual freedom.

A. Legal Protection for the Mentally Ill in Criminal Cases

- Intention to commit a crime necessary for moral responsibility:

   a. Requires knowledge of right and wrong.

   b. Free will to act as he or she chooses.

1. Competence to stand trial

   a. Mentally incompetent to stand trial means a person is not sufficiently rational to understand and assist in his or her own defense.

   b. Essential for trial or legal process.

   c. Mentally incompetent defendants are confined to prison hospitals: confinement without being found guilty.

   d. Competency decisions are influenced by a number of variables.

2. The insanity defense

   a. Insanity defense plea: The legal statement by the accused that he or she is not guilty because of insanity at the time of the crime. Results in defendant going to a treatment facility rather than prison.

   b. Insanity: An old-fashioned term for psychosis; a legal rather than a psychological term for severe mental illness that affects a person's reason and self-control. A diagnosis of a disorder is not the same as insanity.

    c.   Definitions of insanity include

        (1)   Cognitive ability: The mental capacity to know right from wrong.

        (2)   Volition: Ability to exercise free will.

    d.   The M'Naghten rule

        (1)   Accused must know what he or she was doing.

        (2)   Must know it was wrong.

    e.   Irresistible impulse doctrine emphasizes volition. Ability to control behavior is the criterion.

    f.   Diminished capacity refers to mental or physical factors that impaired accused person's ability to understand or control the crime

    g.   The Durham rule absolved the accused if act was product of mental disease. Very inclusive.

    h.   The American Law Institute's (ALI) Model Penal Code incorporates rational and volitional criteria for determining insanity.

    i.   American Psychiatric Association (APA) insanity standard uses a cognitive criterion for insanity rather than volitional.

    j.   Refinements in definition of insanity make a small difference in outcome of cases (volitional criterion for the most part eliminated).

    k.   Insanity plea rarely abused because people adjudged to be not guilty by reason of insanity (NGRI) go to mental hospitals for a lengthy time.

    l.   Some believe that mentally ill people who commit crimes should be found guilty but mentally ill and receive treatment while in prison.

B.   Civil Commitment: Involuntary Hospitalization

    1.   Criminal commitment occurs when a person is confined after being found NGRI.

    2.   Civil commitment is when individuals are held for short periods of time while decision is reviewed and expert testimony sought.

    3.   Need for treatment: Involuntary hospitalization for those that need treatment but are not mentally competent to consent.

        a.   In United States only occurs when persons are dangerous to themselves or others or gravely disabled.

        b.   Persons may only be held if there are signs of imminent danger to themselves or others.

    4.   Problem: Clinicians are only accurate about predicting future violence among the mentally disordered one-third of the time.

C.   Legal Rights of Patients

    1.   The right to treatment

        a.   States cannot hold patients without treating them.

  b. Right to treatment includes active efforts to reduce symptoms and provide humane care.

 2. The right to the least restrictive alternative

  a. Least restrictive alternative: The greatest freedom consistent with personal security and safety of others.

  b. Degrees of dangerousness allow some to live in group homes with some freedom and only more dangerous (to self or others) patients to live in locked hospitals.

 3. The right to refuse treatment

  a. Many states require patients to sign informed consent statements that outline the nature of their treatment.

  b. Patients who refuse treatment (medication) can be overridden.

  c. The refusal is apt to reflect the disorder itself.

 4. Legal right to confidentiality

  a. Confidentiality, the basis for patient trust in the therapist, the protection from disclosure of all personal information.

  b. Limitations of confidentiality:

   (1) Suspected child or elder abuse must be reported.

   (2) Threats to harm others must be reported (cf. *Tarasoff* v. *Regents of the University of California*).

    (a) Therapist has duty to warn the intended victim.

    (b) Therapist has duty to protect potential victim.

II. Consumers' Rights and Therapists' Responsibilities

 • Process in psychotherapy is private and unfamiliar to clients.

 • Confusing array of therapies and therapists.

 A. When to Go for Therapy

  1. Serious mental disorder and great suffering.

  2. Persistent recurring distress.

  3. Impaired ability to carry out important roles.

  4. Uncertainty about goals, a traumatic event.

 B. What's Normal? Social Support and Therapy: Same or Different?

  1. Social support: comfort, support, and advice from friends and family members.

   a. Helps reduce psychological symptoms.

   b. Its absence leads to increased symptoms.

  2. Mild problems greatly helped by supportive relations.

3. Severe problems require professional neutrality, training, unconditional acceptance of a therapist.

C. Choosing a Therapist

1. Licensure helps to protect consumers from unqualified practitioners by requiring training and experience.

2. Financial constraints often limit consumer choice.

3. If medication is required, medical doctor (psychiatrist) must be consulted.

4. Personal characteristics such as gender and ethnicity, as well as therapist flexibility and acceptance, and cultural competence also are important.

D. Maintaining the Client's Welfare: Ethical Conduct

• Ethical standards are the written principles of appropriate professional values and behaviors.

1. Some basic ethical standards (American Psychological Association)

   a. Confidentiality: Essential except in legally specified instances.

   b. Informed consent: Patient must be informed about procedures before agreeing to them.

   c. Competence: The ability to perform effectively. Therapists must limit their services to their training and experience.

   d. No multiple or dual relationships: Unethical for therapist to have a friendship or business relationship with patient outside the therapeutic relationship.

2. Sexual intimacy between therapist and client

   a. Intimacy of therapy process is unique and powerful.

   b. Sexual contact between therapist and client is now explicitly forbidden by professional therapy organizations and is a felony crime in some states.

   c. Such relationships are inherently exploitive.

   d. Obtaining accurate data on prevalence is difficult.

   e. Rates appear to be declining.

   f. Clients should report offending therapists to professional organizations and to regulatory agencies controlling licensure.

III. Barriers to Treatment

A. Mental Health Financing and Access to Services

1. Gap exists between those who need help and resources available to provide it.

   a. Most severely impaired not receiving enough services.

   b. Cost of treating severely mentally ill estimated at $20 billion per year; *social costs* (lost productivity, etc.) an additional $74 billion per year.

      c.   Problem is acute among disadvantaged, children, adolescents, elderly, people living in rural areas, and chronically mentally ill.

    2.   Copayments and preauthorization of services by HMOs or managed care organizations may limit access to treatment.

B.   Deinstitutionalization

    1.   Movement of patients out of mental hospitals back into their own communities

        a.   Reasons include extensive loss of freedom, inadequate treatment, poor conditions, detrimental effects of long-term institutionalization.

        b.   Trend encouraged by court decisions re patients' rights.

        c.   Outcome has been bleak.

           (1)   Insufficient community services.

           (2)   Case management (coordination of total care) not provided.

           (3)   Federal government policies (e.g., welfare benefits) thwart rehabilitation.

        d.   Privatization, the movement away from public funding and nonprofit facilities toward for-profit ownership, has encouraged short-term treatments; chronic cases left untreated or left to underfunded public agencies.

        e.   Seriously ill receive treatment at underfunded, poorly staffed public mental health centers and hospitals.

C.   Mentally Ill Homeless

    1.   Most of the homeless in the United States suffer from alcohol or drug abuse or mental illness.

        a.   Deinstitutionalization a factor.

        b.   Families may be unable to support them.

        c.   Landlords often unwilling to rent to the mentally ill.

        d.   Distinguishing factor between homeless and nonhomeless patients is early history of foster care, disrupted early family experiences, or domestic violence.

        e.   Case management with coordination of services and trained nonprofessionals shows promise.

D.   Family Matters: Children of Mentally Ill Mothers

    1.   Families with children make up a large part of homeless population.

    2.   Large proportion of homeless mothers suffer from mental disorders.

    3.   The children of homeless mothers with mental disorders show significant psychological problems, including externalizing behavior problems, emotional disorders, and learning disorders.

E.   Minority Status and Mental Health Treatment

- Mental health services must recognize different values and standards of conduct in different ethnic groups.

1. Use of services

    a. Differs by ethnic group

    b. Some groups (such as Mexican Americans and Asian Americans) underutilize outpatient services.

    c. Blacks and Native Americans overrepresented in inpatient treatment.

2. Responsiveness to treatment

    a. Ethnic minority patients tend to drop out of or prematurely leave treatment before it can be effective.

    b. Success of treatment influenced by cultural responsiveness, ethnicity of mental health service providers, and language fluency.

    c. Lower dropout rates found when matching therapist and client by ethnicity and language (except for African Americans).

    d. Cultural sensitivity, awareness of different cultural values and customs that affect individuals' behaviors and expectations, important.

    e. Role preparation to teach prospective clients appropriate therapy behaviors, realistic expectations, and problems commonly encountered in therapy increased satisfaction with and outcome of therapy.

IV. Alternatives to Traditional Mental Health Treatments

  A. Self-Help Groups and Self-Care Programs

    1. Individuals united by common experience meet to receive mutual aid and share information and strategies for coping.

    2. Virtually free of charge.

    3. Member-governed, without professional leadership.

    4. Many people are going to self-help groups; 13.3 percent of all U.S. adults at one time have attended a twelve-step program.

    5. Groups cover broad range of problems.

    6. Twelve-step programs, such as Alcoholics Anonymous (AA), are based on 12 central tenets for change.

    7. Many view these groups as the treatment of choice.

    8. Research has shown that nearly all of those studied showed measurable improvement in functioning.

    9. May not be good for those with serious problems.

    10. Self-directed treatments (e.g., manuals and media) may be an inexpensive alternative for mild problems.

  B. Nonprofessionals and Paraprofessionals

1. Nonprofessionals (paraprofessionals): those who lack full training or licensure but who have some specialized training in dealing with specific issues.

   a. Might share circumstances.

   b. Might be ethnically similar.

   c. Able to provide an understanding perhaps not available in highly trained professional.

2. Paraprofessionals have been found to be at least as effective as professional counselors.

C. The Marketing of Mental Health

1. Media psychology is entertainment, not therapy.

2. Shows raise awareness but trivialize serious problems and exploit vulnerabilities.

3. Self-help books, tapes, and seminars have the same potential benefits and pitfalls.

V. Preventing Psychological Disorders

- The number of people who need treatment or are at risk for developing disorders is huge.

- Many do not receive any treatment, particularly youth.

- Prevention is the best hope.

A. Defining Prevention

1. Primary prevention is eliminating or altering the conditions that give rise to problems or changing conditions to allow a person to resist the negative effects of risk conditions.

2. Secondary prevention is aimed at early detection and limiting negative consequences.

3. Tertiary prevention is controlling long-term consequences of a chronic problem.

B. Targets for Prevention: Contributors to Psychological Disorders

- Some of the fundamental roots of mental illness are in social conditions.

1. Poverty, social adversity, and mental health

   a. Risk factors are often directly associated with poverty or are compounded by poverty.

2. Families and mental health

   a. Family dysfunction is a major contributor to mental illness.

   b. Some of the groups at risk because of disruptive family conditions:

      (1) "Crack" babies and those with fetal alcohol syndrome.

      (2) Teenage mothers and their children.

(3)   Abused children.

(4)   Children of mentally ill parents.

(5)   Children of homeless persons (chiefly women).

C.   A Sampling of Preventive Efforts

1.   Preschool programs for high-risk children, such as Head Start. High quality preschool programs bring long-term benefits.

2.   School-based competency training: Aimed at all children; attempts to teach attitudes, values, and skills that support health-enhancing behaviors.

a.   Very costly

b.   Effectiveness is questioned

3.   Adult programs such as rape crisis groups and telephone hotlines are aimed at preventing severe stresses from causing psychological harm.

D.   Focus on Research: Can We Prevent Depression in Children?

1.   Seligman's research suggests that depression can be prevented by programs aimed at reducing maladaptive skills and cognitions.

2.   Treated group had significantly lower depression scores at exit and at follow-up, however, gains may erode over time without additional intervention.

VI.   What Lies Ahead?

A.   Dilemma continues regarding human responsibility for dangerous behaviors.

B.   Laws governing protection for the mentally disabled will continue to change.

C.   Defining and upholding ethical conduct will continue to be important.

D.   Priorities may shift to give more attention and financial support to prevention programs.

KEY TERMS REVIEW

1.   An awareness by a therapist of different cultural values and customs that affect individuals' behaviors and expectations is called _____.

2.   A definition of legal insanity that emphasizes volition by allowing the insanity defense if the accused—even if knowing the difference between right and wrong—could not control his or her actions is the _____.

3.   A definition of legal insanity proposed by the American Psychiatric Association that uses a cognitive approach in which the accused must be judged as "unable to appreciate the wrongfulness of his conduct at the time of the offense" is the _____.

4.   Ability to exercise free will; part of some legal criteria for determining not guilty by reason of insanity is called the _____.

5.   Early detection of people with mental health problems and actions to limit the negative consequences once that problem has manifested itself is called _____.

6. Self-help groups that focus on helping members practice twelve central tenets believed essential for healthy functioning are called _____.

7. A definition of legal insanity that found individuals could not be criminally responsible if their "unlawful act was the product of mental disease or mental defect" is called the _____.

8. The movement away from public funding and nonprofit facilities toward for-profit ownership of hospitals with emphasis on the business aspects of health care is called _____.

9. To _____ is the tendency to seek therapy services disproportionately less frequently than disorder occurs.

10. A definition of legal insanity proposed by the American Law Institute that incorporates both rational and volitional criteria for determining insanity is the _____.

11. The written principles of appropriate professional values and behaviors to which therapists must adhere are called _____.

12. The type of confinement to a mental or prison hospital used for people found not guilty by reason of insanity is called _____.

13. Collections of individuals who are united by common challenges and difficulties who meet to receive mutual aid and to share information and strategies for coping are called _____.

14. A definition of legal insanity—now disallowed in most jurisdictions—that allows the insanity defense if the accused can point to mental or physical factors that impaired his or her ability to understand the nature of the act or to control it is called _____.

15. The principle that anything about an adult patient may not be disclosed by a therapist without the patient's written consent is called _____.

16. Eliminating or altering the conditions that give rise to mental health problems or changing conditions so that a person will be able to resist the negative effects of risk conditions is called _____.

17. People who in the past were institutionalized but now live on the streets because of the lack of care facilities are called _____.

18. The principle that a therapist who knows of a patient's intention to harm another person has the responsibility to take whatever steps are reasonably necessary to protect the other person is called the _____.

19. Conditions that are significantly associated with a disorder and presumed to have causal significance are called _____.

20. The patient's right to turn down physical procedures such as medication; subject to review by professionals who may override the patient's wishes if medically justified is called the _____.

21. The mental capacity to know right from wrong; a component of a legal standard for not guilty by reason of insanity is called _____.

22. Another term for nonprofessional is _____.

23. Controlling the long-term consequences of a chronic mental health problem is called _____.

24. The principle that jurisdictions cannot commit individuals to institutions without providing minimal standards of care, including active efforts to reduce symptoms and provision of humane conditions to support their treatment, is called the _____.

25. A relationship with a patient outside the therapeutic relationship, which is unethical for a therapist to form or maintain, such as a sexual or business association, is called a(n) _____.

26. The ability of a therapist to perform effectively; an ethical and professional requirement is called _____.

27. Prevention programs aimed at all children, not only those thought to be at risk, that attempt to incorporate into the curriculum certain attitudes, values, and skills that support health-enhancing behaviors, are called _____.

28. A period of involuntary confinement for treatment in a hospital when a person is judged by professionals to be dangerous to the self or others; can be required of persons found to be unable to care for themselves due to mental illness is called _____.

29. _____ is a legal, rather than a psychological, term for severe mental illness that affects a person's reason and self-control.

30. A relatively new standard adopted in some jurisdictions that abandons the not guilty by reason of insanity plea, allowing a legal judgment that the accused, though suffering from a psychological disorder, committed the crime, leading to confinement and treatment, is called _____.

31. People who lack full training in psychology and therapeutic techniques but who have specialized training in dealing with specific issues and who can provide assistance to selected populations at considerable savings are called _____.

32. The network of individuals with whom a subject has social or personal contact within a certain time, especially the support related to emotional well-being, the absence of which is thought to be a factor in many stress disorders, is called _____.

33. A cognitive definition of legal insanity of British origin based on the principle that the accused did not know what he or she was doing or did not know that it was wrong is called the _____.

34. The legal statement by the accused that he or she is not guilty because of insanity at the time of the crime is the _____.

35. A phrase applied to an accused person who is not sufficiently rational to understand and assist in his or her own defense is _____.

36. The principle that people can be held in civil commitment only if they are dangerous to themselves or others and show signs of harming self or others in the near term is called _____.

37. The requirement that therapists complete graduate training in an approved institution, complete a certain number of hours of delivery of service under the supervision of licensed professionals, and pass examinations, intended to offer some protection to consumers, is called _____.

38. The principle that a therapist who knows of a patient's intention to harm another person has the responsibility to notify that person is called the _____.

39. _____ is the term used to characterize the environment to which involuntarily committed persons should be confined; it should permit the greatest freedom consistent with their personal security and the safety of others.

40. The principle—which is no longer used in the United States—that people can be involuntarily hospitalized if they need treatment but are unable to consent to voluntary treatment because they are not mentally competent is called _____.

FACTUAL MULTIPLE-CHOICE QUESTIONS

1. The current trend in the law is toward protection
    a. for the community.
    b. for the government.
    c. of individual freedom.
    d. of the medical community.

2. Insanity
    a. refers to schizophrenia.
    b. is a medical term.
    c. is a psychological term.
    d. is a legal term.

3. The concept of "need for treatment" generally leaves the decision of hospitalization to
    a. a physician.
    b. the family.
    c. the patient.
    d. the courts.

4. When choosing a therapist, her or his personal characteristics
    a. should not be a factor.
    b. are the most important factor.
    c. might facilitate the process of therapy.
    d. are only important for ethnic minorities.

5. Which of the following is *not* one of the basic ethical standards?
    a. No multiple relationships
    b. Confidentiality
    c. Informed consent
    d. The right to refuse treatment

6. Sexual contact between therapist and client
    a. has been accurately documented.
    b. is acceptable if the contact is by mutual consent.
    c. is acceptable as soon as therapy has terminated.
    d. is explicitly prohibited.

7. The outcome of deinstitutionalization has been
    a. an unqualified success.
    b. a particular problem for the elderly and mentally retarded.
    c. plagued with problems.
    d. successful because of massive community support.

8. Ethnic minority patients using community mental health services
   a. tend to remain in therapy until they have reached a successful outcome.
   b. tend to drop out of treatment before it can be effective.
   c. are underrepresented in every category.
   d. show consistent rates regardless of ethnic group.

9. Self-help groups
   a. have lost their appeal and are decreasing in number.
   b. focus entirely on substance abuse and alcoholism.
   c. are only used by the most seriously ill.
   d. are often viewed by members as the therapy of choice.

10. Trained nonprofessionals
    a. are a serious source of problems for the mentally ill.
    b. may provide help as well as professional therapists.
    c. must be of the same characteristics as the population they are helping.
    d. must be trained in the broad goals of psychotherapy.

CONCEPTUAL MULTIPLE-CHOICE QUESTIONS

1. All formulations of the legal definition of insanity contain some statement regarding the defendant's
   a. free will.
   b. cognitive ability.
   c. diminished capacity.
   d. delusions.

2. When might a doctor ethically and legally override a patient's right to refuse treatment?
   a. When the family agrees with the patient
   b. When the patient is extremely anxious
   c. When the hospital is understaffed
   d. When the patient is considered dangerous

3. The 1974 Tarasoff ruling held that therapists
   a. had a "duty to warn."
   b. had a duty to protect.
   c. must report suspected child abuse.
   d. must maintain confidentiality at all times.

4. Researchers have found that the mentally ill homeless
   a. are homeless solely because they were deinstitutionalized.
   b. are homeless solely because of their mental illness.
   c. comprise the majority of the mentally ill.
   d. often had disrupted family experiences.

5. Poverty and social disadvantage are associated with psychological disorders because of
   a. poor nutrition.
   b. the lack of material things.
   c. the simplicity of the lives of the poor.
   d. the stressfulness of the disadvantaged person's life.

6. Mr. Simpson brutally attacked and murdered his estranged wife and her companion. His attorney might use as a defense
   a. the M'Naghten rule.
   b. diminished capacity.
   c. the Durham rule.
   d. the irresistible impulse doctrine.

7. When Andrea visited her docile, depressed husband John in the state mental hospital, she was shocked to find that he was only allowed to leave his tiny room for his therapy group. Her attorney is suing the state on grounds of
   a. the right to the least restrictive alternative.
   b. the right to treatment.
   c. the right to refuse treatment.
   d. the legal right to confidentiality.

8. Mrs. Rudner had been living in her car with her daughter for over two months. She had been diagnosed with a mental disorder, but was usually able to function. What type of services would best help her?
   a. institutionalization
   b. psychotherapy
   c. a twelve-step program
   d. intensive case management with coordination of services

9. Miriam worked at the halfway house for recently released drug offenders. She was not a professional, but had training and a sincere interest in helping her clients. Her contact with clients is likely to
   a. cause resentment because they do not have access to a trained professional.
   b. cause a worsening of their condition.
   c. cause her clients to be suspicious.
   d. help as effectively as professional therapists.

10. Julie is in her fourth year of high school. She comes from a low socioeconomic background with a great deal of family dysfunction. She is likely to
    a. receive the proper intervention for her problems.
    b. avoid risky behaviors like the majority of her classmates.
    c. be ignored because the problems of adolescents are not critical.
    d. not receive treatment because few youngsters receive services.

APPLICATION MULTIPLE-CHOICE QUESTIONS

1. Ms. Brendan's second grade class is learning how to deal with stress and overcome pressures to act out in class. Her approach is similar to
   a. Head Start.
   b. school-based competency programs.
   c. programs targeted at high-risk children.
   d. other low-cost, highly effective school-based programs.

2. Mike was a well-known character in the seedy side of town. He would rant at passing motorists about "the day of judgment" and often be seen muttering to himself, occasionally shouting obscenities at unseen antagonists. He is likely to be
   a. arrested.
   b. confined to a mental hospital for the criminally insane.
   c. left alone.
   d. committed on the grounds of "need for treatment."

3. Dr. Johnson's patient Lou was distraught and mentioned several times when he referred to his mother that he was "going to kill the bitch." Dr. Johnson is required by law to
   a. notify his supervisor.
   b. do nothing.
   c. warn the potential victim.
   d. protect the potential victim.

4. Alan was having many problems with his parents as he attempted to choose a career. He was having suicidal thoughts. His counselor recommended
   a. a professional therapist.
   b. more discussions with his parents.
   c. that Alan talk with other members of his family who were objective.
   d. that Alan talk to his friends who had been in similar circumstances.

5. Jamie is a lesbian who is having real problems with her lover about their relationship and living arrangements in the college residence hall. She would probably feel most comfortable
   a. talking these problems over with her father.
   b. discussing these problems with an older male therapist.
   c. discussing her problems with a conservative, anti-homosexual, female therapist.
   d. talking over her problems with a young, lesbian therapist.

6. Dr. Maris was feeling a strong attraction to his client, who was going through a difficult divorce. He explained that it would be unethical for them to have a sexual relationship while she was still his client and suggested that they terminate therapy and begin to see each other right away. He
   a. has taken the proper steps to protect himself and his client.
   b. is in violation of the ethics of his profession.
   c. should wait at least six months before pursuing the relationship.
   d. feels there is nothing wrong because his client is a strong person.

7. Juan is a business leader in the Hispanic Chamber of Commerce. He has been suffering from the effects of a recent divorce. According to statistics on the use of services by ethnicity, Juan is likely to
   a. seek outpatient psychotherapy.
   b. seek inpatient psychotherapy.
   c. begin psychotherapy and stay in treatment until he reaches a successful conclusion.
   d. probably not seek psychotherapy.

8. Mrs. Kim has been told by her minister to seek psychotherapy. Her therapist will have a much better chance of success with Mrs. Kim if she
   a. treats Mrs. Kim just like her other clients.
   b. does role preparation to help Mrs. Kim understand what will happen in therapy.
   c. keeps the course of therapy secret to prevent Mrs. Kim from forming the wrong impression.
   d. tells Mrs. Kim, in order to build her confidence, that therapy will solve her problems.

9. Mr. Alatieri has been attending Al-Anon meetings for six months. After this much time he is likely to believe
    a. that this type program is only for a small number of seriously ill persons.
    b. that this approach is good only for alcohol and substance abuse problems.
    c. this will be his treatment of choice.
    d. the research on this type program confirms his feelings of their efficacy.

10. Wayne's family has been on welfare for three generations. His social worker is working with him to keep him in school. The social worker is engaging in
    a. crisis prevention.
    b. primary prevention.
    c. secondary prevention.
    d. tertiary prevention.

ANSWER KEY: KEY TERMS REVIEW

1. cultural sensitivity (566)
2. irresistible impulse doctrine (552)
3. APA insanity standard (552)
4. volitional criterion (552)
5. secondary prevention (570)
6. twelve-step programs (568)
7. Durham rule (552)
8. privatization (563)
9. underutilize (565)
10. ALI's Model Penal Code (552)
11. ethical standards (558)
12. criminal commitment (553)
13. self-help groups (567)
14. diminished capacity (552)
15. confidentiality (554)
16. primary prevention (570)
17. mentally ill homeless (563)
18. duty to protect (554)
19. risk factors (571)
20. right to refuse treatment (554)
21. cognitive ability (552)
22. paraprofessional (568)
23. tertiary prevention (570)
24. right to treatment (554)
25. dual relationship (559)
26. competence (558)
27. school-based competency training (573)
28. civil commitment (553)
29. insanity (551)
30. guilty but mentally ill (553)
31. nonprofessional (568)
32. social support (556)
33. M'Naghten rule (552)
34. insanity defense plea (551)
35. mentally incompetent to stand trial (551)
36. imminent danger (553)
37. licensure (558)
38. duty to warn (554)
39. least restrictive alternative (554)
40. need for treatment (553)

ANSWER KEY: FACTUAL MULTIPLE-CHOICE QUESTIONS

1. *c. of individual freedom (p. 550)
    a. Community protection was in vogue before the balance tipped toward individual protection.
    b. Government in general is the agency that provides protection through legislation and enforcement.
    d. The medical community protects itself by ethical, educational, and professional standards.

2. *d. is a legal term (p. 551)
   a. A diagnosis of schizophrenia is not the same as insanity.
   b. Insanity is a legal rather than a medical term.
   c. Insanity does not refer to any specific concept in psychology.

3. *a. a physician (p. 553)
   b. Commitment laws were passed to protect a person from anyone, including the family, who would wrongfully commit him or her.
   c. Patients are committed when judged to be incompetent of caring for themselves or possibly injurious to themselves or others.
   d. The courts may become involved when persons show signs of imminent danger to themselves or others, not in the case of "need for treatment."

4. *c. might facilitate the process of therapy (p. 558)
   a. Because trust and cooperation are essential to successful therapy, personal characteristics must be a factor.
   b. They are not the most important factor but should not be discounted in considering a therapist.
   d. Personal characteristics are important for anyone choosing a therapist.

5. *d. The right to refuse treatment (pp. 555, 558)
   a. Therapists may not have any other relationships, such as business or sexual, with clients.
   b. Therapists must maintain the client's confidentiality, except in certain circumstances prescribed by law.
   c. Individuals should be fully informed about procedures before they agree to them.

6. *d. is explicitly prohibited (p. 596)
   a. Obtaining accurate data about the extent and effects of sexual contact is difficult.
   b. Is never acceptable because of the nature of the relationship between therapist and client.
   c. The 1993 Ethical Standards of Psychologists suggests that therapists should never be involved with former clients, but indicates a minimum two-year passage of time after termination of treatment.

7. *c. plagued with problems (pp. 561–563)
   a. Some would say it has been an unqualified disaster for the mentally ill.
   b. Deinstitutionalization has worked best for the elderly and mentally retarded.
   d. Lack of community support is one of the prime reasons it has failed for the mentally ill.

8. *b. tend to drop out of treatment before it can be effective (pp. 564–567)
   a. Ethnic minority patients tend to drop out of treatment before it can be effective.
   c. Blacks and Native Americans are overrepresented in inpatient care.
   d. Use of services varies by ethnicity.

9. *d. are often viewed by members as the therapy of choice (pp. 567–568)
   a. Self-help groups are growing in popularity.
   b. These groups deal with many kinds of problems.
   c. Self-help groups are used by people with varying degrees of severity in their disorders.

10. *b. may provide help as well as professional therapists (p. 569)
   a. Paraprofessionals are a source of real assistance.
   c. Are often identifiable with the populations they serve, but not always.
   d. Paraprofessionals are usually trained in a specialized area.

ANSWER KEY: CONCEPTUAL MULTIPLE-CHOICE QUESTIONS

1. *b. cognitive ability (pp. 552–553)
   - a. Cognitive ability refers to the person's ability to know right from wrong, not to act on it.
   - c. Diminished capacity is an element in one definition of guilt of an intentional act.
   - d. Delusions per se are not part of a legal definition of insanity but may be introduced as evidence of a condition which meets an insanity standard.

2. *d. When the patient is considered dangerous (p. 555)
   - a. The family would not be considered a factor in such a treatment decision.
   - b. Only if the patient is deemed incompetent or dangerous would the right to refuse treatment be superseded.
   - c. Understaffing used to be the reason many patients were overmedicated, even against their will; this is why a patient has the right to refuse treatment.

3. *a. had a "duty to warn" (p. 554)
   - b. The duty-to-protect concept grew out of the earlier Tarasoff ruling and broadened the scope of the therapist's responsibility to potential victims of a threatening client.
   - c. Reporting suspected child abuse is well established in law, but is unrelated to the Tarasoff ruling.
   - d. Confidentiality may be breached in cases of suspected harm that might be done by a client.

4. *d. often had disrupted family experiences (p. 563)
   - a. Deinstitutionalization only accounts for a portion of the mentally ill homeless.
   - b. Overburdened families and lack of affordable housing are other contributing factors.
   - c. Most mentally ill persons do not become homeless.

5. *d. the stressfulness of the disadvantaged person's life (p. 571)
   - a. Poor nutrition has not been found to be a direct cause of mental disorders.
   - b. The lack of material things has not caused mental disorders.
   - c. The lives of the poor and disadvantaged are often quite complicated in the search for the necessities of life.

6. *d. the irresistible impulse doctrine (p. 552)
   - a. The M'Naghten rule suggests "a defect of reason" as central to the insanity defense. It is not clear that this would apply to Mr. Simpson.
   - b. Diminished capacity refers to mental or physical factors that impair a person's ability to understand the nature of the act or to control it.
   - c. The Durham rule states that criminals are not responsible if their "unlawful act was the product of mental disease or mental defect."

7. *a. the right to the least restrictive alternative (p. 554)
   - b. From the description it appears that John is receiving some treatment.
   - c. John apparently has made no attempt to refuse treatment.
   - d. Confidentiality is not an issue in this case.

8. *d. Intensive case management with coordination of services (p. 562)
   - a. She is able to function and does not pose imminent danger to herself or others.
   - b. Psychotherapy is not apt to work for the homeless; they are much more interested in finding housing.
   - c. Twelve-step programs might help once the more immediate problems of housing and child care are solved.

9. *d.   help as effectively as professional therapists (p. 569)
    a.   Her clients might feel more comfortable talking with Miriam than with a professional.
    b.   Paraprofessionals are at least as effective as professional counselors.
    c.   Nonprofessionals might be perceived as an understanding friend or mentor.

10. *d.   not receive treatment because few youngsters receive services (p. 570)
    a.   Fewer than 20 percent of youngsters with current problems actually receive services.
    b.   Growing numbers of youth are engaging in severely risky behaviors.
    c.   The problems of youth are extremely critical, threatening their current and future well-being.

ANSWER KEY: APPLICATION MULTIPLE-CHOICE QUESTIONS

1. *b.   school-based competency programs (p. 573)
    a.   Head Start is a program aimed at very young children.
    c.   Competency programs are directed toward all students, not just those considered to be high-risk.
    d.   Most school-based programs are controversial because of questionable effectiveness and high cost.

2. *c.   left alone (p. 553)
    a.   The tendency is to arrest only on the grounds of imminent danger or actual crime.
    b.   It is unlikely that Mike would be arrested or committed for his actions.
    d.   The "need for treatment" guideline has been superseded by the imminent danger idea, which does not, at this point, apply to Mike.

3. *d.   protect the potential victim (p. 554)
    a.   Notifying the supervisor might be a good idea, but it does not go far enough to protect the possible victim.
    b.   The potential for harm is there, which means the necessity to protect is also evident.
    c.   Warning the potential victim is only one possible step in performing the duty to protect.

4. *a.   a professional therapist (p. 556)
    b.   Family and friends may be loving, but are rarely totally uncritical and objective.
    c.   Other family members are also unable to be completely free from the influence of their own needs.
    d.   Other friends lack the expertise and professionalism that is needed in this serious case.

5. *d.   talking over her problems with a young, lesbian therapist (p. 558)
    a.   Her father may be unable to see his daughter's situation objectively.
    b.   Jamie might be more comfortable with a woman.
    c.   Therapist flexibility and acceptance might be more important than gender identity.

6. *b.   is in violation of the ethics of his profession (pp. 559–560)
    a.   Sexual contact between therapist and client is explicitly prohibited by professional therapy organizations.
    c.   Ethical standards suggest a waiting period of at least two years before considering a romantic relationship.
    d.   Such relationships are inherently exploitive because the client is in a help-seeking role lacking equal power and status.

7. *d. probably not seek psychotherapy (p. 565)
   a. Mexican Americans are significantly less likely than whites to use outpatient mental health services.
   b. Hispanic groups tend to be underrepresented in inpatient treatment programs.
   c. Ethnic minorities tend to drop out of treatment before it can be effective.

8. *b. does role preparation to help Mrs. Kim understand what will happen in therapy (pp. 566–567)
   a. Therapists need to be culturally sensitive to their patients and not treat them all the same.
   c. Providing clients with knowledge about what to expect in therapy is beneficial.
   d. If this expectation is not met quickly, she may be frustrated and terminate treatment prematurely.

9. *c. this will be his treatment of choice (p. 568)
   a. More people attend self-help groups than go for psychotherapy. Participants are not necessarily seriously ill.
   b. These programs reach people with many types of problems.
   d. Collecting appropriate data is difficult and relevant comparison groups may be hard to identify.

10. *d. tertiary prevention (p. 570)
   a. Crisis prevention would be intervention in a situation that demands immediate attention.
   b. Primary prevention is the elimination or alteration of the conditions that give rise to the problems.
   c. Secondary prevention is aimed at early detection and limiting the negative consequences of a chronic problem.